P9-AQL-731

Nation-Building, Propaganda, and Literature in Francophone Africa

Nation-Building, Propaganda, and Literature in Francophone Africa

Dominic Thomas

INDIANA
University Press
Bloomington and Indianapolis

This book is a publication of

Indiana University Press
601 North Morton Street
Bloomington, IN 47404-3797 USA

http://iupress.indiana.edu

Telephone orders 800-842-6796
Fax orders 812-855-7931
Orders by e-mail iuporder@indiana.edu

The paper used in this publication meets the minimum
requirements of American National Standard for
Information Sciences—Permanence of Paper
for Printed Library Materials, ANSI Z39.48-1984.

Manufactured in the United States of America

Library of Congress Cataloging-in-Publication Data

Thomas, Dominic Richard David.
Nation-building, propaganda, and literature in
Francophone Africa / Dominic Thomas.
p. cm.
Includes bibliographical references and index.
ISBN 0-253-34157-4 (cloth : alk. paper) —
ISBN 0-253-21554-4 (pbk. : alk. paper)
1. African literature (French)—History and criticism.
2. Nationalism and literature—Africa, French-speaking.
3. Politics and literature—Africa, French-speaking.
4. Propaganda—Africa, French-speaking. I. Title.
PQ3980.5 .T56 2002
840.9'358'096—dc21
2002003703

1 2 3 4 5 07 06 05 04 03 02

FOR

MY PARENTS,

MY SON DEVEREUX,

AND

MY WIFE, ERIN JOY COONEY

History, despite its wrenching pain, cannot be unlived, and if faced with courage, need not be lived again.

—Maya Angelou

CONTENTS

PREFACE AND ACKNOWLEDGMENTS

I was born in Berlin to a Welsh father and an English mother. My family moved to France when I was two years old and I was raised there until my teenage years when I was transplanted into a boarding school in England. I was eager to maintain a strong connection with France and to keep that component of my identity alive. It was thus with tremendous excitement that I headed off to University College London in the fall of 1984 to read French language and literature. I did indeed spend the first two years at University College much as I had expected, "reading" French literature from the medieval period through to the twentieth century. Then, toward the end of my second year, I noticed a pile of unfamiliar titles on my advisor's table and inquired as to the identity of the authors. "I picked up these books on a recent trip to Senegal," she explained. "They are by African authors and I'm thinking of offering a Special Subject course on their work next year. Do you think people would be interested?" "Absolutely," I answered enthusiastically. "Why don't you take these books with you and let me know what you think." And so I left her office with my first copy of Sony Labou Tansi's *La parenthèse de sang*, Emmanuel Dongala's *Jazz et vin de palme*, Ousmane Sembène's *Les bouts de bois de dieu*, Mariama Bâ's *Une si longue lettre*, Ferdinand Oyono's *Une vie de boy*, Cheikh Hamidou Kane's *L'aventure ambiguë*, and Camara Laye's *L'enfant noir*.

That chance encounter changed the course of my life. Discovering in these extraordinarily innovative (and for the most part living!) authors those very issues that were most appealing to me in literature, politics, anthropology, and sociology, I literally begged my professor to offer such a course the following year. In fact, I ended up directing Sony Labou Tansi's *La parenthèse de sang* at a theater festival at London's French Institute in March 1987, traveled to the Festival International des Francophonies in Limoges in October 1988 to meet with Sony Labou Tansi, and, upon graduation in 1989, started a doctoral dissertation on Congolese literature with a catchy title, "New Writings for New Times"! At a similar time in the United Kingdom, scholars and students across the disciplines came together to found the Association for the Study of Caribbean and African Literature in French (ASCALF) and organized colloquia featuring "specialists" of these literatures. I remember listening to Dorothy Blair, Arlette Chemain-Degrange,

Jacques Chevrier, and Bernard Mouralis discuss a wide range of authors yet being struck by the absence of African voices at these roundtables. I started exploring the shelves of Présence Africaine and L'Harmattan bookstores in Paris and found these other voices I had suspected were out there some-where—Séwanou Dabla, Adrien Huannou, Mohamadou Kane, Jean-Pierre Makouta-Mboukou, Achille Mbembe, Guy Ossito Midiohouan, Pius Ngandu Nkashama, and Mukala Kadima-Nzuji.

Things then took another unexpected turn when I came upon Christo-pher L. Miller's recently published *Theories of Africans: Francophone Lit-erature and Anthropology in Africa*. The whole notion of francophone stud-ies was virtually unheard of in Britain at the time—ASCALF was in fact debating whether to include specialists of Beur and Maghrebi literature at an upcoming conference—and I decided very quickly to embark on a new intellectual journey that would take me to Yale University. Francophone literature was receiving increasing scholarly attention in America, although still facing resistance from conservative departments, but nevertheless texts were finding their way into curricular offerings. Soon I would be exposed to a plethora of postcolonial theorists—Homi Bhabha, Edward Said, Gayatri Spivak—and the work of scholars of multiple national origins working in the American Academy—Koffi Anyinefa, Kwame Anthony Appiah, Rich-ard Bjornson, John Conteh-Morgan, Manthia Diawara, Henry Louis Gates, Kenneth Harrow, Abiola Irele, Eileen Julien, Amadou Koné, Françoise Lionnet, Lydie Moudileno, V. Y. Mudimbe, Elisabeth Mudimbe-Boyi, Jonathan Ngate, Ngùgì wa Thiong'o, Eric Sellin, Aliko Songolo. All too often, I discovered, critics working in different geographic spaces did not read each other's work because of ignorance, but also because of linguistic and disciplinary boundaries. I felt that new research needed to be situated at the intersection of francophone, postcolonial, and African studies, and I sug-gested an approach that would foreground what we have to learn from the multiple voices that come to us from inside and beyond Africa—most im-portantly, writing that would reflect my own intellectual trajectory.

This book then has its origins in research I conducted initially in Lon-don and Paris and then later in New Haven, including fieldwork in the Congo in 1994–95, where I traveled to meet with Congolese authors and scholars. Those meetings in turn radically altered my perspective on African literature and my understanding of the relationship between writers and the state. At that time I became convinced of the imperative of broadening the framework of my study in order to accommodate a multiplicity of voices—from resistance and official literature to newspapers and propaganda—contributing to the construction of the nation-state. Only through a consideration of this polyvocality can one attempt to uncover the postcolonial reality and obtain a more accurate understanding of the circumstances of African decolonization.

Along the way, I have benefited from the generosity and insights of many great teachers, scholars, and writers, many of whom were probably unaware of how much they influenced me. Regretfully, some of the Congolese authors who were most helpful and encouraging have died in recent years: Sony Labou Tansi (d. 1995), who provided all kinds of support for my various projects from 1986 onward; and Sylvain Bemba (d. 1995), who shared with me on numerous occasions his insights on Congolese literature and politics during my visit to the Republic of the Congo. While in the Congo, the various discussions and interviews I conducted with Tchichelle Tchivela, Marie-Léontine Tsibinda, Mukala Kadima-Nzuji, and Claude-Emmanuel Eta-Onka helped transform the project into what it is today. I am especially thankful to Pauline Dongala for arranging my first meeting with her husband, Emmanuel Boundzéki Dongala, who subsequently facilitated the various meetings I had in Brazzaville, who was always available to answer my questions, and whose continued generosity and friendship on both sides of the Atlantic have been a great source of inspiration to me.

At University College London, Annette Lavers was my mentor, providing unconditional support, flexibility, open-mindedness, and an intellectual vibrancy that had a profound influence on me; in turn, Michael J. Worton both inspired and encouraged me to pursue research. Charles Porter was exceptionally kind and receptive to my work at Yale University, and Catherine Cusset offered abundant comments on my dissertation. While at Yale and since, I have considered myself extremely fortunate to have become friends with Jacques Guicharnaud.

My decision to come to the United States to attend graduate school at Yale was premised on my being able to complete a doctoral dissertation directed by Christopher L. Miller. His professionalism and insightful and generous readings of my work have made it all worthwhile. For his continued, indispensable support, I am extremely grateful.

At the University of Notre Dame, generous research funding was provided by the Dr. William M. Scholl Collegiate Chair in Romance Languages and Literatures, which I held from 1996 to 2000, and the Institute for Scholarship in the Liberal Arts (ISLA). This allowed me to conduct research and travel to conferences in Australia, Canada, France, Guadeloupe, Morocco, Tunisia, the United Kingdom, and the United States. In addition to financial support, I am particularly grateful for the intellectual and collegial support I received at Notre Dame from Joseph Buttigieg, Julia Douthwaite, Brian Edwards, Christopher Fox, Louis Mackenzie, Richard Pierce, Donald Sniegowski, Alain Toumayan, and John Welle.

While at Northwestern University as a Visiting Scholar in the Program in African Studies during the spring of 1999, I received constructive input from faculty and Fellows. I am grateful for the welcome extended to me by Akbar Virmani and Mary Ebeling.

My work benefited tremendously from the stimulating exchanges and critiques formulated in different settings by Dominick La Capra, Eleanor Kaufman, Natalie Melas, Kobena Mercer, Jonathan Ngate, and Mark Sanders during my stay at the Society for the Humanities at Cornell University in 1999–2000 as a Mellon Post-Doctoral Fellow.

Grants from the University of California at Los Angeles Academic Senate, along with intellectual and personal support from my colleagues in the Multicampus Research Group on Transnational and Transcolonial Studies (MRG), have allowed me to complete this project; I am particularly grateful to its co-directors, Françoise Lionnet and Shu-mei Shih, and also to Ali Behdad, Karl Ashoka Britto, Jenny Sharpe, and Winnifred Woodhull. My colleagues at the James S. Coleman African Studies Center, and its director Allen F. Roberts, deserve a special thanks for their encouragement. I would like to express my appreciation to Emily Apter for helping me along the way, and for her enthusiasm with regard to my work. Thanks also to Efrain Kristal and Aamir Mufti for their support.

For her unconditional encouragement, energy, generosity, good humor, and warm welcome at UCLA, I am extremely grateful to the chair of the Department of French and Francophone Studies, Françoise Lionnet.

My undergraduate and graduate students at the University of Notre Dame, Cornell University, and UCLA also deserve a special mention; I hope they know how grateful I am for the various exchanges we have had and the intellectual journeys we have embarked upon.

My work has been enriched through dialogue with Mark Behr, by his lucid appraisal of South African and postcolonial politics, but most importantly by his friendship.

Fran Wintroub deserves special thanks for helping me in immeasurable ways.

Special thanks also to my dear friend and comrade throughout, David Carpenter, for the adventures and conversations we have had over the past twenty years, and for those to come.

I owe a particular debt of gratitude to Dee Mortensen of Indiana University Press for her enthusiasm about this book, her engaging collaborative spirit, and the care with which she has guided the project through to publication.

Finally, I am most grateful to my friends and interlocutors in the field of African, francophone, and postcolonial studies, for the immutability of their support, and for their own work from which I have learned so much: Hédi Abdel-Jaouad, John Conteh-Morgan, Anne Donadey, Mary-Jean Green, Alec Hargreaves, Nicki Hitchcott, Lawrence Kritzman, Michel Laronde, Françoise Lionnet, Phyllis M. Martin, Jane Moss, H. Adlai Murdoch, Jean-Christian Pleau, Anjali Prabhu, Mireille Rosello, André Siamundele, Abdourahman Waberi, Richard Watts, Jane Winston, and Winnifred Woodhull.

This book is dedicated to my parents, David and Jean Thomas, my beloved son Devereux, and of course my wife, Erin Joy Cooney, with whom I have navigated and traversed the fragile landscape of emotional sensibility.

For permission to reprint various sections of this book, I am grateful to the editors and proprietors of *La problématique de l'identité dans la littérature francophone du Canada et d'ailleurs* (Editions du Nordir, 1995); *Vanishing Point: Studies in Comparative Literature* 2 (Spring 1996); *Not on Any Map: Essays on Postcoloniality and Cultural Nationalism* (University of Exeter Press, 1997); *Black Accents: Writing in French from Africa, Mauritius and the Caribbean* (Grant & Cutler Ltd., 1997); *South Central Review* (Summer 2000); *Francophonie littéraire africaine en procès* (Editions Nouvelles du Sud, 2000); *Œuvres & Critiques* (Spring 2001); *Rethinking Creative Processes* (Lang, 2001); *Nottingham French Studies* (Spring 2001); and *La Rue Meurt*. In all instances, my work in this book supersedes earlier versions, has been extensively revised, and has benefited from the incisive comments of various—often anonymous but always generous—readers.

NOTE ON TRANSLATIONS

Material included in this book that originally appeared in French has been translated into English using published translations when these were available. Otherwise, translations are my own. Exceptions include the official poems that appear in chapter 2, the original French that appears in figures 1–7 in chapter 6 and that is translated in the text itself when relevant to the discussion, and in instances throughout the book when the meaning of the original version seemed self-evident or its significance critical. In some cases supplemental information has been provided in the notes.

ABBREVIATIONS AND ACRONYMS

AEF	Afrique Equatoriale Française
AND	Alliance Nationale pour la Démocratie
ANEC	Association Nationale des Ecrivains Congolais
AOF	Afrique Occidentale Française
CNR	Conseil National pour la Révolution
JMNR	Jeune Mouvement National pour la Révolution
JRDA	Jeunesse de la Révolution Démocratique Africaine
MCDDI	Mouvement Congolais pour le Développement de la Démocratie Intégrale
MSA	Mouvement Socialiste Africain
OAU	Organization of African Unity
PCT	Parti Congolais du Travail
PPC	Parti Progressiste Congolais
RC	République du Congo
RDA	République Démocratique Africaine
RDC	République Démocratique du Congo
RPC	République Populaire du Congo
TRC	Truth and Reconciliation Commission
UDDIA	Union Démocratique pour la Défense des Intérêts Africains
UE	Union des Ecrivains
UEC	Union des Ecrivains Congolais
UJSC	Union de la Jeunesse Socialiste Congolaise
UM	Union des Musiciens
UNEAC	Union Nationale des Ecrivains, Artistes, et Artisans Congolais
UNTC	Union Nationale des Tradi-Praticiens Congolais
UPADS	Union Panafricaine pour la Démocratie Sociale
URD	Union pour le Renouveau Démocratique
URF	Union Révolutionnaire des Femmes

Nation-Building, Propaganda, and Literature in Francophone Africa

1 INTRODUCTION

Engineering History and Engineering Literature

When an old person dies in Africa, it is the same thing as a library burning. —AHMADOU HAMPATÉ BA

The time will come when Africa will write its own history. —PATRICE LUMUMBA

State involvement in the production and dissemination of ideology has been investigated with specific reference to the ex-Soviet Union and Eastern European countries, China, and Latin America, but it has been ignored in the francophone sub-Saharan African context.[1] *Nation-Building, Propaganda, and Literature in Francophone Africa* attempts to redress this imbalance by exploring a complex African reality and consideration of culture and politics. This book offers scholars and students of African literature, comparative literature, and francophone studies a framework with which to think about the political and ideological consequences of structuring literary works according to the political persuasions of state apparatuses. For political scientists and historians, the book explores those processes that culminated in independence and delineates the complex path of post-independence politics, the transition to democratic rule, and the civil conflict of the late 1990s. In its attempt to engage a broad range of readers across disciplinary boundaries, this book suggests how this approach might in turn stand to impact and influence the future of interdisciplinarity, while also contributing to thinking on nationalism and postcoloniality. In order to obtain a more accurate view of the formation of modern African nation-states and to better understand the complex and complicated mechanisms associated with the process of engineering history and engineering literature, I draw upon a broad range of anthropological, historical, and sociological information. This information offers access to the specificity of the Congolese context, articulates the uniqueness of the Marxist-Leninist era, and locates writings according to the political context in which they were produced.

The construction of cultural and national identities has often been inseparable from the discourse of nationalism in the African context. In an attempt to move beyond Benedict Anderson's groundbreaking book *Imagined Communities: Reflections on the Origin and Spread of Nationalism*, I have adopted what could perhaps be described as a more proactive term, namely the *engineering* of the nation.[2] While my usage of this term shares many of the qualities Anderson attributes to the notion of "imagining," it is also indebted to Stalin's concept of "the engineers of the human soul," which was used to describe state-sponsored writers, and Noam Chomsky's invocation of "consent" as something that can be "manufactured" through propagandist structures.[3] In its incorporation of revolutionary and reconstructive practices, the term *engineering* then has the possibility of situating those voices attempting to exercise control over the various mechanisms of power, while recognizing that this pluralism emerges from often antagonistic coexistence, that its polyvocality inherently functions, negotiates, and competes at different levels, and that various identities are not freely or independently formed but rather mechanically clash in a constitutive framework. Furthermore, this book suggests that Anderson's emphasis on the widespread nature of print culture that allows for the imagination of the nation may not provide an adequate framework with which to explore the complexity of the postcolony. In the case of the Congo, the nation has been engineered top-down by ideologues and state-sponsored official literature, which has in turn been challenged by orality and non-official and diasporic literature.

The fundamental question that emerges concerns the mechanisms through which power is acquired, maintained, and manipulated in colonial and postcolonial spaces. The object of this book is to locate those agents—colonial, national, transnational—responsible for the cultural, political, and social processes explored in the area of investigation. For example, colonial expansionism during the post–Berlin Conference era (1884–85 onward) witnessed the collaborative practices of assimilationist and missionary tendencies for the purpose of deploying the *mission civilisatrice*, while *négritude*, Pan-Africanism, Socialism, and Marxism-Leninism, among other theoretical models, generated particular conditions for the elaboration of post-independence decolonizing objectives. Since the 1980s, numerous political and social transitions have occurred in African states, and this change has been somewhat paradigmatic in terms of the innovative measures it has brought to African conceptions of democracy. The African context offers a unique opportunity for the exploration of the disorientation that has accompanied political transition, and it is taken up in later chapters of this book. Attempts to remedy problems have been provided by truth commissions (South Africa), National Conferences (Benin, the Congo, Togo), and democratization movements (Cameroon, the Côte d'Ivoire, former Zaire) that have allowed for the articulation of new modes of expression, foregrounding testimony as a way of achieving alternative versions of postcolonial events, enabling perpetrators to demonstrate their humanity, but also victims to articulate narratives that official history has declared nonexistent. These testimonies then have the possibility of enacting healing, restitution, reparation, retribution, and reconciliation, and ultimately bringing states to democracy.

To this extent, the Congolese context provides a striking model for the exploration of nationalism and postcoloniality, since having declared itself a Marxist-Leninist state and pursuing relationships with China, the Soviet Union, North Korea, and Cuba, the Congo maintained strong economic links with France. Indeed, Chinese and Soviet influence is often neglected in thinking about Africa but of pertinence to the framework of this book, given the close cultural and political ties enjoyed by many postcolonial African governments and their ideological counterparts in Beijing and Moscow. Through a consideration of official literatures of the state and the influence of cultural paradigms associated with these other discursive realms — notably Socialist Realism and Soviet-style state-sponsored literature, Chinese nationalism and Communist-sponsored literature — this book underlines links with sociocultural frameworks that offer valuable insight to the issues addressed in the African context. Furthermore, this framework broadens considerably the field of sociocultural discourse by insisting not only on imported Occidental aesthetic codes and formulations but also on foregrounding Chinese and Soviet influences in the context of nation-state building located outside of Imperial and neocolonial frameworks. Recognizing the significance of these ideological experimentations, this book reflects on sociopolitical events associated with the reconfiguration of nation-states that coincided with the collapse of the Soviet Union, the end of the Cold War, and the rectification of the Chinese revolution. Links are also made with other communist and post-communist societies, where transitions would ultimately contribute to the demise of the People's Republic of the Congo in the early 1990s, but also through the analysis of the work of Emmanuel Dongala to a more encompassing notion of African history, one that Edouard Glissant suggested in his book *Caribbean Discourse* by incorporating Africa, the Caribbean, and continental America in his framework.[4] Through a focus on texts by official writers and some of the more strikingly original examples offered by the writings of Henri Lopes and Sony Labou Tansi, connections are made to questions of political reform and shifting ideological alignments.

The history that is important to the context of this book is developed in later chapters. Yet, it seems important to highlight that on both sides of the Congo River lie geographic spaces that for most of the twentieth century have traded various forms of the name Congo, often generating considerable confusion among observers of regional politics.[5] Indeed, the genealogies of many of the writers treated in this book and the contextual framework of their texts are located in these respective topographic entities. On the left bank of the river lies the newly established Democratic Republic of the Congo (formerly known as the Republic of Zaire under Mobutu's leadership) with its capital Kinshasa (ex-Leopoldville), while on the right bank is the considerably smaller Republic of the Congo, with its capital Brazzaville. Brazzaville served as the capital of French Equatorial Africa from 1910 to 1960, and, significantly, it was in Brazzaville that General de Gaulle himself staged the famous 1944 Brazzaville Conference that paved the way for debate on decolonization. The confusion surrounding the use of the word "Congo" reflects the interconnectedness of the two "Congos" (French and Belgian), betrays the complex history of the region, and underlines the difficulties associated with the referentiality of African territories, given the complex and complicated historical origins of such alignments.[6]

Questions of dependency are inextricably linked to the postcolonial context where, as Achille Mbembe has argued, "to account for both the mind-set and the effectiveness of postcolonial relations of power, we need to go beyond the binary categories used in standard interpretations of domination."[7] What is more, "it is only through a shift in perspective that we can understand that the postcolonial relationship is not primarily a relationship of resistance or of collaboration but can best be characterized as convivial, a relationship fraught by the fact of the *commandement* and its 'subjects.'"[8] The pertinence of this symbiotic relationship is crucial to the context of recent discourse on African literature and culture because as Paul N'Da has stated in his book *Les intellectuels et le pouvoir en Afrique noire*: "No matter where one finds power relations there will always be inequality; and all power relations are about domination. . . . In the most general sense then, power can be defined as the sum total of the people, structures, public and private mechanisms and means in and through which social domination manifests itself."[9]

The elite nomenclature generated by colonial mechanisms and "promiscuous" power relations in the Congolese postcolony has been unique in terms of the interaction and interplay between the state and literary production, and the connections between prominent political figures and key literary figures.[10] The Congo is thus all the more interesting, given the number of authors who have held and continue to hold important government positions—most notably Jean-Baptiste Tati-Loutard, Antoine Letembet-Ambily, Sylvain Bemba, Henri Lopes, and Tchichelle Tchivela—and because leaders such as Marien Ngouabi and Denis Sassou Nguesso outlined official guidelines for cultural productions and solicited the assistance of writers for the purpose of disseminating their policies. The analysis of Henri Lopes's work provides the occasion to explore testimony and reconciliation while highlighting the problematic status of this prominent author in a somewhat ambiguous position between two spheres of discourse. In an incisive article that explores the relationship between cultural practitioners and the state, Tanella Boni (herself a novelist from the Côte d'Ivoire) stated that "regimes have their writers in the same way that the Kings of Europe once had jesters and the Chiefs of pre-colonial Africa their griots and storytellers."[11]

Indeed, the relationship between literature and politics is especially interesting in the Congo, where the post-revolutionary Marxist-Leninist elite exercising governmental authority between 1969 and 1991 sponsored an official literature of the state. This has made it possible to distinguish between a "nationalist" or "official" literature that is inseparable from the discourse of the state and the imperatives of ideological utility, and a "national" or "non-official literature" that is more concerned with the construction of a nation and which attacks the state for its failure to recognize autonomous political or literary identities. *Nation-Building, Propaganda, and Literature in Francophone Africa* questions this apparently binary structure in order to reveal the complexity of the intersections between these mutually constitutive bodies of literature. While official writers defended a specific vision of society and dedicated their creative activities toward achieving those ends, a competing cultural elite represented by *avant-garde* resistance authors (sometimes censored, and almost exclusively published abroad) menaced this monolithic construct.

Non-official authors subscribe to the nation-building process but attack the state for its failure to effectively construct such a space. Thus, the state rather than the nation comes under attack, since the power mechanisms which come under its aegis determine whether or not an individual can ever have the occasion to "self-realize."[12] While there are many intersections between the diverse body of writings, non-official authors do not participate to the same degree and to the same effect in engineering the nation as the more accessible and affordable texts of their official counterparts.[13] Ignoring and producing texts independently of the hegemonic power of party control, denouncing the homogeneity of official writing, and undermining and exposing the postcolonial political elite to the scrutiny of outsiders, non-official authors stand as testimony to the possibility of producing a literature that remains engaged with the postcolonial reality while nevertheless fore-grounding and allowing for newer kinds of aesthetic articulations. Further-more, as the chapter that focuses on Sony Labou Tansi shows—and this is where Mbembe's work on the postcolony has become so important—orality and popular culture challenge and compete with printed literature, given their non-elitist status, thereby delimiting literature's function in engineer-ing the nation. Thus, while print culture engineers the nation and legiti-mizes it, successive elitist nationalist governments have denied orality its due and valorized instead print culture from a modernity-based perspective. This book insists on the importance of considering the multiple voices that have contributed to the discursive realm since independence, while explor-ing diverse contributions to print culture—novels, plays, poems, newspa-pers, political cartoons, and propaganda.

Following the publication of Jean-Paul Sartre's preface ("Orphée noir") to Léopold Sédar Senghor's *Anthologie de la nouvelle poésie nègre et malgache de langue française* in 1948, even *négritude* became increasingly politicized and came to play a significant role in the politics of nationalism in the post-independence structuring of newly sovereign countries.[14] In fact, early pre-cursors for committed literature were already available in the African con-text through such publications as *L'Etudiant Noir*, *La Revue du Monde Noir*, and *Légitime Défense* (published during the 1930s), and perhaps most significantly with the creation of the publishing house Présence Africaine in 1947. Indeed, political *engagement* was considered a moral, ethical impera-tive at the time. One can measure just how strongly some writers felt about this by considering Mongo Béti's impassioned attack on Camara Laye's novel *L'enfant noir* for what he considered to be its lack, if not even absence, of explicit political commitment.[15] The revolutionary, nationalistic overtones inherent to such a discourse are apparent, and it is this nationalistic dimen-sion that Frantz Fanon fastened on in his critique of Senghorian *négritude* in *Les damnés de la terre*.[16] For Fanon, political independence would pro-vide the necessary circumstances for the autonomous development of na-tional cultures, and African leaders soon recognized the importance of con-trolling both political and cultural mechanisms. Writers such as Ahmadou Kourouma and Yambo Ouologuem at the end of the 1960s and the beginning of the 1970s threatened prevailing political and literary models; Ouologuem in particular set out to demystify and deconstruct the Senghorian view of the African past by juxtaposing the image of a violent, pre-colonial Africa, and arguing that violence was not simply a product of the contact with colonialist powers.[17]

Rather than attempting to provide an exhaustive presentation of Congolese literature—a gesture that would be redundant within the context of this book—I have attempted instead to describe the changing circumstances of literary creativity in the Congo and to situate works in relation to those of their predecessors and African counterparts. Overviews are by definition reductive; in his book *L'idéologie dans la littérature négro-africaine d'expression française*, Guy Ossito Midiohouan criticized the generalizations inherent to such approaches and suggested that we consider instead works according to genre and in relation to the historical context in which they were produced.[18] The framework I have adopted thus acknowledges the appropriateness of Midiohouan's revised historiography and its pertinence to the Congolese context.[19]

The emergence of a considerable body of literature from the region coincided with the Congo becoming a sovereign nation-state.[20] Whereas only a limited number of poems and novels were published during colonialism, production increased dramatically after independence with the publication of some twenty-two novels, twenty-nine volumes of poetry, and nineteen plays, figures that have remained relatively constant with the exception of theater, which has dwindled somewhat since the 1980s with growing production costs and limited financial assistance.[21] While these figures may not be exhaustive, and for the most part do not take into account the works of official writers, they nevertheless provide a clear indication of the changing patterns of literary production in the region.

Gradually, as the revolution became fixed, threatened by change, and less accommodating of provocation and dissent, presidents of the Central Committee of the Parti Congolais du Travail (Congolese Workers Party), Ngouabi (1968–77) and Sassou Nguesso (1979–92), radicalized the politics of nationalism, gestures that were accompanied by considerable governmental interference in the cultural domain as the ruling authorities fastened on both the cultural and political teachings of Marxism-Leninism as a prerequisite to nation-building. Sassou Nguesso was determined to promote political and cultural unity and founded the Union Nationale des Ecrivains, Artistes, et Artisans Congolais (UNEAC) in 1979. While all Congolese artists were automatically members of this organization, one of the paradoxes of the Congolese government's increased radicalization and attempt to sponsor an official literature was to generate a political climate that would stimulate a group of particularly creative authors determined to expose and undermine the authorities' attempts to establish writers' workshops. Counter-hegemonic texts in the tradition of resistance writing began to appear in every literary genre, and a remarkable number of authors would soon receive considerable critical acclaim: Sylvain Bemba, Emmanuel Dongala, Henri Lopes, Caya Makhele, Jean-Pierre Makouta-Mboukou, Guy Menga, Maxime N'Debeka, Sony Labou Tansi, Jean-Baptiste Tati-Loutard, Tchichelle Tchivela, Marie-Léontine Tsibinda (the notable female exception to a predominantly masculine corpus).[22] Congolese authors came to enjoy a particularly close collaborative network, and their concern with eluding attempts to categorize and classify their works according to officially prescribed models or readily identifiable European influences contributed to the elaboration of original literary modes.[23]

The fundamental issue for this book concerns the relationship of writers to the nationalistic agenda of key political ideologues—Ahmed Sékou Touré, Ngouabi, Sassou Nguesso—and their contribution to the creation of a national culture. Since the emergence of sovereign nation-states during the post-independence era of decolonization, it has become increasingly common to talk in terms of national literatures.[24] As Timothy Brennan has argued, "the problem of nation is also the problem of the influence of state policy on national literary production."[25] From the restricted focus of the Congo, the book itself broadens the perspective and establishes pan-African connections to anglophone (Kenya, Nigeria, Somalia, South Africa), francophone (Benin, Guinea, etc.), and lusophone Africa (Angola and Mozambique), thereby providing a framework for thinking in terms of a theory of nationalism in the African context, as well as introducing obvious links to other areas of the world in which issues of national identity are of pressing concern.

The emergence of a national literature coincided with governmental attempts at promoting nationalist sentiment in the Congo and imposing hegemony within the artificial parameters of the newly delineated nation-state. The idea which modern leaders have tried to enforce is, as Edward Said has argued, that "we are still the inheritors of that style by which one is defined by the nation, which in turn derives its authority from a supposedly unbroken tradition."[26] The Senghorian image of the African past, infused with nationalistic fervor, gave African leaders the opportunity of implementing and imposing national unity in the sovereign nation once nation-building had become the responsibility of the state in the postcolony. Whereas assimilationist policy had been the order of the day under French rule, similar philosophies prevailed in the postcolony at the service of nationalistic agendas, and, given the heterogeneous character of newly independent countries, the singularity of unification contained in the one-party system was seen by many leaders as the only way of forging national unity. Marxism-Leninism was therefore embraced as an anti-colonial and anti-capitalist model for the common struggle against imperialism. For Crawford Young, "'Nation' as an imagined community of anti-colonial combat . . . was relatively unproblematic. . . . But 'nation,' once independence was won, required the postcolonial state as vehicle: thus its imperative of 'national integration.'"[27] Leaders were thus able to authenticate their method of rule, outline the tenets of that legitimacy, and then enforce the state parameters.

Country profiles prepared by the Congolese delegation to the United Nations during the 1960s are indicative of the concerns of this period in Congolese history.[28] A cursory overview of these documents provides an official version of Congolese history, reinforcing the idea of a collective memory (through recourse to traditional nationalist and patriotic iconography), shared heritage, and common framework of references—a narrative that is by definition problematic especially when given that the Congo only became an independent nation-state in 1960. As Kwame Anthony Appiah has argued, a "'national heritage' is constructed through the invention of traditions; the careful filtering of the rough torrent of historical event into the fine stream of an official narrative; the creation of a homogeneous legacy of values and experience. . . . The official constitution of a national history bequeaths us the nation, and the discipline of literary history."[29]

The review *Notre Librairie* published three volumes in 1986 which sought to formulate answers, or at least to stimulate discussion around the following question: "Do African literatures, conceived within the framework of the nation-states from which they have emerged, exhibit specificities that allow us to distinguish between them, and if so, what would these be?"[30] In his contribution to the first volume, Elikia M'Bokolo demonstrated how Ernest Renan's definition provided the framework for the organization of nation-states in Africa.[31] The insistence on a sense of common identity as an integral component of a broader network of social relations—a process Jean-Loup Amselle has described as one of "composition, décomposition, recomposition"—duplicates the model adopted by the Congolese state and reproduced in the country profiles.[32] Inevitably, these discussions are linked to the discourse of nationalism, and the various anthologies that appeared in the early 1970s stand today as precursors to these debates. Many questions are raised that serve to illustrate the difficulties, contradictions, and complexities of determining which texts constitute the degree zero of national writing.

When Adrien Huannou published his essay entitled *La question des littératures nationales en Afrique noire* in 1989, he became one of the best-known advocates of national literatures.[33] As his point of entry, Huannou draws upon Alain Rouch and Gérard Clavreuil's notion of "national specificities" in their comprehensive anthology *Littératures nationales d'écriture française*,[34] and he then defines his contextual framework according to Renan's terms, namely "the sharing of a common cultural heritage to different degrees by all members of a given community and the willingness to valorize this cultural heritage" (Huannou, 21). For Huannou, texts produced by a country's nationals automatically belong to the national culture: "Since all that belongs to a nation is national, and since a literature is made up of all the literary works of a country or region, then all the oral and written works produced by nationals of an African state constitute a national literature. There are therefore as many national literatures as there are states in Africa" (Huannou, 34). The problem with this kind of tautological approach is that it fails to consider the sociological circumstances which have contributed to the production of literatures in the postcolonial space, and there is much at stake in discussing African literature within these parameters without adequate treatment of the state's interference in culture and without distinguishing between the literary productions of official and unofficial cultural practitioners.[35] Richard Bjornson's notion of a "universe of discourse" seems the most useful in order to describe "the rules, procedures, assumptions, and conventional meanings that permit verbal communication among individuals from the same community of language users."[36] Such a "universe of discourse" has become increasingly identifiable, given the distinct postcolonial trajectories of African nation-states — the experience of Marxist-Leninist rule as opposed to democratic pluralism — and the particularities these have generated only to be transformed in the writings of nationals.

Foremost among opponents of the concept of national literatures stands Guy Ossito Midiohouan, whose critical writings have addressed the emergence of the national approach to literature.[37] According to him, these frameworks have a tendency to reinforce hostility, of further "balkanizing" African nations, and "*national literatures* as they have manifested themselves over the past decade or so are *still* mythological formations held up by a perverse ideology."[38] Midiohouan makes a necessary gesture in recognizing the ideological dimension of national literatures, something which Bjornson was right to point out Huannou does not sufficiently underscore. Yet, the unified approach to African literature Midiohouan has in mind fails to sufficiently distinguish individual particularities, and his dismissal of the national approach seems unfounded and of course outdated after four decades of decolonization history. Sociological circumstances informing cultural practitioners have grown increasingly specific, and it would be inappropriate to critique African literature from an ideologically neutral position, given that the politics of cultural nationalism are inextricably linked in the African context to the production of literature. As Christopher L. Miller has shown, "when used properly, the national approach should in no way stand as an obstacle to comparative or critical thinking. It should merely provide new ways of understanding the public and hidden transcripts that continue to emerge."[39]

The Congo became an object of public consciousness only with the struggle for independence during the 1950s, but it became a juridical reality with an autonomous government structure and political agenda in 1960. Developments in the Congo under Marxism-Leninism therefore generated radically different sociological circumstances from those in other African countries. *Nation-Building, Propaganda, and Literature in Francophone Africa* stands of course as confirmation of my faith in the fundamental usefulness of the national approach, particularly in order to explore the respective manner in which writers have treated the question of nationalism. My concern is with the relationship between literature and politics, and specifically how cultural production—official, resistance, propaganda—has been influenced by state intervention. In an attempt to avoid the pitfalls inherent in such a potentially determinist approach, parallels between fictional and realistic elements become less important than emphasis on the complicated relationship between autonomous and aligned writings. The writers selected for this book consider themselves Congolese and subscribe to the concept of a national territory within the boundaries left over from the colonial era. Yet, I have distinguished between non-official literary works which criticize the state for its failure to construct the nation, and the productions of official writers who adhere faithfully to the model of partisanship, in a process Roger Chemain has described as "the attempted bureaucratization of Congolese writers and artists as well as the painstaking promotion of a Zdhanovian subliterature characterized by watchwords and hollow slogans."[40]

The choice of restricting the focus of this book to the national framework is, then, prompted by the unique opportunity such an approach offers for a questioning of the nation-state as a category of analysis, rather than simply examining works selected according to authorial nationality or geographical locality. Huannou's notion of national literature is too encompassing and extreme, and my objective is to highlight the potential dangers intrinsic to a national approach that ignores the ideological component, while simultaneously interrogating alternative approaches that refuse to acknowledge the possibilities and potentialities of the nation-state as a valid category of analysis. While it may have been anachronistic to discuss the existence of national literatures during the early years of decolonization, different political regimes, ideologies, and sociological circumstances in each autonomous territory have informed cultural practitioners in different ways and thus generated a certain specificity. By situating these cultural products according to the historical, literary, and political framework in which they are inscribed, one can best identify the various factors that contributed to the present geopolitical entity, and those elements that have come to characterize thinking on issues of postcoloniality.

One must be prepared to acknowledge that the national approach is invested with an ideological component—to ignore this would be nothing less than irresponsible. One of the most disturbing aspects in the promotion of national literatures is the implied attempt to force the cultural practitioner to conform to certain accepted guidelines, which inevitably kill creativity. The works of non-official authors treated in this book examine the disembodiment of cultural references represented by colonialism and nationalism. Their radical new modes of expression and the reform of conventional narrative constitute a gesture of erasure which seeks to challenge state initiatives at building the post-independent nation. Nation-states are in a constant dynamic process of transition, whether criticized by non-official texts for their failure to create appropriately inclusive structures or embraced and praised by official writers who subscribe to the efforts of the governing authorities. In each case, a vision of the national space motivates their respective national and nationalistic efforts at building the postcolonial nation.

While there has been much discussion on the subject of "imagined communities," there has not been enough thinking on the processes through which these communities are more systematically constructed by various individuals and organizations. One needs to explore the role that the state plays in this process and examine the links that exist between the imagination and the representation of cultural and political spaces within the context of decolonization. Not all communities emerge in the same manner and through the influences of the same agents. To what extent are national categories limited by the boundaries of each imagination? Can one say that the sociological reality under investigation is fixed, that is to say permanently circumscribed by the geography that was imagined for it by European colonizers and subsequently enforced by the postcolonial government elite? In other words, should African nations be considered completed entities, finished once the imaginative process comes to an end (if indeed it ever does), or should we consider ways in which cultural productions resist the ruling elite, the political projects or visions contained in their works from which alternative models could or should emerge? This is the era of new alignments—regional, national, transcolonial, transnational, and global. The task will be to determine how these transitions are explored in literature and to continue to monitor the manner in which cultural productions contribute to the future of Africa.

Throughout the book I reiterate the necessity of analyzing those complex mechanisms associated with the process of "truth" telling in a post-independent national space, in light of government intervention, counter-cultural manifestations, and other phenomena employed in the process of narrating and constructing a national identity. By considering the multiple voices competing for authority that have been evidenced in the language of fiction, of official propaganda, of the media, and of historiography, this book attempts to achieve a more encompassing perspective of the cultural dynamics at work in Africa since independence. Furthermore, this approach emphasizes the importance of delineating a framework that calls for better contextualization, indeed one that articulates the specific circumstances in which the circulation of information is regulated by governments, socioeconomic considerations, and particular issues relating to literacy. Such an approach would seem all the more important, that francophone cultures outside of Europe are essentially constituted by nonliterate audiences who do *not* consume print culture as a commodity.[41] The book offers a supranational approach to some of these key questions through an analysis of democratic transition in francophone Africa while also insisting on links to similar processes evidenced since the end of the Cold War in the post-Soviet era, through the Truth and Reconciliation proceedings in South Africa, and post-1997 Hong Kong.[42]

Nation-Building, Propaganda, and Literature in Francophone Africa is a book that incorporates a wide range of voices, and it is structured in such a way as to reflect this polyvocality. It emphasizes the unique perspective provided by official writers and highlights what can be learned from a consideration of alternative forms of print culture (government-controlled newspapers and decentralized media), but it also underlines the diverse contributions of authors as different as Emmanuel Dongala, Henri Lopes, and Sony Labou Tansi. The fact that most cultural practitioners resided in Brazzaville and the immediate vicinity and were able to maintain contact—albeit often clandestine and underground—created a radically different situation from that in countries such as Guinea, Kenya, Mali, Nigeria, Somalia, and South Africa, where many authors were often forced into exile or imprisoned. This book repeatedly insists that monolithic or binary approaches ultimately represent gross oversimplifications of colonial and postcolonial phenomena, and that the distinctions between official and non-official constructs are not always readily identifiable.[43] To argue that colonial and postcolonial literatures only represent critiques of outsiders (colonizers) by insiders (the colonized) and insiders (the postcolonial masses) of other insiders (African dictatorships), respectively, would be to have misunderstood the particularities of the constitutive dimension of colonial contact and of the postcolonial predicament.

While this book is a sociocultural project that reaches into important themes and issues in Africa in general, it is also an artistic project that is representative of something much larger. To this end, the book provides distinctions between the diverse authors and writings that are examined, and it establishes links to a wide range of literary influences, foremost among which figure Latin American authors such as Jorge Luis Borges and Gabriel García Márquez, Sartrean *engagement*, the French New Novel as exemplified by Alain Robbe-Grillet, French experimental and *avant-gardist* writers such as Georges Perec, the Occidental canon, and francophone African literature from *négritude* onward, in addition to various encounters with modernity and modernism. For obvious reasons, the issues raised extend beyond the scope of Africa and are of relevance to all inquiries concerned with the role that intellectuals and ideologues play in nation-state formation.

There is also an urgent need to reconsider aesthetic categories themselves in order to enact less exclusive paradigms for the appreciation of cultural phenomena in Africa, and in order to avoid the drawbacks of a critique that has not sufficiently distanced itself from the concerns and invariably the constraints of Western aesthetic criteria. Indeed, many of these texts were always already contained in divergent aesthetic categories that have informed and continue to inform the relationship between literary production, reception, and categorization, whether in works such as Léopold Sédar Senghor's 1948 *Anthologie de la nouvelle poésie nègre et malgache de langue française*, Léopold Pindy Mamonsono's 1984 *La nouvelle génération de poètes congolais*, or in the more recent, diametrically opposed statements concerning aesthetics made by proponents of cultural nationalism and non-official authors such as Sony Labou Tansi.[44]

Critics and observers need to formulate responsible discursive modes that adequately address the writer's situatedness outside of imperializing, colonizing narratives and discourses, in order to recognize that there continue to be blind spots that will remain incomprehensible if mediated or appropriated through exclusively Western or ethnocentrist critical paradigms that fail to consider the sociological circumstances from which these narratives have emerged. Instead, the articulation of autonomous and specific narratives as an integral component of the creative process needs to be recognized as necessary subversions of colonizing mechanisms and *not* shortcomings on the part of cultural practitioners. Failure or refusal to do this will have serious implications and continue to foster recuperative and canonizing tendencies that hinder authors who struggle to be published and heard.

In his recent book *Nationalists and Nomads: Essays on Francophone African Literature and Culture*, Miller makes an important step toward such an inquiry in his examination of francophone writings by Africans during the 1920s when he suggests that we extend our definition of print culture to include "literary texts that are known or available," "literary texts that have either been lost or neglected," "newspapers," and "miscellaneous works of scholarship."[45] The result is a more encompassing and therefore more accurate representation of the context under investigation, similar to the framework I have adopted through the inclusion of official and non-official voices. Yet, Miller's conclusion in some ways negates the positive dimension implied by his framework: "If so far there are not any rediscovered masterpieces to make us totally reappraise the literary history of francophone Africa, a broadening of our scope to include the 1920s, with all the ambiguities and uncertainties of those years, can only help us toward a more comprehensive understanding of the present and its debt (of blood and ink) to the past."[46] Surely, as I have insisted in this book, one should endeavor to expand the accepted boundaries of cultural inquiries in order to incorporate a more extensive range of cultural phenomena that ultimately will contribute to a better understanding of cultural history, rather than attempting to retrieve from the African archives works that redefine the historiography by fulfilling the requirements and exigencies of a universalist (read Western notion of high culture) aesthetics.

Indeed, the need to move away from such considerations would seem all the more important today as we begin to recognize just how enriching interdisciplinary approaches can be that foreground the unique contributions of individual cultural practitioners. The futility and circularity of the argument between minor and major literatures, Western and non-Western literatures, generate an inclusionary-exclusionary framework that endlessly reproduces the same coordinates that have always been employed to hierarchize and reduce to the periphery non-Western (and of course non-White) cultures. Reinterpretation and recontextualization have become not so much essential gestures but rather methodological imperatives so that multiple voices can be acknowledged. Surely the objective should be to foster productive and responsible approaches that foreground cultural productions in a less exclusive manner, both inside and outside of established Western criteria for the exploration of "literature." Such a framework would allow us to rethink the importance of literary historiography precisely because "official" historiography has failed to consider Africa's particular circumstances for production in the era of European language literacy.

Ahmadou Hampaté Ba's famous statement "When an old person dies in Africa, it is the same thing as a library burning," which serves as one of the two epigraphs to this introduction, underlines the implicit/explicit nature of literacy's violence toward orality. This is intended to serve as a symbol for the heterogeneous nature of cultural production in Africa, and for the urgent need of foregrounding interdisciplinary and multidisciplinary approaches to print culture, while simultaneously serving as an indicator of current debates in the Academy concerning the *cohabitation* of French and francophone studies. These tensions have much to do with perceived or received notions of that which constitutes *literariness* and, therefore, *literary studies.* The implied violence of literacy compels us to engage in broader disciplinary approaches that also influence our relationship to the teaching of African, francophone, French, and postcolonial literature and culture.

Critics in the Academy are increasingly contributing to research in the field of francophone sub-Saharan African studies. This book represents a departure from traditional approaches to non-Western literatures to the extent that it incorporates new lines of investigation in this emerging discourse. These are necessary for the appreciation and understanding of the cultural, social, and political phenomena in complex geographic spaces. The Republic of the Congo has furnished unique colonial, post-independence, and postcolonial processes that have contributed to the elaboration of a rich and diverse body of cultural productions. The fundamental questions addressed in this book are, however, located in a broader context that includes considerations pertaining to the intercultural dynamics of cultural, francophone, postcolonial, transnational, transcolonial, and global studies. Furthermore, recent political events have generated compelling sociological circumstances that enable this book to project the discussion toward contemporary African societies while suggesting a possible framework for inquiry into key cultural and political issues for the twenty-first century.

In many ways, the commonality between comparative and multidisciplinary approaches to culture is located in the respective marginalization of these fields with respect to the curriculum in general. While these disciplines do in fact intersect and share a similar language and discourse, their points of contact also represent sites of contestation and conflict with regard to the broader institutional boundaries of the curriculum, and the relationship between dominant and subordinate cultures. Scholars, students, and teachers share in the responsibility of insisting on the need for innovative responses to these transitions, in exposing reductive categories for what they really represent, while simultaneously refusing to abandon their freedom to the homogeneity of disciplinary control. These suggestions should not be seen as threats to traditional curricular alignments but rather as opportunities to *rethink, revisit, revitalize,* and ultimately *enrich* intellectual inquiries. While this book may not answer to Lumumba's prophecy according to which "The time will come when Africa will write its own history," it is my sincere hope that the book's commitment to incorporate a more inclusive range of narratives through the treatment of a multiplicity of voices will yield a more accurate version of the history of decolonization, which even if ventriloquized through the words of a European scholar will nevertheless constitute a step in the right direction.

2 OFFICIAL WRITERS
The Engineers of the Congolese Soul

Cultural works must treat and reflect in an ample fashion the important problems of the revolutionary edification of our country. . . . This is how cultural values may serve to inspire and mobilize the popular masses to fulfill the tasks assigned by the Party. —DENIS SASSOU NGUESSO[1]

But for the artist . . . art cannot be reduced to the status of a means in the service of a cause which transcends it . . . the artist puts nothing above her/his work . . . the least external directive paralyzes her/him. —ALAIN ROBBE-GRILLET[2]

The relationship between cultural practitioners and the authorities is determined by a multitude of complex phenomena, and governments have been willing to undertake extreme measures to silence resistant authors and other dissenting voices. The execution of the Nigerian writer and environmental activist Ken Saro-Wiwa on November 10, 1995, was a disquieting reminder of the dangers faced by African authors whose courage and conviction drives them to articulate their opposition to the postcolonial power elite.[3] The widely acclaimed Nigerian author Ben Okri asserted in an article denouncing the sentencing of Saro-Wiwa that "the writer is the barometer of the age."[4] Since the process of nation-state formation got under way following political independence, authors have often had to decide whether to align themselves with the new governing elite or maintain their autonomy. In sociological environments in which one is either for or against the ruling authorities, distinct bodies of literature have emerged. I have attempted to distinguish between those "official" writers who adhere faithfully to the party line and "non-official" authors who insist on maintaining an autonomous creative and ideological signification. In many African countries, authors who acted contrary to the objectives of the party were frequently exposed to persecution and censorship and often forced into exile, thus confirming the significance of Okri's statement concerning the author's relationship to changing political circumstances.

Somewhat paradoxically, it was the fight against the shared colonial oppression that brought Africans together and introduced the nation as the object of public consciousness. However, this also created a symbiotic dependency in the need for continued social unity as a deterrent to further exploitative contact. The Marxist-Leninist model thus enabled governments to reject colonialism and imperialism, but also the economic foundations of the colonizer's rule, namely capitalism. Governments were thus able to transform the fight against Western capitalism into an ongoing class struggle. Assimilationist policies were an integral part of French colonialism, and since Socialist Realism begins with the rejection of bourgeois culture, it presented itself as the archetypal model for postcolonial government elites eager to promote national unity. These issues are all the more relevant within the African context, because the introduction of a formalized system of writing coincided with exposure to Western colonialism; in the francophone sub-Saharan African context, this contact was simultaneously accompanied by assimilation to French cultural prototypes.

Assimilationist mechanisms created complicated circumstances for young Africans who, through the acquisition of literacy, often found themselves at odds with those compatriots who had not attended colonial schools. Relinquishing the assimilationist dream of acceptance and incorporation into French society, confronting the impossibility of ever exceeding their hyphenated status as French-Africans, members of the intellectual elite also found re-incorporation into African society problematic. Indeed, these experiences are documented in numerous works, most noticeably in Cheikh Hamidou Kane's novel *L'aventure ambiguë*.[5] For Kane, this disorientation is reflected in his interruption of publication from 1961 to 1995 and symbolized by his entry into politics where he found a more expedient voice.[6] Indeed, this trajectory has not been uncommon for African and other Diaspora authors, foremost among which figure Léopold Sédar Senghor (president of Senegal from 1960 to 1980) and Aimé Césaire (once mayor of Fort-de-France, Martinique), as well as Henri Lopes, Jean-Baptiste Tati-Loutard, Tchichelle Tchivela, among others in the Congo. In a reverse process, political figures have entered the cultural domain in many African countries—following the example of such well-known revolutionary leaders as Mao, Ho Chi Minh, and Lenin—notably Marien Ngouabi and Denis Sassou Nguesso in the Congo, and Ahmed Sékou Touré in Guinea, along with leaders in other anglophone (Kenya, Nigeria, Somalia), francophone (Benin, Burkina-Faso, Zaire), and lusophone countries (Angola, Mozambique).[7] This has served to further complicate the relationship between official and non-official cultural practitioners as the lines of officialdom are often blurred, making the task of determining when a text becomes official inevitably fraught with contradictions.

Racial, political, and social factors that informed colonial relations need to be addressed in order to highlight some of the contributing factors to the emergence of cultural elites and of tenuous intellectual associations. To this end, Henri Brunschwig's compelling and problematic book *Noirs et blancs dans l'Afrique noire française: Ou comment le colonisé devient colonisateur (1870–1914)* seems particularly pertinent.[8] The book is divided into two distinct sections, defined by the racial identity of the subject under investigation; namely "blancs" in part one (pages 13–85), and "noirs" in the second part (pages 89–208). This is an original perspective to the extent that the respective colonial experiences of the colonizer and the colonized were of course radically different; yet, the implied interconnectivity and mutually constitutive nature of the dynamic loses its importance in this framework, something which is in fact not reflected in the actual body of the text, which emphasizes the inter-relational dynamics informing Black and White contact. The work's subtitle—"Ou comment le colonisé devient colonisateur"—contains the key to the challenging and problematic dimension of the work.

Brunschwig's radical thesis and the essential contribution his perspective offers center on a reevaluation of the driving forces behind the colonial project: "If one phrase was to capture the leitmotiv of these chapters, it would be that the 'colonization' of Black French Africa, namely its recent political, economic, and social evolution, was the work of as much and even more Blacks than Whites" (Brunschwig, 11). Indeed, much recent scholarship has argued the importance of shared responsibility as a prerequisite toward reconciliatory objectives—while an extremely sensitive proposition, such formulations have been a dominant component of some of the most challenging thinking on slavery, the Holocaust, colonialism, and apartheid. For Brunschwig, Black contributions to colonial expansionism manifested themselves through varying degrees of involvement:

- Individuals who were "acculturated, literate and *évolués*": "the defining characteristic of these acculturated people was not that they knew how to read and speak French. Rather, it was that they had made a deliberate choice in doing so. They were eager to speed up an evolutionary process that seemed to them to be driving Africa towards an Occidental civilization whose techniques were superior to their traditional ones" (Brunschwig, 92).

- "Collaborator": "an individual who provides assistance to the Black or White colonizer, without for all that abandoning her/his identity, and without considering White ways superior to Black ones, in short, without converting" (Brunschwig, 96).
- "Black peasants": this group tolerated outsiders, while endeavoring to restrict the contamination of their beliefs and practices through exposure to outside influences.

Brunschwig concludes by arguing, "Who will show that the colonizer's excesses were any worse than those of precolonial chiefs? . . . Individual memory does not record the past" (Brunschwig, 212), and that "In reality, the colonial debate was not between Whites and Blacks, but between tradition and innovation, and on the ground, partisans of innovation were often Blacks" (Brunschwig, 212). While the recognition of the role played by Africans in these processes is of course key to registering an authentic version of events, the attribution of blame to opportunistic Africans grossly underestimates the power of the coercive, discriminatory, exclusionary, and assimilationist practices intrinsic to colonial rule. Furthermore, the de-racialization of colonial contact ignores the fact that the racialist discourse of Joseph Arthur Gobineau, among others, was popularly embraced at the end of the nineteenth century in France, and that such pejorative discursive constructs of Africans provided the necessary ideological justification for colonial expansionism and the *mission civilisatrice*.[9] Furthermore, the question of comparing precolonial and colonial violence seems irrelevant. An analogous gesture would be to decriminalize the activities of the World Bank and multinational corporations (such as Shell Petroleum in Nigeria) by claiming that their presence was solicited by the equally corrupt leaders of sovereign postcolonial nations.[10]

Paul Gilroy's argument in his recent book *Between Camps: Nations, Cultures, and the Allure of Race* can surely further enlighten us with regard to the complex influences on identity formations.[11] For Gilroy,

> The organized work of disciplining and training citizens has had to coexist with less formal, involutionary complexes in which the fantastic idea of transmuting heterogeneity into homogeneity could be implemented and amplified outward as well as inward . . . the national principle can be recognized as having formed an important bond between different and even opposing nationalisms. The dominant varieties were bound to the subordinate by their shared notions of what nationality entailed. The forms of nationalism that invoke this mode of belonging exemplify *camp-*

thinking. . . . Politics is reconceptualized and reconstituted as a dualistic conflict between friends and enemies. (Gilroy, 82, emphasis mine)

Gilroy's notions of "camps" and "camp-thinking" are pertinent both to Brunschwig's interpretation of colonizer/colonized contact and to distinctions between official and non-official literature: on the one hand, because a negotiation is implied between two mutually opportunistic "camps" (Black and White) in colonial transactions, and on the other, because "nationalistic" and "national" agendas intersect. In the former instance, Gilroy's juxtaposition of "dominant" and "subordinate" objectives serves to highlight the shortcomings of Brunschwig's account, to the extent that the colonized can never escape his/her inferior status, because the assimilationist objective is of course an illusion. In the latter, Gilroy explains that "the camp mentality of the nationalists is betrayed by its crude theories of culture and might even be defined by the veneration of homogeneity, purity, and unanimity that it fosters. Inside the nation's fortification, culture is required to assume an artificial texture and an impossibly even consistency" (Gilroy, 84).

Many texts resist binary categorization and the implied accompanying "camp" identity contained in the concept of official and non-official literature. For example, while authors may refuse the prescriptive nature of state-sponsored literature, alternative models may prove equally restrictive. Fundamentally believing that productive readings are located beyond binary categories, I have endeavored to refrain from applying binary constructs to complex cultural and social phenomena and from polarizing cultural practitioners, preferring instead to explore the links that exist between the imagination and representation of cultural and political spaces within the context of decolonization and postcoloniality. While literature produced during the colonial era did not consist exclusively in the denunciation of outsiders (colonizers) by insiders (the colonized), postcolonial literature is not made up solely of critiques by insiders against other insiders (African dictators, for example). The circumstances are simply not that Euclidian, because of collaborative practices during the colonial era, because of neocolonial influences during the era of decolonization, and of course because "camps" are fluid rather than fixed entities. The postcolonial reality calls for more rigorous analysis, one that would incorporate a study of (1) those mechanisms that contribute to the political structure of institutions of repression; (2) the newly enfranchised leaders who have been entrusted with the responsibility for governance and power, the dismantling of previous structures, directing new constitutions, and managing new expectations; and (3) the opposition to internal violence in a system that will always be criticized by insiders who, outraged by practices, will be driven to express their moral indignation.

Within the context of nation-building and the pursuit of unifying imperatives, official literatures of the state have flourished at an unprecedented rate in postcolonial African countries under very different political structures as governments have solicited the assistance of cultural practitioners in the process of building the postcolonial nation-state. The Marxist-Leninist political model, as an essentially anti-individualistic and anti-ethnic model, served as a theoretical model for governments endeavoring to promote national unity. In a similar fashion, Stalin's *Marxism and the National and Colonial Question* and Lenin's *Imperialism, the Highest Stage of Capitalism* provided the ideological basis for the rejection of colonialism, and a logical progression was for African governments to sponsor literary productions.[12] The rejection of colonialism coincided with the rejection of capitalism, and Africans were thus able to link this to the struggle against imperialism which provided the fundamental shared sociological experience in the movement toward national autonomy. Independence represented the elimination of one obstacle, namely colonialism, but this then had to be accompanied by radical societal reform since, as Omafume F. Onoge has argued, colonialism consisted in the "incorporation" of the African "continent into the capitalist social order."[13]

This chapter, then, is concerned with exploring the emergence of state-sponsored literature in Africa, with specific reference to its implementation in the francophone context through a consideration of the People's Republic of the Congo during the Marxist-Leninist era (1969 to 1991), and the People's Revolutionary Republic of Guinea under Sékou Touré's leadership. Naturally, this analysis provides insights on similar mechanisms in a pan-African context, where the nation-building imperative has witnessed substantial government interference in the cultural domain.

Francophone sub-Saharan African literature has been politicized from its very beginning, whether in the form of apologist writings such as Ahmadou Mapaté Diagne's 1920 *Les trois volontés de Malic*, *négritude*'s affirmation of African humanity, or, later, the anti-colonial writings of Mongo Béti and Ferdinand Oyono.[14] In his tremendously influential theoretical work on colonialism, *Les damnés de la terre*, Frantz Fanon quoted Sékou Touré in his reflections "On National Culture" in order to underline the importance for artists to participate in the social struggle: "There is no place outside that fight for the artist or for the intellectual who is not himself concerned with and completely at one with the people in the great battle of Africa and of suffering humanity."[15] Sékou Touré, among others, would later draw on Fanon's writings in addition to those of his Martinican counterpart Aimé Césaire in order to outline the usefulness of literature to revolutionary discourse and the ongoing fight against imperialism in the post-independence context.[16] These paradigms were adopted and adapted by the leaders of independent nation-states in conjunction with the Soviet model of partisan literature and Socialist Realism.

On April 23, 1932, all Soviet literary and artistic organizations, including the Association of Proletarian Writers, were dismantled and merged into the new Union of Soviet Writers. The term *Socialist Realism* first appeared in print on May 23, 1932, when the *Literaturnaia Gazeta* published a statement I. Gronskii had made on May 19, declaring Socialist Realism the only acceptable literary form.[17] By August 1934, Socialist Realism had been inaugurated as the official model for literature. As Régine Robin has observed,

> Socialist Realism, as the basic starting point of Soviet literature and literary criticism, requires that the sincere writer offer a historically concrete presentation of reality in its revolutionary development. In this manner, veracity and the historically concrete dimension of the artistic representation of reality should combine with the task of achieving ideological change and educating workers according to the principles of Socialism. (Robin, 40)

The fundamental tenets of Stalinist Socialist Realism included "popular appeal (narodnost'), class-consciousness (klassovost'), ideological orthodoxy (ideynost'), partisanship or adherence to the Party line (partynost'), and typicality (tipichnost')."[18]

Onoge has examined the conflict between aesthetic creativity and ideology in his essay entitled "The Crisis of Consciousness in Modern African Literature." He begins by defining the concept of "art for art's sake" as a model according to which "the artist's responsibility is strictly to the perfection of the form of his craft" (Onoge, 32–33); for him, this particular model's detachment from social considerations precluded it from playing a role in society. The problem for the African writer attempting to position her/himself in society presents itself as a choice between "critical realism," which corresponds to "a literature that is *engaged* with the contemporary reality in a critical way" (Onoge, 35), and Socialist Realism, which goes a step further in that it "implies the artist's or writer's fundamental agreement with the aims of the working class and the emerging socialist world" (Onoge, 36).[19]

The main difference thus originates in the fact that while the critical realist paradigm serves to articulate criticism against a given sociological reality, this gesture is not simultaneously accompanied by a call for programmatic realignment according to Marxist-Leninist, or at least Socialist, criteria. Indeed, one could argue that the refusal of non-official authors to produce texts which follow the model of ideologically aligned literature has accorded them political legitimacy and aesthetic authenticity as artists rather than as activists. For Onoge, it becomes a question of audience, as he argues for "truly revolutionary artistic vehicles" (Onoge, 44). He thus subordinates aesthetics (form) to ideological considerations (content). This argument represents what is probably the central controversy in this area of discourse, namely the decision whether to accord primacy to the ideological concerns of the state-sponsored model of literature or to foreground aesthetic creativity.

In one of the most comprehensive collections of essays on the subject of Marxist aesthetics, *Marxism and African Literature*, Georg Gugelberger (the editor of the volume) argues that the goal of Marxist aesthetics "must be the amelioration of a given society. It is class conscious and anti-metaphysical . . . we have to set out from *real* active men and from the basis of their real-life process."[20] Emmanuel Ngara's comments in his book *Art and Ideology in the African Novel* echo Gugelberger's point, since for him, "Marxist aesthetics is an aesthetics based on content with form playing a subordinate role."[21] These approaches emphasize the importance of raising class consciousness through Marxist dialectics but also situate and define that which constitutes "literature."

Raymond Williams, in his book *Marxism and Literature*, has described the etymological origin of the word "literature."[22] His remarks serve to clarify the various arguments that have characterized the polemics between aesthetics and ideology, and between form and content. There are three fundamental stages, or "tendencies," as he chooses to describe them: "first, a shift from 'learning' to 'taste' or 'sensibility' as a criterion defining literary quality; second, an increasing specialization of literature to 'creative' or 'imaginative' works; third, a development of the concept of 'tradition' within national terms, resulting in the more effective definition of a 'national literature'" (Williams, 48). The third category is the most problematic within the context of African nationalism, since the concept of "tradition" itself would seem anachronistic, given the fact that the degree zero of nation-building dates back only to political independence around 1960 in the case of most other francophone sub-Saharan African countries. According to Williams, the second category gave rise to the distinction between "literature" and "Literature" and led to the "emphasis on 'creative' or 'imaginative' writing as a special kind of cultural practice" (Williams, 145). This is of particular interest to this discussion, because the hasty dismissal of official literature for its predictability is linked to widely held notions of what constitutes "Literature," namely, the criteria we bring to our appreciation and understanding of a text, and which subsequently lead us to hierarchize and canonize various productions. Marxist critics have argued that artistic production is inextricably linked to the social environment and "that artistic forms are socially conditioned and issue from historical circumstances" (Ngara, 4). Ngara has distinguished between "what" the writer says (content) and "how" s/he says it (form); for him, one of the fundamental shortcomings of Marxist aesthetics is its failure to "pay sufficient attention to the *how* of particular works of art" (Ngara, 4). This has been of obvious concern to authors who have expressed their misgivings with regard to the systematic attempt by Marxist critics (and other critics to varying degrees) to project their expectations upon a literary text and reduce it to considerations of content. The interesting dimension comes from the manner in which the model of partisan literature which Lenin had outlined in his 1905 *Partiynaya organizatsiya i partiynaya literatura* (Party Organization and Party Literature) is adapted and transformed in the hands of the Stalinist or Congolese political elite.[23]

Gugelberger advocates Marxist criticism in order to liberate African "literature from wrong formalist colonization,"[24] and as Onoge has argued, "this awareness allows the socialist realists to anticipate correctly that an internal African revolution will also imply structural disengagement from the capitalist structures of Europe" (Onoge, 38). The arguments for the adoption of the Marxist-Leninist political model thus simultaneously provided the basis for adopting the literary model of party literature, since rejecting capitalism also meant rejecting bourgeois cultural criteria. This also justified the unitary paradigm; the fundamental drawback originated in the possibility of resistance to this alignment becoming a treasonable offense.

The official writers selected bring diverse backgrounds and occupations to their writings, although they were for the most part active in their respective party structures as diplomats, soldiers, youth organization leaders, and civil servants. The central focus of the analysis in the Congolese context will be provided by Léopold-Pindy Mamonsono's anthology entitled *La nouvelle génération de poètes congolais*, and the writings of some of the most prolific official writers, including but not restricted to Claude-Emmanuel Eta-Onka and Xavier Okotaka-Ebale.[25] In considering Guinea, attention turns toward

Sékou Touré's impressive body of writings, writers selected by Sikhé Camara for his anthology, *Somme de la poésie guinéenne de combat ou la sirène de la révolution africaine*, and the work of Djigui Camara.[26]

Mamonsono's anthology explores the emergence of an official literature of the state in the Congo and provides an insight into the mechanisms at work in mobilizing and promoting a literature that disseminates messages defined by the state apparatus. In fact, the criterion for inclusion in his volume, which claims to "let our microscope wander in order to shed light on a precise period in the cultural evolution of our country" (Mamonsono, 6) is primarily the degree of revolutionary fervor and commitment to party ideology exhibited by the writers. Indeed, Sikhé Camara's volume echoes this framework:

> we only selected the profound chants of the young voices of Guinea's Révolution Démocratique Africaine. . . . what counts most is the willingness of these writers to produce and make a contribution in whatever modest way they are able in order to inform, enrich, and educate the People; what I am most interested in and what one must remember, is the content of these texts. (Sikhé Camara, 8)[27]

Official texts are to a certain extent predictable, given their prescriptive nature. However, it would be reductive to dismiss them according to that premise alone; instead, these texts should be viewed as products of a complex network of social relations. In that capacity they offer a valuable insight to a given sociological and historical reality. Furthermore, these writings represent the articulation of a specific aesthetics and conception of literary activity and therefore warrant critical attention and dialogue.

Official writers offer a vision of society in terms that are devoid of ambiguity, in that "they *name* the existing reality—capitalism" and accept that "these problems can be overcome only by the *liquidation* of the capitalist state" (Onoge, 37–38). This has created an environment in those African countries that have sponsored an official literature of the state in which, as Paul N'Da has observed,

> the leaders' discourse, particularly that which emphasizes "nationalist" issues, often uttered so as to overshadow the various regional and ethnic differences and disparities, mask inequalities, encourage the tolerance of injustice and reduce class conflict, must be "applauded" by all those who participate in domination: nationalist discourse in particular must rejoin another self-legitimizing discourse, that in turn must reach all members of the national collectivity.[28]

These circumstances raise important questions pertaining to the particular elaboration of a postcolonial aesthetics adapted to the African context. While it may seem somewhat ironic that independent African leaders and authors may have borrowed from Western literary traditions (Socialist Realism, Sartrean *engagement*) to serve their respective nationalizing tendencies, the most interesting information lies in the manner in which these *adopted* influences have been *adapted* to the African context.[29] Roland Barthes's essay "Ecrivains et écrivants" ("Authors and Writers"), while not of course written with the African context in mind, nevertheless goes a long way toward circumscribing the distinctions between official and non-official cultural practitioners.[30] For Barthes, "the author performs a function, the writer an activity" (Barthes, 144), and the fundamental difference stems from the fact that

> the author existentially forbids himself two kinds of language, whatever the intelligence or the sincerity of his enterprise: first, *doctrine*, since he converts despite himself, by his very project, every explanation into a spectacle: he is always an inductor of ambiguity; second, *evidence*, since he has consigned himself to language, the author cannot have a naïve consciousness, cannot "work up" a protest without his message finally bearing much more on the working-up than on the protest. . . . But what he obviously gains is the power to disturb the world, to afford it the dizzying spectacle of *praxis* without sanction. (Barthes, 145–46)

While the "écrivant" (writer) "posits a goal (to give evidence, to explain, to instruct), of which language is merely a means; for him language supports a *praxis*, it does not constitute one. Thus language is restored to the nature of an instrument of communication, a vehicle of 'thought.' Even if the writer pays some attention to style, this concern is never ontological" (Barthes, 147).

The situation becomes increasingly complicated in the African context as one explores the question of political commitment. Official writers disseminate state-sanctioned ideology while the political concerns of non-official authors come close to a more specifically Sartrean model of responsible political commitment. Barthes objects to the demands and expectations of Sartrean *engagement*, since for him, "a 'committed' author claims simultaneous participation in two structures, inevitably a source of deception" (Barthes, 146). Alain Robbe-Grillet echoes Barthes's perspective, because for him, "Socialist Realism or Sartrean 'engagement' are difficult to reconcile with the problematic exercise of literature" (Robbe-Grillet, 38).[31] However, Robbe-Grillet does acknowledge Sartre's recognition of the potential dangers of such a literary program, and the importance of avoiding the propagandist, programmatic imperative or tendency through which the interpretation is fixed by the party. For Sartre, it becomes a question of authorial responsibility, of commitment as *praxis*, and not a simple distinction between content and form/style.[32] As Steven Ungar has pointed out, from "Qu'est-ce que la littérature" ("What Is Literature") to "Orphée noir" ("Black Orpheus"), Sartre's preface to Senghor's *Anthologie de la nouvelle poésie nègre et malgache de langue française*, Sartre "revises the program of *littérature engagée* in two significant ways. First, it allows for poetry [and not exclusively prose] to be reconsidered in the context of colonialism, thereby transposing its marginal status . . . into a meaningful function tied to social change."[33] Subsequently, for Sartre, this poetry comes to represent "the most authentic revolutionary plan and the purest poetry [originating] from the same source."[34] For reasons similar to those registered by Sartre, poetry was later to be adopted by the adherents of governmental orthodoxy as a contribution to revolutionary ideals.

In the case of non-official authors, their works stand as a concerted effort to promote the creative dimension in order to distance their writings from Western literary models and traditions as well as the official "langue de bois." This is inherently what is contained in the title of Bernard Geniès's article, "Africain d'accord, écrivain d'abord," in which he discusses the insistence of contemporary African authors on foregrounding the aesthetic dimension of their works.[35] While Robbe-Grillet underlines what he perceives as the irreconcilability of politics and art: "art cannot be reduced to the status of a means in the service of a cause which transcends it . . . the artist puts nothing above his work . . . the least external directive paralyzes him" (Robbe-Grillet, 37), his statement is in fact close to the agenda of non-official authors whose primary focus is style and form, but who, while refusing to abandon their freedom to the homogeneity of party control (presumably what Robbe-Grillet would refer to as an "external directive"), nevertheless do not attempt to avoid the responsibility of engaging themselves with the contemporary reality.

Non-official authors challenge the picture offered by official writers, but while official writers are at the service of the government, non-official authors are not. Tanella Boni has stated that "to create does not consist in reproducing reality—the colonial or post-colonial condition—as it presents itself. To create is to suggest a meaning, a certain vision of this same reality . . . the absurd world s/he stages becomes the work for which we are all responsible."[36] While both literary bodies are concerned with and informed by the sociological realities of the country in question (even when it is veiled in a topographically imaginary space), the simple reproduction of that reality precludes the visionary dimension evoked by Boni. Thus, in a context in which nationalism is indissociable from the discourse of the state, an author may refuse an ideological alignment that is not there if s/he feels that a nationalist dimension is being accorded to his/her work.[37] Non-official authors may suggest an alternative "national" model (which of course gives credence to the state as a governing body) yet not be "nationalistic" in that they refuse the existing model that is being promoted. Thus, while it was acceptable to challenge Western colonialism because there was unity and consensus against colonization, the imperative of embracing the national model adopted by government leaders has generated persecution, silencing, and what Salman Rushdie has described as attempts to "shackle creativity" by the authorities who control the various power mechanisms.[38]

Non-official authors may focus on aesthetic considerations explicitly as they attempt to distance themselves from reductive official guidelines, in which concern for the message articulated kills creativity. Non-official authors challenge the official picture and the power structures which the governing authorities depend on. As Elisabeth Mudimbe-Boyi has argued, "the writer threatens established power through the exercise of writing: her/his work destabilizes, since through writing, an alternative and autonomous discourse emerges."[39] Of course, this constitutes one of the fundamental differences between the official and non-official literary bodies, since official writers do not engage in autonomous discursive modes. The Kenyan writer Ngùgì wa Thiong'o, while embracing a Socialist view of society, further underlines this point when he insists on the importance of adversarial narratives: "our pens should be used to increase the anxieties of all oppressive regimes. At the very least the pen should be used to 'murder their sleep' by constantly reminding them of their crimes against the people, and making them know that they are being seen. . . . Let our pens give voices to silence."[40]

For Ngùgì wa Thiong'o, cultural practitioners must endeavor to paint a picture which negates all previous ones in order to denounce official ideology, and in order for the political discourse their texts promulgate to invalidate existing government attempts at controlling the nation-state. In doing so, these authors can deconstruct the existing national project and attempt to undermine it by exposing its repressive practices. The contestatory, oppositional nature of writing that is indebted to a model of *engagement* literature is exemplified in the work of Sony Labou Tansi. The persecution of those who refuse the party's guidelines has ominous implications since, as

Alexandre Mboukou has argued, "without a functioning group of intellectuals, a society is deprived of a certain level of consciousness and insight into vital problems."[41] Current attempts to construct the nation are presented as achievable only at the expense of individual, cultural, and traditional aspirations, and non-official literary works therefore stand as attempts to reinscribe these and to offer alternative structures upon which society can build its future.

In the Soviet context, non-official authors were commonly referred to as "litterateurs" or "saboteurs." As Sue Curry Jansen has argued, "ideologues claim (or simulate) a monopoly of explanatory powers by asserting that their position articulates a single vocabulary of truth."[42] However, the *litterateurs* "dissimulate. They maintain that they are only playing: just telling stories. Their dissembling counter-claim allows litterateurs to retain metaphoric resilience, the equivocal powers, necessary to subvert or transcend the absolutism of the linear discourse of ideology" (Jansen, 194). Non-official texts challenge the univocal discourse of the state, such that in addition to differences with regard to party ideology, differences are also located at the level of narrative voice and style. One could perhaps further elaborate this distinction by arguing that official writers follow a theory that is developed for them. However, while the works of non-official authors represent models for change that do not necessitate theory, their incorporation of various authorial forewords and prefaces generates a space in which important statements of purpose are articulated and from which one can begin to discern the articulation of an autonomous postcolonial aesthetic theory.

Non-official authors of course hold diverse political views; some embrace a Socialistic world view while nevertheless exercising artistic activities independently and outside of the principle of alignment to the party line. The Kenyan writer Ngùgì wa Thiong'o and the Senegalese novelist and filmmaker Ousmane Sembène are the most striking examples, both of whom are widely recognized as among the most interesting and talented cultural figures in Africa. As Ngara has argued with reference to these two authors, they "are evidently aware not only of the necessity to present a Marxist interpretation of reality but of the need to meet the *requirements* of socialist art" (Ngara, 116, emphasis mine). The determining factor in the writings of Ngùgì wa Thiong'o and Ousmane Sembène is the concern with exposing neocolonial practices and dismantling capitalist societal structures in favor of Socialism. The central protagonists have assimilated these ideals and undertake the task of raising class consciousness among the oppressed masses.[43]

Ngùgì wa Thiong'o and Ousmane Sembène are of further interest to the extent that they have both felt the need to redefine their cultural productions in response to questions of accessibility given social considerations specific to Africa. Both authors have come to the realization that "written" literature has proved insufficient in eliciting the type of popular revolt they had envisioned. In the case of Ngùgi wa Thiong'o, he decided to renounce writing in the colonizer's language (English) in favor of Gìkùyù, a language which is today one of Kenya's most widely spoken languages. As for Ousmane Sembène, the question of audience has also been of crucial concern and is a direct product of his Marxist aesthetics. His decision to focus his artistic endeavors on filmmaking is a response to considerations of widespread illiteracy, to the economics of inaccessibility to the written text in Africa, and of course to governmental interference with the process of distribution. Indeed, as Walter Benjamin has argued: "the representation of reality by the film is incomparably more significant than that of the painter, since it offers, precisely because of the thoroughgoing permeation of reality with mechanical equipment, an aspect of reality which is free of all equipment. And that is what one is entitled to ask from a work of art."[44]

Official literature is not of course specific to Africa, and similar models of unswerving allegiance can be found on every continent. The analysis of official texts and of the manner in which Socialist Realism, political commitment, and state-sanctioned guidelines for writing have been adapted and transformed will begin with the Guinean context and continue with the Congo.[45]

Sékou Touré and Revolutionary Writers in Guinea

Sékou Touré, in his capacity as president of Guinea until 1984, defined culture and the role of the writer in the construction of the post-independence Socialist nation-state. Ideological guidelines were outlined in his abundant body of writings and disseminated in some 224 volumes of the Guinean Democratic Party's monthly review, *Révolution Démocratique Africaine*, between 1966 and 1984, and other publications such as the tri-weekly *Horoya*, weekly newspapers such as *Horoya-Hebdo*, FONIKEE, and *Recherches Africaines*, and the *Bulletin d'Information du Bureau Politique National du PDG*, a monthly publication of the Jeunesse de la Révolution Démocratique Africaine (JRDA). Sékou Touré underlined the indissociability of culture and the masses;[46] this is emphasized in the introduction to his collection of poems, *Poèmes militants*, a volume that provides the paradigm for revolutionary poetry in Guinea and in which he develops the following argument:

"within a given Nation, culture constitutes a decisive factor of national unity, not so much through its mode of expression that can be more or less perfect, more or less elaborated, but rather through its language, which is to say its content, which explains it."[47] This argument is underscored by additional comments: "culture thus becomes the manifestation of life in society, simultaneously translating the foundations and the rules on which various societies are based, and whose creative activities it directs towards values it considers a postulate" (*Poèmes militants*, 19).

As early as 1959, Sékou Touré addressed the question of aesthetics: "Who has not heard the theory of art for art's sake defended, the theory of poetry for poetry's sake, the theory of every man for himself."[48] Naturally, Sékou Touré is, effectively, outlining his own aesthetic codes, dismissing what he identifies as the individualistic concerns of those for whom the focus is with form above considerations of content, a gesture that would therefore be contrary to the concerns of the community. The usefulness of artistic creativity lies, as Sékou Touré has argued, in its ability to "work towards the good of the people, if it is integrated in a fundamental manner to action, thinking, and the aspirations of the people" (*La Guinée et l'émancipation*, 170).

Sékou Touré's poems are easily reducible to their political message and often represent mere adaptations of his political rhetoric. The predictability of the content is partly contained in the titles themselves; these have evolved according to the shifting party line: in 1963 one could read "Hommage au Parti Démocratique de Guinée" (*Poèmes militants*, 29); later, this progressed toward the 1969 poem "Travailleurs du monde unissons-nous et agissons" (*Poèmes militants*, 119), and in 1976, "La lutte de classes" (*Poèmes militants*, 117). Some of his more notable poems reveal this development. In "Le Peuple et la Culture," he writes:

> La Culture partout est Une dans son fond
> Mais multiple dans ses formes d'expression
> Car partout c'est le Peuple unique,
> Partout ce sont ses activités multiples. (*Poèmes militants*, 21)

and in "La lutte de classes":

> La roue de l'Histoire doit tourner,
> Et aucun ennemi ne pourra la détourner
> De son objectif de bonheur populaire
> Car, elle est guidée par de vrais prolétaires
> Qui, par la révolution socialiste
> A jamais anéantiront l'exploitation capitaliste. (*Poèmes militants*, 118)

There are of course inherent limitations to this type of discourse, the most important being its inability to validate any form of expression which deviates from the ideological dimension. In his preface to Sikhé Camara's anthology, Sékou Touré introduced the volume's objectives as follows:

> Literature requires a spirit of synthesis and a capacity for research and analysis that calls for the continent's intellectual elite to show greater interest and better devote themselves to specific activities. The immediate advantage comes from being able each time to take stock of the situation, of always and consciously enlisting emerging generations in literary production appropriate for the continent, to offer the outside world the possibility of getting a precise idea of intellectual and moral values, ideological and political principles, as well as of artistic forms of expression that indicate both the ethical and aesthetic level and essence governing African society.[49]

For him, literature stands at the service of ideology and party policy: "This poetry is a weapon for the mobilization of the People and a call for individual and collective participation in the task of national construction, while also being a bridge of fraternity and solidarity between Guinea and other Peoples."[50] In the introduction to the anthology, Sikhé Camara underlined the importance for these "committed poets, faithful and uncompromising in the service of the revolution" (Sikhé Camara, 3) to produce accessible, revolutionary texts glorifying the nation's heroes, the nation, the party, and its leader Sékou Touré. Important connections are established to a wide range of European authors—Du Bellay, Rousseau, Hugo—and African and Caribbean cultural figures—Mongo Béti, Aimé Césaire, René Depestre, Frantz Fanon, Ferdinand Oyono, Jacques Roumain, Léopold Sédar Senghor, Ousmane Sembène, and Joseph Zobel—whose writings indicted colonialism and embraced national liberation. The paradigm they offered for committed writing is recuperated by Guinean revolutionary writers in the context of post-independence nation-state formation. These analogies also extend to an international political framework that is associated with similar anti-imperial and class struggles—from Ho Chi Minh's political strife and writings from prison as a symbol of Vietnamese resistance against Japanese, French, and American imperialism; Mao's writings; but also Che Guevara, Fidel Castro, and the conflict in Angola, Benin, and Mozambique. Indeed, the fact that both Césaire and Senghor had represented the intelligentsia and in turn become key political personas served to justify the entry into the cultural domain by the new leaders of decolonizing Africa.

These references to what are widely acknowledged as French and francophone canonical authors raise some interesting questions. Indeed, in the preface to Djigui Camara's *Chronique de la révolution*, Ibrahima Khalil Diaré addressed this particular question: "Written in the form of didactic recitals, his poems appear repetitive, chanting the same facts in their limpid simplicity. This is the voice of the popular singer who makes use of French, deliberately neglecting the canonical texts of classical French poetry."[51] The French and francophone canon is dismissed by these official writers, yet important links remain in terms of influences that lead us to question what they may signify with regard to their agenda as writers. Although the anthology is essentially restricted to works of poetry, some novelists and non-Guinean authors are mentioned in the preface. Yet, while many authors are mentioned, those who are excluded both from the preface and from Sikhé Camara's anthology itself are equally interesting. Their omission is thus more indebted to a deliberate exclusionary gesture, one that attempts to drive to the periphery those Guinean authors who have refused to adhere to the party line. The most significant absences among authors who had published by the time the anthology went to press include Camara Laye, who was forced into exile after his novel *Dramouss* was published in 1966, Tierno Monénembo, who had taken up residence in Algeria in 1973 to escape Sékou Touré's regime, Alioum Fantouré, and Williams Sassine.[52] Thus, while Guinean revolutionary writers may locate their influences in anti-colonial or liberationist authors, the model for political *engagement* does not extend to those authors who continue to question oppressive power in the postcolonial context and who do not share their commitment to the ideals of the Guinean revolution.

Nenekhaly Condetto Camara, for example, was influenced by the works of Soviet writers Vladimir Vladimirovitch Maïakovski, Khlebnikov, and Ilya Ehrenbourg.[53] For Sikhé Camara, Nenekhaly Condetto Camara insists on writing because "the poet must be a hero, a gatherer and catalyst of energy, using her/his art to transform society, reflect its ideals and aspirations, while rediscovering traditional literary forms and infusing them with a new revolutionary content."[54] In his "Conscience nationale et poésie négro-africaine d'expression française," Nenekhaly Condetto Camara critiques Césaire's work as insufficiently anti-imperialist, while with reference to Senghor he asks, "Does his poetry really aim to stir the most legitimate sentiments of a People aspiring to a better life and future? . . . Through the grace of his poetry, towards what destinies does this writer intend to shepherd the African

People?"[55] The lack of a programmatic project and clear revolutionary message comes under attack—Césaire and Senghor's oppositional framework is thus embraced but the literariness of their work denounced for its lack of political utility. With Alpha Colyah Diallo, writing consists in

> reaffirming and rehabilitating the value of popular literary creation. . . . The writer must be an educator, a paladin of the liberty of mankind and the People, and will refuse to be merely a poet preoccupied with sterile aesthetic poetry in the coziness of a salon. . . . Her/his poetry will in every way be one of combat, transformed by the ideals of the Party and the People. (Sikhé Camara, 34)

His poems glorify the revolution, for example, in "Jamais dans la nuit": "Le Guinéen révolutionnaire / A opposé le Non / Le Non historique qui a jailli de l'union / De tout le Peuple voulant désormais / Ejecter l'oppresseur pour jamais" (Sikhé Camara, 38); and in "Je ne veux pas de votre estime": "A cette Afrique / Que du bout du canon vous avez tuée / Et qu'au bout de mon Idéologie / Populaire et orthodoxe / J'ai ressuscitée" (Sikhé Camara, 46). Similar criteria are reiterated in the work of Onipogui Zeze, Mamadou Lamine Conde, whose objective is to "interpret Socialist doctrine" (Sikhé Camara, 309), and Wolibo Doukoure, for whom "Artists cannot rest as long as their work has not reached the soul of the People they serve and from whom they expect no recognition, the Revolution alone being their raison d'être" (Sikhé Camara, 299).

In the case of N'Daw Pascal Leno, we find a poet "who definitively locates his literary or poetic action according to a single system of reference and resource: the People" (Sikhé Camara, 68). His poem "La mission du poète révolutionnaire" is paradigmatic in this sense: "Si un jour par noble ambition, / Quelque Guinéen se propose / D'écrire des vers ou de la prose, / Que ce soit en l'honneur de la Révolution!" (Sikhé Camara, 72).[56] Parallel themes are found in Ibrahima Khalil Diaré's publications, *Chants et larmes, de foi et de joie* and *Les dits de nul et de tous,* and Roger Goto Zomou's poetry, "Elégie d'une combattante" (Sikhé Camara, 143), "Ma patrie" (Sikhé Camara, 150), "Noble combat" (Sikhé Camara, 152–57), and "Le combattant": "Je m'appelle Combattant / Je suis l'ouvrier aux bras d'acier / Je sens des mines de toutes les couleurs / Que chante la fierté des usines" (Sikhé Camara, 58).[57] Almany Oumar Laho's comments on revolutionary poetry are revealing. According to Sikhé Camara, his framework is based on the view that

> the theory of art for art's sake, the theory of political art, conceal a profound class signification. That of the aristocracy and the bourgeoisie that are nourished and kept by the People at whose expense they live. For this writer, art for art's sake is little else but a practical joke and evidence of the hardening of sensibility at the heart of a retrograde and decadent system. (Sikhé Camara, 227)

The fundamental distinction between official and non-official writers is contained in the way in which this writer situates himself with regard to creative autonomy, juxtaposing "individual creativity" with "the spirit of the Party" (Sikhé Camara, 236).

Djigui Camara was an active member of the revolutionary intelligentsia, contributing regularly to *Horoya* and frequently heard on the national radio network, *La Voix de la Révolution.* For him, writing provides the opportunity to "outline his philosophical conception of the world, that of Guinea's Democratic Party, and therefore to reaffirm his political convictions" (Sikhé Camara, 197). In his *Chronique de la révolution*, according to Ibrahima Khalil Diaré, "Djigui narrates the story of the Revolution's heroes and heroines so as to offer them up as examples for posterity. In his poems, he tells of the liberation of the African People, and in his international flights of oratory poetry, sings praises to the homeland of Lenin and Socialism."[58] The founding of the Guinean Democratic Party in 1947 and Guinea's political independence in September 1958 after voting against continued links with France in a referendum are celebrated in his poetry. In "Je m'appelle révolution," he writes "Je m'appelle REVOLUTION / Ceux qui m'adorent / Ensemencent les champs de l'avenir / Travaillent aux choses utiles / Ouvrent à la communauté entière / Les portes du bonheur authentique" (Djigui Camara, 30); in "Les héritiers de la révolution": "Sur le chemin du soleil avancent fièrement, / Résolument les héritiers de la Révolution. / Allons, marchons camarades / Sur le chemin sublime / Des pionniers de Septembre" (Djigui Camara, 49); and "Ma patrie": "La patrie! C'est un tapis immense que tisse chaque génération d'hommes unis par l'histoire et le commun devenir. C'est le fruit du combat paysan, ouvrier . . ." (Djigui Camara, 77).[59] While so many young writers joined the revolutionary struggle, Sékou Touré's increased activities and involvement in the cultural sphere culminated in what Christopher L. Miller has described as "Sékou Touré's personal dominance of Guinean discourse."[60] When publications did not carry original contributions by the Guinean leader himself, the message and discourse articulated effectively ventriloquized the omnipresent leader. While no

Congolese leader has played such a central role, government authorities and agencies have carefully monitored cultural activity.

The Intellectual Nomenclature: Ngouabi and Sassou Nguesso

Fulbert Youlou was forced to resign in 1963 following widespread dissatisfaction among trade unions and the military. These events culminated in the transition of power and were subsequently reframed in the myth of Congolese identity as a popular, revolutionary movement whose *a priori* objective had been the creation of a People's Republic. When Ngouabi outlined new ideological guidelines in 1968, he described these events as the period "during which Congolese revolutionary forces, under our guidance, embarked upon the readjustment of the Congolese Revolution born on August 13, 14, 15, 1963."[61] Ngouabi was the first leader to advocate radical ideological positions, coining the party "caption," "Tout pour le Peuple— Rien que pour le Peuple," to go along with the Parti Congolais du Travail (PCT) emblem, "Unité–Travail–Progrès."[62] He was also the first to address the importance of these radical concepts and their projected contributions to the process of nation-state formation. While in Dakar on January 15, 1975, he described a number of key policy issues in a speech entitled "Le socialisme scientifique en Afrique: L'expérience congolaise" (Scientific-Socialism in Africa: The Congolese experience). Some of these are included in the following excerpt:

> In our eyes, the state is not, on the level of the nation, a neutral instrument. . . . The state is an instrument of dictatorship par excellence. It is not the head of a family, because class relations are not affectionate, but rather violent. Following dictatorship, the Marxist hypothesis anticipates the decline of the state once the superior phase of evolution has been attained by mankind and society. (Ngouabi, 49)

The state apparatus literally engulfed the political realm, and for Ngouabi the "national" approach was of course essential: "The objective of this stage consists in overthrowing French imperial domination that controls the national economy and consequently and objectively controls the political situation. This stage also aims to establish objective and subjective conditions for the Congolese nation, by destroying the erroneous foundations of tribalism and regionalism" (Ngouabi, 52). His thinking and ideological framework enabled him to reduce the Congo's problems to matters of tribal rivalry and conflict and to threats of imperialism, all of which could be dispelled through national unity and a Marxist-Leninist model. Although he was assassinated in 1977, the legacy of Ngouabi's ideological alignment prevailed long after his death, as did his declarations concerning culture in which he developed the concept of partisan literature: "the Party leader, the revolutionary intellectual and the true patriot's role, is to place his knowledge at the service of the people so that it may become determining at the intellectual stage of the revolution."[63] The official newspaper of the PCT, *Etumba*, had also outlined the strict requirements of partisan literature, insisting on "revolutionary rigor and discipline" as a pre-condition for the Commission Nationale de Censure to grant distribution authorization.[64] Later, Sassou Nguesso would employ a similar discourse: "In the present economic circumstances, in which the weak are victims, it's advisable for Africa to hear those forces that have joined in unison, and walk resolutely towards the unity so wished by the masses throughout our country. . . . The theoretical justification for this unity is no longer in question. Every effort must now be made to achieve it."[65]

Scientific-Socialism thus offered an anti-imperial, anti-colonial, and even anti-neocolonial political model with which to fight "against imperialism and its instruments: local valets, including the bureaucratic bourgeoisie, tribal chiefs, and the nation's traitors" (Ngouabi, 588) and thereby engineer the nation.[66] Naturally, this dialectic was denounced as a weapon of oppression. President Sassou Nguesso actively instigated the sponsorship of state literature and prescribed guidelines for production:

> Cultural works must treat and reflect in an ample fashion the important problems of the revolutionary edification of our country. They must treat and propagate powerful motives: the heroism of the people and those heroes who, through their example, assume an avant-garde role in life, work, science, school, everywhere. . . . This is how cultural values may serve to inspire and mobilize the popular masses to fulfill the tasks assigned by the Party. (Sassou Nguesso, 44)[67]

One of the most significant measures implemented by Sassou Nguesso's government was the creation in 1979 of the Union Nationale des Ecrivains, Artistes, et Artisans Congolais (UNEAC), in order to "answer to the Party's concern with establishing a group that would bring together all the creators and producers of cultural goods for the purpose of engaging in an anti-imperialist struggle at the cultural level, in order to preserve and promote the cultural heritage."[68] Sassou Nguesso also emphasized "The importance of unity among revolutionaries is that much greater since it has to serve as the foundation to national unity; a lack of unity always engenders tension at the heart of the nation, generating conditions that would not be favorable to revolutionary struggle."[69] Membership in this union was mandatory, and Sassou Nguesso mobilized and solicited writers to serve government propaganda, ideology, and the imperative of national entity. While not all members of the UNEAC followed the guidelines outlined in Sassou Nguesso's manifesto, those uncooperative authors for whom the state symbolized the incarnation of repressive and dictatorial power were systematically labeled anti-African and elitist.

The situation was of course further complicated by the existence of competing elites, broadly constituted of a cultural elite represented by non-official authors published almost exclusively abroad—a fact that served only to support the allegation of elitism and to discredit their productions—and a post-revolutionary political elite exercising governmental authority and sponsoring an official literature of the state.[70] These circumstances generated considerable antagonism between official and non-official cultural practitioners. Congolese publishing houses were all essentially vanity or state-subsidized publishing establishments in Brazzaville, often simply offering printing and distribution services. Different types of literature were being produced in the Congo during the scientific-Socialist era. My primary interest is to focus on those official writers who established themselves as representatives of an identifiable political elite with a Marxist-Leninist rhetoric in the name of a classless society, and whose writings fulfill the requirements of state-mandated cultural productions.[71] Adrien Huannou has, with specific reference to writings from Benin, described this body of literature as "revolutionary literature."[72]

The situation is further complicated by the fact that some Congolese authors fundamentally subscribed to Socialism but did not necessarily manifest solidarity with the party line. The poet and playwright Maxime N'Debeka's predicament was, arguably, closer to that of Ousmane Sembène. N'Debeka was an active member of the Jeune Mouvement National pour la Révolution (JMNR) and a member of the Central Committee of the PCT until he was arrested and sentenced to death in 1972 (later amnestied and placed under house arrest) for his supposed involvement in plotting a failed coup d'état. He has published a number of volumes of poetry, including *Soleils neufs* and *Les signes du silence.*[73] His most famous poem, "980.000," in the collection *L'Oseille des citrons*, exhibits pronounced solidarity with the masses. The idea he develops is that there are some twenty thousand out of every one million Congolese who manipulate power and wealth without any consideration for the remaining number:

> 980 000 nous sommes
> 980 000 affamés
> brisés
> abrutis
> Nous venons des usines
> Nous venons des forêts
> des campagnes
> des rues
> Avec des feux dans la gorge
> des crampes dans l'estomac
> des trous béants dans les yeux
> des varices le long du corps
> Et des bras durs
> Et des mains calleuses
> Et des pieds comme du roc
> 980 000 Nous sommes
> 980 000 Ouvriers
> chômeurs
> et quelques étudiants
> Qui n'ont plus droit qu'à une
> *fraction de vie.*[74] (Emphasis mine)

N'Debeka's discourse is indebted to Marxism-Leninism or at least Socialist rhetoric and attacks the elite in the name of the masses. His vision of a classless society corresponded in theory to that of the governing authorities in the Congo. As an outsider (albeit a discredited "insider" following his brief involvement in government), N'Debeka subscribed in all sincerity to a Socialist vision of the world and formulated criticism against the "20,000" who manipulated power.

Political events made it increasingly evident that the enemy was in fact "within" the structures that were being glorified. The "nous" which N'Debeka describes becomes those "qui n'ont plus droit qu'à une fraction de vie" at the end of the poem, namely, the victims of a system in which the official Marxist-Leninist discourse of the state was employed as a weapon of oppression. Indeed, Sassou Nguesso was described as a "Cardin-Communist" (to indicate his fondness for the French designer Pierre Cardin's clothing). The common fight against oppression and the implied need for solidarity is contained in the repeated use of the subject "nous" (namely, the masses), a category that fails to describe the status of official writers as a post-revolutionary elite. Thus, while N'Debeka sympathized with Socialism as a political model, his writings were inadvertently serving the official state ideology of an increasingly repressive monolithic dictatorship that had nothing to do with Socialism. N'Debeka has commented on this phenomenon: "at a given time, I wrote texts that earned me medals, at a given time I wrote texts that were taken up literally word for word by the Congolese people who had no idea by whom they had been written. And these texts were then used to make demands, to assist the struggle."[75]

Jean-François Obembe, a Congolese ambassador to the German Democratic Republic, wrote a number of texts. The most notable was his *Problèmes liés à l'édification du Parti Congolais du Travail: Premier parti marxiste-léniniste au pouvoir en Afrique* (a comprehensive description of the historical origins of the PCT, and an outline of the manner in which the Soviet-based Marxist-Leninist model was adopted and implemented).[76] I mention Obembe by way of an introduction to the work of Léopold-Pindy Mamonsono (the editor of the 1984 anthology entitled *La nouvelle génération de poètes congolais*). Obembe prefaced one of Mamonsono's collections of poems, *Héros dans l'ombre*. This anthology focuses on the period during which the government authorities began to actively sponsor a literature of the state, inaugurating the Union Nationale des Ecrivains, Artistes, et Artisans Congolais (UNEAC), organizing the First Exhibition of Congolese Books in December 1977, and founding the Congolese Cultural Circle in March 1978. As Mamonsono declares, "for the first time in Africa, Artists and Writers came together to form a union for the defense of their interests, sponsored by the established government power" (Mamonsono, 7).[77]

The volume includes a wide range of poets who are assessed by Mamonsono as "the prototype of the committed poet, who chooses to come down from his 'ivory tower' and to take in hand the control tower of society by mingling with the people in their joy and sorrow" (Mamonsono, 64). An ideological framework to which most writers answer is imposed on the anthology. The reference to the "ivory tower" confirms some of the antagonism between official and non-official cultural practitioners with regard to their respective understanding and interpretation of "Literature" and "literature." Mamonsono's comment reveals his fundamental belief in a literature for the people, although his dismissal of the cultural elite conceals a degree of envy for the status they have acquired. His own poem "A nous deux maintenant, Goliath," in his collection *Héros dans l'ombre*, stands as the ultimate model of committed militancy:

Je vous jette à la figure
L'éponge rouge du contestataire
Le pagne rouge de la couleur de sang
Le gant rouge du défit
Celui du boxeur poids-plume de 1958
Qui défie le boxeur poids-lourd de 1976
Tel David bravant Goliath.[78]

Mamonsono has transformed the conflict between David and Goliath to the context of a boxing match itself adapted to colonialism, the struggle for political independence, and subsequently decolonization. The aim is to demonstrate that the initial situation of weakness (the status of the colonized as "poids-plume" [feather weight]) and dependency has been reversed through scientific-Socialism (the emancipated subject has become a "poids-lourd" [heavy weight]: by 1976 the Congo had become a People's Republic under Marien Ngouabi's leadership). However, in his concern with communicating this politicized message, certain technical problems surface. For example, the word "rouge" is repeated three times in as many lines to emphasize his political sympathies, and then in an attempt to further underline this dimension, he informs the reader that the "rouge" in question is "couleur de sang." This poem is one example, but there are many others in which the elementary rhyme scheme, images, and facile ideas would have led us to the same conclusions, namely, that the unswerving commitment to the party line has precluded the possibility for creativity. Huannou's comments with reference to Benin are pertinent to this context: "revolutionary writers from Benin will begin to produce works that are aesthetically worthwhile once they have understood that the essential component of literary creation is not the message, but rather the manner in which it is delivered, namely the style."[79]

In the preface to his book entitled *La femme africaine*, Xavier Okotaka-Ebale has been described by Christian Ndinga of Marien Ngouabi University in Brazzaville as an "Educator and militant poet."[80] His main body of work is contained in his *La pensée conscientisante d'un progressiste*. This work contains two texts that outline his political thoughts, "La jeunesse congolaise et la révolution" and "Dix pensées révolutionnaires et éducatives," and a collection of poems entitled "La pensée d'un militant."[81] The titles of these poems are immediately indicative of the content: "De la conscience socialiste," "Du patriotisme," "De l'unité nationale," "De la jeunesse," "Des vertus prolétariennes," "De la discipline révolutionnaire," "Du sacrifice nationale," and "Le Congo socialiste." As Okotaka-Ebale states in the preamble to this collection, "the primary goal then of this opuscule is assuredly to contribute, even in the remotest consequential and modest manner, to the so very unrewarding but benevolent task of educating the popular masses in order to awaken in them a more revolutionary national conscience" (Okotaka-Ebale, 53). The poem "Du patriotisme" is one such example:

> Je suis un Congolais patriote.
> Je suis un militant conscient.
> Je suis un Congolais révolutionnaire.
> Je le suis et tiens résolument à le demeurer.
>
> A bas, l'égoïsme et l'individualisme!
> A bas, le tribalisme et le régionalisme!
> A bas, le sentimentalisme et le favoritisme!
>
> Vive l'altruisme!
> Vive le patriotisme!
> Vive l'unité nationale! (Okotaka-Ebale, 60)

In the case of Okotaka-Ebale, the fundamental objective of his writing is to promote the official party line. He simply has a world view that he wants to communicate and his poems merely reproduce political propaganda. Claude-Emmanuel Eta-Onka's poems are different from Okotaka-Ebale's to the extent that Eta-Onka does at least attempt to respect certain forms. However, the primary concern of official writers in the Congo during the Marxist-Leninist era is contained in Eta-Onka's statement: "I write in a given context, and I must attempt to be *useful* to my country" (emphasis mine).[82] The notion of usefulness is of course linked to the writer's aesthetic and ideological agenda. Through a brief consideration of his poems and short stories some of these concerns will become evident.

Eta-Onka is, arguably, the most interesting and indeed intriguing example of an official militant writer in the Congo. His commitment to official government ideology and the nationalist fervor exhibited in his writings are unparalleled in the body of official writing. Recourse to biographical information is useful to our understanding of Eta-Onka's texts, given that the facts of the author's life are inseparable from his writings. Eta-Onka was born in 1946 and has made his career as a soldier after being trained at the prestigious French military academy of Saint-Cyr. Until recently he held the most important military position in the Congo, commander-in-chief of the Congolese Armed Forces, and in March 1995 was appointed as a government minister by Pascal Lissouba.[83] In addition to his remarkable military and political career, Eta-Onka played basketball and handball for the Congo. This biographical information is crucial to the image of the ideal patriot he develops in his writings. In 1991 he published a collection of poems, *Insomnies*, and in 1993 eight short stories in a volume entitled *Les tandaliennes*.[84] Eta-Onka has specific notions of what artistic productions should seek to achieve, and in the interview I conducted with him in January 1995 in Brazzaville, he defined his position as a writer:

> As men of letters, I believe we are patrons, precursors. Our conscience is superior to that of ordinary mortals. I would even say that we are visionaries, and this allows us to see . . . I think that all Congolese writers, our elders and those from my generation, products of a nation that had just emerged from political independence and that was in full construction, had a duty to adopt this national conscience. (Interview, 1995)

This statement clearly underlines the fact that Eta-Onka considers himself to be a writer of standing, without seemingly distinguishing his productions from those of other Congolese cultural practitioners. The fundamental distinction lies in the fact that Eta-Onka's "vision" is inseparable from the official party line, such that the element of originality is immediately voided. While Eta-Onka's writings effectively promote a national model that is determined by the state, non-official authors are able to subvert the national space in their representations of it, to deny it in its present form, and thereby to offer alternative models.

Eta-Onka's poems in the volume *Insomnies* are divided into four sections: "Elans," "Regrets," "Folies," and "Fibres." The first category, "Elans," contains what are primarily his political poems, anchored in propagandist and nationalist discourse. The last three sections of *Insomnies* broaden the scope of his writing as he incorporates a number of stereotypical poetic themes—love, death, and memory—but invariably lack originality to the extent that the structure is determined by the ideological message articulated. In the poem "Jeunesse," for example, he defines the framework for nation-building according to the Socialist model:

> Tu es ce Congo en construction
> Cette terre bantoue en évolution . . .
> Ton devoir est socialiste,
> Ton honneur Congolais,
> Et ta conscience nationale. (*Insomnies*, 15)

Eta-Onka has commented on his training as a soldier and described the manner in which that experience has influenced his poetry:

> There is a certain military rigor to my poetry, and I have been criticized
> for this. People have asked me why I continue to produce rhyming verses
> when the trend is towards free verse. I tell them that I am from the old
> school, that I would have liked to celebrate mass in Latin rather than
> French, that I believe one must seek out difficulty and overcome it, and
> that that is what yields beauty. (Interview, 1995)

Yet, with so little attention devoted to the linguistic domain, selecting instead to underscore the message, there is little to differentiate his poetic text from reported speech. The same conclusions apply to the poem "Hymne des diables-rouges," which links sporting activities to patriotism:

> A travers le sport pour toi Congo
> J'userai toujours dix douze chaussures l'an
> M'écorcherai coudes et genoux
> Et me foulerai poignets et chevilles.
> Pour ton honneur et ton renom Congo
> Je supporterai mille maux et internats,
> Et *l'abstinence pré-compétitions*. (*Insomnies*, 23, emphasis mine)

The willingness to suffer for the benefit of a cause is of course a noble gesture and represents the central idea behind this poem. However, Eta-Onka's attempts to raise his own endeavors to the status of martyrdom become somewhat burdensome and reach their ultimate expression in the ridiculous implications of the conclusion: "Je supporterai mille maux et internats, / Et l'abstinence pré-compétitions." Congo provides a constant source of poetic inspiration, reaching almost obsessive levels, as the poem "Ma passion" reveals:

> C'est ma passion, ma volonté d'être utile
> A ma Patrie, à ma Patrie fertile . . .
> Une, *indivisible* et prospère
> Nation Congolaise, terre bantoue
> Envers et contre tout. (*Insomnies*, 35, emphasis mine)

The word "indivisible" is taken directly from the Congolese constitution and is of course a key word in nationalist discourse. Patriotism, nationalism, and nation-building provide the framework to the majority of his poems, whether in the context of the Socialist revolution or at the service of government. When I asked him whether his poetry would survive the Marxist-Leninist context in which it is so firmly anchored, he argued that his work was timeless: "I think that if one removes the word *Socialist*, the rest of the text remains topical, because the notion of fatherland continues to be pertinent. . . . The text can survive from one generation to another" (interview, 1995, emphasis mine). Furthermore, this statement raises questions about Eta-Onka's own commitment to the ideology he is defending and of course leaves him open to the charge of opportunism. The whole premise upon which his writing is based consists in advocating Socialism and conveying a clear political message. His narrative is so firmly anchored according to the sociological circumstances in which it was produced that it becomes problematic to describe the product as anything but a historical document. Indeed, as Terry Eagleton has demonstrated in his discussion of aesthetics in *Criticism and Ideology: A Study in Marxist Literary Theory:*

> Some works of art certainly survive their contemporary moment and others do not; but this is not determined by something called the "aesthetic level." It is determined . . . by the aesthetic "producibility" of the concrete ideological conjunctures in which they inhere — conjunctures of which the available, relatively autonomous lineages of literary form are a crucial structure.[85]

Mamonsono is of course full of praise for Eta-Onka, declaring in his critical appraisal of his poetry that he considers him to be "among the most gifted poets of his generation to the extent that he has succeeded in harmonizing *military ardor* and the *finesse of the athlete*, themselves combined to a contemplative meditative reverie that is so essential for a man who controls the destiny of a school as important as the Ecole des Cadets pour la Révolution" (Mamonsono, 51, emphasis mine).

Eta-Onka's professional experiences have translated themselves into his literary works, and he has been eager to underline this point: "one should not differentiate between the conscience of a writer and that of a soldier, because I believe a soldier is the ultimate patriot: the one who can give his blood for his country" (interview, 1995). "Military ardor" and "the finesse of the athlete" have nothing to do with a notion of aesthetics in which creativity provides the defining framework but do nevertheless contain and reflect the aesthetic and political guidelines prescribed by the party. Indeed, as Huannou has argued, "a number of them [i.e., revolutionary writers] threw themselves into poetic creation without seemingly knowing that the very essence of poetry resides in imagery, rhythm and music. . . . they practice an art form whose aesthetic requirements they are completely unaware of."[86] Later in the poem, there would seem to be a contradiction between the socially constructed masculine exigencies of his professional military duties and some of his poetic lamentations; one such example arises in the second section in the poem "Larmes du self" (*Insomnies*, 51), when he is driven to tears in a self-service restaurant in Paris as a struggling artist wanders unsuccessfully from table to table trying to sell his work. Eta-Onka has addressed the ambiguity faced by the "poet who is misunderstood by his brothers" (*Insomnies*, 51); according to him, this misunderstanding stems from the fact that he wears both "velvet gloves" and "iron gloves."

Antoine Letembet-Ambily's "Préface" is full of praise: "Eta-Onka proves to be a real creator in his collection of poems, a master of the word, at once charming and vivifying; transmitting to his brothers a message quivering with romantic humanism" (*Insomnies*, 7). Letembet-Ambily was himself an established writer who received some critical attention and was once a minister of culture. The fact that he should be called upon to preface an official text is indicative of the complicated power structure in place, of the complex relationship between official and non-official practitioners, and confirms the existence of a cultural elite with the ability to confer recognition on a work that would probably go unnoticed outside of a "nationalistic" framework. Additionally, this underlines the point concerning the impossibility of delineating absolute boundaries between official and non-official spheres. The disquieting aspect of this phenomenon stems from the impossibility of bringing (or refusing to bring) independent critical assessment to texts; for to criticize the "literariness" of a text could be interpreted as criticism of the state model according to which it has aligned itself.

Eta-Onka's writings represent important historical documents and have much to reveal with regard to the sociological reality in the Congo during the scientific-Socialist era. He received two literary prizes for his poems at a time when some non-official texts were censored. These prizes included the First Prize on the occasion of the tenth anniversary of the Congolese Revolution in 1973 for his most militant poems ("Ma passion," "Jeunesse," etc.), and the First Prize in 1986 on the twentieth anniversary of the National Popular Army. Eta-Onka has described both the purpose and the audience (what Onoge has termed the "writer's constituency" [Onoge, 38]) for his writings. The question of accessibility is paramount, and he announces in the "Avant-Propos" (preface) to *Les Tandaliennes* his refusal to take part in what he calls "the quarrel between writers on the subject of stylistics in short stories" (*Tandaliennes*, 7). This measure effectively represents a dismissal of *Literature* as contrary to Marxist or Socialist aesthetics, in favor of an alternative conception of production: "I always have my stories read by high school children. I believe that most Congolese citizens and people elsewhere in Africa are at a level that does not exceed the ninth grade" (interview, 1995). Rather than identifying this gesture as a pretext for mediocrity, it introduces instead the tenuous dynamic concerning differing perspectives on culture's objectives and roles.

All of Eta-Onka's short stories are set in Brazzaville and explore a number of everyday circumstances and events in the lives of the inhabitants of Brazzaville: family rivalry, sporting loyalties, and so forth, and Eta-Onka attempts to offer an educational message. He is concerned with educating and elevating class consciousness through a literature for the people. There is no attempt to transcend the sociological reality which informs his writing, to offer any alternative, or invariably to challenge the reader. Robin's conclusion, in her meticulous investigation of Socialist Realism, underlines the specific historical situatedness of these contributions: "Socialist Realism is over. It marked a historical period in Soviet society with an aesthetics of transparency and clarity as its driving force, *a monologic dream of cultural and ideological homogeneity,* and a very specific model, that of the positive hero" (Robin, 323, emphasis mine). This "monologic dream of cultural and ideological homogeneity" is precisely what has served postcolonial nation-building unitary discourse, and the constitutional "indivisibility" hailed by Eta-Onka and other official writers. This homogeneity has been denounced by non-official authors as exclusive, anti-pluralistic, and repressive in its implied attempt at precluding the development of radically distinct approaches to literature.

The works of non-official authors expose the manner in which members of the postcolonial political elite acquire, maintain, and manipulate power, and in doing so undermine these processes and subject them to the scrutiny of outsiders. In the case of official writers, their texts are circumscribed by the sociological reality. For non-official authors, that same reality serves as the point of entry to the process of artistic creativity, but the text then distances itself from that reality to suggest another. Official writers defend a specific vision of a post-capitalist society and dedicate their creative activities to achieving those ends. Sony Labou Tansi addressed the tenuous relationship between fiction and reality in his novel *L'état honteux,* stating that "The novel is, supposedly, a work of the imagination. However, this imagination must find its place somewhere in reality."[87] Sony Labou Tansi's position and that of many of his contemporaries gains proximity to Barthes's conclusion: "literature is always unrealistic, but its very unreality permits it to question the world" (Barthes, 145). This may explain why official writers have for the most part restricted their productions to poetry. While novels have been successfully written in other literary traditions by French, Soviet, and Eastern European Communist writers, the writing of a novel without some reference to a reality that exceeds the reproduction of an ideological agenda is an extremely difficult task.

These fundamental problems are the product of a process in which ideology is foregrounded above all else. Non-official authors have succeeded in producing texts which are firmly rooted in the tradition of resistance writing but where the primary concern is with aesthetic considerations, while a Zhdanovite paradigm for Socialist Realism has compelled official writers, as Robert Porter has demonstrated, to employ writing in such a manner that "the notion has come to mean unanswering allegiance to the demands of the Party."[88] In the latter context this has been enacted through the imposition of a theoretical model according to which cultural practices are inextricably linked to the imperatives of constructing the nation.

The move toward democratization in the Congo coincided with the gradual disintegration of the Soviet Union and the reduction of Soviet interest and activity in Africa — indeed, these transitions are addressed in the final chapter of this book. However, culturally, Socialist Realism continued to serve as the official paradigm long after it had been relinquished in the Soviet Union and Eastern Europe, and it was only with governmental transitions after 1991 that control over literary production was effectively decentralized. The spirit of reform and the newly drafted post–National Conference Congolese constitution of 1992 offered some degree of optimism in its emphasis on democratic principles. However, political conflict has continued to compromise social stability and the Congolese playwright and novelist Guy Menga's 1993 book, *Congo: La transition escamotée*, was a good indicator of the conflicts that would follow.[89] State control over literary production may have been eliminated, and while some established authors — Dongala, Lopes, and Tchichelle Tchivela — have continued to publish, the deaths of Sylvain Bemba and Sony Labou Tansi represented considerable losses for both Congolese and African Letters, and new voices emerging in the Congo are being hindered by a lack of publishing opportunity.[90]

While this chapter has focused on the concept of official writing in specific sociological and political contexts, the implications are far-reaching. By underlining the influence of cultural paradigms associated with other discursive realms — notably Socialist Realism and Soviet-style state-sponsored literature, Chinese nationalism and Communist-sponsored literature, and the colonial liberation struggle — connections are established with other sociocultural frameworks. While the demands for unyielding loyalty to the party line have generally precluded the potential for creativity and more often than not served as a straightjacket on literature, one cannot ignore the fact that these texts constituted an essential component of print culture. For the most part, these texts were the only affordable and available works of literature in the Congo, Guinea, and elsewhere, and one can only begin to surmise the importance and contribution of these cultural, political, and social phenomena to the discursive realm of the postcolonial nation.

One needs to reflect on the extent to which writing is only about the advancement of a political doctrine or world view. To a certain degree, all cultural practitioners prescribe a way of writing and use literature to advance a cause. Generally speaking, official writers also abide by a strict set of aesthetic codes — Socialist Realism, accessibility, communicability, simplicity, glorification of heroes — and have a clear understanding of what constitutes literature. Non-official authors subscribe to an aesthetics of *avant-gardism* in which stylistic experimentation is foregrounded, while maintaining an independent agenda and positing or suggesting alternative alignments that may find a place in the future — these works provide the focus of discussion in chapters 3, 4, and 5. The danger emerges of course when governments claim that their aesthetic constitutes the only acceptable one — frequently, in environments that produce and impede authors, attention focuses primarily on what one *cannot* write rather than on what one *can* write. In this process, production is located in the here and now, thereby voiding individuality and transforming the writer into a domesticated cultural practitioner.[91]

Writers will continue to face difficulties as long as postcolonial nation-states are controlled by monolithic, repressive governments determined to mobilize consent. As Nurrudin Farah has poignantly written with regard to Somalia, what we have is "A nation regimented, militarized. A nation disciplined and forced to obey the iron-hand directing the orchestra of groans and moans."[92] While Africans insist on their plurality and diverse aspirations being recognized and their struggles legitimized, one could argue that the only fundamental change that has taken place is at the level of the terminology, and that the old discourse is merely being reiterated in different terms. Indeed, as Edward Said has convincingly argued in his book *Culture and Imperialism,* "in the formerly colonial world, the prospect for a culture with strongly liberationist components has rarely seemed dimmer."[93] As long as cultural, political, and social configurations continue to be formulated in this manner, the possibility of autonomous and adversarial narratives being subjected to the hegemonic influences of the dominant power structures in the process of engineering the decolonized postcolony will continue to exist.

3 SONY LABOU TANSI
Commitment, Oppositionality, and Resistance

Ever since culture became this instrument to impress,
ever since culture became a pretext for holding on to the
right of speech even when one has nothing to say, we
have lost the wisdom to utter a single word that is not
polemical. We have lost all poetry. Discourse has
become a bitter site. —SONY LABOU TANSI[1]

My writing will be shouted rather than simply written
down, my life itself will consist of groans and screams
and being pushed around, and never being allowed
simply to live. —SONY LABOU TANSI[2]

While Congolese authors are informed by similar sociological circumstances, they have nevertheless succeeded in developing radically different approaches to literature. Sony Labou Tansi's attempts at dismantling traditional narrative linearity, his lexical and syntactical creativity, and his concern with the dissipated civil authority characteristic of disintegrating postcolonial states have contributed to the creation of a subversive body of writings. The fundamental axis of his work is provided by the objective of undermining the repressive exercise of dictatorial power that has resulted in the assault on human dignity, and with the elaboration and articulation of political commitment, oppositionality, and resistance.

Marcel Ntsoni or Sony Labou Tansi

I would say that Sony lives in the Congo, but that the
Congo lives in me. —TCHICAYA U TAM'SI[3]

Sony Labou Tansi (pseudonym of Marcel Ntsoni) was born on June 5, 1947, in Kimwanza in the Belgian Congo.[4] His father was Zairian and his mother Congolese, and while there has been some confusion surrounding his nationality, he was a citizen of the Republic of the Congo.[5] He spent his early childhood in Zaire, where he was educated in Kikongo; in fact, he did not begin to learn French until much later when he started school across the river in Brazzaville in the context of an exclusively French-language curriculum. He completed his studies and then worked as an English and French teacher for a short period before devoting his time and energy to his literary and theatrical activities.[6]

The publication of six novels with the prestigious Paris-based publishing house Editions du Seuil (between 1979 and 1995)—*La vie et demie, L'état honteux, L'anté-peuple, Les sept solitudes de Lorsa Lopez, Les yeux du volcan*, and *Le commencement des douleurs*—and the staging of more than a dozen plays during what was approximately a twenty-year period from the mid-1970s to the mid-1990s established Sony Labou Tansi as one of sub-Saharan Africa's most innovative playwrights and novelists.[7] He founded the internationally acclaimed Rocado Zulu Theater company in 1979, and his plays and repertoire were regularly performed in Africa, Europe, and the United States, at the Festival International des Francophonies in Limoges, at the Festival d'Avignon, and at the Théâtre National de Chaillot and L'Espace Kiron in Paris. These productions have been officially recognized through the awarding of numerous prizes, including awards from Radio France International's Concours théâtral interafricain and the Prix Ibsen for *Antoine m'a vendu son destin*.[8] Sony Labou Tansi also published short stories and poems, and important literary awards were bestowed upon his works, including the Prix Spécial du Premier Festival de la Francophonie in 1979 and the Grand Prix Littéraire de l'Afrique Noire in 1983. He is unquestionably one of the most prolific authors Africa has ever had, and the manner in which he sought to combine political commitment with artistic creativity was both an example and an inspiration to an entire generation of artists, as he paved the way for the emergence of an innovative literary corpus.

However, critical acclaim for his work was treated with suspicion by the government authorities with whom he maintained an ambiguous relationship. According to Jean-Michel Dévésa, "it is patently obvious that Sony Labou Tansi served as a cultural showcase for Sassou Nguesso's regime throughout the 80s, allowing him to sweep aside in a swift gesture of the hand any accusation of authoritarianism" (Dévésa, 15). Recognizing the futility of censoring Sony Labou Tansi's work in what essentially constituted a non-book-consuming society, the authorities proceeded instead to discredit him by underlining and questioning the appropriateness of his links with the former colonial powers: "this was tantamount to turning the writer into a supporter of the old colonial power, into an agent of imperialism"

(Dévésa, 13–14). Yet Sony Labou Tansi himself was acutely aware of his international profile and successfully circumvented various governmental attempts at recuperating and mainstreaming his dissidence.[9] The most notable instance concerns those efforts that were made to incorporate him in the political nomenclature. He was asked the following question by David Applefield in an interview in 1993: "Your books carry a political message, yet at the same time you are a popular author and your country is obviously proud of your reputation. You've even been offered ministerial positions in the government. How do you manage to reconcile political symbolism and serious art, political activism and official acceptance?" Sony Labou Tansi replied that "For many years, I pretended I was politically naïve, which helped quite a lot. They took me for an idealist, a dreamer, and that served to pacify their fears. Generally speaking, the structure of political power in Africa is precarious: those who rule are afraid of the situation and this can incite them to act dangerously."[10]

Sony Labou Tansi evidently became increasingly adept at manipulating the official structure. While recognizing the inherent dangers to his oppositionality, he negotiated a space for himself within this framework and found innovative ways of bypassing potential strictures. A striking example of this is contained in the following statement he made regarding the issue of censorship:

> a few years ago the plays performed by my own troupe were invariably banned. In those days, it was forbidden to put on a play without written authorization from the Board of Censorship. One day, I got together with some friends and we decided to invite the members of the Board to attend rehearsals. So this guy came along and it was really funny. I got one of the cast to keep on saying: "No, that's not it. When you say that line, you step forward and place your left hand on your chest." For a whole hour! Well, as you can imagine, the guy soon got bored and after a few rehearsals, they told us that in future they would automatically give us the go-ahead. (Applefield, 97)

Somewhat paradoxically, it was in his capacity as a school teacher from 1971 to 1976, and therefore as a civil servant, that Sony Labou Tansi began to get involved in the theater. His play *Je soussigné cardiaque* becomes all the more revealing if one considers this biographical information, since his oppositionality seems to be symbiotically linked to his experiences during this period in his life. His growing disenchantment with officialdom is partly associated with the system for which he worked, while his activities within that system (including active involvement in producing plays) served only to further complicate matters. As Abel Kouvouama has noted, "due to his intense critical activities, Sony would once again be transferred to another college; in an attempt to prevent him from exercising his influence directly on school children, the educational administration appointed him head of this college."[11] Sony Labou Tansi's account of events during 1971 and 1972 substantiates this statement, as when officials attended a performance of Molière's *L'avare* which he had produced with some of the schoolchildren:

> The authorities were intrigued by the fact that everything was working out so well. And so one day, and this was at the time when all anyone spoke of was "revolution," an official delegation demanded to see the play, and they concluded that it was not sufficiently "red" . . . I'm not quite sure what they considered as "red." But the fact remains that they wanted to cancel the show and replace it with a Chinese film. We did in fact stop the performance, but announced to the audience the reasons for the interruption and invited them to join us elsewhere and see the end. An impressive upheaval ensued. The following year I was transferred to another institution.[12]

After being repeatedly moved around the Congo to new teaching appointments, Sony Labou Tansi finally abandoned his occupation as a teacher in order to gain greater autonomy and became the director of the Rocado Zulu Theater company in 1979. He explained to Bernard Magnier the opportunities contained in such a venture:

> It was born of a conviction: theater leaves us ample space while the world around us unrelentingly seeks to take it over.
>
> I started producing plays with my pupils. Everywhere I taught I created a little theater company.
>
> And then in 1979, I wound up with some old pupils at a Cercle Littéraire in Brazzaville. Nicolas Bissi already had a troupe, and so we joined forces. That is how the Rocado Zulu Theater company came about.[13]

A lengthy statement from Sony Labou Tansi is worth quoting at this juncture, since his comments have much to reveal concerning the unique possibilities and potentialities of theater for establishing the necessary framework for the elaboration of oppositionality:

> We wanted things to be this way. Uncertainty is very much a part of the work we do, from an aesthetic point, but also in artistic and social terms.

It is this uncertainty that drives us to want to live differently. We are also brought together by a lack of means. Our troupe is made up of actors, civil servants, and people who work in the private sector.

What brings us together is a common dream. We allow ourselves to believe that it is possible to make the world into a smaller place.

African wisdom tells us that we cannot be right all by ourselves. One is always right with someone else. As artists, we endeavor to be right with others. I am afraid of things that are permanent. I am drawn to things that are accepted for a few days. . . . I can write a whole play starting from a few words that are accessible to everyone.[14]

The sentiment of communality clearly constitutes an integral part of the motivation to be involved in theater, but beyond this important factor, theater represents a powerful medium in which political opposition can be enacted in an accessible manner. Indeed, as the playwright and director of the Théâtre de la Fraternité from Burkina Faso, Jean-Pierre Guingané, has argued:

A quick glance at the themes treated in plays over the past ten years confirms the essentially political character of African theater . . . inspired by revolt against the deplorable economic, social and political circumstances in Africa. . . . And more so than just being political, this theater is militant. It advocates for a societal model based on justice and freedom, for a new world. This world can only exist if society is prepared to rid itself of its flaws. The role of theater then is to urge on the world towards this objective by helping it to identify its troubles, determine their origins, and situate individual and collective responsibility.[15]

Sony Labou Tansi's works relentlessly attacked repressive postcolonial African governments and were thus subject to a certain degree of censorship in the Congo while it was a people's republic. Yet it was not until he was involved with the powerful opposition party, the Mouvement Congolais pour le Développement de la Démocratie Intégrale (MCDDI), that he experienced the most serious recriminations. In the newly achieved pluralist democracy, this party was led by Bernard Kolélas, and Sony Labou Tansi was elected in 1992 as a deputy for Brazzaville's heavily populated neighborhood of Makélékélé. His activities had clearly exceeded the boundaries deemed acceptable of an author, and various attempts were made to silence him right up to his untimely death. As he stated in a letter to the French newspaper *Libération* in 1994, "My freedom has been taken away. . . . I wrote two letters to the President of the Republic [Pascal Lissouba], and that exercise of liberty cost me my passport, my professional position, such that I now have to hide out like a rat in order to safeguard my life."[16] This harassment was particularly disquieting since both he and his wife were very sick at the time and therefore unable to receive appropriate medical attention. An international committee responded to these apparent violations of human rights, and the new Congolese administration was finally forced, in January 1995, to allow Sony Labou Tansi and his wife to be hospitalized in Paris. Their medical condition had worsened, and it was unfortunately too late to stabilize. They returned to the Congo in April, and both died of complications from AIDS in June 1995.[17]

Aesthetics and Creativity

Sony Labou Tansi's earliest publications were concerned with the question of repressive power, and this theme remained central in his writings throughout his productive career as he sought new ways of exposing the abuses. While he remained a politically committed author, his writings made considerable inroads toward the articulation of an *avant-gardist* project by foregrounding literary creativity. This dimension is of course crucial to the broader framework of this book, given that this constitutes one of the factors that serves to distinguish Sony Labou Tansi's writings from the paradigms embraced by his official, propagandist counterparts, for whom Socialist Realism was the primary tool. Sony Labou Tansi has underlined this distinction: "Art calls people to their most sacred obsessions and awakens their wildest hopes. The rest is nothing but polemics. Art lacks the malicious dimension of propaganda, and I think that is the reason why tomorrow will be another day for the artist. And I think that is also the reason why art touches us more easily and profoundly than propaganda."[18]

In the case of Sony Labou Tansi, the *avant-gardist* quality of his work begins as early as the title. One only has to sample a handful of his writings to substantiate this point: *Conscience de tracteur, La parenthèse de sang, Je soussigné cardiaque,* and *La vie et demie.* Thus, by way of the cover, the reader is prepared from the very first point of contact for the initiation that the experience of reading will provide. These titles also constitute attempts to distinguish his literary productions from the more prescriptive titles of some of his African literary predecessors that, to a certain degree, followed the evolution of philosophical themes. Some of these include Bernard Dadié's *Un Nègre à Paris* (an account of Dadié's observations and experiences during a visit to Paris), Ferdinand Oyono's *Une vie de boy* (the trials and tribulations of Toundi—a houseboy—during the colonial era), Cheikh Hamidou Kane's *L'aventure ambiguë* (where the young African protagonist, Samba Diallo, is forced to choose between an Islamic upbringing and Western education), and Ahmadou Kourouma's *Les soleils des indépendances* (which explores the manner in which political independence generated widespread disillusionment and floundering hopes rather than fulfillment and happiness).[19] However, some of Sony Labou Tansi's most strikingly original statements are achieved through a number of paratextual devices that include lengthy "Avertissements" (forewords), prologues, prefaces, dedications, and epigraphs, culminating, arguably, in a theory of African literature. These spaces allow Sony Labou Tansi to describe his approach to literature while anticipating potential reactions from censors, confusing the authorities, and underlining the necessary distinction that has to be made between fiction and reality. While historically, political authorities have often been unable to make this distinction, Sony Labou Tansi has insisted his texts be identified as products of the creative imagination.

In the "Avertissement" to *La vie et demie*, Sony Labou Tansi writes, "*La vie et demie* becomes this *fable* that sees tomorrow with today's eyes. And let no political or human concern of the day interfere. This would only generate confusion. The day when I am given the opportunity to talk about some nondescript today I'll get straight to the point, and most certainly not through as convoluted a way as the fable" (*La vie et demie*, 10). A reading of the novel in fact reveals that Sony Labou Tansi has had recourse to the fable in order to expose the activities of the Providential Guide and the disorder characteristic of disintegrating postcolonial states. As Lydie Moudileno has demonstrated in her essay on *La vie et demie* as a fable, "as soon as the tyrant is made into a character in the tale, he immediately loses the exclusiveness of authority by becoming the subject of an author who can now have him suffer the whims of his imagination. Displacing the tyrant into the narrative space therefore appears as the first potential reversal of power."[20] Sony Labou Tansi underlines his concern with the act of creativity as he distances himself from any established school of writing but does not lose sight of political issues, claiming to invent "a post of fear in this vast world" (*La vie et demie*, 9), and achieving a political text in the tradition of resistance literature while simultaneously avoiding the programmatic mode associated with Socialist Realism or partisanship.

The "Avertissement" to his fourth novel, *Les sept solitudes de Lorsa Lopez*, can be seen as a further attempt to define literature:

Art is the strength to make reality say what it would not have been able to say by itself or, at least, what it might too easily have left unsaid. In this book, I argue there should be another center of the world, that there should be other reasons for naming things, other ways of breathing. . . . My writing will be shouted rather than simply written down, my life itself will consist of groans and screams and being pushed around, and never being allowed simply to live. (*The Seven Solitudes*, foreword)

Sony Labou Tansi refuses to be a mere bystander and to be silenced by the authorities. Instead, he insists on acting as a true witness to his age. After dedicating *L'état honteux* to three people, two of whom—Henri Lopes and Tchicaya U Tam'si—were acclaimed non-official Congolese authors, Sony Labou Tansi affirms his commitment, "we will fight" (*L'état honteux*, 5). This further politicizes their activities as authors and calls upon them to join forces in the fight against oppressive political regimes. In *L'état honteux* as well, the "Avertissement" plays an important role in defining the framework of the novel: "The novel is, supposedly, a work of the imagination. Yet this imagination must find its place somewhere in reality. In a way, I write, or scream, to force the world to come into the world. . . . *L'Etat honteux* is the summary in a few 'maux' of the shameful situation in which humanity is engaged" (*L'état honteux*, 5).[21] The novel itself subsequently analyzes the various "maux" that have contributed to the "shameful situation" and provides a striking indictment of totalitarian rule. A closer look at this theme in the corpus of works will better contextualize the various forms of power— physical, sexual, governmental—that Sony Labou Tansi challenges, exposes, and undermines.

Undermining Official Discourse

In his novel *L'état honteux*, Sony Labou Tansi tells the story of Colonel Martillimi Lopez, the President of an imaginary African nation. The early reference to the Flemish, essentially interchangeable with the Belgian colonizers, allows the reader to circumscribe the action to contemporary Zaire, without Sony Labou Tansi actually having to name the country. President Lopez states his intention to rid his territory of the colonial powers: "I insist that the Flemish colony that has set itself up over the expanse of my hernia leave the territory" (*L'état honteux*, 26). There are also a number of references to their "flamanterie" (*L'état honteux*, 25), which combines their national status as "flamand" with the "connerie" (damned stupidities) they commit.[22] This is an effective device, since by transposing his narrative in Zaire, Sony Labou Tansi can attack authoritarianism without actually naming the People's Republic of the Congo; this enables him to at least attempt to bypass censorship, or perhaps even to claim innocence should he be accused of treason. However, the reality he describes and the interconnectedness of the respective colonial and postcolonial histories of the two Congos are close enough for the criticism to apply to both spheres.

Sony Labou Tansi's writings criticize existing political systems, and the void that he generates is filled by an alternative political discourse, one that is diametrically opposed to what he has deconstructed and which suggests less exclusive alignments. In *L'anté-peuple* we are told that "they called the river the Congo here, the Zaïre over there. But all that was the result of man's foolishness" (*The Anti-People*, 112). The fact that the point of reference from which all else is measured is provided by the Congo is significant and discreetly reveals Sony Labou Tansi's primary concern. Indeed, the Congo and Zaire have acquired an almost synonymous status that reflects their shared historical trajectories; in many ways, this is contained in the body of water they both designate, while also delineating the boundaries of their respective sovereign states. As Kenneth Harrow has argued, "if there is one archetypal figure that has both defined and been denied as the border, it is the river, the river between—the river with two names. . . . The river is the quintessential border that refuses to be fixed" (Harrow, 320–22).[23] In *L'anté-peuple,* characters travel from Zaire to the Congo, and from the Congo to Zaire. In his incisive reading of *L'anté-peuple,* Jonathan Ngate has underlined the significance of Dadou's flight from Zaire to the Congo: "The Bakongo (singular, Mukongo) live on both sides of the river in Zaïre, in the Congo and in Angola. . . . For them . . . the international border is just a bothersome aberration. . . . It is therefore not surprising that Dadou and Yealdara should feel sufficiently 'at home' in the Congo to become active in the guerrilla movement there."[24] Ngate's anthropological explanation for this phenomenon underlines the complexity of the sociological reality and confirms that linguistic and cultural communities can achieve continuity outside of juridical borders. However, the central question that is asked in *L'anté-peuple* is crucial to Sony Labou Tansi's attempts to challenge and undermine the postcolonial ruling elite: "People from over there were coming here. People from here were going over there. Fleeing from one bank to land on the other. But which was the more to be fled from? It was hard to say. One just went ahead. Life was much the same on both banks. The frontier was for papers" (*The Anti-People*, 133). Dadou's problems originate in Zaire, and it is this national space that comes predominantly under attack. By deliberately confusing the two spaces (Zaire/the Congo), the respective otherness is gradually reduced to sameness, and whatever criticism is formulated against the one simultaneously becomes applicable to the other. In other words, "which was the more to be fled from?" Topographical considerations are extremely important and inextricably linked to the dichotomy contained in the relationship between fiction and reality. Sony Labou Tansi discussed this dimension with Applefield:

> **Sony Labou Tansi:** The book [*La vie et demie*] was written in somewhat painful circumstances. In 1977 Brazzaville was the scene of a major social and political crisis following the assassination of President Marien Ngouabi. . . . Innocent people were blamed for the killing and were subsequently eliminated. I was aware of the conspiracy because I knew some of the victims personally; they were friends of mine. . . . I was so upset by the situation that I decided to write *La vie et demie.*

> **David Applefield:** So it's fiction based on a historical reality?

> **Sony Labou Tansi:** Yes. The starting-point of the story was the death of these friends. . . . I wrote the book because I wanted to rehabilitate people like Cardinal Byayenda, Luti Nganga and the former president Massamba-Débat. (Applefield, 93–94)

In *La vie et demie*, Sony Labou Tansi explores the question of dictatorial power by concentrating on the particularly violent succession of Providential Guides in the imaginary African nation of Katamalanasie. The closing sentences of this novel, "My body remembers you. It is dead, Mister Minister of His Most-Greasy-Hernia" (*La vie et demie*, 192), find their literary sequel in the opening words of Sony Labou Tansi's next novel, *L'état honteux:* "This is the story of my Colonel Martillimi Lopez son of Maman Nationale, who came into the world holding his *hernia,* and who left the world still clutching it" (*L'état honteux*, 7, emphasis mine). A thematic continuity and intertextuality can be seen to link these presentations of the postcolony, located in this particular case in the evocation of the grotesque body.

The relationship between the body and nationalist discourse, along with the tenuous associations between gender and nationalist identities, provide important sites at which power is explored and in turn the elaboration and articulation of protest and resistance located. Indeed, writing from postcolonial francophone sub-Saharan Africa has consistently denounced governmental attempts to render the body as what Michel Foucault has described as both mentally and physically "docile."[25]

Power and Popular Culture

Achille Mbembe's book *De la postcolonie: Essai sur l'imagination politique dans l'Afrique contemporaine* represents one of the most comprehensive and engaging studies of the postcolony.[26] Part of Mbembe's analysis concerns the burlesque and carnivalesque elements of popular culture, and for him the "grotesque" and the "obscene" are characteristic of the postcolony. He situates his argument in relation to Mikhail Bakhtin's writings, for whom these factors constitute "a means of resistance to the dominant culture, and as a refuge from it, obscenity and the grotesque are parodies that undermine officialdom by showing how arbitrary and vulnerable is officialese and by turning it all into an object of ridicule" (Mbembe, 103–104).[27] Sony Labou Tansi incorporates these attributes of popular culture into his novels, thereby crossing the boundaries between orality and literacy, but also simultaneously redefining and transforming the parameters of the novel as genre in order to accommodate these voices. Mbembe suggests that we go one step further and show how these factors are in fact an integral component of the power mechanism itself by analyzing: "1) the timing and location of those occasions that state power organizes for dramatizing its own magnificence; 2) in the actual materials used in the ceremonial displays through which it makes manifest its majesty; and 3) the specific manner in which it offers these, as spectacles, for its 'subjects' (cibles) to watch" (Mbembe, 104). The symbiotic nature of the relationship between the *dominator* and the *dominated* is exemplified in a multitude of linguistic practices; Mbembe highlights the popular use of the Rassemblement du Peuple Togolais Party acronym RPT, in a such a way as to underline the onomatopoeic dimension contained in the sounds "PT," which resemble the French verb "péter" (to fart).[28] The important point for Mbembe is that "the public affirmation of the 'postcolonized subject' is not necessarily found in acts of 'opposition' or 'resistance' to the *commandement*. What defines the postcolonized subject is the ability to engage in baroque practices fundamentally ambiguous, fluid, and modifiable even when there are clear, written, and precise rules" (Mbembe, 129).

In Sony Labou Tansi's novel *La vie et demie*, there is a similar example, whereby the party acronym PPUDT in the allegorical nation is itself transformed to signify the "Parti Payondi pour l'unité des dettes et des tueries" (*La vie et demie*, 60). Mbembe's analysis is both stimulating and convincing, and its pertinence to a reading of postcolonial writings is unquestionable, indeed implicit to the literary projects of many francophone sub-Saharan

African authors such as Sony Labou Tansi, Thierno Monénembo, Ibrahima Ly, and Alioum Fantouré. Yet, while I struggle to share the implied faith he has in the population's consciousness of their subjectivity and of their capacity to appropriate this role in order to modify a given social reality—a point that is underlined in *L'état honteux* when the President is informed that "in this country, only those who have nothing to lose speak the truth" (*L'état honteux*, 9)—I do agree with his formulation to the extent that "the question of whether humor in the postcolony is an expression of 'resistance' or not, whether it is, a priori, opposition, or simply manifestation of hostility toward authority, is thus of secondary importance" (Mbembe, 108). While such instances of popular resistance undermine official discourse both inside and outside the written text, the masses occupy an economic, political, and social status unlikely to generate the type of consciousness susceptible to generate systematic revolutionary action. Furthermore, they lack the means—education, access to media, literacy—to articulate opposition outside of the parameters of popular culture, fearful of potential retributions, and aware that dissent exposes them to recriminations.

Koffi Anyinefa's book *Littérature et politique en Afrique noire: Socialisme et dictature comme thèmes du roman congolais d'expression française* offers a particularly insightful reading of Sony Labou Tansi's early novels; his analysis and critique of the scene when President Lopez, disguised as a peasant, interacts with the masses during a visit to a "densely populated neighborhood" in order to apprehend what his people are saying about him illustrates the argument I am formulating concerning the contestatory effectiveness of popular culture (Anyinefa, 164). President Lopez listens to the masses sing a song which openly mocks him:

> If I were a little mouse
> I would burrow into his greasy hernia
> If I were a little cat
> I would go and hunt in his hernia. (*L'état honteux*, 42)

His stupidity is underlined when he joins in with the singing, thereby providing a further case of counter-discursive ridicule. Thus, while these moments exemplify Mbembe's "baroque practices," undermine official discourse, and have much to reveal concerning the popular imagination of state violence, their limited effectiveness in overthrowing the power mechanisms manipulated by the monolithic dictatorship is confirmed by the fact that the state structure itself is not ultimately threatened. I propose to elaborate upon some of these issues and focus on Sony Labou Tansi's analysis of the methods employed in establishing national dominance and nationalistic discourse, and the masculinist constructs that accompany this gesture.

Nationalism and Masculinity

The body and sexual activities are crucial to Sony Labou Tansi's thinking on power. Anyinefa has argued the centrality of this theme in Sony Labou Tansi's writings, given that it is the "bas du corps et politique" and the "conjunction of these two domains that 'generate' the *shame*, and suggest the collapse of the country's political morals" (Anyinefa, 157). János Riesz extends this analysis since for him "the hernia not only expresses the game or the stakes of the game of power, it also becomes itself the object of a game, a parodic element of a discourse that allows other discourses to emerge and thus reveals the character of the usurpation of this Hernia-Power-State."[29] Dysfunctional sexual behavior functions as a parallel to the dilapidated postcolonial sphere itself in which President Lopez feels that "the consumption of vagina can interfere with the smooth running of the affairs of the state" (*L'état honteux*, 41).

By linking violence and decay to sexuality, the traditional qualities associated with such activities undergo a radical variation. As Anyinefa has signaled, "sex is never synonymous with love" and "the sex/power relationship is always a violent one" (Anyinefa, 158–59). Where there was once life and pleasure there is now death and pain. Indeed, Article 7 of the Congolese constitution decrees that "human beings are sacred. The state has an obligation to respect and protect this sacredness."[30] This fundamental constitutional guideline—upon which the nation-state is founded—has been ignored, and the phallus as a traditional source of procreation transformed into a weapon of masculine dominance.

President Martillimi Lopez in *L'état honteux* is indissociable from his hernia, an aspect Anyinefa has described with reference to Bakhtin's analysis of Rabelais, for whom "protruding bodily parts . . . are key components in the relationship to the grotesque, since they lend themselves admirably to hyperbole in order to become autonomous bodies" (Anyinefa, 159). While Anyinefa's reading incorporates issues pertaining to the President's obsession with various bodily functions (foremost among which would feature those activities related to sex), the phallic quality of this hernia needs to be further underlined. Sexuality in Sony Labou Tansi's work links desire to authoritarian impulses in a complex process of bodily and territorial dominance.

The opening pages introduce the notion of territory as the leader asserts his right to delineate national borders: "what kind of a people are we if we do not have the liberty to fabricate our own borders?" (*L'état honteux*, 10–11). Significantly, the logic informing his decision making is inseparable from his hernia:

> For the first time he let out his loud father's laugh, splitting his sides with laughter and how stupid you are: you've left the homeland in the same shameful state as the Flemish left it, you've left the nation as if the pale power was still there, how shameful mother, and how stupid you all are! Fetch me some red ink. And he started outlining the homeland's new dimensions: put the *tirailleurs* to work, and he drew four straight lines that joined up two by two, leaving some areas of our national territory with our neighbors, and taking from our neighbors sections of their territory because, my brothers and beloved compatriots, that's the decision of my hernia: the homeland shall be square. (*L'état honteux*, 10)

A similar process leads to the elaboration of the constitutional document that will guarantee the sovereignty of the borders he has structured:

> Article 1: the homeland shall be square.
> Article 2: down with demagogy.
> Article 3: Maman Nationale is everyone's mother.
> Article 4: no strikes, and no damned stupidity. (*L'état honteux*, 13)

Indeed, for what corresponds to a ridiculous constitution, we also have a ridiculous leader, obsessed with the power his genitals and hernia confer upon him. This power is contained in his declaration, according to which "the genitals are not an object of courtesy: they are material for governance" (*L'état honteux*, 82), a dimension that is further underlined when he appoints a "Minister of Testicles" (*L'état honteux*, 79). This ministerial post further foregrounds phallocratic power, as masculinist identity is inextricably linked to the exercise of political power. The colonial phallocracy is transferred here onto President Lopez as a defining element, characterized by Mbembe in the following terms: "Without a phallus, the colonizer is nothing; has no fixed identity. Thanks to the phallus, the colonizer's cruelty can stand quite naked: erect. A sliver of flesh that dribbles endlessly, the colonizer's phallus can hardly hold back its spasms, even if alleging concerns about tints and odors" (Mbembe, 175). Naturally, this has implications for the relationship between gender and sexuality to the extent that the public is further inscribed as a traditional male space, while the private one remains female.

President Lopez's identity is constructed according to his sexual persona, to the extent that only those physical attributes located in his lower region serve to differentiate him from the otherwise undifferentiated masses. President Lopez has even gone so far as to install loudspeakers in every neighborhood in order to ensure that his omnipresence transcends the public space to enter the private one as well, "while they are busy riding their wives, while they are busy cursing me and conspiring against me, as they are busy insulting me, at least let them hear me and let my voice deflower them, so that if I cannot be loved, at least I will be feared, known, smelt" (*L'état honteux*, 22). Such great importance is attached to the phallus that it may not be surprising to note the manner in which emasculation comes to signify the removal of the possibility of exercising power. There are repeated threats and indeed castrations carried out to this effect. When a prisoner comes before the President to beg for a pardon, he is granted his request but at the expense of his sexual organs: "I'm taking your male utensils away from you: it is for them that you seized power. . . . I'm severing the trunk and both nuts" (*L'état honteux*, 99). Another character's penis is cut off and the President "walks over his testicles" (*L'état honteux*, 31), a fate shared by a fellow countryman, "in my name, I disconnect your willy" (*L'état honteux*, 151). These "utensils" are a prerequisite to anyone wishing to manipulate power, such that their removal also eliminates the possibility for resistance. Any positive dimension that could traditionally have been associated with the notion of sexuality has thus been evacuated and replaced by a type of behavior that is devoid of any constructive dimension and voided of any affirmation of moral value.

Cruelty and Sexuality

Sexuality, cruelty, and violence are everywhere in Sony Labou Tansi's vision of the postcolony, and his treatment of the theme is considerably more forceful than that of his literary peers.[31] Acts of torture are consistently breaking new boundaries and presented as an integral component of sophisticated governmental attempts at achieving docility and submissiveness, while simultaneously controlling and eliminating dissent. Page duBois, in her book *Torture and Truth*, has argued that

> Torture is no longer performed to obtain truth from a victim. Rather, torturers torture to punish, to offer examples of the pain to be suffered as a consequence of certain actions. They torture to send back out into the

world people broken, destroyed, to serve as living warnings. They torture because of their own rage, their own sadistic desire to punish, to offer for themselves the spectacle of conversion, the body of the other so abused that the tortured gives up a belief and thus comforts the torturer who can then himself believe that he has triumphed, that his cause will triumph over resistance.[32]

Torture, humiliation, subordination, and dominance thus serve to duplicate the images of decay, dilapidation, and degenerate behavior that have come to characterize the sociological reality.

While orders such as those given by Sergeant Cavacha in Sony Labou Tansi's play *La parenthèse de sang* — "cut off his right hand. Put out his right eye. Don't fool around with useless loss of blood. He must die piece by piece. Cut off his ears, his nose" — may seem disturbing, primacy is accorded to wounds of the sexual order as the ultimate form of disempowerment.[33] Sony Labou Tansi innovates with a powerful metaphor that comes to represent the fate of the postcolony, a metaphor that can help us interpret ongoing problems and their treatment in his writings. Traditionally, human behavior has been presented as a dynamic involving rational thinking and sexual desire. Yet, in Sony Labou Tansi's postcolony, the degree of dysfunctionality is so pronounced that one can only deduce that the self-perpetuating (or reproducing) power structure may need to be castrated or radically rehauled prior to there being any possibility of positive transition.

President Lopez describes in one of his speeches how "the death penalty is for women, what men need is the penalty of my hernia, because it is their shameful male function that is behind everything, it is their hernia that drives them to sell themselves to the nation" (*L'état honteux*, 51). Death, in and of itself, constitutes an insufficient mechanism for the elimination of dissent in Sony Labou Tansi's narratives. This serves to further emphasize the symbiotic link established between sexuality and the exercise of power, to the extent that dissenting voices are silenced only after sexual mutilation is complete; life itself does not constitute the point of resistance, but rather it is the capacity to assert sexual control that creates the conditions for protest and resistance. Torture becomes a gendered activity in which men mutilate women and each other to affirm the supremacy of the phallocratically controlled public space over the private space. Significantly, for example, when Chaïdana assumes the role in *La vie et demie* of what Arlette Chemain-Degrange has described as "justicière" (dispenser of justice), she does not become masculinized, nor does she target her own gender.[34] Rather, as

Moudileno has argued, "Chaïdana's function consists in serving as bait in her father's revenge in such a way that the bridal room is substituted for the torture chamber. . . . The feminine body assimilated to both the national and textual space constitutes one of the sites where the demiurgic battle between the masculine figures takes place" (Moudileno, 27–29).

Sexual mutilation and ambiguity play a central role. Carvanso, in *L'état honteux*, claims that "former colonel Fetranso almost became my wife" (*L'état honteux*, 36), and at the end of the novel we have a new "national aunt" since "that's what I call my colonel Loufao who has a woman's voice" (*L'état honteux*, 156).[35] There is an interesting play on words here, to the extent that French colonial leaders were commonly referred to as "oncles" (uncles); in this instance, the character's nationalist identity is contained in the inclusion of the term *national* in the title that he is granted, but his gendered identity—colonel Loufao—is subverted by the emasculation contained in the feminine title of "aunt."[36] The character's assumption of a feminine identity appears to void the possibility of his constituting a threat to the power structure in place, although of course the character of Chaïdana in *La vie et demie* provides a fascinating subversion of this precept. When the soldiers arrive at Libertashio's home in *La parenthèse de sang*, they are ordered to "make sure the men are men, and the women women" (*Parentheses of Blood*, 10). Similarly, Sergeant Cavacha's words to Ramana contain obvious implications that go beyond his concern that she be a virgin, "I presume you *are* a girl" (*Parentheses of Blood*, 10).

Examples of mutilation and deviant sexual behavior are everywhere in Sony Labou Tansi's texts. In *L'état honteux*, the penis is described as a "rape utensil" (*L'état honteux*, 153), and in *La vie et demie*, Martial "had such a terrible fit of rage that he beat his daughter like he would a beast and then slept with her, no doubt in order to administer an internal slap" (*La vie et demie*, 69). Rape represents the ultimate violation of the private sphere by the public, thus reinforcing the notion that power itself encompasses both spheres. Violent sexual contact is the order of the day, as when President Lopez declares that "he searched her so thoroughly that he pulled a piece of intestine out of her vagina" (*L'état honteux*, 31). Whereas sexuality informs, indeed determines, President Lopez's exercise of authority, Chaïdana resorts to prostitution as a mechanism for resistance, using her body to lure ministers, officials, and powerful military men to the private space she has secured at the Hôtel La Vie et Demie. From here, she is able to subvert gender constructs as she proceeds to poison these public officials after performing sexual favors. Her gendered identity is transformed into a weapon of resistance allowing her to record her opposition to the existing power structures while simultaneously participating in the nationalist struggle in which she is engaged. The indissociability of gender and nationalist identities is thus unambiguously registered through her political commitment. Sexuality becomes synonymous with alienation and rejection as the experience of Shaba in Sony Labou Tansi and Caya Makhele's play *Le coup de vieux* clearly illustrates: "The story goes that my mother injected herself with metergin for three months to try and kick me out of her abdomen; and then when I came into the world she tried to cause me to have a drug overdose by putting mescaline in my bottle. By some unspeakable miracle I survived all these dirty tricks."[37]

Violence and torture even assume aphrodisiac qualities, as when a character announces that "when I have to hit out, I . . . I have an erection just like when I'm with a woman" (*L'état honteux*, 115).

In what constitutes a gesture of resistance in *La vie et demie*, Martial starts a campaign to discredit the Providential Guide by spreading rumors that he is impotent. The objective, indeed intended consequence, of such a misinformation campaign is to challenge the President's capacity for leadership without the prerequisite emblematic exigency of masculinity.[38] A national role model in the postcolonial community is no longer simply referred to as a hero but rather as "herotic" (*L'état honteux*, 27), in which the performance of nationalism is inseparable from the humiliating, subordinating, and dominating tendencies of eroticism.

Random, arbitrary acts of violence in general are portrayed as characteristic of the postcolony in Sony Labou Tansi's writing, thereby reproducing the parameters of the colonial model. For Mbembe, "at the root of colonization is thus an inaugural act, within a jurisdiction all its own, that of arbitrariness. That act consists not only in ordaining without limits, but also in freeing oneself from reality's limits" (Mbembe, 188). I shall draw parallels later between this violence and Sony Labou Tansi's linguistic practices in order to reveal how these function as part of his broader literary project. First though, I propose to explore Sony Labou Tansi's plays. These plays provide important thematic links to the novelistic corpus, and unfortunately, like so many performance arts in Africa, their extraordinary originality has not been matched by sufficient critical attention.[39]

Patrick Chabal has addressed the question of power and violence in postcolonial Africa and distinguished between two types of violence, namely, "active violence" and "passive violence."[40] Article 7 of the Congolese constitution decrees the human body to be sacred, such that violation of that body represents a serious infringement of that document. Sony Labou Tansi's writings offer recurrent scenes in which "active violence" is perpetrated by the state against Article 7—assuming that we are willing to investigate beyond the veil of allegory contained in the fictional product in order to recognize that the text does not attempt to avoid dialogic engagement with a contemporary reality in which such a decree would be a fairly standard component of most constitutional documents. In fact, such scenes provide a genuine conflation between real and fictive material.

La vie et demie takes the violation of the body to its most extreme form. Martial and several other prisoners are brought before the Providential Guide who "gave off a very simple little smile before sliding the table knife" into Martial's throat and then proceeded to devour a large piece of meat (La vie et demie, 11). We are dealing here with a bloodthirsty monster who declares "I am carnivorous" (La vie et demie, 18), and whose cruelty knows no bounds. Each act of violence he engages in inevitably adopts sexual overtones: "The Providential Guide plunged the table knife in one and then the other eye, extracting a blackish gelatinous substance that trickled down his cheeks and of which two tear-shaped drops joined up at the wound in his neck, while the old wreck-father continued to breathe as a man does after finishing the act" (La vie et demie, 13). However, no matter how much the Providential Guide dissects Martial's body, his soul refuses to die; the blood and fluids that come out of his body stain the presidential floor, and these indelible bodily markings—referred to as "Martial's stain" (La vie et demie, 16)— ultimately stand as a symbol of rebellion. For Mbembe, "colonial violence . . . participates in the phallic gesture: a phallic and sometimes sadistic gesture, insofar as the colonizer thinks and expresses himself through his phallus" (Mbembe, 175). The Providential Guide does all that he can to disempower Martial and finally decides that he will eat him: "he ordered that the human termitary be taken away, divided up, and prepared as pâté and a nice casserole for lunch the following day" (La vie et demie, 16). The authorities have no respect for the sacredness of the body as outlined in the constitutional document upon which its power has been legitimized and are prepared to do anything to maintain their power base. The public body may be able to do whatever it chooses to the private body, but it cannot control or eliminate the mind and thought processes that challenge the leadership. They seem to find ways of mutating in Sony Labou Tansi's texts, of resurfacing in different forms, even beyond "la vie et demie" (life and a half) and the parentheses; indeed, the implication is that they will continue to do so until the "world that is called modern" and that is "shameful and a scandal" (*L'état honteux*, 5) ceases to be so. This is perhaps what is implied in Sony Labou Tansi's claims in *La parenthèse de sang* that there was no "nothingness," and in *La vie et demie*, when we hear of "two worlds, that of the living, and that of the dead" (*La vie et demie*, 17). The "in betweenness" he alludes to seems to suggest the possibility of resistance, underlining his faith in protest as an agent of change and confirmed in the oppositional dimension of his writing.

Performing Violence and Power

> We all live for theater: the theater of existence and that
> of the stage. —SONY LABOU TANSI[41]

Perhaps nowhere has the concept of power been staged more powerfully than in Sony Labou Tansi's theatrical works.[42] Mbembe has defined the baroque in the postcolony in terms of "its unusual and grotesque art of representation, its taste for the theatrical, and its violent pursuit of wrongdoing to the point of shamelessness" (Mbembe, 115), and many of these qualities are to be found in *La parenthèse de sang*. The handling of these themes in dramatic works is all the more interesting to the extent that postcolonial governments have literally engaged in the act of "staging power"—through military parades, visits by heads of state, inauguration ceremonies —in an effort to "dramatize its importance" (Mbembe, 115). In addition to explicit public activities, there is also evidence of implicit private mechanisms—rules of terror, networks of lies, insinuations, and allusions.

The introductory remarks made by Sony Labou Tansi in the published edition of *La parenthèse de sang* provide an indication of the theme of the play: "And so that was coming out of 'raw life' so as to go forth and believe in all these hearts [cœurs] that become a chorus [chœur] in us! And so that was the proof that there was no such thing as nothingness. All my flesh leans into me: we have created the anti-hole; the soul is us without words."[43] The juxtaposition of "cœurs" (hearts) with "chœur" (chorus) reveals Sony Labou Tansi's fondness for lexical experimentation, innovation, and amusement (a dimension that is lost in translation here). Furthermore, the invocation of a "vie brute" (raw life) serves as a forewarning to the alternative space Sony Labou Tansi will erect in the parentheses. Mbembe's discussion of the temporality that designates the colony and "what comes after" (Mbembe, 196) can serve to illustrate what Sony Labou Tansi may have in mind:

> Since changing time is however not really possible, we must firmly place
> ourselves in another space to describe our age, the age and space of *raw
> life* (vie brute). The age of raw life as an alternative space has a number
> of properties at which we must briefly look. First, it is a place and a time
> of *half-death*—or, if one prefers, *half-life*. It is a place where life and
> death are so entangled that it is no longer possible to distinguish them,
> or to say what is on the side of the shadow or its obverse. (Mbembe, 197)

The second sentence provides what is arguably the affirmative message of
the play, namely, that there is no such thing as "nothingness." This exclusion of nothingness, of nihilism, and of the possibility of reducing the individual to insignificance represents an avowal in the direction of resistance
and engagement. This notion is reiterated in Sony Labou Tansi's novel *L'anté-
peuple*, in which the dedication reads:

> To my dead ones . . .
> Because to die
> Is to dream a different dream. (*The Anti-People*, 5)

The frame of reference grows increasingly strange and unfamiliar, for in
reaching beyond this vacuum which could embody the soul (through verbal extravagance), the possibility arises of transcending the status quo.

The opening stage directions are disquieting: "The evening angelus rings
in the distance. Bursts of a tommy-gun. Bugle calls. An atmosphere of war"
(*Parentheses of Blood*, 5), thereby anchoring the action in a situation of conflict. The prologue then introduces the notion of parentheses: "It's begun—
in this sad century. Whether opened or closed—this *parenthesis of blood*,
this *parenthesis of the intestines*, it's begun, but won't end" (*Parentheses of
Blood*, 1, emphases mine). The performance of the text compels the spectator to decipher the significance of the parentheses contained in the title
itself, *La parenthèse de sang*. While the prologue sets up an opposition between blood and intestines, primacy is accorded to blood through its inscription in the title. For Kouvouama, the prologue affords Sony Labou Tansi
a space in which to "construct the paradigm of violence and subversion, to
fix collective norms and the rules of Libertashio's family history, hero of
freedom, and to reinvent a free world on the ashes of collective madness"
(Kouvouama, 101). These parentheses serve as metaphorical representations
for national boundaries, territories, or geographies. Whether they are of blood
or of intestines, they echo the violence, brutality, and disemboweling that
we have come to associate with Sony Labou Tansi's images of conduct by
the postcolonial authorities. But they also contain an allusion to the resis-

tance struggle, namely, an affirmation of survival and a refusal of being reduced to nothingness.

The stage directions and prologue, compounded with the presence on stage of three graves and of a character called "le Fou" (fool, madman), confuse the reader and spectator, forcing them to grant the dramatist's text undivided attention. According to Kouvouama, "in this violent world in which all emancipative language is outlawed and condemned to death, only the fool's words echo at the heart of the group. His words attempt to reveal the meaning of things without nevertheless providing the interpretive key" (Kouvouama, 103). One of the graves contains Libertashio, while his three daughters, Ramana, Yavilla, and Aleyo, his wife Kalahashio, and his nephew Martial are together on stage. Yavilla tells them that she can see a group of soldiers approaching, to which Martial immediately interjects: "this country's the land of soldiers" (*Parentheses of Blood*, 7).

As the soldiers arrive on stage, the family is rigid with fear, only too aware of the reputation that precedes them. Indeed, as Kouvouama has commented, "the logic behind the terror instigated by the arrival of the soldiers serves to invent death on a permanent basis in order to erode any free conscience, any vague liberation impulse that might be burgeoning" (Kouvouama, 104). The dialogue subsequently concentrates on denouncing the soldiers for their stupidity and the system they represent for its ineptness. The following exchange between a Sergeant and one of his soldiers, instigated by Ramana's probing questions, is perhaps the most indicative:

Ramana: What are you looking for?

The Sergeant: Mark! Mark! Help me remember what we're looking for.

Mark: (*from inside the house, where the body searches are taking place*) We're looking for Libertashio.

The Sergeant: (*to Ramana*) We're looking for Libertashio.

Ramana: Since when?

The Sergeant: Mark! Mark! How long have we been looking for him?

Mark: Six months or more.

The Sergeant: (*to Ramana*) Six months or more.

Ramana: Who sent you?

The Sergeant: Mark! Mark! Remind me again, who sent us?

Mark: The capital.

The Sergeant: (*to Ramana who's pouring wine into the helmet*) The capital. (*Parentheses of Blood*, 10–11)

The image conveyed is of a country given over to soldiery, with these men in turn at the beck and call of the fictitious center of power, namely, the capital. Even when the family confirms the death of their father, Libertashio, the soldiers refuse to question the capital's official position and insist on obtaining fingerprints. As Mark declares, "They tell us to search for him, and that's what we're doing" (*Parentheses of Blood*, 19). For Moudileno, the Providential Guide's "hegemony is maintained through the physical elimination of all opposition and by the subordination of the minds to the arbitrariness of the State" (Moudileno, 22–23). Ramana assures them that he is well and truly dead and the Sergeant finally concedes that they must be telling the truth. However, when he shouts out his newfound conviction, "Libertashio is dead" (*Parentheses of Blood*, 14), Mark instantly shoots him, claiming that "a deserter is a uniformed soldier who says Libertashio is dead" (*Parentheses of Blood*, 15). This is the first in a series of killings among the interchangeable military ranks. The arbitrary nature of the killings and the random selection of victims contribute to the fear of the alarmed masses who are only too aware of the dangers they face when in the presence of these men. The soldiers are further ridiculed by their inability to use terminology correctly, as when Mark talks of their responsibility to find Libertashio: "Any number of Libertashios will do. We'll find fifty or a hundred if we have to, as many as the capital wants. (*Pause*). We aren't looking to find anyone, we're looking for the sake of looking" (*Parentheses of Blood*, 19). Martial ends up handcuffed when the soldiers decide that he resembles the picture they have of his uncle Libertashio. The overriding image we have of these soldiers is that of mere pawns in the wider, more complex manipulations of power. They show signs of limited education and ignorance of the fundamental workings of the political process; in the electoral processes they evoke, ballot boxes are referred to as "balling boxes" (*Parentheses of Blood*, 21).

In this sphere of arbitrary violence and random executions, questions concerning life and death that are central to Kongo custom find themselves inextricably linked to Sony Labou Tansi's theatrical project. Pius Ngandu Nkashama has shown how *La parenthèse de sang* is deeply rooted in Kongo tradition.[44] According to Nkashama, the inclusion of references to a kambala tree, graves, and a fool in the opening stage directions serve to anchor the text in Kongo tradition. Nkashama explains that the "dream-death conjunction is of primordial importance. It has provided the essential framework of those plays that established Sony's reputation."[45] For Sony Labou Tansi, Kongo performance practices are contained in "the specificity of tradition-al Kongo theaters prohibited by missionaries and the colonial administra-tion,"[46] the key tenets of which include "1— The theater of the Kings or public insults; 2— Kingizila or the theater of healing; 3— Lemba or the cult of re-birth; 4— Yala-Yala or Nsimba: theater of twins; and 5— Nkoloba or the theater of little wooden dancers (marionettes) that is developed around a story."[47] Indeed, as Kouvouama has argued, *La parenthèse de sang* can be considered a variation of Kingizila theater, whereby "the reinvention of a free world via a collective healing of fear is enacted by Sony Labou Tansi on a symbolic level through the principle of self-sacrifice that combines the renunciation of terrestrial life and the principle of elevation by releasing oneself to a spiritual humanity" (Kouvouama, 101).

There is a continuous play on these notions, as Ramana talks of "A ballet called *The Death of Life*" (*Parentheses of Blood*, 10), and the parson claims that "life on this earth is dead" (*Parentheses of Blood*, 52). In *La vie et demie* we hear that "Hell, hell. Do people know that hell corresponds to the death of Life, that it corresponds to the death of liberty? . . . We must con-quer the death of life, because it is even more unbearable than the death of beings" (*La vie et demie*, 152). As Henri Lopes wrote in his "envoi" (send off) to Sony Labou Tansi's play *Conscience de tracteur*, "Westerners think their lives through, we dream ours" (*Conscience de tracteur*, 10). Sony La-bou Tansi distances himself from the framework of Cartesian logic which he understands as being against instinct and intuition.[48] The atrocities he describes, along with the dreams and nightmares of his characters, escape the rule of logic. In Sony Labou Tansi's words, "I think that Descartes killed an excellent part of the European soul, he invented a kind of spiritual frigid-ity."[49]

The next scene introduces the concept of life and death in a more di-rect fashion when each member of the family is asked to state his or her last wish. Martial's request to "stay alive" (*Parentheses of Blood*, 30) is the most original and constitutes a refusal to give up hope. In *La vie et demie*, similar concerns were raised, and as Tchicaya U Tam'si has argued, "the authorities are the worst enemy. In Sony's first book, there is an attempt to kill this hope in the character of Martial, who is killed, assassinated, but who does not die."[50] Martial's defiant behavior results in torture, while Aleyo's wish to marry the Sergeant generates the greatest response. Compelled to respect her re-quest, Aleyo is referred to as the "future late Madame Sergeant Cavacha"

(*Parentheses of Blood*, 47) during the rapidly improvised and extravagant wedding ceremony. While this is of course comical, the horrifying absurdity is further underlined.[51]

Following these events, the family is confined to a room, unable to sleep yet showing no signs of fatigue. There are parallels here to Jean-Paul Sartre's play *Huis-Clos*, in which the inability to sleep forced the three characters condemned to eternal life in hell, Garcin, Inès, and Estelle, to reflect on issues of life and death and to confront the circumstances of their imprisonment.[52] As with Sartre's play, life and death are no longer clearly distinguishable. The third evening (the first four acts are "evenings," and the final act is a "morning") begins with a prologue that is included in the published version of the text in addition to the stage directions. This paratextual element further complicates the relationship between terrestrial and other spaces. Indeed, as Mbembe asks, "How, then, does one live when the time to die has passed, when it is even forbidden to be alive, in what might be called an experience of living the 'wrong way round'?" (Mbembe, 201). The prologue then raises a crucial question, shifting the burden of responsibility to the protagonists: "the parenthetic pass, which either opens or closes; you must *choose*" (*Parentheses of Blood*, 44, emphasis mine).[53] The choice of political activism thus rests with the individual. By analogy, Sony Labou Tansi sought to distance himself from the traditional narrative structures he critiqued for their failure to provide adequate frameworks with which to describe the contemporary sociological reality. In his book *Thresholds of Change in African Literature: The Emergence of a Tradition*, Kenneth Harrow has described this process in the following terms:

> [Sony Labou Tansi] has repeatedly affirmed his intention to write a literature of combat while at the same time choosing a literary style that is not easily accessible, that denies the techniques of realism. We can say that his protest is anchored in a reality whose images he refuses to recast in realist terms. . . . [This] gives Sony Labou Tansi access to a discourse whose multifaceted features lend his protest far greater force than would be the case had his work remained circumscribed by the narrow bounds of realism.[54] (Harrow, 315–16)

While his writings may exceed the bounds of realism and thus distance him from the tradition of realist writers, Sony Labou Tansi could be said to be describing realistically—albeit in an exaggerated manner—a situation that defies realism and Cartesian logic. As Harrow has argued, Sony Labou Tansi "rejects the boundaries and distinctions upon which a fiction of realism is erected, and creates in its place dialogic discourses of postrevolt magical realism" (Harrow, 331).

Rebellion functions as proof of life in an environment where death is a part of everyday existence. Ironically, President Lopez acknowledges this in *L'état honteux* with reference to a character's determination, stating that "he must have realized that the dead are more fortunate than the living" (*L'état honteux*, 63). However, for Dr. Portès in *La parenthèse de sang*, "you don't kill betrayal by killing the traitor" (*Parentheses of Blood*, 62). At this point, one could argue that the ice has been broken and that the acquaintance with death has been made in the realization that the individual is, literally, killable. Here lies part of the significance of the parentheses: they symbolize enclosure but also imply that there is something beyond them, something that is accessible through individual empowerment and the assumption of personal responsibility. As Mbembe has argued, "But then, chasing behind one's shadow, one must still know how, each time, to open or close the parenthesis in which these parts will take their place" (Mbembe, 203). While the parentheses may also represent imprisonment and the restricted framework of the theatrical stage, they can, in a broader context, include a plethora of oppressive frameworks offstage—colonialism, nationalism, or military rule. Sony Labou Tansi is effectively staging the process through which people convert to revolt under pressure. Aleyo and the family want to persuade themselves that they are dead, a gesture that contrasts with Dr. Portès's deflating, realistic, and scientific tone: "I'm in pain. I'm in pain, and so I'm alive" (*Parentheses of Blood*, 60), words that rejoin his declarations of love, and whose buoyant nature represents a surrealist mixture of love and revolution. Ultimately, as Mbembe has argued,

> To think about the end of being and existence . . . is to be interested in what lies *this* side of the lifeless material thing—not necessarily to establish the status of the dead person or even the survivor, but to see how, in Africa after colonization, it is possible to delegate one's death while simultaneously and already experiencing death at the very heart of one's existence. (Mbembe, 201)

When a messenger arrives to announce that the capital has reversed its policy and declared Libertashio dead, Cavacha executes the family. Such policy reversals and inconsistencies are characteristic of the general confusion in the postcolony, as new alliances are forever being forged. Nevertheless, Yavilla's words contain a positive message and imply a degree of hope through commitment: "As long as we're not dead, we have to stay alive"

(*Parentheses of Blood*, 40). When Cavacha opens fire and yells "We'll destroy the state radio station. We'll tear down the capital" (*Parentheses of Blood*, 74), his statement reveals the self-importance of the soldiers but also underlines the importance of the "imaginary society that must be healed of its collective madness; for it is in healing the sick body that one also heals those individuals who carry the seeds of violence" (Kouvouama, 105). However, Cavacha is clearly disillusioned and reacts violently with the affirmation of some sort of faith and consistency in his behavior, the futility of which is contained in his final statement of violence. The utter hopelessness is expressed in the last spoken dialogue of the play, when Dr. Portès, a formerly privileged person representing conservative Western humanism, realizes that he will inevitably return to the status of inert matter: "No, death. You can't. You have no right. No. You can't close me off in these parentheses. No, flood! You can't take me. No-o-o-o-o. I will remain barren! No!" (*Parentheses of Blood*, 74). The closure of the parenthesis represents the final stage in the life cycle for him, given that entry to the kingdom of the dead corresponds to a metaphysical nothingness from which the option of resistance is forever excluded. Dr. Portès's rejection of this closure, his "no," symbolizes a call to rebellion.[55] As Mbembe has shown, "between the moment of execution and the moment when he hit the ground of death, there was a delay, a stretch of road along which the tongue of the dead man began to speak in memory of what had been left behind, of life" (Mbembe, 205). Furthermore, prior to being shot himself, the Fool exclaimed "Libertashio! Twelve who will eat no more. Twelve in your body. Libertashio! Twelve in your body" (*Parentheses of Blood*, 69), thereby, as Kouvouama has explained, allowing Sony Labou Tansi to invite the spectator "to enter into the initiatory world of lemba in which the individual must first transition through twelve stages that correspond to the twelve degrees of wisdom prior to reaching the light" (Kouvouama, 105). Thus, refraining from locating death as a finality allows for an alternative reading of Sony Labou Tansi's play, one that contains the possibility for counter-insurgency.

The family's execution winds up making martyrs of them. There are obvious similarities to be drawn here between the fictional character Libertashio and the influential political activist and leader of the "other" Congo after the end of Belgian colonial rule, Patrice Lumumba—the man in the picture which the soldiers believe to be Libertashio has a mustache and goatee, physical traits that are immediately identifiable with Lumumba. Sylvain Bemba's novel *Léopolis*, in which a political leader by the name of Fabrice M'Fum is assassinated, has further contributed to Lumumba's status in the "universe of discourse" of the region.[56] Similarly, Aimé Césaire's play *Une saison au Congo* was inspired by events surrounding Lumumba's assassination.[57] Sartre's comments in his essay on Lumumba seem to underline the status which he had acquired: "The dead Lumumba ceased to be a person and became Africa in its entirety, with its unitary will, the multiplicity of its social and political systems, its divisions, its disagreements, its power and its impotence: he was not, nor could he be, the hero of pan-Africanism. He was its martyr."[58]

Consideration of *Je soussigné cardiaque* can allow for further elaboration of some of these issues. The play's characters constitute an interesting hierarchy: Bala Ebara, the director general of education in the imaginary Republic of Lebango, stands as a symbol for the government infrastructure; Mallot Bayenda, a young schoolteacher and civil servant with a slightly different relationship to authority than the aforementioned director; Perono, a wealthy businessman whose status allows him to exercise influence over the corrupt governmental structure; and, finally, Dr. Manissa, chief medical officer at the main hospital in the capital, Hozana. Other characters play secondary roles and will be referred to as necessary.

The play opens in a prison cell as Mallot writhes on the floor, handcuffed, with mice crawling over his body. He stirs and gradually brings himself to his feet, lamenting his actions and choices, and expressing his frustration concerning his incapacity to overcome the praetorian system to which he has fallen victim: "They will come at dawn. They will operate the law on the limpid sound of my breathing—on the virginal warmth of my entrails. It has to operate, the law does. . . . By killing him, I will have found a path to jail, a path, my path; and I'll die even. Even but empty. Oh, *if* only I had such a story to tell myself" (*Je soussigné cardiaque*, 78). The use of the conditional symbolizes the motivation behind his oppositional situatedness. While he has been unable to have an impact on the political status quo, writing provides the occasion for exploring the possibilities of resistance. The artistic project thus becomes invested with an oppositional component aimed at destabilizing and exposing the authorities.

Divided into four "tableaux" and multiple scenes within these section breakdowns, the main body of the play in fact becomes a reconstruction of the events that culminate in Mallot's incarceration. As Nkashama has argued, "In *Je soussigné cardiaque*, 'passion' constitutes a theatrical space for the *metamorphosis* of the teacher Mallot Bayenda, who appears to be taken over by an 'insane force,' right in front of the firing squad. He had wanted to stand up for a 'metaphysical meat.' The text clarifies this point: *'The rest of the play takes place as a dream, and the actual awakening only occurs at dawn with the arrival of the firing squad.'"*[59] The second scene thus opens with Mallot's arrival at his new assignment in an unidentified rural location, accompanied by his pregnant wife and daughter Nelly. The reader discovers that Mallot has been relocated on numerous previous occasions, "I've been working for eight years, and during that time, I've been moved twelve times" (*Je soussigné cardiaque*, 97), and witnesses his complaints relating to the educational structure he works for: "Ah! What a life! What a job! And all this for the thirty-two C.F.A. francs they throw you at the end of the month. . . . The little teaching machine" (*Je soussigné cardiaque*, 82–83). This does, of course, lead one to question the reasons for such frequent moves, although it is only later that one begins to understand that Mallot's oppositional nature is responsible for these. As I mentioned earlier, the parallels with Sony Labou Tansi's own experiences are striking when one considers the biographical information available to us concerning the author.

As Mallot complains about his circumstances, his wife, Mwanda, comments on his attitude, from which it becomes evident that oppositionality constitutes an integral part of his persona: "Oh, you know. Silence, well it drives me crazy. I've got to make a noise. Any noise. Just to convince myself that I am still there" (*Je soussigné cardiaque*, 84). The first indication that we have that Mallot is going to encounter some difficulties with his new assignment emerges when he is taken to Perono's house in order to solicit some petrol. He ignores the cautionary words of the young boy who accompanies him, "If you want to live in peace you shouldn't go bothering Mr. Perono. Because if you do you'll have the whole country on your back in five minutes" (*Je soussigné cardiaque*, 87). Perono lives in a luxurious modern villa and has a servant. These material possessions, as physical manifestations of the power he holds, are compounded by an understanding of power that he has personalized and which Mallot challenges at the first opportunity. When Perono states that "Here, you see, Mr. Teacher, I am everything. Absolutely everything" (*Je soussigné cardiaque*, 93), Mallot responds with "Almost everything" (*Je soussigné cardiaque*, 93), which leads Perono to further qualify and ultimately clarify his status in the following terms: "I am the flag, the law, liberty, the devil and the good Lord. And so you see—everything. . . . So much so that the entire region listens to me and obeys me, how I shall I put it, blindly" (*Je soussigné cardiaque*, 93–94). This conception of totalitarian power and denial of autonomous agency challenges everything that Mallot stands for, and he begins to articulate his opposition to Perono in more forceful terms.

Perono appears to find the schoolteacher challenging and does not seem to have encountered this degree of opposition before—indeed, three previous instances of resistance have, according to him, been dealt with accordingly. Perono goes on to explain the manner in which it has become customary for him to be obeyed because of people's "laziness" (*Je soussigné cardiaque*, 95). This term is important in its invocation of the disempowered postcolonial masses, while simultaneously underlining Mallot's own oppositionality. Postcolonial narratives have consistently portrayed the masses as relatively helpless in their subjectivity, conscious that dissent would expose them to immediate recriminations, and also questionable with regard to their capacity to systematically appropriate power. Mallot seemingly has nothing to lose since existence for him is predicated on a Sartrean model of political commitment in which the assertion of freedom is a precondition for authenticity.

The relationship between power and oppositionality is further problematized by its symbiotic construction, one that resembles other models of dominance. Dissent is ultimately considered a treasonable offense by the postcolonial government authorities who necessitate the type of "laziness" evoked by Perono in order to exercise power—where "laziness" symbolizes the acceptance of a marginalized status and the refusal to participate in oppositional activities. As Perono argues: "No one resists me. No one. I distribute the right to oxygen. I crush everyone. But you must try and understand me. This thirst for power, I need it to build my very own way of breathing; I need it to operate. Yes! All my flesh and all my blood implore me to suffocate others" (*Je soussigné cardiaque*, 96). Mallot, however, frustrates him by refusing to play the role he is expected to play: "I am impregnable. Impregnable, do you hear me? I operate naturally and straightforwardly. In the most straightforward manner in the world. You say you want to tame me? Well that is your right. The right of a villain. . . . No, Mr. Perono: I will be impossible to can" (*Je soussigné cardiaque*, 99). Perono makes one last attempt to subjugate him by offering him money. He claims "To possess, that is the only reality in this world. There are two kinds of people in this world, yes, two: those that possess and those that want to possess. And justice, or at least what one refers to as such, well that is the work of those who possess illegitimately against those that want to possess" (*Je soussigné cardiaque*, 104).

Perono attempts to simplify this complex situation by reducing it to two categories, namely, those who have power and those who do not—those who already wrongly possess placed before those who seek to possess. Accompanied by threats and menaces, Perono vows to crush Mallot's oppositionality and is convinced that he will achieve this objective: "I am going to cancel you out" (*Je soussigné cardiaque*, 106). Mallot's response, his resolution, will be to resist, to refuse to play the role that Perono needs him to play: "I will fight" (*Je soussigné cardiaque*, 108). In fact there is a precedent to this oppositionality, as when Mallot states to his wife: "Do you remember? Four months ago they chased us out of Kwamou because I spoke the truth to the regional chief, and because I showed the governor that he was swindling illiterate people" (*Je soussigné cardiaque*, 109).

There is a rapid shift in topography between tableau one and tableau two—some twenty-eight days have elapsed between the two—and the action is now situated in the capital, Hozana, where Mallot has undertaken the task of identifying the individual in the Ministry of Education who accepted Perono's money and moved him "to the other end of Lebango" (*Je soussigné cardiaque*, 118). In order to do this, Mallot attempts to obtain a note from a doctor certifying that a medical condition will require him to remain in Hozana—this would, effectively, remove him from the classroom and result in his appointment to a desk job at the ministry. This becomes a complicated procedure, one that will expose Mallot to the workings of a corrupt bureaucratic order.[60] While those who manipulate power want Mallot to be kept at a distance, Mallot himself is all the more eager to remain in their presence and subject them to his scrutiny: "No, I would like to stay. Let them smell me in their champagne glasses, let them breathe me in in their beef stock and on the women they ride" (*Je soussigné cardiaque*, 118). Manissa demands an explanation of the circumstances that led to Mallot's presence in his office and seems to sympathize with his cause by agreeing to write him a note. As Mallot explains: "I am the only poor old bastard in my family to climb my way up in society to the level of a teacher. But, unfortunately, one evening, Perono said to me: kneel down. I'd already seen my father do that too many times. And so I spat on him. He sold me to the system" (*Je soussigné cardiaque*, 127). Mallot is determined to protest, to stand in opposition to oppressive structures, and refuses to remain silent: "As for me, well I'm going to bellow out. That way, one day, things will be different" (*Je soussigné cardiaque*, 131). This affirms his belief in protest as a tool with which to combat the deeply entrenched corrupt political and social order. However, the director of education refuses to acknowledge the note. Mallot is provoked into asserting his existential freedom as defined by his oppositionality: "I won't leave. I have come to kill you. Just like that. For no reason. Simply to bring myself into the world. You must understand, I have to try and exist now, don't I. I've had it with·*nothingness*" (*Je soussigné cardiaque*, 144, emphasis mine).

Mallot's elimination becomes necessary, given that he cannot be domesticated, tamed, or converted in a social environment in which there is no platform for dissent. As David Mavouangui has argued, "he refuses to give himself over to the system, to be who he is as an object subjugated to the laws of desire, to the laws of a universal mechanism."[61] Having asserted his autonomy, "I am not another's thing, I belong to myself" (*Je soussigné cardiaque*, 108), his integrity is preserved and his death need not be seen as an assertion of the futility of revolt but rather as an affirmation of the validity of oppositionality in a system in which the "laziness" evoked earlier can never lead to emancipation. Indeed, some of these themes are interesting in a broader contextual framework, in which one could incorporate an analysis of more prevalent state involvement in oppressive practices aimed at fostering nationalizing imperatives.

The governing authorities dominate the private space, but this constitutes a mere component of their wider influence over the national territory. Governments appear to be content to run "economies that are reduced to consume that which they do not produce and to produce that which they do not consume."[62] To have power is one thing, but one must simultaneously be seen to have it; this secondary aspect, contained in Chabal's notion of "passive violence," is vividly presented in postcolonial literature and has generated the corruption and financial impoverishment of the nation-states in question. Jean-Claude Willame has described this mechanism in terms of the "increasingly accelerating cannibalization of the state and its economic appendices"[63] and shown how in Zaire, "mobutism" literally "ate the state."[64] Mbembe has also described this process, demonstrating how those who are able "to monopolize will effectively be spared from famine."[65] This observation emphasizes several elements, the most significant of which would include the survivalist instinct that requires control over power mechanisms in order to ensure their continuity; the hunger for power; and finally hunger as a weapon of oppression whereby leaders are well fed while the masses struggle on a daily basis to make ends meet.

Power is structured as a corrupting phenomenon, the appetite for which appears to grow: this can manifest itself as sexual appetite or as an appetite for power and its various emblems. There are numerous textual examples of the political nomenclature enjoying the material components of power: luxury palaces or villas, unlimited access to sexual partners, food. These are contained in the acronym "VVVF" Sony Labou Tansi coins in *La vie et demie*, and which he explains in a footnote as "villas, voitures, vins, femmes" (*La vie et demie*, 36).[66] The whole "political psychiatry" Mbembe describes is dysfunctional at every level, "for it is every aspect of social pathology that is deteriorating when one looks at it from the perspective of a history marked by centuries of slavery and colonization."[67] The omnipresence of the state and its power to engulf parallels in a number of ways the pre-colonial fluidity that characterized the relationship between various ethnic groups, characterized by what Jean-Loup Amselle and Elikia M'Bokolo have described as "sociétés englobantes" and "sociétés englobées."[68]

The fundamental problem confronting the postcolony resulted from the failure of various leaders to achieve national integration and unity. The national project has achieved little with the exception of exacerbating ethnic rivalry and conflict, and the power mechanisms employed by governments to consolidate their power bases have been responsible for many of the difficulties in the postcolony today: pronounced differences in economic standards and entrenched corruption that hinders any possibility of progress and development. National Conferences that were held in many francophone sub-Saharan African countries from 1990 onward endeavored to establish new constitutions and frameworks for development but soon generated renewed disillusionment and disorientation as these alternative structures inevitably failed to resolve complex circumstances. As Willame has pointed out, "a political system that reproduces itself through the arbitrariness and instability it engenders at every level, also authorizes the outgrowth of large spaces it will neither be able to absorb nor regulate."[69] The consequences would be similar to those documented in Sony Labou Tansi's representations of power in his novels and plays since "when the law slips from the grasp of those who control it, it becomes a matchless killing machine" (*The Anti-People*, 120).

Individuality and autonomy are shown to be absorbed and engulfed by the state apparatus in the postcolony, voiding the possibility for the construction of identity within the imposed national culture and underlining the futility of the integration process in its relentless pursuit of the unitary paradigm and philosophy it has imposed. Rather than promoting dialogue and building a nation in which communal existence is the primary objective, government authorities are presented as having rejected the rights of their subjects in order to concentrate instead on extermination, massacre, and torture, in the effort to obtain popular support for their monolithic dictatorship. The measures they have been willing to adopt to achieve this end have often been so alarming that Sony Labou Tansi has found it difficult to accurately convey them using existing syntax and language. A consideration of Sony Labou Tansi's use of language will provide the conclusion to this chapter. This particular aspect represents a central element in what is a strikingly original and innovative corpus.

Verbal Extravagance

> *At a time when man is more than ever determined to kill life, how else can I speak to you if not in flesh-pass-words?* —SONY LABOU TANSI (LA VIE ET DEMIE, 9)[70]

> *The* Larousse *and* Petit Robert *dictionaries allow me to look up, verify, and explain vulgar words in French from France to Africa's indigenous Black people. The* Inventory of Lexical Particularities of African French *explains vulgar African words to French* toubabs *from France. And* Harrap's *dictionary explains vulgar pidgin words to any French-speaking person who doesn't know a thing about pidgin.* —AHMADOU KOUROUMA[71]

The symbiotic link introduced between the body and language in the words "flesh-pass-words" (*La vie et demie*, 9) in the "Avertissement" to Sony Labou Tansi's first novel underlines the inextricable link between the multiple degrees of violence evidenced in his writings. While other Congolese and francophone sub-Saharan African authors—Emmanuel Dongala, Henri Lopes, Ahmadou Kourouma, Thierno Monénembo—are linguistic innovators in their own right, Sony Labou Tansi's linguistic practices and experimentation with language constitute the greatest distinction between his work and theirs, given the integral role these considerations play in his literary activity.[72] His originality emerges from what the late Congolese author Sylvain Bemba has described as "the unprecedented art of what I would call literary recombination."[73] For Bemba, Sony Labou Tansi "writes as he invents and invents as he writes," a factor that differentiates him from other writers to the extent that there is "a certain distinction between invention, that I associate with the ingenuous usage and reconstruction of pre-existing forms in new ways, and discovery that consists in finding something precisely where there was nothing before."[74] Language, then, assumes a key position in order to function as an elaborate component of a radically new literary project, enabling him to achieve the status of pioneer.

Arguments, explanations, or justifications as to *why* Sony Labou Tansi uses the French language are not so much of concern as is the question of *how* he uses it.[75] The question of language remains an important issue in discussions on African literature, and the choice of language has raised questions with regard to identity and authenticity.[76] Sony Labou Tansi has been one of the most outspoken on this issue, insisting on the plurality and cultural diversity of linguistic practitioners, and substituting the plural form of "francophonies" for the hegemonic "francophonie."[77] As Alain Ricard has argued, "Sony Labou Tansi totally assumes *francophonie*, yet without exalting the values of what remains an instrument . . . instead, he attempts to appropriate the language."[78] On the one hand, Sony Labou Tansi explains how the sociological circumstances of his environment have shaped his writing in French: "I am African. My reality is African. I am comfortable as an African wherever I happen to be. However, I have things I want to say, and I want to say those things to those people who have chosen French as their fellow traveler,"[79] while on the other he has claimed that "when I speak French, I speak it with my concepts and my images, images that may not be those of a French person."[80]

For the most part, Sony Labou Tansi perceives his relationship to the French language as one of violence. In his stimulating book *In My Father's House: Africa in the Philosophy of Culture*, Kwame Anthony Appiah alludes to the manner in which Sony Labou Tansi's "colonial teachers daubed him with human feces as a punishment for his grammatical solecisms."[81] Sony Labou Tansi's experience with the *mission civilisatrice* and the concern with assimilation to French cultural prototypes was inseparable from a context of violence:

> I write in French because that is the language in which the people I speak for were raped, that is the language in which I myself was raped. I remember my virginity. . . . One must say that if between myself and French there is anyone who is in a position of strength, it is not French, but I. I have never had recourse to French, it is rather French that has had recourse to me.[82]

The association between language and rape is of course an extremely powerful one, albeit one that is located within a linguistic domain; nevertheless, his views on language have implications for the way in which sexuality and nationality are treated. For Sony Labou Tansi, the original violence finds its marker in the classification of colonialism as rape. His fellow countryman Tchicaya U Tam'si made a similar connection in his statement, "The French language colonizes me, and so I in turn colonize it right back."[83] Colonialism, rape, and violence are employed almost coterminously and remain all the more pertinent to questions of gender and nationalist identities whether anti-colonial or those specific to the era of decolonization.

Sony Labou Tansi's usage of language is a response to the shortcomings of language—in this case French—as a communicative tool with which to express and depict his perception of the postcolony. For him, the problem lies in the fact that even metaphors have proved insufficient or incapable of accurately describing, reflecting, or portraying the political dislocations evidenced in the postcolonial space. This linguistic redundancy has generated the linguistic and syntactical devices that equip him to protest and resist. In a sophisticated reading of these questions, Elisabeth Mudimbe-Boyi has argued that "confronted with the destructive violence of power, a counter-violence born of the act of writing establishes itself as a constructive force,"[84] thereby heralding Sony Labou Tansi's *avant-gardist* literary project. The radical use of language also stands as a concerted attempt to distance his narrative from the official *langue de bois* that characterizes the slogans and propagandist works of his official counterparts.

Sony Labou Tansi's writings have relentlessly denounced the oppressive and tyrannical nature of the postcolonial elite. Political commitment has remained an integral part of his work, yet he has endeavored to reconcile this agenda with artistic ends, refused to subordinate aesthetic considerations to those of content, and ensured that the message articulated has not killed creativity. Determined to concentrate on contemporary Africa, insisting on adopting an oppositional mode to official nationalistic discourse, refusing to engage in prescriptive formulations, and rejecting ideological agendas, Sony Labou Tansi provides in his writings powerful explorations of the challenges Africa faces in the twenty-first century. The syntactical and lexical upheaval which has led critics to characterize Sony Labou Tansi as "a magician with words, a juggler of phrases, a syntactical trapeze artist"[85] has coincided with a modification of traditional narrative linearity. In fact, even normal punctuation has disappeared. With Sony Labou Tansi's *La vie et demie*, as Séwanou Dabla has argued, we have a much more adventurous text, functioning around a triple "mis-en-abyme."[86]

Writing as an act of violence enables Sony Labou Tansi to re-inscribe an alternative to the power mechanisms that are at work and to undermine officialdom. Simultaneously, the act of writing is gradually empowered as it appropriates the violence of the postcolony, transforming it into a source of creation and renewal. The dismemberment of syntactical and lexical alignments and the disfigurement of traditional literary forms and linearity come to echo the dismemberment and disfigurement of bodies in the postcolony. This situation is contained in Mudimbe-Boyi's observations, "if in the hands of power, theft and rape function as negative elements in an autocratic and manipulative system, they nevertheless offer, through the exercise of writing, a space for freedom in which the writer can insert a political and aesthetic claim."[87] The crucial thing for Sony Labou Tansi is that the use of normal language suggests a degree of normality that is absent in the postcolony and in the behavior of those who control power. Sony Labou Tansi feels compelled to dismantle traditional linguistic practices and inquire into the manner in which these have coincided with the dismemberment and disfigurement of both the physical body and the body politic. For Harrow, the "unnamable topos beyond the scope of words is evoked by oxymorons . . . in which the trope's conundrum, its condition of impossibility, is the condition of possibility for expression" (Harrow, 336).[88] Sony Labou Tansi has thus invented a new language to describe the postcolonial realities and to suggest new alignments. His contribution, as Georges N'Gal has shown, is to generate the conditions for lexical, semantic, and linguistic "rejuvenation."[89] The use of degrading or defiled terms and the omnipresence of extreme violence — rape, mutilation, torture, cannibalism — constitute, as Anyinefa has argued, "a complete appropriation of language upon which the creative freedom and the power of the writer are based" (Anyinefa, 117).[90]

There is a certain spontaneity to these practices that is prompted by a desire to seek revenge against a language with which both Sony Labou Tansi and his people have enjoyed a relationship that is itself defined by violence — slavery, colonialism, neocolonialism. His writing shares points of commonality with the techniques associated with the work of Raymond Queneau, Georges Perec, the OuLiPo ("ouvroir de littérature potentielle") school of writing in France, or the *nouveaux romanciers* (notably Alain Robbe-Grillet, Michel Butor, Robert Pinget) but moves beyond the limited dimension of these projects that emerges from their emphasis and concern with form. Sony Labou Tansi's writings criticize existing political systems, and the multiple innovative devices he employs attempt to distance his work from the prescription and entrapment that could accompany resistance literature. Indeed, as Justin Kalulu Bisanswa has argued, "Sony Labou Tansi's novels clearly present themselves as the entry of a literary manifesto. The novelist is elaborating an aesthetic project that is able to destroy dominant styles; but he does not want to produce an antagonistic work of art or a novel that can be easily linked with other writings of crisis, that is, another manifesto."[91]

National identity is an artificial construct, albeit one that has become a sociological reality; alternative identity models nevertheless do exist and therefore challenge the national in the ethnic, regional, and transnational alignments they suggest. Sony Labou Tansi's contributions to the circulation of representations in cultural productions explore the problem of constructing a legitimate identity in a constantly mutating postcolony, challenge hegemonic integrational measures that have exacerbated ethnic rivalry, and suggest mechanisms that will have to be negotiated in order to prevent new paradigms and democratic laws from disintegrating in the disorientation that may ensue once power has, through protest and resistance, in fact been overthrown.

4 HENRI LOPES
Collaboration, Confession, and Testimony

I would ask my reader not to waste time endeavoring to recognize Daddy in the portrait gallery of African leaders, but rather to kill the Daddy in them. —HENRI LOPES[1]

The possibility we face is of a confession made via a process of relentless self-unmasking which might yet be not the truth but a self-serving fiction. . . . The more coherent such a hypothetical fiction of the self might be, the less the reader's chance of knowing whether it is a true confession. We can test its truth only when it contradicts itself or comes into conflict with some "outer," verifiable truth, both of which eventualities a careful confessing narrator can in theory avoid. —J. M. COETZEE[2]

Henri Lopes's position is especially intriguing and problematic because, while establishing himself as one of francophone sub-Saharan Africa's most critically acclaimed authors, he has simultaneously occupied influential diplomatic and governmental positions as a representative of the Republic of the Congo. This presents somewhat of a contradiction, given the inevitable collaborationist complicity that such a position entails with the ruling elite, and in light of the complex dynamic that characterizes relations between authors and postcolonial authorities. Of particular interest in this chapter will be those fundamental and complicated questions raised by Lopes's ambiguous status inside the very power structure his work subverts and challenges by exposing it to the scrutiny of outsiders; the primary focus will be provided by his 1982 novel, *Le Pleurer-Rire (The Laughing Cry)*.[3] Furthermore, I want to consider the novel as a confessional and testimonial narrative that further problematizes this relationship, while raising important questions relating to collaboration and reconciliation.

Henri Lopes is legally Congolese (that is to say a citizen of the Republic of the Congo), although he was in fact born in 1937 in the Belgian Congo (formerly the Republic of Zaire, but today the Democratic Republic of the Congo). Both of his parents were born of European fathers and African mothers, although Lopes has always identified himself as Congolese: "I am first and foremost Congolese, and then a *métisse.*"[4] The question of *métissage* is a recurring theme in Lopes's writing and receives its most complete treatment in his novel *Le chercheur d'Afriques.*[5] However, the multiple dimensions of this hybridity also function metaphorically to designate Lopes's status as a politician and writer constantly negotiating between these identity markers.

There is an important point of intersection between the writings of Bessie Head and Lopes. In a letter Head wrote, she stated that "I could have been born a white man. I have no control over it. I shake with terror at the thought. Say, some merciful fate put me on the receiving side of brutality and ignorance, but what if I were born to mete this out to others."[6] As Jacqueline Rose has indicated, "Since Head is half white, this moment of terrified imagining has its concrete foundation. But it is also part of a capacity for psychic crossover and identification which adds a further dimension of 'universality' to her writing."[7] The analogy I draw to Lopes concerns his own ethnic identity as *métisse*—as both colonized subject (the Black dimension) and colonizer (the White component)—such that the "Tonton" ("Daddy") in us that is alluded to in the first epigraph to this chapter represents a very real concept for Lopes and his own struggle with his authoritarian impulse. For him, it contains the ambiguity of his biographical identity in which the tenuousness emerges through constitutive components. It designates and underlines his belonging to both sides: on the one hand the postcolonial nationalists, and on the other, the non-official resistance authors.

Between 1969 and 1981, Lopes held a number of high-ranking ministerial positions under three presidents: Marien Ngouabi (until his assassination in 1977), Joachim Yhombi-Opango in the interim administration between 1977 and 1979, and finally Denis Sassou Nguesso. His appointments included that of minister of foreign affairs in 1972, prime minister from 1972 to 1975, and minister of finances from 1976 to 1981. Until recently, he worked for the United Nations Educational, Scientific, and Cultural Organization (UNESCO) in Paris, abandoning his position to become the Congo's ambassador to France in 1999.[8] Lopes's literary and political careers are inextricably linked, and the relationship between the two has helped shape both the man and the writer.[9] His first publications coincided with his initial involvement in politics and, given the political tone of his writings, it has become almost impossible to talk of the polemic writer without considering his professional activities. Lopes has published a collection of short stories and seven novels (the last four with the Editions du Seuil), and he was able to remain productive while in political office.[10] This is somewhat problematic, given the fact that other Congolese authors experienced difficulties with the authorities during this period (notably Sony Labou Tansi and Maxime N'Debeka). Furthermore, Lopes has argued against the politicization of African literature, stating that "in general, a work of art does not lend itself to a political program."[11] The expected political dimension of a literary work in Africa has clear historical roots, and texts by African authors have often coincided with the various political circumstances in which they were produced. Lopes's work stands as an affirmation of something that is different, in that he has succeeded in maintaining a political dimension, while avoiding the programmatic mode. As Lopes has argued:

> many of our authors had become accustomed to confusing the political struggle with artistic creation. Thus, they set out to defend and to illustrate our cultural identities, but they foundered on a sort of nationalism which, when we encounter it in other people, seems anti-humanistic. In actual fact, true literary creators are never chauvinists or lackeys. They solve their problems within the context of their own society and their own time. By their nature they are not content.[12]

His involvement in government is of course a paradox, since it places him at the crossroads between official and non-official cultural practitioners.

The relationship between literature and politics, and between fiction and reality, is of central concern to any critical reading of Lopes's literary productions. Indeed, Lopes himself is acutely aware of this relationship and has gone so far as to deliberately disorient literal-minded readers. In an article he wrote in 1993, "My Novels, My Characters, and Myself," Lopes addressed the inherent pitfalls of a determinist reading that relies too heavily on biographical data; for him, "readers who devote themselves primarily to detective work are in danger of missing what is essential in a book. An artist's life is one thing; the life he creates in his fiction is quite another" ("My Novels," 86). However, having said this, Lopes proceeds to confuse the boundaries between fiction and reality by adding that "as an unrepentant liar myself, I never reveal my sources, and whenever people think they are about to pin me down, I step neatly aside" ("My Novels," 81). This recurring tenuousness between the biographical information one can infer from the author's life and the fictional product is a constant feature of Lopes's writings. In fact, Lopes complicates the situation in order to further confuse the government authorities responsible for censoring the work, while also forcing readers to make inferences about the author's ability to distinguish between those elements that originate in the imagination and those that are transposed from experience into fiction. This has become an elaborate game of hide-and-seek and will provide the central locus of this discussion—because it warrants further exploration, given Lopes's repeated allusions to its implications, and because it provides the space in which complex notions pertaining to witnessing and testimony are evidenced.

Lopes's experiences as a politician have afforded the writer a unique perspective on the manner in which power mechanisms in the Congo are manipulated, indeed one that has not been available to other Congolese authors who, while they may have collaborated at some point in history, certainly did not enjoy the same degree of exposure as Lopes. Rather than merely attempting to gauge the extent to which Lopes's involvement in politics has translated itself into the fictional product, I propose instead that we investigate Lopes's objective in adopting a testimonial narrative in order to examine his experiences as a witness.

Paratext and Politics

The relationship between truthfulness and lying is central in *Le Pleurer-Rire*, particularly in the paratextual devices Lopes employs, and through the novel's own self-reflexivity. Indeed, one could argue that the whole text is made up of an intricate network of paratextual connections. Table 1 provides a breakdown of the text's composition and paratext. I refer to this process as "polyvocality," in order to designate the multiplicity of competing voices both within the text and outside of it—official, propagandist, and resistant—cohabiting with different claims to narrative and political authority. Achille Mbembe's characterization of the postcolony as "chaotically pluralistic" functions well here as a symbol for the orchestration of this plurality.[13] In a political environment in which the articulation of political opposition constitutes a transgressive act, Lopes's multiple registers give voice to those subjects who have no voice because of questions of literacy, censorship, fear of repression, or government control and monopoly over public discourse (through official party newspapers such as *Mwéti* and *Etumba*). Indeed, as Paul Ricoeur has observed, "language itself is from the outset and for the most part distorted: it means something other than what it says, it has double meaning, it is equivocal."[14] The information we receive as readers comes to us in the text from journalistic and propagandist sources, radio broadcasts and *radio-trottoir*, the text and paratext, and it is from these multiple voices that we attempt to construct some kind of linear reality and formulate a historical narrative.

In many ways, the class struggle through language is located in the polyvocal hierarchy and serves to further underline the manner in which colonial/postcolonial, official/non-official, and insider/outsider constructs are not independently formed but rather mechanically clash in a mutually constitutive dynamic. This echoes colonial discourse, characterized by Mbembe for its capacity of "picking up rumor and gossip, amplifying them in the telling, it claims to throw light on things that haunt and obsess it, but about which, in truth, it knows absolutely nothing" (Mbembe, 178–79). In *Le Pleurer-Rire*, the Maître d'Hôtel (narrator), for example, is an *insider*, but as a servant occupies a position in the hierarchical order below that of his master, President Bwakamabé. Although the latter is an obvious *insider* whose social rank places him at the top of the hierarchy, he can be both subverted and ridiculed through language and various carnivalesque gestures, thereby altering the Hegelian master-slave relationship according to which the master inevitably controls knowledge. Thus, the articulation of the tenuousness between high culture and low culture is inextricably linked to the postcolonial predicament, as it becomes almost impossible to distinguish between the competing voices that oscillate in Lopes's ventriloquism.

Essentially relinquishing chronological linearity, the body of the novel is broken down into five categories; these are distinguished by different font shapes and sizes (see table 1).[15] Prior to exploring the most significant breakdowns, I will briefly comment on the significance of the title and editorial layout of the work, and how this is relevant to questions of production and reception.

Le Pleurer-Rire is somewhat disorienting as a title, capturing the reader's attention and interest for a text that resists and subverts novelistic convention while ultimately affirming its faith in the novel as an effective mechanism for the exploration of postcoloniality.[16] The juxtaposition of "pleurer" with "rire" evokes two possible responses to the circumstances generated by colonialism and post-independence politics. On the one hand, a consideration of this reality could lead only to "crying," while an alternative coping mechanism would be simply to "laugh" at the situation. In addition to these interpretations, the "rire" can also serve as a metaphor for the collaborationist dimension that is implied in the notion of going/laughing along with the oppression, and acknowledging the lie. Nevertheless, both responses are

Table 1. Polyvocality in Henri Lopes's *Le Pleurer-Rire*

CATEGORY	PAGES	FORMAT	FONT
Le Pleurer-Rire	83 sections, 315 pp.		
Epigraphs 1. Beaumarchais 2. Voltaire 3. Boris Vian	7	Italics	Small
Sérieux avertissement	9–12	Italics	Regular
Main text	13–315	Regular	Regular
Narrator's memoirs	43, 59–60, 66, 86, 96, 104–105, 117–19, 124, 127, 150, 154–55, 174, 193, 203–205, 217, 264–67, 272–73, 280, 288–89, 294–96, 304–305	Italics	Regular
Correspondence from exiled friend	51–52, 77–78, 102–103, 123, 179–81, 249, 272	Regular	Small
Denis Diderot: Jacques le Fataliste	254–56	Italics	Regular
Quand Soukali enjambe la fenêtre du roman ou (au choix) de la réalité	313–14	Italics	Regular

indicative of more complicated processes that have much to do with the experience of trauma and the burden of witnessing. Indeed, the narrator's concluding words in the novel (to which I shall return subsequently) emphasize this dimension: "Here I end the telling of a rosary of dreams and nightmares that have followed one another with the cadence of a chronicle and from which I cannot be free until the last word is written" (*The Laughing Cry*, 259). This is perhaps also what is contained in Nicolas Martin-Granel's assessment of contemporary francophone sub-Saharan African literature as a form of "crier-écrire."[17]

While an author's contribution to the actual editorial process can vary tremendously, and while my concern here is not with determining Lopes's role in editing the manuscript, the published product has much to offer this analysis. Lopes's Paris-based publisher, Présence Africaine, has insisted on the fictional nature of the work by including the word "roman" (novel) under the title on the cover page. An interesting transformation takes place in the English edition, published in the United Kingdom in 1987 by Readers International, given that *Le Pleurer-Rire* becomes *The Laughing Cry: An African Cock and Bull Story*. Lopes's "pleurer" is interpreted as a "cry"—thereby partly voiding the psychoanalytic dimension that was contained in "pleurer" (crying)—and additionally transformed by the "novel's" migration toward a "cock and bull story." While a novel is traditionally defined by its fictitious nature, a cock-and-bull story commonly refers to "an absurd, improbable story presented as the truth" (Webster's dictionary). Lopes's text problematizes and complicates notions of truthfulness while also ultimately refusing traditional criteria employed for analysis and categorization. M. H. Abrams has attempted to illustrate the specific intricacies that emerge from the multiple ways in which fiction is used, and these may serve to elucidate the complexity of the framework Lopes adopts:

> In an inclusive sense, fiction is any literary narrative whether in prose or verse, which is invented instead of being an account of events that in fact happened. . . . Both philosophers and literary critics have concerned themselves with the logical analysis of the types of sentences which constitute a fictional text, and especially with the question of their truth, or what is sometimes called their "truth-value"—that is, whether, and in just that way, they are subject to the criterion of truth or falsity.[18]

For Lopes, each of these considerations proves to be central to the broader parameters of his *avant-gardist* project.

Significantly, a long quotation from a canonical French writer provides the paradigmatic framework for Lopes's experimentation with narrative. The passage in question (*Le Pleurer-Rire*, 254–56) is drawn from Denis Diderot's *Jacques le fataliste et son maître* (Jacques the Fatalist) and introduced as a response to the narrator's exiled friend who has just recorded his objections concerning the narrator's recent account of an erotic encounter he had with his mistress.[19] The most pertinent section from this long quotation juxtaposes "contes" and "histoire," as Diderot announces to the reader, "Premièrement, lecteur, ce ne sont pas des contes, c'est une histoire" ("To begin with, dear reader, these are not fables, but history") (*Le Pleurer-Rire*, 254, and *The Laughing Cry*, 209, respectively).[20] In the English translation, "conte" is rendered as "fable" and "histoire" as "history," effectively eliminating the ambiguous territory covered in the French by "histoire" as both "history" and "story." The translation is a document that has nothing to do with Diderot himself, yet the translation interprets Diderot's "histoire" as history, and therefore as something more truthful than a fable. As Lydie Moudileno has argued with reference to Sony Labou Tansi's novel *La vie et demie*, "in pretending to operate in a realm outside reality (and realism), the fable as a genre has always constituted a means of outmaneuvering official censorship."[21] Truth is constructed as both fact and fiction, such that history comes to be accorded preference over fiction. Distinctions established by Tvetan Todorov have particular pertinence in light of Lopes's schema, since for him "We must distinguish between at least two senses of the word: truth-adequation (la vérité d'adéquation) and truth-disclosure (la vérité de dévoilement). . . . Novelists aim only for this latter type of truth; nor do they have anything to teach historians about the former."[22] Lopes's work appears to underline various interconnections and intersections that exist between history and literature, whereby fiction can be used to make truth claims, or, alternatively, historical research to make fictional claims. In Lopes, "truth disclosure" is set in motion through the text's polyvocality. As Alice Fredman has noted, "The great man, Diderot had said in the *Salon* of 1767, is not the one who tells the truth; he is the one who can best reconcile truth with falsehood."[23]

The implications of Lopes's use of Diderot are far wider reaching in their suggested analogy between the master and servant relationship of Jacques and his master, and that of the central narrator, the Maître d'Hôtel, and President Bwakamabé. The authors are similar in that they resist, subvert, and ultimately challenge aesthetic convention, a dimension on which the narrator's exiled friend comments: "Whilst reading your work, I was constantly asking myself how to classify it. Sometimes you aspire to the precision of a historian or a sociologist; sometimes you resemble more the *griots* in whom some see only dream-peddlers and entertainers, and others a key to decoding the life of the village" (*The Laughing Cry*, 34).[24]

The multiplicity of genres adopted by Lopes is of course significant and constitutes a logical continuity to the polyvocality and paratextual devices he employs. The exiled friend is clearly struggling to locate the work according to a specific genre; at those junctures when he recognizes events, he is comforted by the truthfulness of the narrative. Yet, while he identifies the fictional component and is willing to acknowledge what may be its allegorical dimension (namely, the key that is employed by *griots*), he remains ultimately confused by the storytelling dimension which for him lacks verisimilitude. Indeed, as Shoshana Felman has demonstrated, "If narrative is basically a verbal act that functions as a historiographical report, history is, parallely but conversely, the establishment of the facts of the past through their narrativization."[25] Perhaps one could follow Charles Maier's questioning, "Why focus on narrative? Because both history and the trial are based on a highly ordered recitation of reports that makes sense of 'events' by placing them in a sequence structured by time. Witnesses have stories to tell. The narrator—single or collective—arranges testimonies in an order that seems self-evident, but is necessarily artful."[26] In *Le Pleurer-Rire*, objective truth is forsaken for a relative truth that functions as a parallel for the system and society at large in which self-deception and delusion cohabit in a complex network of interwoven lies. As Koffi Anyinefa has argued,

> With *The Laughing Cry*, Lopes surely wanted to write a "certain" history of his time, a history from a very subjective point of view, that of the butler. It is in this way that *The Laughing Cry* is postmodern, in the sense that historiography is no longer considered an objective activity but rather a performance filtered through a consciousness that in no way seeks the Truth behind events; this consciousness relates, instead, how it lived those events and reserves the right to be selective. ("Postcolonial Modernity," 16)

My approach shares points of commonality with Anyinefa's in that my reading also identifies a movement in Lopes's text toward abandoning the imperative of truth seeking and objective truth—but differs in that I do not locate a narration of history exclusively in the "butler's" (Maître d'Hôtel) "subjective point of view," but rather in the relative truth offered by the polyvocal agenda.

Further similarities can be established between the works of Diderot and Lopes, and it is no coincidence that the passage quoted by Lopes should deal with questions of veracity: "And your Jacques is only an insipid rhapsody of events, some *real* and some *imaginary*, written without grace and arranged without order" (*The Laughing Cry*, 210, emphasis mine). There is, furthermore, a clear absence of seriousness on the surface of Diderot's work, exemplified as early as the title *Le Pleurer-Rire* of Lopes's work, although each work does of course treat a serious subject. Lopes is clearly familiar with Diderot's work, and the intertextuality was instrumental in framing the various relationships between reality and fiction, master and slave, and narrator and reader. Marx and Hegel also read Diderot's text and discussed the significance of the master-servant relationship.[27] In fact, during the Marxist-Leninist era in the Congo, the works of Enlightenment authors were very popular. One of Lopes's earlier fictional characters, Gatsé, in his second novel, *Sans tam-tam*, declared: "A close reading of Diderot and Voltaire can contribute to the crystallization of national sentiment."[28]

The most striking analogy between the two authors concerns the symbiotic nature of the master-servant relationship, and the particular manner in which this is played out in *Le Pleurer-Rire* where President Bwakamabé (aka Tonton) does not exist outside the narrator's manuscript and observations. The hierarchy that is at first defined by their respective status as President and Maître d'Hôtel is thus considerably more complex than their social rank may suggest. The main body of the text is structured using normal script and provides the space in which the narrator's descriptions and comments are articulated. President Bwakamabé's personal servant, the Maître d'Hôtel, is selected as the principal narrative voice and thus able to witness and comment upon every public and private activity in which both the President and his entourage engage.[29] The advantages associated with such a privileged voice can by association be extended to Lopes himself who, as a high-ranking government official, also occupied a position from which to formulate insightful observations. Indeed, one has to wonder about the extent to which the narrator's voice is in fact Lopes's own. A consideration of Lopes's comments concerning his "technique" can perhaps bring us closer to understanding this dynamic:

> My "technique" is actually a very simple one: it consists of intentionally attributing some of my own traits to my narrators. Starting with a rudiment of myself, I create wholly imaginary characters and then slip inside of them for the period during which I am writing. These characters are

no longer me. If there is a resemblance, it is that of a son whose features
and gestures and habits seem like those of the father. ("My Novels," 85–86)

Lopes is of course free to make this claim, but one cannot overlook the fact
that he previously described himself as an "unrepentant liar." He would
have nothing to achieve (or prove for that matter) were he to deliberately
exclude his experiences; on the contrary, they add weight to the narrator's
observations and accord Lopes a perspective other authors do not have. If
Lopes's text is to be categorized as a work of resistance, aligned with other
non-official authors, then one could argue that his objective to undermine
the authorities becomes all the more effective, given his understanding of
the workings of power. Lopes may reduce identifiable similarities to a mere
"resemblance," but the fact that a certain veracity can be accorded to the
narrator's observations serves to further legitimate them as we begin to sense
their proximity to Lopes's own sentiments.

The question of legitimacy recurs throughout the text. One such example is provided when Lopes adopts a smaller font in order to delineate
the text's shift to the epistolary genre. This space allows one of Bwakamabé's
exiled cabinet ministers and close friend of the narrator to formulate his
comments on the manuscript in which the narrator has recorded his account of political events. The exiled friend plays a very important role, given
that his observations corroborate and substantiate the narrator's narrative as
truthful; like all witnesses attempting to testify, the narrator questions his
memory of events and, accordingly, resolves to consult his friend: "Feeling
some lack of confidence in myself, I have consulted a compatriot, the former
Cabinet Secretary to Daddy, now living in exile" (*The Laughing Cry*, 33).
As Felman has argued, "witnessing does not provide narrative knowledge,
since one cannot be sure, in one's position as a witness, either if one is in
reality perceiving what one believes oneself to be perceiving or if one is in
effect speaking in . . . one's own voice" (Felman, 139). The exiled friend is
then, perhaps without even fully understanding his contribution to the testimonial process, able to assist the narrator in his attempt at "telling" his story:
"However, my position in Bwakamabé's regime and my relations with Yabaka
enable me to speak with authority about this matter. It is even possible that
my absence from the country that day will confer on my analysis a distance
and objectivity which are lacking in many other accounts" (*The Laughing
Cry*, 143). In order to further underline the legitimacy of his own account,
the exiled friend further constructs himself as a privileged witness: "On this
point, I have seen documents which make it incontestable" (*The Laughing
Cry*, 143). There is thus an additional attempt to confuse the relationship

between truth and fiction to the extent that the exiled friend authenticates the text as truthful. The discussion concerning their respective involvement in Bwakamabé's power structure is also crucial to the framework of this chapter and will receive additional attention in a consideration of Lopes's collaborationist politics, and of *Le Pleurer-Rire* as a testimonial document.

In the concluding section of the novel, a note from Soukali, the narrator's mistress, is included in italics under the following heading: "When Soukali climbs through the window of the novel or (if you will) reality" (*The Laughing Cry*, 257). Soukali's extra-textual interjection at the end of the novel adds legitimacy to the narrator's argument to the extent that her recognition of the fictional space in question lends veracity to the narrative:

> Despite a few transpositions, your friends will have no difficulty in recognizing every one of the actors under their masks. . . . If the names and places sound strange to our ears, even though you leave here and there in the text the words of an imaginary dialect of your invention, the most myopic of moles would recognize "the country." . . . There is scarcely as much difference between your story and our lives as between a Van Gogh, a Cézanne or a Modigliani and a photograph of the original model. But the magic and teaching power of art, isn't it less to resemble reality than to lend reality the colors of the painter's heart? (*The Laughing Cry*, 257–58)

By association, of course, this only slightly veiled sociological reality would be identifiable to most observers, including the authorities. Soukali's position is interesting in that her comments pertain to two spaces that are in fact one and the same: she has recognized the "fictional" entity, but simultaneously the process of "climbing through the window of the novel" represents a passage into another space, namely, reality.[30] Once again, Lopes has deliberately blurred the line between fiction and reality—or perhaps one could argue that his text is more *realistic* than those of his *socially realistic* compatriots. A further example of this confusion emerges from a consideration of the topographical situatedness of the novel. Lopes's narrative is anchored in an imaginary setting referred to simply as "the Country":

> Ah yes! The Country, the Country, the Country—but which Country? Somewhere on this continent, for sure. Choose for yourself, after a hundred calculations, or just follow your hunch, take a point on the equator, and steer either northward or southward, keeping your nose with the wind, and at a slightly oblique angle. Your craft then, after surviving airpockets and overcoming tornadoes, will arrive, after a certain time, at a point from which you can just discern the capital of our country. (*The Laughing Cry*, 34–35)

Although, as the narrator says, "To tell the truth, I must say the country concerned is not on any map" (*The Laughing Cry*, 40), Soukali has had no problem identifying the country in question. While Lopes has resorted to the veil of allegory to structure his narrative, a number of references do nevertheless make the text specific to the Congo—as Lopes has claimed, "there are a few winks that can only be picked by Congolese readers."[31]

Additional textual and paratextual components warrant commentary. There are three epigraphs in *Le Pleurer-Rire*, and each one addresses a theme which the text subsequently explores. The first epigraph is a quotation from the French dramatist Beaumarchais and reiterates the opposition contained in the title itself between the words "pleurer" and "rire": "It's no use my crying, the laughter will always slip out somehow" (*The Laughing Cry*, epigraph). This epigraph thus serves to underline the text's playfulness, pervasive humor, and often comical treatment of the question of dictatorial power, while introducing the fiction-reality dichotomy. Commenting on the relationship between laughter and oppositionality in the postcolony, Mbembe has argued that "instead of keeping silent in the face of obvious official lies and the effrontery of elites, this body breaks into laughter. And, by laughing, it drains officialdom of meaning and sometimes obliges it to function while empty and powerless" (Mbembe, 129).

The second epigraph, taken from Voltaire's 1772 *Lettre à Valentin Philippe de Rocheret*, introduces the conflict between the concerns of the imaginative writer and the expectations that are made of the writer to be politically committed, and also the question of testimony: "Whoever writes the history of his times must expect reproaches for all he has said and all that he has not" (*The Laughing Cry*, epigraph).[32] The third and final epigraph, from Boris Vian's novel *L'écume des jours* (The Froth of Days), is also important to our understanding of the dynamics between reality and fiction: "The argument of the following pages draws all its force from the fact that the story is entirely true, since I have imagined it from beginning to end" (*The Laughing Cry*, epigraph). As Moudileno has shown, the "difference between the work of the tyrant and that of the novelist resides in the fact that while the tyrant insists on the 'truth' of the History he is imposing, the writer's fable recognizes itself as such, thereby 'making sense' on the already confused boundaries between reality and dream (or nightmare), life and death, the spoken and the unspoken, and the rational and the irrational" (Moudileno, 24).

Rather than using these epigraphs to clarify some of the ambiguity introduced by the title, Lopes has preferred to confuse and disorient the reader. Somewhat paradoxically, the epigraphs themselves forewarn rather than enlighten the reader as to the subject of the text itself. Further confusion is achieved through the inclusion of a preface ("Sérieux Avertissement") written by the imaginary Association Interafricaine des Censeurs Francophones (Inter-African Association of Francophone Censors), which serves as an additional obstacle separating the reader from the body of the novel. It comes as no surprise then that one of the criticisms leveled at the novel by the imaginary censors concerns the disorientation it creates: "Africa begs for clarity, and this book brings confusion" (*The Laughing Cry*, preface).

Prefaces and various other paratextual devices have become common features in the novels of francophone sub-Saharan African postcolonial authors, most notably Sony Labou Tansi, Tchichelle Tchivela, and Caya Makhele, and have provided the site for describing and defining the *avant-gardist* aesthetics and political commitment of their respective projects—a tradition that hardly seems surprising, given the precedent set by French writers rendering francophone texts legitimate through their prefaces and introductions—the surrealist poet André Breton writing about Aimé Césaire's *Cahier d'un retour au pays natal,* Jean-Paul Sartre introducing Léopold Sédar Senghor's *Anthologie de la nouvelle poésie nègre et malgache de langue française,* and so forth.[33] In *Le Pleurer-Rire,* we do not find the same kind of preface, since Lopes has, this time, introduced a "Sérieux Avertissement." Lopes's version constitutes one of the most revealing documents concerning the relationship between writers and the government authorities in postcolonial Africa. A strong sense of irony characterizes the language of this preface, as Lopes has the reader believe that it was drafted by a body of censors on behalf of "an independent and non-governmental organization. It draws its resources from its own contributors, from gifts and from various legacies" (*The Laughing Cry*, preface). Significantly, this official preface comes after the epigraphs, thereby disrupting the traditional chronological sequence and locating the preface "within" the text rather than "outside" it, which is where such prefaces would traditionally be found. While this preface is of course Lopes's creation, it serves to further confuse real and fictive elements, given that similar organizations did exist. While "imagined," it nevertheless provides important insights into censorship mechanisms operating during the scientific-Socialist era in the Congo.

Printed in italics, the preface warns potential readers of the contents of the work. The organization's status as an independent body is also somewhat questionable, since it seems difficult to imagine who would constitute its membership. However, its originality lies in its inclusion in the published product, for it is in that capacity that it underlines the political dimension of the novel and anticipates the official reaction to nonaligned literature. This allows Lopes to demonstrate the futility of such a response, while simultaneously confirming that the work depicts a recognizable and therefore authentic or truthful rendering of a given sociological reality.

The preface describes the various options censoring organizations have employed, and it serves to illustrate the type of responses authors came to expect during the scientific-Socialist era. Lopes reveals his own understanding of these mechanisms and deconstructs them one after the other by revealing the criteria considered by censors in reaching a decision:

- One option available to censors was to simply ban the text. However, after years of experience, censors have come to realize that "banned books always sell, under the counter, better than good ones" (*The Laughing Cry*, preface). Socioeconomic circumstances rendered most books published in France inaccessible to the vast majority of the population; however, copies did circulate, and while censorship physically removed texts from the shelves of bookstores, the attention it brought to a work often contributed to underground circulation.
- Another solution consisted in purchasing every copy of the book directly from the publisher and then burning them. However, as the censor remarks in *Le Pleurer-Rire*, "But, all things considered, that would merely be to enrich in record time a wretch who really deserves a dungeon, a few good lashes and oblivion" (*The Laughing Cry*, preface)

The censors are thus forced to consider the options they have at their disposal, and as a last resort they decide to preface the book. Lopes successfully demonstrates the ineffectiveness of their measures by further confusing the relationship between the sociological reality in which censorship occurs and the fictional literary product in which this discourse has been articulated.

The comments made by the censoring organization are of further interest, because they outline their expectations of a literary text and thus confirm the official line of the "real" party on aesthetic creativity. One of the more disquieting aspects which underlies this preface concerns its attempt to question the sociological and political environment that is depicted by adopting a literal approach to the various textual representations: "all sane readers know that no President exists so flippant, burlesque and cruel as Daddy" (*The Laughing Cry*, preface). The dismissal of Lopes's novel by censors is part of a more complicated process (which has its roots in reality) that consists in discrediting resistance authors by manipulating public opinion and placing them at odds with the population. This objective is achieved by describing the literary productions of non-official writers as anti-governmental (and therefore anti-national), and linking them to the activities of the Western colonial powers. This device has been used since independence within the context of nation-building and has created a number of complex issues and ethical dilemmas for writers. Josaphat B. Kubayanda has explored this problem: "The writer, in his/her absolute attachment to the 'real,' attempts to reconstruct history and to create what some readers might tend to regard as a discourse of despair, or a mere rehashing of the ex-colonizer's racist representations of 'Third World' regime types."[34] Indeed, some prominent writers (Ferdinand Oyono, Cheikh Hamidou Kane) who were active during the colonial period abandoned their literary activities once power was transferred to the African leaders of sovereign nations.[35] The types of representations evoked by Kubayanda are contained in the following argument made by the censoring organization:

> Daddy is the image of a black president such as the racist and nostalgic whites, still dreaming of a vanished colonialism, imagine him. They hope, by means of this gross example, both to demonstrate the incapacity of blacks to govern themselves without barbarity, and to discourage all forms of cooperation between the developed world and ours, so as to let us founder in misery. (*The Laughing Cry*, preface)

Government authorities continue to persecute authors, particularly in nation-states that have sponsored an official, propagandist literature. This dimension is underlined in the concluding remarks in the preface: "We know we can count upon the wisdom of our literary critics and the vigilance of our masses to raise a wave of *counter-propaganda* that will obliterate, beneath a sea of sanity, this drop of anti-African poison" (*The Laughing Cry*, preface, emphasis mine). This counter-propaganda designates the body of official writing (official writers, statements by leaders, government-controlled media, etc.), to which Lopes's text stands in direct contrast. Both censorship and counter-propaganda effectively constitute preemptive strikes against what the state has anticipated will be projected toward it in non-official texts. In a somewhat paradoxical manner, government measures aimed at disenfranchising oppositional agents generate precisely those circumstances conducive to the production of resistance works by clandestine authors. In his essay on censorship, the South African novelist J. M. Coetzee has described this as a "paranoid dynamic of blaming," in which

The suspicion that the censor acts on the basis of unadmitted impulse itself belongs to the mode of paranoia. It is answered by the suspicion of the censor, also paranoid, that the call for the end of censorship in the name of free speech is part of a plot to destroy order. Polemics around censorship tend all too soon to fall into a paranoid mode in which every argument presented by the other is seen as a mask for a hostile intention. Once paranoid discourse is entered upon and its dynamic takes over, the intentions of the other cannot but be hostile, since they are constituted by one's own projections.[36]

The inclusion of this preface is one example of Lopes's acute awareness and understanding of the manner in which power is manipulated. In his attempt to deconstruct, expose, and undermine those mechanisms that have contributed to confusion within the postcolonial sociological reality, Lopes has felt compelled to invent a text capable of incorporating this confusion. The title, epigraphs, and preface function as indicators of what the narrative, delineated by the parameters of the work, will reveal.

Collaboration, Confession, and Testimony

The implications of Lopes's involvement in the operation of government structures are far-reaching, and the question of participation in the apparatus is addressed in *Le Pleurer-Rire* primarily as a means of controlling the abuses of power, influencing policies, and of course explaining and justifying the reasoning behind involvement. Comments formulated by the narrator's exiled friend provide some insight on this phenomenon: "It is true that about this time Yabaka had begun to question the whole basis of our tactics, whose objective was to remain within the state apparatus, the better to control it, penetrate all its parts, and gradually remove it from the effective control of Bwakamabé himself" (*The Laughing Cry*, 143). However, the narrator and exiled friend are forced to admit that they underestimated President Bwakamabé's ability to manipulate power:

> We certainly made a grave tactical error in accepting government posts under Bwakamabé. That's because we underestimated the fellow, believing that our self-confidence, our level of education, our experience of militant politics, would easily prevail over a peasant blockhead. But do these errors justify such a biting condemnation of our group as you seem to invite? (*The Laughing Cry*, 34)

The dialogue with the friend in exile allows the narrator, and by association Lopes as well, to reflect and comment upon political experiences. Indeed, as early as Lopes's first published text, the collection of short stories *Tribaliques*, a character stated that "if you are not in politics, you will have to endure it."[37] Furthermore, in *Longue est la nuit*, a collection of short stories by the Congolese author Tchichelle Tchivela, this same argument is reiterated by one of the protagonists: "After careful analysis of the situation, I understood that in order to bring down Tongwétani's corrupt regime, one had to penetrate it and attack it from within."[38] Given that Tchichelle Tchivela was appointed minister for tourism and environmental issues in Pascal Lissouba's post-scientific-Socialist government, these initial remarks have gained additional significance. When I interviewed Tchichelle Tchivela in Brazzaville in January 1995, I asked him how he could reconcile this statement with his current ministerial position. Given the manner in which the relationship between fiction and reality is exploited in Lopes's writing, Tchichelle Tchivela's response was particularly interesting: "Well you know, one must not confuse the writer and the man."[39] Tchichelle Tchivela and Henri Lopes's respective positions imply faith in participation as a means of achieving change and curbing oppression. The narrator's correspondence thus provides a crucial space in which Lopes can, indirectly, justify his own political choices and actions, as well as legitimize his writing as a further source of political commitment.

Lopes's statement, which is the first epigraph to this chapter, serves as a transition to some of the issues relating to collaboration, confession, and testimony I want to address. His words have much to reveal concerning the situatedness of the individual articulating a confession: "I would ask my reader not to waste time endeavoring to recognize Daddy in the portrait gallery of African leaders, but rather to kill the Daddy in them."[40] Lopes is of course warning the reader against the futility of identifying such details, but perhaps more importantly he is suggesting something about his own authoritarian impulse, a dimension of the psychology of human behavior that may represent a genuine struggle for him. Discussions of the postcolony have traditionally attributed disorder to sociological and political circumstances resulting from incompetent and totalitarian leadership; instead, Lopes's text offers the occasion to focus on an alternative approach that would allow for an exploration of history from a psychological perspective.

While this may serve as the point of departure for Lopes's confessional and testimonial narrative (assuming we are willing to agree that the novel in fact represents such a document), authentic and productive reconciliation can be successfully enacted only from the point at which the reader, the judge, and the victim are willing to accept that we all struggle with these impulses. While some may collaborate and others rebel, such a step would at least be accompanied by the recognition of the other's humanity even when the other is a perpetrator. Lopes himself adopted some of the characteristics of a Tonton (Daddy) figure, invented himself a space within the existing power structure, and attempted to use his influence to curb the oppressive practices of the postcolonial elite competing for control. Thus, *Le Pleurer-Rire* could also be read as an attempt by Lopes to demonstrate his humanity. If this is the case, then Lopes has effectively challenged us, as readers, to withhold judgment and hear his confession and testimony. Indeed, as Felman has convincingly demonstrated in her discussion of Paul de Man and the Holocaust, "It is easy to pronounce lapidary judgments from within today's belated and anachronistic clarity, with the self-complacent self-assurance of history's hindsight" (Felman, 122).

The task of establishing what effect, if any, Lopes had on the administrations in which he served would most likely be unproductive. In terms of cultural activities, Sony Labou Tansi has described the manner in which some high-ranking ministers used their authority to protect non-official authors: "there were personalities like Henri Lopes and Jean-Baptiste Tati-Loutard, who worked for the ministry and who regarded us as their protégés. They used to say: 'Don't mess around with the young ones.'"[41] In an interview with David Applefield, Sony Labou Tansi was asked whether he considered anyone to have served as a "mentor," to which he responded by claiming to have received "strong moral support" from Sylvain Bemba, and "financial backing" from Henri Lopes.[42] The context in which Lopes effectively facilitated the underground production and dissemination of a non-official adversarial literature was of course highly significant, given that the authorities were actively sponsoring an official literature of the state and censoring the works of non-official authors. While the history of censorship under scientific-Socialist rule in the Congo confirms that authors were not subjected to the same type of reprisals as their counterparts in countries such as Guinea, Kenya, Nigeria, and South Africa, this is hardly the occasion to engage in an analysis of comparative standards of repression.

Rather than focusing on the actual impact of Lopes's collaborative activities, a more productive inquiry can be located in a consideration of *Le Pleurer-Rire* as a confessional and testimonial narrative. These terms are not employed coterminously in this context; Lopes's text becomes a confessional document when, mediated through the narrative invocation of the failure of participation, he locates his transgression as participation and subsequently shifts to the testimonial mode as he asserts the authenticity and legitimacy of the narrative through the introduction of a reliable witness who can provide the authentication he seeks. This witness may, alternatively, become Lopes himself as we sense a narrative voice whose proximity to Lopes's own is unquestionable, and when we engage with the author outside the power structure as he assumes the role of witness to corrupt governmental mechanisms. In Lopes's case, collaboration was a public activity, such that the confessional act for him does not consist in *revealing* collaboration. His narrative thus becomes a testimony to his involvement and is closer to a process that would include explaining, justifying, and even apologizing. However, while not providing the testimony of a victim as such, his unique perspective within the power structure has afforded him a standpoint from which witnessing becomes possible.

Lopes's narrative (the telling of *his* story) is also polyvocal to the extent that his position as an insider allows him to address the question of the exercise of political power in a francophone postcolony while also justifying his participation. In other words, and with specific reference to the latter voice, one has to ask whether redemption lies in speaking culpably. Testimony and collaboration become symbiotically linked in what Felman describes as the "Impossible Confession" precisely because of "the demand for absolution that every confession necessarily implies" (Felman, 149). Reparation could be provided by a "public confession" (Felman, 141) and a "public declaration of remorse" (Felman, 141) that in turn demonstrates repentance. However, this in itself introduces a complicated dynamic within which the perpetrator continues to control power since nothing ultimately separates the crime from the testimony when the perpetrator is the author (Lopes) writing *his* version of events (his *story*, that is). The question therefore remains as to whether Lopes attempts to manipulate the reader through his objective of explaining away his involvement. As Felman argues in the case of Paul de Man, his "essay shows how all these possibilities of excuse (of a confession asking for absolution) *are not at the disposal* of its author, who knows that no excuse, and confession, can undo the violence of his initial wartime writing" (Felman, 150). Felman's analysis of Rousseau and de Man remains pertinent to Lopes in the "distinction between the confession stated in the mode of revealed truth and the confession stated in the mode of excuse" (Felman, 145). There is more tension between the terms "confession" and "testimony" than Felman is willing to attribute to them. My investigation focuses on the possibility of confession without offering an excuse, without an excuse enacting a justificatory mode, and on establishing preconditions under which one could elaborate such a model. For confession offers the individual the occasion to accept responsibility, absolute responsibility, without having to formulate excuses, and in order to learn about the circumstances that have triggered the confession.

These observations do not, of course, negate the importance of testimony as "a crucial mode of our relation to events of our times — our relation to the traumas of contemporary history" (Felman, 5). Lopes's concluding words in the novel address the question of trauma in a very significant way, situating his writing as a liberating act: "Here I end the telling of a rosary of dreams and *nightmares* that have followed one another with the cadence of a chronicle and from which I cannot be free until the last word is written" (*The Laughing Cry*, 259, emphasis mine). To the extent that there can be no closure, this becomes a delusionary quest, because the circumstances are recursive, given the cyclical dynamic of testimony. In many ways, this process duplicates the novel's own cyclical dimension, whereby the penultimate sentence, "In fact I have borrowed nothing from reality, nor yet invented anything" (*The Laughing Cry*, 258), rejoins the implications of the epigraph from Vian, according to which "The argument of the following pages draws all its force from the fact that the story is entirely true, since I have imagined it from beginning to end" (*The Laughing Cry*, epigraph).

Our attention should then, perhaps, focus on the nightmares he alludes to as the site of trauma, and from which he seeks to liberate himself by committing to a therapeutic process and recounting his experiences. As Dori Laub has argued, "the testimonial enterprise is yet another mode of struggle against the victim's entrapment in trauma repetition, against their enslavement to the fate of their victimization," whereby witnessing allows the individual to come to terms with the past.[43] Testimony provides the escape, the potential for interrupting the cycle and erasing the nightmare. According to Laub, the process functions as follows:

> The testimony is, therefore, the process by which the narrator . . . reclaims his position as a witness: reconstitutes the internal "thou," and thus the possibility of a witness or a listener inside himself. In my experience, repossessing one's life story through giving testimony is itself a form of action, of change, which has to actually pass through, in order to continue and complete the process of survival after liberation. The event must be reclaimed because even if successfully repressed, it nevertheless invariably plays a decisive formative role in who one comes to be, and in how one comes to live one's life. (Laub, 85–86)

This raises a number of complex issues, given that the silence of the perpetrator will most likely be treated with suspicion and understood as a refusal
to repent or accept responsibility. In the case of de Man, Felman has argued
that the "complex articulation of the impossibility of confession embodies,
paradoxically enough, not a denial of the author's guilt but, on the contrary,
the most radical and irrevocable assumption of historical responsibility"
(Felman, 152). Indeed, much of the work of the Truth and Reconciliation
Commission (TRC) in the Republic of South Africa, of the National Conferences in francophone sub-Saharan Africa, has underlined what we have
to learn from hearing all voices, and not just those of victims. Lopes has
argued that "An author's task should not be to tell the plain truth; on the
contrary, he should proclaim his own truth, that no one else sees clearly but
which he himself feels intensely during his fleeting moments of insight. To
do so, he must be a good liar, a fine illusionist. He must succeed in creating
what Louis Aragon called the 'lie-truth'" ("My Novels," 86). His explanations for political collaboration are problematic, given the manner in which
his continued insistence on supposed honorable intentions does not provide for any degree of accountability and responsibility. As Felman has argued, "the trouble with excuses (with confessions) is that they are all too
readable: partaking of the continuity of conscious meaning and of the illusion of the restoration of coherence" (Felman, 151). Coherence is disrupted
and displaced in Lopes's novel by the polyvocality, and the formulation of
excuses can be seen as an attempt to inscribe the type of order evoked by
Felman. Lopes continues to justify his involvement as a self-imposed mission to impose checks and balances on those who manipulate power. But
this positioning is problematic, given that he systematically refuses to entertain any kind of atonement for his participatory role (no matter how limited
it may have been) as a step toward absolution. To a certain extent, Lopes's
case exemplifies some of the more ambiguous and paradoxical aspects faced
by the TRC. Given that conditions of amnesty were essential, as Wole Soyinka has argued, in order "to encourage revelation, to establish truth," these
were inextricably linked to the "implicit, *a priori* exclusion of criminality"
and therefore the possibility of abandoning "responsibility."[44] Jean-Michel
Dévésa cites Lopes's words to Sony Labou Tansi explaining his decision to
leave the government: "I told him that it was becoming increasingly evident
to me that I was not cut out to be a political animal, that I didn't feel right in
these apparatuses, and that I needed to free myself of them if I wanted to
express myself and follow my heart."[45] However, Lopes's continued involvement since the publication of *Le Pleurer-Rire* as a high-ranking international

civil servant in UNESCO and since 1999 as the Congo's ambassador to France and the European Union only further complicates any attempt at understanding him.

Furthermore, Lopes has even gone so far as to claim that "I myself have not collaborated with anyone who resembles the Daddy character in my novel" ("My Novels," 83). Historical facts do not corroborate this statement and many Congolese citizens who lived under the authoritarian rule of Ngouabi, Yhombi-Opango, and Sassou Nguesso would disagree with Lopes's comparative standards for abuse. Such statements effectively deny victims of oppression the right to exercise judgment, and they ultimately void the possibility for reconciliation that could be offered through an acknowledgment of accountability. Perhaps this type of tension is contained or suggested in one of the epigraphs, whereby "Whoever writes the history of his times must expect reproaches for all he has said and all that he has not" (*The Laughing Cry*, epigraph). One should note that Lopes has been severely criticized for his involvement, and for the publication of a polemic and critical novel so soon *after* he left political office. David N'Zitoukoukou's 1983 review of Lopes's novel in *Peuples noirs, Peuples africains* is indicative of the type of criticism and accusations leveled at Lopes:

> When all is said and done, *Le Pleurer-Rire* should be read as a self-critique by its author whose hands, for having collaborated with those very people he criticizes today, are forever dirty. As far as this novel representing some kind of indictment, it is nothing of that. Rather, it is a speech for the defense, since it is highly likely that the narrator undertook the initiative of drafting this lampoonist narrative after a painful examination of his uneasy conscience. For it is not that easy to forget a decade of service in a regime that described itself as "popular and revolutionary." These long years of collaboration with the regime in Brazzaville have left an indelible mark on the novelist's conscience. It is not that hard to understand why Lopes was careful enough to wait for his retirement from politics before turning his pen against his friends whose "blunders" he apparently was so disapproving of deep down inside.[46]

Lopes represents a manipulative witness for N'Zitoukoukou, and his criticism seems perfectly warranted, given that the tone adopted in *Le Pleurer-Rire* is considerably more acrimonious than in his previous publications. While Lopes himself can be attacked for what he has chosen to articulate and what he has kept silent in the narrating of *his* story, his testimony should not attempt to silence other testimonies as integral and necessary stages of the reconciliation process. For, as the South African novelist Mark Behr has argued and observed through the confessional/testimonial voices he has adopted in his novels, *The Smell of Apples* and *Embrace*, as well as in his 1996 "Fault Lines Speech" and subsequent written submission to the TRC, it is essentially only from incorporating the narratives that emerge from multiple voices that we can ever hope to obtain some appreciation and understanding of the cultural dynamics at work since independence.[47] Indeed, as Robert Rotberg has argued with reference to South Africa, "the story of the past could not therefore be just one story."[48] The confessional mode can be further complicated to the extent that an individual may well *feel* guilty but in fact not *be* guilty while, alternatively, a witness may demonstrate repentance but not *feel* guilty. As Njabulo Ndebele has argued, "Guilt, in this situation, may be healthy. It may represent a healthy recognition of the moral flaws of the past and the extent of one's responsibility for them."[49] Lopes's guilt or innocence are not, of course, irrelevant to the contextual framework of the novel, but they are, ultimately, undecidable. Our attention should focus on the manner in which Lopes's circumstances further obscure the geometry between insider and outsider.

I want to further consider these notions by incorporating Coetzee's superb 1985 essay "Confession and Double Thoughts: Tolstoy, Rousseau, Dostoevsky" into the discussion.[50] This essay is particularly pertinent to my argument because Coetzee complicates the confessional mode by underlining the multiple layers that inform such a gesture. "Confession," he argues, "is one component in a sequence of transgression, confession, penitence, and absolution. Absolution means the end of the episode, the closing of the chapter, liberation from the oppression of the memory. Absolution, in this sense is therefore the indispensable goal of all confession, sacramental or secular" ("Confession and Double Thoughts," 252). This is clearly contained in the closing words of Lopes's novel where the narrator evokes the nightmares that have been plaguing him. Coetzee is referring to a different context, but his claim that "what calls to be confessed is something that lies behind the theft, a truth about himself he does not yet know" ("Confession and Double Thoughts," 252) has relevance to Lopes, for whom the transgression itself may be located in the collaboration, but the "unconscious truth" may be closer to his authoritarian impulse. Coetzee's readings of Tolstoy, Rousseau, and Dostoevsky could also apply to Lopes, in his objective of exploring how "authors confront or evade the problem of how to know the truth about the self without being self-deceived, and of how to bring the confession to an end in the spirit of whatever they take to be the secular equivalent of absolution" ("Confession and Double Thoughts," 252).

Lopes's objective is contained in the desire to "raconter," to tell a *or* his story. However, similarly to Pozdnyshev, Tolstoy's central protagonist in his 1889 *Kreutzer Sonata,* "the strain of articulating one truth with one voice ('consciously') while another truth speaks itself ('unconsciously')" ("Confession and Double Thoughts," 258) reflects the polyvocality of Lopes's novel and can serve to designate the complexity of the multiple voices competing in him. As Coetzee's analysis shifts to Rousseau's confessional writings, further points of contact emerge that pertain to that "element of *confession* whose purpose it is to reveal a verifiable truth, and an element of *excuse* whose purpose is to convince the reader" ("Confession and Double Thoughts," 266).[51] While Coetzee accepts that binary constructs—such as those that would juxtapose "good intentions" and "bad acts"—fail to sufficiently incorporate the multiple layers inherent to each category (namely, that "good" and "bad" aspects can in fact cohabitate simultaneously, as for example when Rousseau claims that his transgression contained a positive dimension), he further complicates the dynamic when he asks: "How can he know that that part of himself which recalls the good intention behind the bad act is not constructing the intention *post facto* to exculpate him?" ("Confession and Double Thoughts," 266).

In Lopes's case, collaboration represents the transgression, the "blameworthy act." However, through a justificatory mode, exemplified in the comments formulated by the friend from exile, the "bad act" (collaboration) contains a "good intention" (participation), whereby working within the power structure held the possibility of curbing authoritarian excesses. However, these circumstances can be further complicated because of the possibility that Lopes is "recalling" the "good intention" in order to exculpate himself, thereby allowing him to exercise the authoritarian impulse that corresponds, effectively, to the unconscious "real truth." In this model, "The 'truly shameful' desire that Rousseau is too ashamed to confess is the desire to expose himself . . . this process of shame and exposure, like the process of confession and qualification, entails a regression to infinity" ("Confession and Double Thoughts," 267), one that is partly contained in the interconnectedness of paratextual devices and Lopes's insistence on escaping categorization. Indeed, the circularity of Lopes's novel contains this "regression to infinity," from the epigraph selected from Vian's work, "The argument of the following pages draws all its force from the fact that the story is entirely true, since I have imagined it from beginning to end" (*The Laughing Cry*, epigraph) to the novel's penultimate sentence, "In fact I have borrowed nothing from reality, nor yet invented anything" (*The Laughing Cry*, 258). The following question therefore remains: Does Lopes indulge in the transgressive collaborative act primarily to *confess* it? Or, as Coetzee phrases it,

> a cause or reason or psychological origin is proposed to explain the crime; then a rereading of the confession yields a "truer" explanation. The question we should ask now is: What must the response of the confessant be towards these or any other "truer" corrections of his confession? The answer, it seems to me, is that to the extent that the new, "deeper" truth is acknowledged as true, the response of the confessant must contain an element of shame. ("Confession and Double Thoughts," 273)[52]

For Lopes, this "deeper truth" is located outside the context of collaboration, and by attributing it instead to his authoritarian impulse, he would gain proximity to the shame and disgrace associated with a "truer explanation." However, this dynamic is further problematized by Coetzee, for whom "there is something literally shameless in this posture. For if one proceeds in the awareness that the transgressions one is 'truly' guilty of may be heavier than those one accuses oneself of, one proceeds equally in an awareness that the transgressions one is 'truly' guilty of may be lighter than those one accuses oneself of" ("Confession and Double Thoughts," 274). And this, I believe, captures the spirit of Lopes's intellectual struggle with the Tonton in him.

The notion of truthfulness is of course central to any discussion of confession. For Coetzee, the problem presents itself in the following manner:

> The possibility we face is of a confession made via a process of relentless self-unmasking which might yet be not the truth but a self-serving fiction. . . . the more coherent such a hypothetical fiction of the self might be, the less the reader's chance of knowing whether it is a true confession. We can test its truth only when it contradicts itself or comes into conflict with some 'outer,' verifiable truth, both of which eventualities a careful confessing narrator can in theory avoid. ("Confession and Double Thoughts," 280)

In Lopes's text, this dynamic is evidenced in and through the polyvocal structure and inner contradictions that inform the text from the inside and the outside simultaneously: historical verifiable facts, letters from the exiled friend that authenticate his narrative, Lopes's statements concerning his nature as an "unrepentant liar," and the tenuousness of the epigraphs. In fact, Lopes "steps neatly aside" when anyone gets too close to him, or perhaps to the truth. The quest for closure and ultimately healing for Lopes, of being finally unburdened, lies in the telling (in the disclosing): "until the last word is written" (*The Laughing Cry*, 259). As Coetzee has demonstrated, here lies the shortcoming of the "secular confession" ("Confession and Double Thoughts," 291) and the paradox for Lopes, since the "self cannot tell the truth of itself to itself and come to rest without the possibility of self-deception" ("Confession and Double Thoughts," 291).

Acquiring, Maintaining, and Manipulating Power

> *Marshal Bwakamabé Na Sakkadé, in short, was not*
> *only a great leader, but an artist and director of the first*
> *rank. —The Laughing Cry, 69*

The emphasis in the final section of this chapter will shift toward exploring the manner in which Lopes has undertaken the complicated task of exposing and undermining the various power mechanisms he has observed, along with the various circumstances which have enabled a figure such as Tonton to acquire, maintain, and manipulate power. In his concern with exploring the Tonton in each of us, Lopes sets up a symbiotic relationship between the narrator (who recounts the trauma) and the reader (or listener in psychoanalytic terms). A productive reading can be registered by accounting for Lopes's status as witness, whereby, as Laub has argued, "a witness is a witness to the truth of what happens during an event" (Laub, 80). It is this *truth* that I propose to explore.

The President of "the Country" has so many titles that instead of conferring upon him the legitimacy he seeks, they transform him into a farcical figure: "For who can forget the entrance of Marshal Hannibal-Ideloy Bwakamabé Na Sakkadé, President of the Republic, Head of State, President of the Council of Ministers, President of the National Council of Resurrection, Recreating Father of the Nation, holder of many ministered portfolios" (*The Laughing Cry*, 64).[53] Most of the time, however, he is simply called Tonton, which is the name used by young French children to describe their uncles. This is of course significant, since French paternal colonialist leaders were commonly referred to as "uncles." While Bwakamabé's renaming inscribes him as the postcolonial descendant of the former colonial powers, the process nevertheless subverts the paternal colonialist figure.

Indeed, a parallel to Hergé's 1930 comic *Les aventures de Tintin au Congo* could provide us with an insight into the process through which Bwakamabé is himself transformed into a caricature.[54] As Philippe Met has shown in his discussion of Hergé's book, "The greater part of the most prevalent stereo- types and tropes of the primitivistic 'canon' are indeed to be found in this album."[55] Hergé's book reproduced representations of Africa that had been widely disseminated in Belgium and France for decades thereby contribut- ing to the popularization of such images and providing additional justification for colonial expansionism. Mbembe's insistence on such discourse origi- nates in the fact that

> colonial discourse ends up producing a closed, solitary totality that it
> elevates to the rank of generality. . . . How could it be otherwise, since
> the actual is no longer perceived except through the mirror of a perver-
> sity that is, in truth, that of the subject uttering this discourse? Colonial
> language thus advances deaf to its silent vibrations and endlessly repeat-
> ing itself. In its grip, the Other is never him/herself, but is always the
> echo of our irreducibility. (Mbembe, 178)

Through various devices, Lopes transforms his protagonist into a caricature, visiting upon him the type of ridicule associated with such figures.

Tonton has succeeded in establishing absolute rule over the fictitious nation he governs. Mbembe has analyzed the plural nature of the *commande- ment's* power structure, arguing that

> the general practice of power has followed directly from the colonial
> political culture and has perpetuated the most despotic aspects of ances-
> tral traditions, themselves reinvented for the occasion. This is one rea-
> son why the postcolonial potentate was hostile to public debate, and
> paid little heed to the distinction between what was justified and what
> was arbitrary. Because the potentate's normative source now lay only
> within itself, the potentate arrogated the right to "command." It is true
> that such a right to "command" sought legitimacy from several sources,
> drawing simultaneously on the imaginary worlds both ancestral and im-
> ported. (Mbembe, 42)

Tonton's political discourse is thus inherently contradictory to the extent that he endeavors to accord legitimacy to his authoritarian rule over the nation-state he controls. His power is anchored in customary beliefs (offer- ing cultural legitimacy through the ethnic and spiritual foundational com- ponent), and a Marxist-Leninist paradigm is adopted while simultaneously maintaining strong neocolonial ties with France.[56] The cohabitation of political models exemplified here serves to further underline the "promiscuity" evoked by Mbembe, transposed here into the postcolony in order to designate how the pre-colonial survives in the colonial, and how the colonial in turn survives in the postcolonial framework. In an atmosphere of secrecy and intrigue, and through the observations of the omniscient narrator, the narrative assumes the position of an authentic record of power in its every manifestation from a perspective we have not yet been afforded in other francophone works. In *Le Pleurer-Rire*, the narrator's status as an inside observer enables him to articulate his observations as a first-hand archivist of political intrigue.

Tonton's omnipresence evokes the Orwellian image of a surveillance state in which "Big Brother is watching you": "From then onwards, these eyes watched the whole country, under the sun's rays, under those of light bulbs and kerosene lamps, as well as in the dark. Whenever we passed a public building, they gazed down on us. Whenever we entered shops or offices, we met their stare" (*The Laughing Cry*, 26).[57] The Maître d'Hôtel, through his false modesty and ironical statements, demonstrates a capacity for insightful observations and an uncanny ability to analyze political events and those mechanisms through which power is acquired, maintained, and manipulated. These interjections gain authenticity and legitimacy as they are registered, and one begins to attribute them instead to Lopes, effectively further blurring the distance between fiction and reality.

Tonton is disdainful of all forms of legal jurisdiction: "It was all very nice to dream of elections. No doubt that would legalize the regime. But that would be to fall into the weakness of *legalism*" (*The Laughing Cry*, 74). From the moment Tonton assumes control over the presidency, he imposes a tough regime: "My word for it — nothing to fear. Ther'll be political stability. No opposition" (*The Laughing Cry*, 21). Torture is used to convert people to governmental philosophies and ideologies, and Captain Yabaka explains why it has become a prerequisite for efficient governance:

- Torture is obligatory. It exists even in revolutionary regimes. How can you force a bandit to talk, unless you make him suffer?
  The other did not hesitate in his reply.
- But are you not in danger of making an innocent man confess to God knows what, by putting him to the question? (*The Laughing Cry*, 138)

The answer to this question is provided by the arrest of a group of rebels whose resistance and attempts to undermine the government take the form of graffiti. Torture successfully breaks them down and converts them to the official ideology: "They were well beaten, threatened with the most exquisite tortures, and wasted no time in spilling the beans" (*The Laughing Cry*, 83).[58] One of the most disquieting aspects of the treatment of torture in *Le Pleurer-Rire* comes from its presentation as an enjoyable activity, characterized as "the sheer pleasure of killing" (*The Laughing Cry*, 113), and performed by people devoid of feelings: "Men with a crab for a heart, who could kill without blinking a member of their own tribe, or their mothers and fathers, just like that. Simply for the sake of obeying their superiors, so that society can be preserved in the good order they love. Specialists" (*The Laughing Cry*, 246). For Mbembe, "To colonize is, then, to accomplish a sort of sparky clean act of coitus with the characteristic feature of making horror and pleasure coincide" (Mbembe, 175).

People are only too aware of the fate that awaits them if they transgress official guidelines. For example, Tonton seeks to punish his Foreign Secretary for offering unsolicited advice, and his assistant Monsieur Gourdain has to plead with him to spare the man from prison: "Punish him, Mr. President, but, I beg, not the prison" (*The Laughing Cry*, 45). There are no specific guidelines according to which individuals are punished; when Captain Yabaka is indicted for his supposed participation in a coup d'état, we learn that "The meeting of the Tribunal took place at night. Scarcely a few hours after the nomination of the lawyers" (*The Laughing Cry*, 252). As a defendant he had no time to prepare the defense, but in legal proceedings in which criminality is established *a priori*, this would have been futile anyway: "They introduced some witnesses, fabricated for the occasion" (*The Laughing Cry*, 252). Deposed leaders and the alienated masses are helpless before the legitimate and constitutional power of the state. As Anyinefa has argued:

> The success of Bwakamabé's coup d'état is also due to the fact that the majority of the country's citizens were completely indifferent to public affairs. . . . The people do not identify with the authorities since the latter neither represent nor work towards their interests that are above all those of survival. . . . For the inhabitants of Moundié, politics not only represents hostile, strange, and repellent territory, but also the Mecca of corruption and violence from which it is wise to keep one's distance. (Anyinefa, 189–209)

The Congolese constitution, as was the case for other francophone sub-Saharan African countries, was structured according to the model provided by the French constitution and the French declaration of human rights. Tonton's "Country" is clearly and unequivocally indicted as a sovereign African nation whose constitutional principles are repeatedly violated through extrajudicial practices and the actions of those who manipulate power. Lopes's text has engaged in a dialogue with the constitution in which the reader's awareness of this subtext (and of the basic universal guidelines of such a constitutional document—sanctity of human life, protection against arbitrary detention, etc.) serves to discredit and thus deconstruct the constitutional parameters upon which the "Country" is founded. Characters are consistently denied legal representation, imprisoned, tortured, and executed, while the ruling postcolonial elite's sponsorship of an official literature of the state and control of the media have precluded and voided the possibility of free speech. Ultimately, Lopes denies the "Country" its status as a nation worthy of the name by revealing that the constitutional document upon which it is based is an official lie. The alternative model for political agency and representation one could extricate from this critique would emerge from inclusive political practices in which the foundational constitutional document was enforced as the inviolable framework for the national entity.[59]

Lopes has undertaken the complicated task of exposing and undermining the dynamics of power mechanisms that have contributed to the engineering of a sub-Saharan African dictatorship. The innovative narrative structure and the intricate network of paratextual devices have served as a parallel to the disjointed postcolonial sphere and enabled Lopes to criticize postcolonial governments and their policies while reconciling and reflecting upon his own choices and their consequences. Le Pleurer-Rire is firmly anchored in the tradition of resistance writing and addresses questions of confession, testimony, and reconciliation. The harsh critical tone and polemic nature of the novel can, in part, be attributed to the author's disappointment and disillusionment concerning his futile attempts at disrupting the ruling elite from the inside. In his concern with exploring the Tonton in each of us, Lopes sets up a symbiotic relationship between the narrator and the reader, thus forcing the latter to simultaneously consider the Tonton in him or her. Writing for Lopes has become a therapeutic and purging experience, enabling him to confront his feelings of guilt and of helplessness. Perhaps the reconciliation process, in its objective of allowing both victims and perpetrators to tell their stories of respective "disgrace," is both a *private* and a *public* process, one that compels us, as Lopes has suggested, to examine the Tonton in us but also to take up the challenge that is contained in Coetzee's question: "If you had the lyrical, we would not be where we are today. But I say to myself, we are all sorry when we are found out. Then we are very sorry. The question is not, are we sorry? The question is, what lesson have we learned? The question is, what are we going to do now that we are sorry?"[60]

5 EMMANUEL DONGALA
History, Memory, and Reconciliation

Death brings its own freedom, and it is for the living
that the dead should mourn, for in life there is no
escape from history. —MARK BEHR

Emmanuel Boundzéki Dongala's work is concerned with establishing a narrative that challenges official history and questions the intolerance for multiple versions of history. Whether the focus is provided by a discussion of the relationship between Africa and France, Africa and the transplanted people in the Americas, or more recent concerns relating to the complicated path toward democratization since the collapse of the one-party system, his writings address the various mechanisms through which history is recorded and memory constructed, in order to suggest ways in which reconciliation could be achieved. While my argument thus far has attempted to delineate the respective contributions of official writers, the oppositionality of Sony Labou Tansi, and the testimonial mode adopted by Lopes, this chapter begins with an analysis of Dongala's fascinating trajectory as an author and scholar, gradually expanding the framework in order to focus on the challenges he has articulated in his work against authoritarianism, sketching his contributions to the mapping of a history in which multiple voices are foregrounded, and finally connecting his agenda to the objectives of the National Conferences.

In 1960, after obtaining his *baccalauréat* in Brazzaville, Dongala competed for a scholarship that was being offered for the first time by the United States to African students from francophone sub-Saharan African countries. Dongala became the first Congolese recipient of that scholarship and left for the United States later that year. The traditional destination for African students and those from the francophone Diaspora in general was France or other French-speaking countries (such experiences are well documented through the writings of Léopold Sédar Senghor, Aimé Césaire, Camara Laye, and Bernard Dadié, among many others); this unique and unusual itinerary has played an integral part in building his world view and in shaping the future writer.

After spending nine years in Connecticut, New York, New Jersey, and at Oberlin College in Ohio, Dongala returned to the Congo at the end of the 1960s. The country was undergoing radical transition toward a scientific-Socialist government, and Dongala found it difficult to adjust to this environment. Barely a year passed before he left again, for France this time, in order to pursue his scientific training as a chemist. Dongala returned to Brazzaville in 1979, where he worked as a professor of chemistry at the University Marien Ngouabi, later becoming the university's dean. In one of history's curious and paradoxical turns, Dongala and his family were dislocated from Brazzaville because of civil unrest in 1997 and transplanted across the Atlantic to the United States, where Dongala was offered a teaching position at Simon's Rock College of Bard in Great Barrington, Massachusetts.[1]

Dongala is primarily a novelist, although he has also written poetry and theatrical works and directed the Théâtre de l'Eclair in Brazzaville. His first novel, *Un fusil dans la main, un poème dans la poche*, was published in 1973 and awarded the Grand Prix Ladislas Dormandi. A collection of short stories, *Jazz et vin de palme*, followed in 1982; a second novel, *Le feu des origines*, in 1987 (for which he was awarded the Grand Prix Littéraire de l'Afrique Noire and the Prix Charles Oulmont); the novel *Les petits garçons naissent aussi des étoiles* in 1998; and his most recent novel, *Johnny, chien méchant*, in 2002.[2] To varying degrees, these works will provide the central focus in this chapter, in an attempt to demonstrate their inextricable link in the process of narrating a version of colonial, post-independence, and postcolonial Congolese history that is not included in official constructs.

Congo-Kongo

In addition to biographical information, one should consider the influence of Kongo culture on Dongala, since it accords a certain anthropological specificity to the literary text by anchoring it in a restricted cultural context.[3] Dongala has acknowledged this influence, stating: "in my novel, *The Fire of Origins*, I really started out from Kongo civilization."[4] To this end, the research and findings of Wyatt MacGaffey and Simon Bockie, among other specialists in the field of Kongo culture, are particularly useful to the discussion. The conflict between traditional beliefs and the modern secular world — in this case a scientific-Socialist environment — provides the fundamental power struggle examined. The inconsistencies Dongala identifies and draws upon from the political reality become the problems faced by the various protagonists. The authorities are presented as having failed to eradicate traditional beliefs, given that the alternative models they have proposed—scientific-Socialism, Marxism-Leninism, and so forth—are shown to be contrary to customary belief in animate nature, founded on elements that are devoid of scientific and rational explanations. Bockie has explained this phenomenon in the following manner: "Traditional systems of belief have proved to be extremely tenacious in Africa and resistant to basic change. This is due in large part to the fact that they are inseparable from communal life."[5] As MacGaffey has argued, Kongo culture primarily consists in a "belief in the land of the dead and the spirits who inhabit it"[6] and therefore, by definition, is fundamentally opposed to scientific rationalism. The axis provided by these themes is in itself a source of polemics, since by association, the failure of science and reason to explain everything simultaneously leads us to question the political structures that are depicted. Key tenets of Kongo culture will be described only when they serve to elucidate and illuminate textual elements and will not lead to any questioning of the implied discourse or context.

Dongala's collection of short stories, *Jazz et vin de palme*, provides the point of entry to my discussion in this chapter. His second novel, *Le feu des origines*, will serve to further explain certain elements and outline important themes. The last section of this chapter will establish links between *Le feu des origines* and a number of significant developments in Dongala's more recent work, *Les petits garçons naissent aussi des étoiles*, that include a gradual globalization of the francophone sub-Saharan African novel along with various paradigms for reconciliation in post-scientific-Socialist Africa.

Censorship

Eight stories make up the collection *Jazz et vin de palme*; of these, the first five are set in Africa. By resorting to topographical references and actual historical and political events, Dongala has chosen to anchor his narrative in post-independence Congo. This is confirmed in interviews he has given, where he has stated that "I deliberately chose to situate these short-stories in the Congo, and you can even identify specific topographic landmarks. I really wanted to call Congolese society to witness and actually name it."[7] The fact that the action clearly takes place in the Congo is very unusual. Under the most repressive regimes, postcolonial African authors have found it necessary to resort to the veil of allegory to conceal their narratives, even if everyone sees through it and knows that the fictional state being described is in fact the real state. This has been the case for a number of francophone sub-Saharan African authors, such as Ahmadou Kourouma's (Côte d'Ivoire) imaginary République Populaire de Nikinai (sounds like "Guinée") in his novel *Les soleils des indépendances* (The Suns of Independence); Aminata Sow Fall's (Senegal) "La Ville" in *La grève des bàttu* (The Beggars' Strike); Alioum Fantouré's (Guinea) "Les Marigots du Sud" in *Le cercle des tropiques* (Tropical Circle); Ibrahima Ly's (Mali) "Béléya" in *Toiles d'araignées*; and Calixthe Beyala's (Cameroon) "Iningué" in *Tu t'appelleras Tanga* (Your Name Shall Be Tanga).[8] If one looks to the Congo, there are many examples: Henri Lopes's "Country" in *Le Pleurer-Rire* (The Laughing Cry); Sony Labou Tansi's "Katamalanasie" in *La vie et demie*; and Tchichelle Tchivela's "Tong-wétani" in *Longue est la nuit* and *L'exil ou la tombe*.[9] As the Guinean novelist Tierno Monénembo has stated in the foreword to his novel *Les crapauds-brousse* (The Bush Toads), in what is an innovative transformation of the traditional language used in authorial disclaimers, "places and people in this novel *should* only exist in my imagination" (emphasis mine).[10] Monénembo is of course playing with convention, but in particular with the government authorities who will eventually be responsible for censoring the book in Guinea. A heuristic interpretation would be straightforward, namely, that the repressive postcolonial environment that provides the discursive framework of the novel "should" never exist beyond the realm of the imagination. However, by introducing the conditional "should," Monénembo has deliberately subverted the function of such a disclaimer in order to confuse the relationship between fiction and reality (the work is advertised as a novel), and to present the images he projects as anchored in an identifiable reality. This enables him to undermine and expose that reality, but also to further inculpate those who identify themselves and ultimately censor the work.

With the struggle for independence, national spaces became the object of public consciousness, and geographical considerations were foregrounded. The "degree zero" of the history of decolonization coincided with political independence, namely, the official recognition of sovereignty. However, resistance to the postcolonial elite soon became a treasonable offense in many countries—or has at least resulted in censorship, imprisonment, and forced exile. These conditions have compelled writers to reflect on the effectiveness of artistic production as a tool for resistance, and to resort to innovative ways of bypassing censorship and the various guidelines delineated by the ruling elite for artistic creation. Non-official authors have attempted to negotiate identity through the use of imaginary topographical spaces; this device has served to question the existing postcolonial juridical territories, while simultaneously re-inscribing these alternative utopias/dystopias within the artificial, imagined boundaries. Authors have deliberately attempted to blur the lines between fiction and reality, but the fact that their imagined topographies correspond to an identifiable, recognizable reality has been vindicated by censorship. The act of challenging these territorial alignments acknowledges them as a sociological reality, but to challenge them with another name is to deny them what they have come to represent under their official name.

For obvious reasons, the national setting unanimously and unambiguously provides the context in the case of official writers. Given the repressive nature of the regime which comes under attack and the degree of censorship at the time, Dongala's position was obviously a courageous one, one that effectively underlined the extent to which he sought to vindicate his opposition to the leadership of the nation-state. *Jazz et vin de palme* was, however, banned in the Congo upon publication in 1982. In interviews I conducted with Dongala in Brazzaville in December 1994 and January 1995, he described the process in the following manner:

> It was still the era of Marxism-Leninism, and that is when I wrote *Jazz et vin de palme*, while I was in the Congo, where there was a one-party state and fierce censorship. The book was censored throughout the one-party era and was only allowed into circulation again after the National Conference. But everyone still read it, it circulated clandestinely, and even politicians read it on the sly. (Interview, 1994–95)

Somewhat paradoxically, censorship in this case generated an interest in the work and increased circulation. Indeed, as we saw in the previous chapter, the preface to Henri Lopes's novel *Le Pleurer-Rire* (The Laughing Cry) reiterated this same argument. While one would have expected Dongala to be sanctioned more severely than he was, it seems that his refusal to resort to a fictional setting and overt treatment of Congolese reality somehow, in a similar fashion to Henri Lopes's preface, anticipated the official reaction and left the censors with limited options. Dongala has commented on this dimension:

> The censors selected random references, random clichés, and if they came across material they didn't like, well then they censored the book. But as far as *Jazz et vin de palme* is concerned, there was a legitimate reason, because the book was violently anti-regime, it was genuinely against the system in place. But what is extraordinary is that I was never arrested or interrogated, nothing was ever done to me, but the book was banned and every copy was seized from the bookstores. . . . What really

saved me was the fact that I wrote the book while I was there, under my name, and everyone knew that it was me and I even said it was, and I don't think they knew how to handle the situation. (Interview, 1994–95)

Dongala's literary works are a product of the imagination, and while the unofficial universe resembles the sociological reality, the text establishes a distance from it. The reality serves as a point of entry to the literary and imaginative product represented by the literary text, and it is particularly important to underline this dimension since it serves to distinguish Dongala's texts from those of the official writers. In the case of official writers there is no effort to transcend that level of awareness, and of distancing the fiction from the reality.

The last two stories in the collection are set in the United States, and the story that bridges the African and American spheres bears the title of the collection itself and introduces a group of extraterrestrials.[11] Humor and irony play a determining role in this text, but a strong sense of pathos pervades this irony. Indeed, irony is a highly effective device for truth telling. As Sue Curry Jansen has observed,

> ironic assertion requires far more linguistic craftsmanship and precision than the propositional language of univocal discourse. Ironic messages require "double reading" . . . there could be no irony without the univocal pretenses (*hubris*) of established systems of power-knowledge. The ironic probe seizes upon the gaps—the anomalies or contradictions—in established explanatory systems.[12]

The tone can thus be seen as somewhat pessimistic, although the surface is of course very comical. When confronted with this idea of pessimism, Dongala has responded by saying that "the word 'pessimism' is perhaps too strong but nevertheless, it does not prevent us from asking: is there a future? In my work, this is compensated for with humor."[13] In a gesture of intertextual recognition of Henri Lopes's novel *Le Pleurer-Rire*, Dongala evokes his desire to "laugh so as not to cry."[14]

The African Stories

In each of the African stories in *Jazz et vin de palme*, Dongala examines the various mechanisms that have been employed as a component of the imperative to engineer the nation. Indeed, one could argue that the real axis of the work is the individual-collective one. Dongala's writing, particularly in the case of his novel *Le feu des origines*, stands as a striking example of the attempt by an author to examine the dangers of such a collective memory. Memory serves to construct identity and thus empowers the individual, and this is portrayed as unacceptable to the dominant political order. Government propaganda has sought to demonstrate that the Congolese share a common history, when in fact the creation of a modern, independent nation-state dates to the year 1960. Authors thus warn against the dangers of the discourse of assimilation, suggesting instead that we look beyond this and seek alignment within the framework of a multitude of identities. In this particular case, Dongala's novel represents a departure from the official version of history (employed within the context of nation-building rhetoric), in order to inscribe a historical version that is not mediated through the imperatives of a state-sanctioned ideology.

Dongala attacks the governing authorities for having ignored ideas of individualism, individual liberty, and the ideology of civil rights. The influence of the American experience is evident. As he explained recently, "because of the time I had spent in America, I developed a certain way of seeing things, a certain concept of freedom, a way of saying what one thought, of reading, and I had a lot of trouble adapting when I went back to the Congo" (interview, 1994–95). In the story "A Love Supreme," Dongala describes the 1960s in America in terms of "those trying times during the 60s when life in America was scarcely tolerable for people of *our race*" (*Jazz et vin de palme*, 135, emphasis mine). In this description, Dongala does not distinguish between African Americans and Africans, and he even identifies with their struggle. This sentiment is reiterated in the story: "Later, when we became political militants and supporters of Black Power and fellow travelers with the Black Panthers, his music [i.e., John Coltrane's] would take on new meaning for us, it would become the artistic avant-garde of *our struggle*" (*Jazz et vin de palme*, 150, emphasis mine). Dongala sees a parallel between the political climate and issues that were in question while he was living in America and the situation he found when he returned to the Congo. During the late 1960s, political reform in the Congo, established under the hegemony of the party, is shown to have created alienating circumstances for postcolonized subjects.

Old World, New Order

In the first story, "L'étonnante et dialectique déchéance du camarade Kali Tchikati" (The Astonishing and Dialectic Downfall of Comrade Kali Tchikati), the eponymous hero has fallen out of political favor and is concerned about a paternal uncle whom he claims is trying to "eat" him. The etymological and anthropological significance of the notion of "manger" is partly explained by Jean-Claude Willame's definition, according to which "The notion of 'eating' refers to two specific and intricately linked cultural registers in the African context: namely munificence which, for example, turns physical corpulence into a political asset, and particularly the realm of the invisible, that is to say the nocturnal world of the ancestors, of dreams, divination, magic, and witchcraft."[15]

The invisible quality is in question here. After attending indoctrination classes in Moscow, Tchikati marries a girl who has a doctorate in sociology and therefore seems to possess all the necessary ideological attributes to become the wife of a high-ranking government official. However, the one "blemish" (*Jazz et vin de palme,* 15) on her otherwise faultless résumé stems from the fact that she does not belong to the same ethnic group as he: while he is from the northern Sangha region (therefore either Sangha, Mekee, or Kota), she is from Pointe-Noire (Kouilou, Kongo sub-ethnic group). He argues in vain with his family to obtain their consent, but the only thing he is successful in obtaining is a procreation curse, whereby "you will have no children, your wife will be barren, we don't want offspring from the belly of this outsider . . . we don't wish you any harm, and nothing will happen to you except for the fact that this woman's blood will have no lineage in our family" (*Jazz et vin de palme,* 15). Tchikati mocks them for their superstitious beliefs, but he is soon forced to reconsider the situation when he fails to produce any offspring.

Kongo society is structured along matrilineal lines and, as Bockie has explained, "in Kongo culture 'mother' is a broad category that includes not only the biological mother but her sisters and brothers as well" (Bockie, 20). In this system, "marriage is the responsibility of a young man in concert with his uncles" (Bockie, 23–24). Thus, while having chosen a supposedly ideal wife according to the ideological demands of the new system, he has violated custom by ignoring his family's wishes. Traditional attitudes, practices, and world views have remained integral elements of contemporary society. According to Bockie's observations, a curse in a case similar to Tchikati's would "not refer to an act performed by someone but to the blockage of blessings caused by going against communal and ancestral wishes" (Bockie, 9). This would have considerable implications, since marriage "is at the very center of the flow of blessings into both the family and the larger community, the creating of a new life and carrying on the lineage" (Bockie, 31). The manner in which ethnic considerations influence human relationships is significant here, since it underlines the futility of government efforts to promote national integration in a context in which inter-ethnic links cannot be freely formed due to their increased politicization and thus serves to question the feasibility of the construction of the national space along these lines. Similarly, the government's status as an all-knowing, all-powerful body is put into question by its inability to solve Tchikati's problem through its dialectic reasoning process. The inability to reproduce serves to intensify ethnic animosity and enables him to expose the government's futile attempts at eradicating customary beliefs.[16]

Significantly, Tchikati never questions his own capacity to procreate, blaming instead his wife's reproductive potential. When he does finally consult medical experts, he is overjoyed (and ridiculed) when they are able to conclude that his "lazy spermatozoa" (*Jazz et vin de palme*, 17) are to blame. His wife, however, grows increasingly impatient and finally persuades him to take part in an "obscurantist ceremony" (*Jazz et vin de palme*, 18) to which he brings expensive gifts and asks for the forgiveness and blessing of his family and elders. The following month his wife is finally pregnant. This discovery coincides with a reassessment of his faith in party ideology. When his father dies, he meets with his uncle again and they argue over the inheritance of the deceased's car. The concept of inheritance is of course contrary to Marxist principles (in its implied accumulation of personal wealth), but Tchikati is more concerned with recovering what he considers to be his legitimate claim than with his ignorance of the most basic ideological precepts. Only two weeks after the incident, he has a road accident in his recently serviced, inherited car, and the only injury he sustains is a speech impediment that prevents him from pronouncing the letter "I"! This has serious professional implications for him, since he is henceforth unable to properly employ words such as "praxis"—now "praxs"—and of course "Lenin"—now "Lenn" (*Jazz et vin de palme*, 24). The only explanations that experts are able to come up with are somewhat questionable in scientific terms in that they refer to "invisible lead shot that had hit my optic nerves" (*Jazz et vin de palme*, 25). The boundaries and effectiveness of scientific theory are thus put into question once again.

Endeavoring to confirm the source of his affliction, he arrests and attempts to try his uncle. However, he is confronted with a problem that is a product of his own making, namely, "how can you try someone for a crime that *cannot exist*?" (*Jazz et vin de palme*, 27). A similar situation arises in Dongala's novel *Le feu des origines*, in which Mankunku is told by his family elders that he will not be able to have children with the woman he has chosen. The power of the elders and of their curse would be confirmed were he to have no children. Thus, the fact that his wife eventually gives birth to an albino child leaves the situation deliberately ambiguous. We feel some of Dongala's own frustrations at times through the words of Mankunku, when he claims that "The foreign doctor's science is stronger than your sorcery; he explained to me that this was nothing but a banal accident" (*The Fire of Origins*, 218). However, as a family member points out, "why did you summon us if you don't fear our power?" (*The Fire of Origins*, 218). The text is forced to remain ambiguous, conceding that "you can never be too careful" (*The Fire of Origins*, 211) and, in *Jazz et vin de palme*, that "Africa had its mysteries" (*Jazz et vin de palme*, 34). He is, however, permanently torn between two cosmologies, stating that "between what are commonly held opinions and submitting oneself blindly to ancestors that have long since departed, there is quite a margin" (*Jazz et vin de palme*, 52). Compromise is chosen as the path forward: "He, Bunseki Lukeni, had a scientific approach to the world through knowledge, the old man a holistic sapience. . . . The ideal would be to combine these two approaches" (*The Fire of Origins*, 233).

Tchikati calls upon a *nganga*, whose importance lies in his capacity to identify the origin of a curse. Dongala employs the term in an all-encompassing manner to designate, in *Le feu des origines*, "the one who knows, the savant, the sorcerer, the healer . . . the priest, the magician; he had the ear of the ancestors and could penetrate their secret" (*The Fire of Origins*, 31–37). The key tenets are *kinganga*, which denotes magic, and *kindoki*, which corresponds to witchcraft. As MacGaffey has indicated, "these concepts in turn presupposed a cosmology of divided worlds in which the holders of these powers mediated between the dead and the living" and constitute, according to Kongo custom, "so many responses to the possibility of obtaining power from the world of the dead and using it in this world with violent or therapeutic effect, for altruistic or selfish ends" (*Modern Kongo Prophets*, 4–12).[17] A person who is able to obtain power in such a manner and use it to adversely affect someone is described as *ndoki*. According to Bockie, "it is believed that ndoki mystically eats his victims. . . . he invisibly attracts their psyche, their inner source of life and vitality" (Bockie, 46–47). The *nganga*, as a healer, is able to remove or dissolve the *ndoki* curses. MacGaffey's comments are pertinent to the situation depicted by Dongala, since these activities are today "usually limited to witchcraft or the injudicious use of magic. This change means that therapy is usually a matter of adjusting interpersonal tensions directly . . . [and] the commonest causes of trouble were family resentments . . . usually that the mother's or father's relatives disapproved of the client's marriage" (*Modern Kongo Prophets*, 149–68). The *nganga* will have recourse to *nkisi* (objects used for ceremonies), which represent "a personalized force from the invisible land of the dead; this force has chosen, or been induced, to submit itself to some degree of human control effected through ritual performance [by the] initiated expert . . . the nganga."[18] Tchikati thus willingly submits to the *nganga* he has called upon, who is able to confirm, after contacting Tchikati's dead father in the land of the dead, that it is in fact the uncle who is responsible for his misfortunes. This "land of the dead" is *Mpemba* (the world of the ancestors) and represents for Bockie "the embodiment of spiritual reality, a reality present everywhere, at all times. . . . This community furthermore extends through all life to include not only the visible beings but also those who are unseen" (Bockie, 1). So as to undo his uncle's power, the *nganga* orders him to get undressed. However, by igniting some gunpowder he was using for the ritual, he creates enough of a distraction to be able to take off with Tchikati's belongings, leaving him stranded in the forest. This supposed *nganga* turns out to be little else but an impostor, thereby indicting the entire fabric of this postcolonial society.

Tchikati gains consciousness of alternative models, in which diversity is recognized as the key to social progress:

> When all is said and done, what are a society's realities? Are they not, ultimately, determined by the way a society behaves, the acts it posits in relation to what it stands for? Which is tantamount to saying that there is nothing to be gauged from knowing whether what it believes in is true or false . . . what really counts is that this conviction translates itself into a social, psychological, and cultural reality. (*Jazz et vin de palme*, 34)

He redefines his position, corrects his political illusions, distances himself from dogmatic party ideology, and begins to understand the importance of achieving a reality that is acquired rather than imposed, and in which dissent is acceptable.

Leviathan in the Postcolony[19]

In the second story, "Une journée dans la vie d'Augustine Amaya" (A Day in the Life of Augustine Amaya), Dongala denounces the bureaucratic order that has developed in the postcolony. Inherited from the colonial era, the bureaucratic system has mutated and grown under postcolonial regimes, becoming a powerful, oppressive, and corrupt mechanism. While the surface appears to suggest governmental incompetence at running the bureaucracy, the bureaucrats are in fact portrayed as having mastered only too well the intricate workings of this powerful body, and they have found ways of using it to their advantage.

As its title indicates, the story is about a day in the life of Augustine Amaya, a poor saleswoman (*revendeuse*) who travels across the river to Kinshasa to purchase a variety of goods for resale back in Brazzaville. On this particular day (the fourth consecutive one of its kind), Augustine attempts to retrieve her "identity card" from the customs officials to whom she was forced to surrender it. Rising early and having fought her way on the overcrowded *foula-foula* (mini-bus for public transport in Brazzaville), she finds herself in line shortly after daybreak. After waiting for almost four hours for the office to open, she finally realizes that "today was her lucky day because the office manager arrived earlier than usual, at ten o'clock. By the time he had arranged his paperwork, filed away his folders, and given out instructions to his subordinates, it was eleven o'clock" (*Jazz et vin de palme*, 37). The official finally asks her to state the reason for her visit, and she explains how she followed instructions and handed over her card. His reply, "well you shouldn't obey absurd orders" (*Jazz et vin de palme*, 37), reveals the lack of consistency in policies, and how these serve to confuse the population. Their deliberate or real ineptness serves to make sure that nothing actually gets done, and that the status quo is preserved. Augustine makes no progress with this particular official, who orders her to return that afternoon, since it is already time for his lunch break. The description of his office is revealing:

> Amaya followed the movement of his sturdily built body, swollen with authority. A portrait of the Immortal President, youthful and thick-lipped, was hanging to the right of the clock, assassinated by whom she was not so sure, given that the numerous versions circulating had been so contradictory. Whilst to the left, the wall was plastered with slogans that meant nothing to Amaya for the very simple reason that she did not know how to read. (*Jazz et vin de palme*, 38)

Those who have power find ways to flaunt it. This is an integral part of the power mechanism, as the repeated references to effigies reveal. The citizens are presented as illiterate and uneducated and therefore able only to repeat the vocabulary of the official *langue de bois* they have overheard. They also know that authority is to be feared and respected and are therefore willing to say anything, even when it is as ridiculous as to claim that the Immortal President has been assassinated. Official party lines are constantly changing

as new leaders, new governments, and new cabinets seek to distance themselves from their predecessors. This further contributes to the general confusion among the people.[20]

The consequences of this bureaucratic inefficiency are clear. In this
particular instance, they represent a loss of needed income for Augustine,
who, without her official papers, cannot cross the border and thereby work.
By having to wait until the afternoon for further attention, she does not have
sufficient time to go home and carry out other essential tasks. While she
waits for the official to return from his lunch break, she goes for a walk.
From the water's edge, she observes small commercial boats pull in and
contend with customs officers, shown to have ultimate control over the situation. Augustine notes that "the women found nothing unusual in this drub-
bing, these insults, and the insulting behavior these customs officers subjected them to, because ever since they had been born, the authorities . . .
had treated them with the same contempt" (*Jazz et vin de palme*, 38–39).
The implications are disquieting, to the extent that oppression in the postcolony is presented as a mere continuation of colonial practices. In the case
of Augustine, the consequences are devastating because she is left to fend
for herself and her children.

Furthermore, Augustine is a victim of her social condition, in that she is
not aware of the legal mechanisms supposedly available to her, because "she
was not sufficiently educated to know that there were such things" (*Jazz et
vin de palme*, 40). This underlines the system's failure to fulfill its promise to
educate the people and redistribute wealth according to the ideological principles it embraces. When the official finally returns from his break, he informs her that he has discussed her case with his assistants and that she
should return the following day. All that is left for her to do is to wonder,
"will tomorrow be another day?" (*Jazz et vin de palme*, 43).

The element of pessimism in this story emphasizes the helplessness of
the individual before the powerful governmental body. Without adequate
resources (educational, legal, and financial), Amaya and, by association, other
Congolese citizens have little hope of achieving satisfactory living standards.
Dongala reproduces this socioeconomic reality in order to reveal the effectiveness of government mechanisms (in this case bureaucracy) in curbing
eventual dissent, by increasing the dependence and subordinate status of its
people. The fictional text thus becomes an effective medium for articulating criticism of the sociological reality, and for exposing those practices that
have contributed to the failure of postcolonial Congolese governments to

create social structures conducive to economic progress and adequate standards of living. Instead, the government officials have placed their energy in propaganda and in strengthening power bases, in the name of national integration and unity, but have never really attempted to create spaces in which these objectives can ever be successfully achieved. Augustine's plight questions the validity of existing government guidelines, and of course the wisdom of borders and control mechanisms between two countries whose histories are so closely intertwined (thereby rejoining Sony Labou Tansi's novel *L'anté-peuple*, in which similar identitarian issues were raised).[21]

Legal Processes

In the third story, "Le procès du Père Likibi" (Old Likibi's Trial), a drought lasting some four months has had devastating consequences on the village of Madzala. Someone in the village has even suggested that the only solution is to sacrifice someone. However, as the narrator points out, "one no longer killed someone just like that without a scientific reason. . . . That was the rule since the last coup d'état which, after having adjusted the revolution, *imposed* on all the villages the scientific-Socialism the people had *freely chosen*" (*Jazz et vin de palme*, 48, emphasis mine). The conclusion to the story serves to contradict this statement in its inscription of violence, epitomized as a continuation of colonial rule. The contrast between "imposed" and "freely chosen" is evident here, and the tone is deliberately ironical, since it is precisely in the name of scientific-Socialism as the path to unity that those who dissent have been eliminated. Questions pertaining to law and testimony will be addressed in the concluding section to this chapter.

After considerable reflection on the matter, Ikounga, a village elder, traces back the last rainfall to the night before the wedding of Likibi's daughter. Likibi had held a short ceremony, in which he asked for the rain to stop, chanting "Oh sky you can remain dark, but you the rain do not fall" (*Jazz et vin de palme*, 49). Along with the considerable losses in crops and livestock, the fact that both Ikounga and the village chief, Mouko, were turned down as possible suitors by Likibi plays an obvious part in their eagerness to see him take the blame. Ikounga informs Mouko of his suspicions, but by suggesting that a person could be responsible for this, Mouko is forced to remind him that he cannot entertain such notions as the party's representative in the village, notions which are fresh in his mind after a recent all-expenses-

paid trip to the capital for an "ideological bath" (*Jazz et vin de palme*, 52).
However, he thinks back to the day he returned from the capital and delivered his scientific speech and handed out photographs of Marx and Lenin.
Likibi questioned his reasoning: "if the priests and all the Whites who were
here along with their *mbouloumboulou* failed to make us give up the customs of our founding ancestors, it's not you or your little soldiers in power
who are likely to succeed" (*Jazz et vin de palme*, 53).[22] This statement underlines the people's initial unwillingness to subjugate their individual aspirations to a state body whose policies and actions they perceive as a continuation of the Western colonial model.

Dongala's decision to structure a story around a trial allows him to highlight the contradictions within the system and to indict people's greed. The
following description of the proceedings illustrates some of the confusion:

> The government commissioner, Konimboua, his eyes reflecting the cor-
> rect line for the anti-imperial and anti-obscurantist struggle, took a mo-
> ment to look around and assess the impact of his demonstration on the
> illiterate audience he was judging. Old Likibi seemed perplexed rather
> than impressed, like someone who was beginning to question the men-
> tal health of his interlocutor. (*Jazz et vin de palme*, 75)

Those who conduct the trial ignore the fundamental workings of a court of
law and are as such no more enlightened than the confused villagers attending the proceedings. At least in theory, the trial should allow for a fair exploration of the accused's culpability. However, the predetermined guilt of Likibi
(the accused) excludes the possibility of a fair trial. The contradictions stem
from the accusation itself, since it is contrary to dialectical reasoning. Failure to prove his guilt would undermine the omnipotence of the state, but
yet confirmation of his ability to influence the weather defies the very logic
upon which the system has established its power base.

Konimboua Zacharie is recruited by the Central Committee to oversee
the proceedings. He arrives in a Land Rover, and his "revolutionary stom-
ach, accustomed to the rigors and sacrifices required of a scientific-Socialist
praxis," serves as a striking contrast to the physical signs of malnutrition epitomized by the "few rachitic children with swollen bellies that surrounded his
car" (*Jazz et vin de palme*, 59).[23] His opening words make it clear that the
notion of a fair trial was itself erroneous: "we are going to make an example
of Old Likibi, we are going to conduct an exemplary trial, as much in its
unfolding as in the verdict. That way, people will understand that we can

use force when we choose to" (*Jazz et vin de palme*, 60). Villagers witness the manner in which their spiritual leader is treated, and this serves to intimidate them further as their own vulnerability is exposed. Likibi, however, "clearly had no clue what was going on" (*Jazz et vin de palme*, 63), because the concept of a modern trial is alien to him. The situation presented by Dongala stands in contrast to similar juridical proceedings in Ousmane Sembène's novel *Les bouts de bois de dieu*, where the character Bakayoko successfully raises the political consciousness of his fellow workers.[24] As MacGaffey has pointed out, "the elite, owing their success and prosperity to their participation in urban, European institutions, are driven to accept the European evaluation of their way of life. . . . [An] assumption prevalent among the elite is that evolutionary progress from rural to urban is dependent on the evolving mentality of individuals."[25]

Under local customary law, the responsibility lies with the accused to prove their innocence. As MacGaffey has shown, the *nganga* can recommend an ordeal, which would usually consist of "the administration of a vegetable strychnine poison (in Kongo, made from the bark of the nkasa tree) . . . which was supposed to pierce the witchcraft substance (kundu) of the suspect and cause him to defecate and faint."[26] Bockie describes a similar situation, whereby a victim is administered a poisonous drink, and "if he prevailed over it, he was immediately acquitted; if it downed him, he was guilty and was to be burned alive" (Bockie, 40). There is a textual usage of this practice in Dongala's novel *Le feu des origines*, when Uncle Bizenga accuses Mankunku of being a sorcerer and requires him to disprove the accusation, "Yeah, Mankunku, prove you're not a sorcerer, take up the challenge, the trial by *nkasa*" (*The Fire of Origins*, 112). Likibi can only be found guilty, since a continued drought or sudden rainfall would only serve to confirm his powers. Through a series of ridiculous arguments, each one more absurd than the last, the prosecution criminalizes Likibi and orders his execution.

In *Le feu des origines*, a similar problem challenges the authorities' ability to employ scientific criteria. An overloaded train is forced to interrupt its journey (the reader knows why it has been forced to stop, but the object is to underline just how firmly entrenched traditional customary beliefs are). The people believe that this is the work of the rebel Moutsompa, whose name and mythic associations are similar to that of the religious leader and resistance figure André Matsoua.[27] The authorities seek to disprove popular belief by conducting a ridiculous scientific experiment, in which a scapegoat of very limited physical strength is ordered to lift some weights. His inability to lift these light weights confirms that he could not possibly stop a considerably heavier train. The authorities may have, at least scientifically, proved their theorem, but that is of little significance to the Kongo people whose beliefs are firmly rooted in animate nature, and for whom the interconnectedness of the world of the living and the dead is central: quite simply, "Moutsompa has simply disappeared until the day he returns to set us free" (*The Fire of Origins*, 168).

Vulnerable Leaders

The fourth story, "L'homme" (The Man), describes the successful assassination of a president and the ensuing attempts to identify the perpetrator.[28] This story is particularly interesting in that it stands as an analysis of extravagant security mechanisms implemented in a number of African countries as a response to repeated coups d'état and assassinations since independence. These mechanisms are also shown to be a part of the more sophisticated measures employed by leaders to justify security expenditure, as a constituent part of a policy of internal stability. Indeed, as this fictional story reveals through its inclusion and description of government activities, purges, and recriminations (documented by human rights organizations, newspapers, etc.), these were an integral component of the rule of fear. The arbitrary nature of decisions—including extra-judiciary executions—serves to remind the citizens that their fate lies in the hands of the state.

The presidential compound in this story is protected by state-of-the-art surveillance equipment. However, the central protagonist, referred to simply as "the man," crosses the supposedly impenetrable boundaries and assassinates the leader. This generates a pathological response from the military forces, who engage in a campaign of violence and torture.[29] The soldiers finally select a man at random from a group of villagers they have rounded up. By pure coincidence, the man they select for execution happens to be the culprit. The irony of his death stems from the fact that they will never actually identify the man that they are looking for and therefore live in fear that he will strike again. However, an alternative interpretation would be located in an analysis of the power structure, and of its recourse to intimidation in the construction of a rule of fear. The fact that the assassin has effectively eluded them serves to justify the ongoing nature of their searches and reign of terror. Of course, optimism could also come from the implied threat of eventual revolt that is contained in the hero's martyrdom.

Ethnicity and Ideology

The last story set in Africa is the most revealing in terms of the analysis of those mechanisms that determine political alignment, and the manner in which ideology is utilized to serve these ends. Irony is a device which Dongala handles in a remarkable fashion, a dimension that is also prevalent in his novels.

The focal point of the action in "La cérémonie" (The Ceremony) is a "modest militant" who has hopes of being appointed to the vacant director's position in the factory in which he works. Such a position would of course be accompanied by considerable financial benefits. However, a fellow worker who belongs to the same ethnic group as the President is appointed. While the militant does all that he is in theory supposed to do to obtain recognition (he reads the writings of Marx and Lenin, for example), he is confused and at odds with a system that does not practice what it preaches. His faulty use of party jargon underlines the failure of party education programs, as, for instance, when he calls for "a development program that is auto-managed and auto-centered . . . now, to achieve this automobile development—sorry, auto-centered, we have to fight against bourgeois democracy—sorry, bureau-cracy (please forgive me, I learned so many things in so little time that it's all a tad bit mixed up in my head)" (*Jazz et vin de palme*, 91). Political authen-ticity is limited to the wearing of a "Mao collar," and, as Anyinefa has shown, "when civil servants dress in the style of Mao while ostentatiously gorging themselves at public expense during an official function, the ironic com-mentary on their behavior derives in part from the contrast between their attitudes and those of Mao" ("Intertextuality," 8).

The confusion is partly located in the discrepancy between that which is described in public speeches and through various propaganda mecha-nisms (official texts, radio, television, posters, slogans, party newspapers, and pamphlets), and the actual behavior of government officials. At one point, the militant attempts to decode the concept of a "bureaucratic bourgeoisie" in light of what radio broadcasts have been saying: "What misled me was that when I looked around, I saw that all our Ministers, our political tenors, the members of our glorious Party's Central Committee, they all had luxury air-conditioned cars, and their wives and children didn't roast in the sun waiting for an unreliable bus so as to get to the market or to school" (*Jazz et vin de palme*, 97–98). The material signs of corruption are readily identifi-able. The people only have to compare their misfortunes, lifestyles, and sociological environments to those of the leaders who manipulate power. Dongala employs a series of binary oppositions to illustrate this dimension: crowded public transportation and luxury automobiles, villas and corrugated iron shacks, overweight men and children suffering from malnutrition. The dictatorship of the people is achieved through a rule of fear, and nepotism is rife in this environment. Through the militant's comments pertaining to the trade union leader's speech at the ceremony, Dongala is able to formulate one of the most perceptive and striking commentaries of the contemporary situation:

> He started by saying that we had to fight against tribalism. That made me laugh, because all three of them, the Secretary-General of the Trade Union, the new director and the President of the Republic all came from the same area. . . . Oh, careful now, this is not an attack, since it is perfectly natural that the country be dominated by people who come from the same area and ethnic group as the President since, just like in a garden, some patches yield better vegetables and fruits than others. . . .
> In Africa you know, competence, like genius, always manages to suddenly flourish in the area or ethnic group of the person in power. (*Jazz et vin de palme*, 104–105)

By transposing a given reality into his fictive production, Dongala is able to demonstrate the manner in which ethnicity undercuts the integration process and is utilized as a political tool by those who are endeavoring to consolidate their power bases. When the tire of a passing Renault 4 bursts and bystanders suspect gun fire, the militant is alone in offering his body to shield the President, who by then "was scared stiff" (*Jazz et vin de palme*, 109).[30] However, the militant ends up being taken into custody and beaten for his act of bravery. His courageous act is juxtaposed with the vulnerability and weakness of government officials, who repress their own weakness and shame in accusing him of conspiracy. Indeed, as we shall see, this act of deflecting responsibility very much characterized the discursive realms during the 1991 National Conference and transition away from Marxism-Leninism toward democratic rule.

Dialogue with the Diaspora

The sixth story, "Jazz et vin de palme" (Jazz and Palm Wine), bears the title of the collection itself.[31] The narrative moves to a universal dimension as world leaders gather to solve a common threat presented by the invasion of extraterrestrial colonizers. The story ends on a distinctly positive note though, as world leaders share in the enjoyment of listening to John Coltrane's and Sun Ra's music, while consuming palm wine. By association, the outcome of this story serves as a model for the type of national space Dongala envisions for the Congo and in many ways stands as a precursor to the reconciliatory objectives of the 1991 National Conference and 1994–95 Forum national pour la culture et la paix. The conclusion to this story and its strategic positioning at the juncture between the African and American (and of course African American) spaces underline Dongala's understanding of the symbiotic links between these respective historical trajectories:

> People began to dance with one another, to embrace and to sing of their newly-won freedom. In this way, Sun Ra became the first black man, and a Jazz-musician to boot, to occupy the post of President of the United States; in the same way, the best palm wine drinker of the year is regularly appointed Secretary-General of the United Nations, and Jazz has conquered the world. (*Jazz and Palm Wine*, 201)

The penultimate story, "Mon métro fantôme," takes place on the New York City subway, as Dongala explores alienation in the American context in a city he has described in terms of its "infernal" qualities (interview, 1994–95).[32] A connection is made to the next story, "A Love Supreme," which tells of Dongala's encounter with the jazz musician John Coltrane during the 1960s. In a recent interview, Dongala declared that this marked a time when the popular image of Africa was undergoing a number of changes: "Black Americans only had a stereotyped view of Africa through Tarzan and Hollywood cinema. The attempt to return to origins claimed to be realistic . . . but a new myth emerged from this thinking in which Africa became the birthplace of humanity, the continent of every virtue. And of course this was disturbing to those of us who knew what things were really like."[33] Given the instability and increasing violence that was becoming characteristic of the postcolony, this view of Africa was problematic for him. Furthermore, in its continued mythic presentation of Africa, this perception constitutes a barrier to progress. Anyinefa is right to point out the importance of Mayéla's statement in Dongala's first novel, *Un fusil dans la main, un poème dans la poche*, whereby "Africa is a reality for me as an African, but a myth for you as a Black American" ("Intertextuality," 12). However, he does find a parallel between the civil unrest in America during this period in history (namely, the violent repression of civil rights activists by the authorities along with the assassinations of John F. Kennedy in 1963, Malcolm X in 1965, and Martin Luther King in 1968) and that of Africa, with the assassination of

Patrice Lumumba, for example, in 1961. As Anyinefa has pointed out with reference to *Un fusil dans la main, un poème dans la poche,* "African nationalist movements are presented as sharing the same goals as the civil rights movements in America" ("Intertextuality," 13). These events lead Dongala to question the significance of artistic creation within this context, and specifically to a reflection on the importance of John Coltrane's music. As Séwanou Dabla has argued, the "narrator reveals the aesthetic and individual quest of the Black musician who pursued his entire life and through his music 'those marvelous and extraordinary things' that are Liberty, Love, and Elevation in this harsh and cruel world."[34] For Dongala—as narrator— the occasion is characterized by a deep psycho-emotional response: "I watched the closest companions of my generation sacrificed, massacred for the beliefs they held: believe me, J.C., your music upheld their faith. That is the artist's triumph . . . allowing each individual the pleasure of self-discovery as well as those marvelous and extraordinary things that must exist somewhere out there in the universe" (*Jazz et vin de palme,* 152). Dongala's combination of references to both sides of the Atlantic further underlines the interconnectedness of these people, in which the musical project of jazz captures the fracturing of humanity but reconfigures it by inaugurating a new paradigm of harmony. The repeated usage of the initials "J.C." in order to refer to John Coltrane compel us, as readers, to establish links with Jesus Christ, thereby further underlining the musician's martyrdom. This reflection, by implication, affords Dongala the space to define his own artistic vision, whereby art allows "each individual the pleasure of self-discovery as well as those marvelous and extraordinary things that must exist somewhere out there in the universe" (*Jazz et vin de palme,* 152). This creates a striking contrast to the writings of official authors, since the faithfulness of official writings to the dissemination of an uncompromising world view precludes this dimension.

The ultimate conclusion we can draw from these stories is that the irresponsible exercise of power has denied individuals their aspirations, that is to say the possibility to become fully participating citizens. Government authorities are shown to pursue their ideological policies, which exclude dialogue, while, as Dongala observes, the artist "neither tries to persuade nor to bring happiness" (*Jazz et vin de palme,* 152). Anna Ridelagh's criticism of Dongala's writings for his failure to "propose solutions" therefore seems all the more problematic, since the absence of such programmatic guidelines has accorded originality to non-official productions.[35] In fact, faced with such criticism, Dongala would undoubtedly refer us back to a statement he made in 1979: "Let's be quite clear about this: I am not a spokes-man for the 'people,' I am no one's messenger, and I don't have a Guide or any heroes (in fact, as Brecht once said, 'Woe betide a people who need heroes')."[36] Dongala clearly employs realism as the framework to a satirical and polemic text and is concerned with distancing himself from the *langue de bois* paradigm exemplified by the texts of writers such as Claude-Emmanuel Eta-Onka and Xavier Okotaka-Ebale who faithfully followed the model of Socialist Realism and partisanship. Dongala is first and foremost a writer of fiction and as such free to channel his creative and imaginative inspiration without any consideration for prescriptive guidelines. While Dongala has chosen to explore a given sociological and political reality, the fictional product transcends that reality in order to generate a text that is firmly anchored in the tradition of resistance writing, exposing and ridicul-ing the targeted authorities—a fact confirmed by the text being banned for almost a decade.

The title of the collection deserves some comment. As Dongala has claimed, "there are two parts to this collection, an African one and one that takes place in the United States. On the one side 'Jazz,' and on the other 'palm-wine' that symbolizes an African façade for me" (interviews, 1994–95). Black people and their history are captured in this title, in which jazz emerges in the framework of transplantation and displacement, while palm wine establishes associations with the non-transplanted African cultural roots. Perhaps this is what is contained in Dabla's suggestion, according to which, "from symbol to symbol, is Dongala not throwing down a bridge over the Atlantic to link two different universes contained in the Black American? Is he not reconciling two peoples separated by history?"[37] Indeed, as Homi Bhabha has observed, it is "the intervention of the 'beyond' that establishes a boundary: a bridge, where 'presencing' begins because it captures some-thing of the estranging sense of the relocation of the home and the world—the unhomeliness—that is the condition of the extra-territorial and cross-cultural initiations."[38] Furthermore, Edouard Glissant's triangular framework for the exploration of the African Diaspora in his book *Caribbean Discourse* provides an excellent framework for the contextualization of these multiple points of contact and the deconstruction of these intercultural dynamics.[39] Glissant establishes a plethora of links between Africa, the Caribbean, and continental America: musical (jazz, reggae, salsa); cultural (*antillanité, négritude*, Harlem Renaissance, return to Africa); political (Algeria, Black Power, Black Muslims, Fanon, independence, decolonization, pan-African-ism, slavery, Toussaint Louverture); artistic (poets and storytellers, indigenism, contemporary writing).[40] The interconnectedness of the African and American spheres is thus further underlined, as Dongala's text can be recontextualized within broader geographical and political parameters.

While African America may provide a working model, Dongala recognizes the prevalence of interracial tensions in that space. His own experiences in America have afforded him this perspective, and, through a number of extra-textual acts, some of these experiences are factored in. Writing becomes a space in which to explore his own ambiguities, and he is deliberately not judgmental and arbitrary. In *Le feu des origines*, the great-grandson of Lukeni, Bunseki Lukeni (the resemblance to Dongala's middle name, Boundzéki, is of course evident), studied in the United States and returns to the Congo with his African American wife, Muriel (Murielle was the name of the woman with whom the African American Meeks was in love in *Un fusil dans la main, un poème dans la poche*). The implications of the following statement are clear: "Nothing was impossible for them: Lukeni had married a woman from the other side of the world without any problem whereas Mankunku couldn't marry the woman he loved on the pretext that she was a foreigner and that her city, a day's walk from his village, was too far from his village for him" (*The Fire of Origins*, 236).

Dongala emphasizes the quest for common ground, epitomized in his writings by the title of his collection of short stories, *Jazz et vin de palme*, and the story by that name in which people come together by overcoming differences. The search for unity and community finds its most striking manifestation in *Le feu des origines* when the central protagonist, Mankunku, declares that "a state between the world of the forgotten ancestors and us the living, between life and non-life; that's the transition I've been looking for" (*The Fire of Origins*, 232). This union is expressed symbolically through the character's discovery of mercury (a substance that is neither liquid nor solid), which he describes as "Water which doesn't make things wet!" (*The Fire of Origins*, 232), and perhaps most memorably when his wife gives birth to an albino child.

During interviews in 1994–95, Dongala confirmed that the stories included in the collection *Jazz et vin de palme* were all written at different historical junctures, a fact that does not in any way diminish the significance of the organizational structure of the collection and subject matter of each story, and that respectively calls upon the reader clearly and unambiguously to address those links that exist between the African, American, and African American framework. In *Le feu des origines*, Bunseki suggests that Mankunku record his memoirs: "You could dictate them to Muriel, and it would make an extraordinary document for our children" (*The Fire of Origins*, 228). As an African American woman, Muriel has a different perspective "because of the cumulative experience of her people's short history in America" (*The Fire of Origins*, 225). The importance she attributes to recording history through writing captures the fundamental paradox between orality and literacy, given that the gesture of writing history down will serve to both preserve it and simultaneously deny it its dynamic dimension. Nevertheless, it suggests a way in which the past can be employed for the purpose of testimony.

There is an added urgency in writing this down before it is, literally, lost forever. As the Nigerian author Wole Soyinka recently claimed, "A people who do not preserve their memory are a people who have forfeited their history."[41] This dimension acknowledges and underlines the importance of memory in the nation-building process, and in an intertextual gesture to Ahmadou Hampaté Ba and his famous statement "when an old person dies in Africa, it is the same thing as a library burning" Mankunku is described as "this old man, a living museum and library of the past" (*The Fire of Origins*, 225). By further extending the analogy to the word "fire" in the title of *Le feu des origines*, Dongala's cyclical novel becomes that document, thereby reproducing the African *gnosis* according to which the circular nature of time is underlined. The younger generation comes to him for sources and origins, creating a symbiotic dependency which serves to counteract government attempts to eradicate customs and traditions. As Lukeni tells the child Mankunku "'The story of a people shouldn't die with those who have lived it, it should be transmitted from mouth to mouth, from memory to memory to the grandchildren of our grandchildren'" (*The Fire of Origins*, 41). The text is thus both a testimony to history and a critique of history, in which the week changes from four days to seven days, altering memory, the past, and of course storytelling itself as the reader moves from the bush as locus for the indigenous world to the urban topography that symbolizes the modernity-obsessed perspective. The urban space provides the occasion for the encounter with the technological dominance of the colonial enterprise, culminating in the building of the Congo–Ocean railway (1921–34), whereby "the train, that immense fuming monster brought here by the foreigners" (*The Fire of Origins*, 111–12) links the "fire" of the technological machinery with the engineering of history.

Genealogy is thus presented as a key tenet to the construction of identity, and as an essential component in the fight against amnesiac revisionism. For Anyinefa, "national construction is a difficult task that requires the mobilization of all the country's citizens" ("Intertextuality," 7). For this to successfully occur, Dongala provides a distance from artificial constructs, and a broader contextualization of historical events. As Mankunku's mentor wisely states, "The search for wisdom does not mean breaking with one's heritage, my child, all things follow each other" (*The Fire of Origins*, 45).

Rewriting African History

The most fundamental contribution Dongala makes through his novel *Le feu des origines* comes from his engagement with the complicated process of telling history. Connecting with Patrice Lumumba's claim in one of the opening epigraphs to this book, namely, that "the time will come when Africa will write its own history," Dongala's text suggests ways in which one may begin to respond to the dual dimension of Lumumba's statement: first, by locating an African version of historical events in oral history that distances itself from the authoritative attempts of ethnography to delineate the parameters of an Occidental interpretation of events; and second, by insisting on foregrounding a version of African history in which complicity and collaboration are acknowledged as an essential step toward achieving reconciliation. Dongala's text thus attempts to chart a historical narrative that begins with an exploration of pre-colonial times, colonial contact, and finally the path to independence, autonomous rule, and the emergence of the one-party state.

Dongala's text plays a crucial role in incorporating multiple voices and in challenging the binary constructs that too often characterize discursive treatment of the colonizer/colonized dynamic. In shifting the exclusive burden of responsibility away from the colonizer, Dongala makes an important contribution toward the demystification of the Golden Age myth associated with pre-colonial Africa and extends this gesture by insisting on the importance of approaching the colonizer/colonized dynamic as a mutually constitutive network of relations, thereby rejoining the framework provided by Mbembe's notion of "promiscuity."[42]

The eight chapter divisions correspond to broad historical categories that range from accounts of pre-colonial relations, the arrival of Western explorers, travelers, missionaries, and colonizers, to colonization, anti-colonialism, nationalism, independence, and revolution.[43] In each section, Dongala highlights moments of complicity and collaboration between various power structures and social actors that serve to accentuate social tensions and rivalries. This is important in recognizing how colonialism was able to exploit this conflict and capitalize upon the authoritarian impulses of the colonial subjects themselves.[44] Commenting, for example, on the discord that accompanies Mankunku's mysterious birth, Lukeni exclaims: "Do you know what precipitated this chaos? Well, it was because of the clans, the bloodlines, the families, who fought, killed each other in competition for the throne; clans which made and unmade alliances with the whim of the wind, men who went so far as to make pacts with strangers against their own people" (*The Fire of Origins*, 11). Indeed, what is so original about Dongala's text is the manner in which he seeks to reflect the diversity of voices offering alternative versions of historical events, thereby further complicating the construction of memory in the oral sphere as well: "People said: 'They come from the bottom of the waters, from the land of shadows where the dead abide. . . .' or else: 'They came in great whales breathing smoke, they emerged from the ocean where the spirits live . . .'" (*The Fire of Origins*, 51). "People also said: 'It's better not to fight them because they use extraordinary weapons which spit thunder . . .' and others added: 'It's better to welcome them, to ally ourselves with them and their power in order that we, in turn, may conquer neighboring ethnicities'" (*The Fire of Origins*, 52). And finally, marking the collaborative moment itself, the "convivial" relationship between "the *commandement* and its 'subjects,'"[45] Dongala insists on the native subject's willingness to exercise complicity and to follow orders: "Go into the villages catch all the holdouts and all the lazy bastards who don't want to harvest rubber take them prisoner whip them until the village pays its taxes understand dirty monkeys if not it's you who'll pay for them but if you do your job well you'll be chiefs we'll make you chiefs like us" (*The Fire of Origins*, 53).

Significantly, in his commitment to presenting a version of history that is always heterogeneous, Dongala also underscores the emergence of pan-African consciousness and the coexistence of complicity and oppositionality:

> If entire villages were destroyed or subdued, entire ethnicities dispersed or conquered, if chiefs rallied to join newcomers, it didn't all happen in the same way or to the same degree. There were those who failed to struggle and abandoned in their flight everything they had, or, taking the foreigners for long-awaited ancestors, kneeled before them; there were those who struggled a little, or rather, pretended to struggle before submitting; there were those who, either due to their naivete or their sense of hospitality, were duped; there were those who struggled heroically and were massacred; and finally, there were those who knew how to resist, taking militiamen as prisoners. (*The Fire of Origins*, 57)

Indeed, in discussing the relationship between the colonizer and the colonized subject, the question of translation serves as a symbol of the "promiscuity" Mbembe alludes to. Straddling two spheres of influence, the *évolué* translator and the process of translation itself inevitably alter the original narrative through choice, selection, and omission, thus influencing the outcome of negotiations and ultimately the process of writing and recording history.[46] The process of negotiations and exchanges and the "signing" of legal treaties and contracts heralded the introduction of print culture in a nonliterate environment that enabled the colonizer to capitalize on local greed and enact an effective policy of divide and rule: "It is finished, it was finished. A simple sign had just changed the history of the world, of their world. Years later, when their descendants would gather in front of the governor's mansion to protest against their exploitation and victimization, this very piece of paper, now yellowed and dog-eared, would be shown to them" (*The Fire of Origins*, 71).

Dongala insists on exploring and denouncing authoritarianism without actually naming the topographic space, on unveiling the machinery in place and analyzing how authoritarian systems reproduce themselves—because, as Lukeni argues, "all people bent on conquest of other people are alike" (*The Fire of Origins*, 77). A truthful treatment of events is of paramount importance to Mankunku: "The foreigners have made their contribution to our present misery, perhaps, even for sure, but we also have to look the truth in the eye, Father. Without our cooperation things wouldn't have gone so badly, they wouldn't have had such an easy time of it. . . . We'd better do everything we can to see that future generations don't assume that all of this was the fault of the foreigners. We must never forget, father, our own appetites and our own weaknesses" (*The Fire of Origins*, 90–91). The objective consists in expanding the parameters of the dualistic rhetoric associated with accounts of colonizer/colonized relations, in order to establish a discursive realm in which reconciliatory objectives can be addressed more honestly.

For Mankunku, the nation becomes an object of public consciousness with the sudden realization that "All of a sudden, for him this land whose borders had been set at random by a foreign conquest, this land made up of ethnic mixtures and fragments of disparate ethnic groups, took on an actual existence, a soul" (*The Fire of Origins*, 209). While embracing the construction of a nation within the juridical boundaries determined by colonial powers, he has nevertheless clearly expressed his opposition to the current state model for its failure to transcend the model of unity and to recognize and validate ethnicity and diversity. As Mankunku tells his father, "Our society [pre-colonial] was also a violent society. . . . Do you think that a society lacking the flexibility to hold on to those who are different is a good society, a just society?" (The Fire of Origins, 90). Dongala has successfully created fictional environments that allow the reader to articulate the obvious answer to this question, namely, that flexibility is an absolute prerequisite to accommodating and accepting the other and promoting successful communal existence.

Mankunku relentlessly questions the new direction Africa is taking: "would this new Africa being born add intolerance to the conformity already suffocating everything?" (The Fire of Origins, 210). The anachronistic nature of this statement enables him to pose and simultaneously answer questions that have, at least historically, already been answered. In the final chapter of Le feu des origines, the repeated use and play on the word "feu" (in French, the word "feu" also means "the late" when alluding to a deceased person and thus serves as a further gesture inscribing the importance of the past and of memory in building the future) culminates in the phrase "to rediscover, as on the first morning of the world, the primitive brilliance of the fire of origins" (The Fire of Origins, 247–48), that rejoins the epigraph to Dongala's novel. The cyclical pattern is now complete, and from this fire the implication is that one can hope for new growth. Similarly, from Un fusil dans la main, un poème dans la poche, to Jazz et vin de palme, and then to Le feu des origines, from Meeks to Mankunku, and through the African stories, Dongala traces a historical path that ends with "these things moving and burning like a wave surging from John Coltrane's saxophone, these things pure as a cry on the first morning of the world" (The Fire of Origins, 248), thus rejoining the North American sphere, and the end of the story "A Love Supreme." Dongala imposes a pan-Diasporic dialogue with the transplanted people which does not end with the transatlantic voyage. These multiple points of reference are perhaps most convincingly expressed by Paul Gilroy in his book The Black Atlantic: Modernity and Double Consciousness, where experience is conceived as "rooted in and routed through the special stress that grows with every effort involved in trying to face (at least) two ways at once."[47]

Dongala's statements concerning his writing underline his concern with confronting the contemporary political situation in the Congo. The sociological reality of the scientific-Socialist era in the Congo informed Dongala's writing until 1991, and he was determined to articulate his opposition to the oppressive monopoly of power. For him, alienating government practices precluded the possibility of transcending the concept of national unity in order to achieve a social environment in which diversity could be validated without fracturing community. Political commitment remains central to Dongala's artistic project, yet as a committed artist, he has not subjugated the artistic dimension to ideological utility. As Dongala stated recently:

> The problem is that no matter what people might say, the writer is not there to preach and provide a guide indicating how people should be-have. . . . you always start from somewhere in order to write something, but the writer's artistry is to take something that belongs in a little corner somewhere and make it accessible so that someone in say America can understand it. (Interview, 1994–95)

In some ways, the difference between official and non-official writers might just reside in the distinction one could delineate between *reproducing* and *producing*. The former could be seen as governmental objects with the capacity to *reproduce* doctrine much like a record player can reproduce recorded sounds, while the "artistry" of the latter would be premised on *producing* that which was not there before.

The Road to Reconciliation

Dongala's work has always incorporated a transatlantic and transnational dimension, foregrounding the importance of maintaining dialogue with the transplanted people and arguing that much can be learned from charting the respective sociopolitical trajectories and experiences relating to the displacement of the African people. His novel *Les petits garçons naissent aussi des étoiles* (Little Boys Come from the Stars) marks an interesting shift in perspective as Dongala also addresses the impact of global cultural and economic influences on francophone sub-Saharan Africa. Having denounced the authoritarianism of Marxist-Leninist regimes in his previous work, Dongala now questions Americanization and Western capitalism, thereby attributing a more sinister influence than he had previously accorded to America. These influences include television (CNN), radio (BBC World Service), videos, cinema (James Bond, the Ninjas, Arnold Schwarzenegger, Rambo, Goldorak, etc.), athletic clothing (Nike, Reebok, etc.), music (Michael Jackson, rap, raggamuffin), the Internet or the information superhighway, and CD-ROMs. These elements come to symbolize some of the more significant transitions that have accompanied the democratization of post-scientific-Socialist Congo and are all the more significant to the extent that they suggest the incorporation of francophone sub-Saharan Africa in shifting global alignments that no longer automatically duplicate established colonial and neocolonial alignments.

Dongala's work has always been concerned with the question of reconciliation, and with recording a historical narrative that challenges official versions. While *Les petits garçons naissent aussi des étoiles* is located in an imaginary African country, the sociological circumstances treated clearly restrict the focus to francophone sub-Saharan Africa and even, arguably, to the Congo itself. This question is marginal, however, in comparison to those raised by the novel pertaining to reconciliation during post-independence rule, and more specifically, since 1991.

In *Les petits garçons naissent aussi des étoiles*, the narrator is a young man of fifteen years of age, named Matapari (meaning "trouble"), born on August 15, 1980, a date that coincides with the twentieth anniversary of the fictitious country's political independence (as indeed the year also did for most francophone sub-Saharan African countries). The novel is constructed around this young man's narrative, adopting an ironical voice that is similar, in many ways, to that of the militant in the short story entitled "La cérémonie" (The Ceremony). However, the voice has matured somewhat to produce a narrative that skillfully exposes and denounces the inauthenticity of officialdom. This device allows for the fictitious country's historical narrative to be recounted, one that incorporates the path to political independence and the emergence of scientific-Socialism, and which culminates in the staging of a National Conference as a transitory step toward democratization. The young boy's uncle, Boula Boula, undertakes the task of relating to him a version of the country's history that has been subjected to numerous revisionist gestures with each political transition. A somewhat lengthy quotation will serve to illustrate this point as Matapari organizes what he has learned:

> He explained to me that our country had once been occupied by white people, who had arrived here by accident on ships whose sails had been pushed by the tropical winds toward the African coast. The white people then began systematically scouring our coastland and even our inland regions, stealing people and selling them as slaves. . . . Then there were missionaries who came to chase our ancestors out of their graves, out of the groves and rivers, and out of the huts they inhabited, to replace them with Jesus Christ, the Bible, and the cross; and the armed men who came along with them and installed themselves. In these parts they were French. They ruled over us, ran the country, exploited us, taught us their language, sent us to their schools, and gave us new ancestors called

Gauls. . . . These French so exploited us that twenty years ago we re-volted against this exploitation called colonialism and became indepen-dent, that is, masters of our destiny. . . . Unfortunately, the three or four leaders who took over from the French kept obeying these same French and other whites, having sold out to what uncle called imperialism and neocolonialism. That's why the young military men overthrew these lead-ers in a series of coups d'état, killed them off, and took over. But these army men weren't any better, and so other army men plotted and over-threw them, and so on and so forth, until this day of my unexpected birth on the twentieth anniversary of the day that one of these military men . . . set up a "revolutionary" system based on something called scien-tific socialism. . . . He didn't tell me what that meant exactly but ex-plained enough to indicate that this was something completely new, a definitive break with slavery, colonialism, neocolonialism, imperialism. (*Little Boys Come from the Stars*, 6–7)

This historical narrative serves to underline similarities between various authoritarian models that have successively denounced their predecessors in order to adhere to their own official versions of history. The historical narrative Matapari has registered is itself erected on a fiction upon which the post-independence Congolese nation has been engineered. As the young narrator grows up, he exposes contradictions and gradually rejects the official lie, effectively enacting the paradigm suggested by Soyinka and thereby al-lowing for "a truthful but critical embrace of our past" (Soyinka, 61). This is achieved most effectively through the focus on legal proceedings.

Testimony and Law

Matapari has elected to record televised trials on his VCR, and he re-plays them in order to ensure that his account is accurate: "I taped the most dramatic episodes on a VCR, and as I tell you this story I'm reviewing a few scenes so that my account, even if I don't keep to the precise chronological order, will be as faithful as possible" (*Little Boys Come from the Stars*, 126). This technology suggests radically new modes of treating historical data but has significant implications, given the process of selection and the editing criteria employed. For while the transcript of legal proceedings would be available from the initial broadcast, the narrator's decision to record and comment upon only selected moments voids his initial statement concern-ing the imperative of sustaining accuracy, given that he privileges only those episodes of the trial he finds "the most dramatic." The trial in question concerns a man named Bissila, accused of conspiracy against the authorities and of detonating an explosive device.

In theory, at least, the courtroom should provide the opportunity for testimony, for the accused to "tell his story," his version of events. Based on evidence gathered by the defense and prosecutor, two (at least) versions of events are narrated, in an attempt to reconstruct a *truthful* account of historical events. The burden thus lies in the respective ability of these juridical representatives to recount a convincing, plausible story, to arrange and manipulate the evidence into a coherent narrative that will be rendered believable and compelling to a judge or jury who were not present at the historical moment the transgression was committed. These circumstances are problematized in Dongala's work to the extent that the accused is always denied the opportunity of telling *his* story. For example, when his narrative (testimony) challenges received notions, the prosecutor appeals to the judge to strike the account from the official record of the proceedings: "'Comrade Magistrate,' the prosecutor continued, 'I ask that you strike the defendant's statement from the record'" (*Little Boys Come from the Stars*, 133). The justificatory premise for striking the defendant's statement is that it is *untruthful*. The judge's response, "'Objection sustained,' the magistrate concurred while rolling up his sleeves. 'This entire section will be stricken from the record'" (*Little Boys Come from the Stars*, 133), underlines the collaborative relationship between the judge and prosecutor who refuse to accommodate multiple versions of history. The prosecutor's position is based on the discrepancy between the spoken testimony and the written confession: "Comrade Magistrate, there is no point continuing. This man lies like he breathes, and he will never tell the truth. You have read his signed confession" (*Little Boys Come from the Stars*, 135). The defense lawyer's insistence that the confession was obtained by forcible means is ignored. The verdict, the accepted version of the *truth*, has already been determined; the only opportunity the accused has of negating this predetermined verdict is to offer evidence in the form of eyewitness testimony: "Can you give us the name of a witness who can confirm that you were really at Punta Negra that day?" (*Little Boys Come from the Stars*, 135). When the defense produces such a witness, the judge violates customary procedures by preventing the defense's witness from assuming that role: "General, you have not been accused, you are not even a witness in this trial. You are here only to clear up a point or two; it is thus unnecessary for you to take the oath" (*Little Boys Come from the Stars*, 139). The witness is denied the right to testify on behalf of the accused, and when he does actually speak, it becomes evident that his narrative is tainted, altered by official instructions.

Similar corrupt practices are evidenced in the trial of Old Likibi in the short story by that name. In that case, the proceedings are structured as a truth-finding exercise, but when Old Likibi speaks he is immediately interrupted and asked to be more selective in the organization of his testimony. He is not therefore free to tell *his* story, and the version he does recount is dismissed as untruthful: "it really is a terrible shame, for you have told us nothing but lies!" (*Jazz et vin de palme*, 72). There is no space for the accused's testimony to be recorded as a constitutive component of the historical narrative. The transition to democracy in the Congo was accompanied by a National Conference in 1991 as an attempt to promote inclusive dialogue and to chart the path to democracy.

Democratization and National Conferences

> *After slavery, colonialism, neocolonialism, and scientific*
> *socialism, democracy descended upon us one August*
> *morning, in the middle of the dry season.*
> —Little Boys Come from the Stars, 155

The transition to democracy in the Congo generated an explosion of political pluralism and the formation of political organizations and parties, phenomena Dongala has incorporated and transposed into fiction in the concluding section of *Les petits garçons naissent aussi des étoiles*. The National Conference was televised, and the degree of irony is captured by the narrator as he undertakes the task of describing the reasoning behind such a gathering:

> We were told that just as an astronaut could not go from the high pressure of his cabin to the low pressure of space without first going through a decompression air lock, so we could not go from single-party rule to liberal, pluralist democracy without passing through a sort of political air lock, meaning a national convention. This convention was a decontamination zone (just as astronauts were put in quarantine when they came back from the moon), without which we risked transplanting the totalitarian virus onto the new democratic soil that lay just over the horizon. It enabled all the sons and daughters of the nation to learn from a past unworthy of a civilized land, from all these years of blood and tears under the thumb of the Single Party. We would then commit to never let

it happen again, to never lie again, never steal again, never kill again, never covet our neighbor's wife. Finally we would part with an embrace in the spirit of brotherly love. (*Little Boys Come from the Stars*, 195–96)

In this description of the discourse that characterized the National Conference, reconciliation is underscored as the primary objective, yet there is no attempt to confront history in the way Dongala does—acknowledging authoritarianism, complicity, and collaboration. These essential measures are strikingly absent from the official transcript, as participants abdicate all responsibility for the disintegration of the postcolony, preferring instead to subscribe to a revisionist narrative that reproduces patterns of behavior indissociable from previous attempts at achieving political reform. Indeed, the futility of the National Conference was vindicated by the collapse of the democratic experiment, the exacerbation of ethnic conflict, and finally the violent civil conflict from June to October 1997 that resulted in thousands of deaths. One of the most significant aspects which the narrator fastens upon concerns the manner in which history is actually *rewritten* by the conference delegates:

Then they began their speeches. . . . Why were all these people pretending that all the wrong that had been done to this country, the chaos, the political murders, the economic crimes, the divorces, and poor harvests, had been the fault of one man alone, our current President, whom no one considered the Enlightened Guide of Our Revolution anymore? He was now evil incarnate. Apparently, he had seized power and then ruled for close to twenty years all by himself, and none of them had contributed to keeping the system in place. (*Little Boys Come from the Stars*, 198)

The narrator attempts to make sense of proceedings but is clearly confused and disoriented by the attempt to produce a revised official history of the scientific-Socialist era:

You do understand, as I told you, that I'd been born fourteen years earlier, and I had known only one president, the very one we were now spitting on. . . . I had been told that adults hardly ever changed their convictions, so what triggered their about-face—what was the kick in their ass that now propelled us into democracy? (*Little Boys Come from the Stars*, 198)

The narrator's disorientation stems from the fact that there is nothing in his cumulative life experience that corroborates the delegates' observations.

The fundamental question remains to determine whether or not Dongala's texts bring us any closer to the truth than other narratives and official transcripts. Indeed, if any analogy can be established between the objective of Dongala's work and that of a truth commission, such an analogy may reside in the contribution such exercises can make toward the future of the nation-building imperative. Soyinka's observations on this dimension are useful, since for him,

> the necessity of such commissions is surely vindicated—to enthrone, once and for all, the desirable goal of Truth. Beyond Truth, the very process of its exposition becomes part of the necessity, and, depending on the nature of the past that it addresses, the impact it has made on the lives of the citizens and the toll it has taken on their sense of belonging, it may be regarded as being capable of guaranteeing or foundering the future of a nation. (Soyinka, 11–12)

Perhaps one should consider abandoning and relinquishing the imperative and indispensability for absolute truth and accept that such agendas can offer only limited results. The refusal to adopt such a framework may, as Soyinka has suggested, potentially have represented the most significant shortcoming of the Truth and Reconciliation Commission (TRC): "Truth as prelude to reconciliation, that seems logical enough; but Truth as the justification, as the sole exaction or condition for Reconciliation? That is what constitutes a stumbling block in the South African proceedings" (Soyinka, 13). Then, by incorporating the polyvocality, we would be free to recognize the fallacious nature of truth itself and accept that reconciliation need not consist in establishing one official voice or master narrative. In fact, as Charles Maier has argued with reference to truth commissions, "a truth commission is thus predicated on the idea that establishing the historical record, more precisely, and securing its public acknowledgment, is a requisite for successful democratization. But what is the relation of that record to 'history' or to what a historian does?"[48] This would constitute a step toward renouncing the quest for power that enables us to wash our hands of guilt, and to claim that the authoritarian impulse could not live in us. Instead, each side relinquishes power and authoritarianism in order to allow reconciliation to transform itself into compromise and synthesis. In this paradigm, reconciliation would not then be so much about truth as it would be about giving voice, incorporating multiple narratives to the process of telling history.

Indeed, Mankunku appears to have understood the implications when he takes the initiative to meet with his family for a frank discussion in order to "open up the sin, just as one lances an abscess. Thus the infection would be publicly cleaned up. . . . Mankunku remembered old Lukeni the just, who, in every dispute, tried to re-establish equilibrium" (*The Fire of Origins*, 214). This framework gains proximity to the agenda of the TRC in South Africa, according to which the notion of justice itself was expanded in order to become part of a different project, insisting instead on the distinction between *retributive* and *restorative* justice. In the words of the chair of the TRC, Archbishop Desmond Tutu, restorative justice "is concerned not so much with punishment as with correcting imbalances, restoring broken relationships—with healing, harmony and reconciliation."[49] Restorative justice then, according to Elizabeth Kiss's analysis, offers a framework in which it becomes possible "(1) to affirm and restore the dignity of those whose human rights have been violated; (2) to hold perpetrators accountable, emphasizing the harm that they have done to individual human beings; and (3) to create social conditions in which human rights will be respected."[50] Soyinka has been critical of the degree to which the TRC has engaged in "correcting" the "imbalances" alluded to in Tutu's statement. For him, the restorative dimension lacks the reparative and restitutional one, in that "the essential is to establish the principle: that some measure of restitution is always essential after dispossession" (Soyinka, 36), since "reparations, we repeat, serve as a cogent critique of history and thus a potent restraint on its repetition" (Soyinka, 83).

The period of transition in the Congo from one-party rule to a pluralist democracy shared many parallels with the earlier South African context evoked by Nadine Gordimer in her essay "Living in the Interregnum." Taken from Antonio Gramsci's writings, the notion of the interregnum designates that point of transition where "the old is dying, and the new cannot be born," which Gordimer goes on to further qualify as existing "not only between two social orders but also between two identities, one known and discarded, the other unknown and undetermined."[51] Subsequent attempts at establishing what Njabulo Ndebele has described as a "reconstructive national environment" following political transition often require the type of radical social and political reformulation suggested in the conclusion of Dongala's novel *Le feu des origines*.[52] Dongala's own actions are paradigmatic in this context, as exemplified by his recent comments in an introduction to a lecture by former South African president F. W. De Klerk during a visit to Simon's Rock College of Bard. While in actuality Dongala would surely attribute only a limited role to the former South African leader in the process of social reform, he nevertheless accredited him with his "vision to pull South Africa out of a political dead end—his courage to rise above the [apartheid] ideology he was nurtured in—and his political skill to translate his vision into acts to help transform South Africa into a multi-racial society."[53] Dongala effectively demonstrated the type of imaginative step necessary (what Mark Behr has termed "moral imagination") in moving toward a reconciliation that would incorporate everyone in a broader network of relations in which all judgments would be prefaced with statements of complicity.[54] For Soyinka, this imaginative prerequisite is contained in the notion of "inventiveness":

> Truth alone is never enough to guarantee reconciliation. It has little to do with crime and punishment but with inventiveness—devising a social formula that would minister to the wrongs of dispossession on the one hand, chasten those who deviate from the humane communal order on the other, serve as a criterion for the future conduct of that society, even at times of stress and only then, heal. Memory—of what has been, of acts of commission or omission, of a responsibility abdicated—affects the future conduct of power in any form. (Soyinka, 81–82)

Dongala's words in 1994–95, "we missed our turn towards democracy, from the one-party system to democracy" (interviews), have proved prophetic as the Congo has struggled to establish post–National Conference social and political stability. The fundamental questions raised in Dongala's writings concern the disorientation that accompanies political transition, whether it be from the colonial to the postcolonial, or from scientific-Socialism to democracy. The inclination to construct binary categories between the colonizer and colonized, or African leaders and their opponents, and the accompanying ethical labels and arbitrary divisions into categories of "good" and "evil" are themselves tremendously problematic. While the construction of the colonizer as a negative entity was of course justified, this dynamic has been further complicated during the post-independence era, since once emancipation had been achieved, once the enemy (the colonizer) had been overthrown and removed, this allowed for the "good" (the colonized) to control power. The additional degree of complexity was introduced when the "good" in turn became "evil." Indeed, this has been the case in many independent francophone sub-Saharan African nations and has been documented in works as diverse as Ousmane Sembène's novel and film *Xala*, Sony Labou Tansi's novel *L'état honteux*, and Alioum Fantouré's novel *Le cercle des tropiques*.[55] These transitions have created a disorientation that a National Conference or Truth and Reconciliation Commission could seek to remedy. Truth telling allows for perpetrators to demonstrate their humanity but also simultaneously allows for victims to articulate narratives that official history has declared nonexistent. Confession then has the possibility of enacting healing, restitution, reparation, retribution, and ultimately, reconciliation.

6 NATIONAL CONFERENCES AND MEDIA DECENTRALIZATION IN FRANCOPHONE AFRICA

*You had to read foreign newspapers to be troubled
about our fate.* —HENRI LOPES[1]

*Of my soul the retina leans to expand
daily because by a thousand stories
I was scorched
A new skin.* —ANTJIE KROG[2]

Africa was not, of course, unaffected by the realignment of global powers that took place during the last decade or so of the twentieth century. Indeed, these events served to further underline the singularity of the francophone sub-Saharan African context as countries underwent remarkable cultural and political transitions. Although this concluding chapter does not offer an exhaustive account of these transitions, issues pertaining to governmental reform and the particular circumstances generated for political dissidence by media decentralization will be addressed and connections established to some of the book's general themes—orality and popular culture, official literature and propaganda, resistance and democratization mechanisms.

While African countries had experimented with and adopted a plethora of political models in the immediate aftermath of independence—monarchies, military rule, Marxism-Leninism, African Socialism, and so forth—various experiments with democratic and electoral reform took place from 1990 onward throughout francophone sub-Saharan Africa (Burkina Faso, Cameroon, the Central African Republic, Guinea, Senegal, etc.), and National Conferences were held in the spirit of reconciliation in countries with political histories as diverse as Benin, Chad, the Congo, Gabon, Madagascar, Mali, Niger, Togo, and Zaire.[3] As Patrick Manning has shown,

> the strong common roots and the shared traditions of francophone African nations brought close interactions and commonalities to the experi-

ence of their democratization movements. . . . The demands for conven-
ing conferences of the "forces vives de la nation" and for establishing
pluralistic political order became the most prominent elements in this
wave of contestation.[4]

Yet, while optimism may have characterized the initial sentiment during
the preliminary stages of sociopolitical transformation, entrenched postcolonial alignments and configurations would more often than not prove
resilient to the multifarious attempts made toward their displacement. As
John F. Clark has argued, "in the cases in which political transitions took
place, it became clearer that political change did not necessarily spell an
end to corruption or undemocratic politics."[5]

National Conferences and Reconciliation in Francophone Africa

Benin was the first country to hold a National Conference, February
19–28, 1990, and then to conduct multiparty elections in 1991 in a country
where Mathieu Kérékou's Marxist government had been in power since 1972.
Similar attempts at political transition occurred across francophone Africa—
Gabon's conference was held in 1990, and others followed in 1991 in the
Congo, Mali, Niger, and Togo. Marien Ngouabi had already held a National Conference in the Congo in 1972, but unlike their historical precursors, these new National Conferences were not conceived as platforms for
the ruling parties to outline their policies and guidelines but rather as *Conférence nationale souveraine,* that is *sovereign* National Conferences, invested
with the power to issue new constitutional and governmental directives.

Since independence and up until the 1991 National Conference, power
had changed hands in the Congo on five occasions. Fulbert Youlou remained
in power until 1963 when, following widespread demonstrations, riots, and
a general strike that came to a head between August 13 and 15—days that
are now commemorated each year as the *Trois Glorieuses*—he was replaced
by Alphonse Massamba-Débat. Massamba-Débat's own presidency lasted
only until 1968. The Congo's first great ideologue, Marien Ngouabi, then
became president and remained in office until his assassination in 1977.
The fourth administration, headed by Joachim Yhombi-Opango, lasted only
until 1979 when he was voted out of office by the Central Committee, leaving the way to Denis Sassou Nguesso's twelve years as president.

A number of events triggered the movement away from Marxism-Leninism toward a multiparty system. As Clark has demonstrated, "both an economic crisis and a crisis of legitimacy were responsible for the collapse of

the ancien régime in Congo,"[6] and "Benin's stunning National Conference in 1990, which promised transition to democracy through elections, strengthened cries for *multipartisme* in francophone Africa" (Clark, 66). Of course, the dismantling of the Berlin Wall in 1989 and the fracturing of the Soviet Union contributed toward political transition in the Congo, and as Sassou Nguesso has remarked, "the consequences of the end of the Soviet empire and the collapse of the Berlin Wall were debated in a Central Committee session of the Party."[7] Thus, on July 4, 1990, the Central Committee of the Parti Congolais du Travail (Congolese Workers Party) decided to abandon Marxism-Leninism, advocated a multiparty system, and finally agreed to hold a National Conference that would get under way on February 25, 1991. The conference would end up lasting longer than in any other francophone country, with proceedings officially adjourning on June 10, 1991.

The appointment of a religious figure, in the guise of Catholic Bishop Ernest Kombo, accorded the proceedings the semblance of neutrality, a measure that duplicated the model adopted in Benin and that would subsequently provide the framework for the South African Truth and Reconciliation Commission (TRC) under the chairmanship of Archbishop Desmond Tutu. As Manning has argued, the initial focus of the conference was essentially provided by attacks on Sassou Nguesso's regime, and "the apologies offered by Sassou Nguesso for the excesses of his regime matched and went beyond those of Kérékou in Benin" (Manning, 198). The conference nevertheless did allow for a partial reconfiguration of the political landscape. As Clark has shown, "the Congolese National Conference resulted in a widely accepted transitional government and the unequivocal commitment of the political class to establish a new order" (Clark, 69). André Milongo was appointed prime minister at the head of an interim government, and presidential elections were scheduled for June 1992. The preamble to the document produced by the commission on June 4, 1991, read as follows:

> Under the one-Party system in particular, the dignity, liberty, peace, prosperity, and love of the homeland were signed away or set back by totalitarianism, the confusion of the authorities, nepotism, tribalism, regionalism, social inequalities, the violation of basic liberties. . . . Intolerance and political violence, the violation of individual and collective rights, arbitrary executions of real or supposed political opponents, and the villainous assassination of peaceful citizens have plunged the country into mourning, and fueled and exacerbated divisions between the various ethnic communities that make up the Congolese nation.[8]

After acknowledging these facts, the commission proceeded to ratify a series of resolutions:

> Consequently, the Congolese people:
> Assert their firm commitment to build a legal state and a united and fraternal nation; solemnly proclaim their right to resist and engage in civil disobedience should any individual or group seize or exercise power through a coup d'état or any other form of violence; reaffirms its attachment to the principles of democratic pluralism. . . . (Boulaga, 196)

The emphasis on culpabilizing Sassou Nguesso during the conference itself hindered the objective of achieving genuine reconciliation, precisely because widespread complicity was not acknowledged and the political elite never held accountable for their participatory role in governance. Instead, the tone of the conference was characterized by the articulation of an accusatory, denunciatory, and renunciatory language, a dimension Emmanuel Dongala fastened upon and satirized in his novel *Les petits garçons naissent aussi des étoiles*.[9]

Nevertheless, the National Conferences constituted a unique forum for discussion in their objective of creating a more inclusive discursive site, one that would incorporate a broad range of voices in the process of defining and even imagining the country's post-Marxist trajectory, to account for history, and project toward future alignments. In theory at least, the National Conferences delineated the parameters of political reform and confronted the past, insisting on the return to multiparty government, elections, and constitutional reform associated with early post-independence initiatives. The National Conference in the Congo allowed for the failure of decolonization to be partially addressed, and systematically that of both colonial and post-independence rule. In one of the first books about this phenomenon, *Les conférences nationales en Afrique noire: Une affaire à suivre*, Fabien Eboussi Boulaga argued that "The determining characteristics of the African National Conferences were definitely therapy and dialogue. These represent a ritual for restoration. . . . After any destruction, fall, distraction or alienation, one needs to return to sources, to origins, with a new beginning in mind" (Boulaga, 151). While analogies to the South African TRC could be conceived as anachronistic in a discussion of francophone Africa, important parallels and intersections can be established between the National Conferences and the TRC.

The TRC was established under the Promotion of National Unity and

Reconciliation Act, No. 34 of 1995, and as Antjie Krog has explained in her compelling book *Country of My Skull: Guilt, Sorrow, and the Limits of Forgiveness in the New South Africa* "was designed to help facilitate a 'truth recovery process.' It was unique in the history of such commissions around the world in that it called for testimony before it to be held in public."[10] Already, elements found later in the South African model informed the francophone sub-Saharan African context, the most striking of which centers on the public nature of proceedings and the insistence on incorporating multiple voices (what I have described as a polyvocal framework) in the narration, recording, and confrontation of history—a radical gesture in many francophone African countries where public discourse had been the privileged domain of a hegemonic authority. Indeed, as Archbishop Desmond Tutu has argued, "We could not make the journey from a past marked by conflict, injustice, oppression, and exploitation to a new and democratic dispensation characterized by a culture of respect for human rights without coming face to face with our recent history."[11] However, he readily points out that "the trouble is that there are erroneous notions of what reconciliation is all about. Reconciliation is not about being cozy; it is not about pretending that things were other than they were. Reconciliation based on falsehood, on not facing up to reality, is not reconciliation and will not last."[12] Unfortunately, one might concur, the failure to subject the Congo's past to a process of engaged and critical scrutiny would inevitably hinder the potentiality of such a National Conference with regard to generating future stability. Comments made by South African writer Njabulo Ndebele offer a particularly insightful appraisal of circumstances, since for him "the past is knocking constantly on the doors of our perceptions, refusing to be forgotten, because it is deeply embedded in the present. To neglect it at this most crucial of moments in our history is to postpone the future."[13]

The motivating factors for National Conferences were similar, at least on the level of rhetoric, to the South African model. The cathartic dimension has been underlined in what Boulaga has described as "cathartic effervescence" (Boulaga, 171), a therapeutic component of the National Conference. Interesting parallels exist between the structure of proceedings and traditional forms of dialogue and conflict resolution in the African context. For Boulaga, "the National Conference is a re-using of the African *palabre* for its logo-therapeutic values. . . . To simply participate already constitutes an implicit commitment to renounce violence and to consent ahead of time to conciliation. . . . The *palabre* closes with a communal feast that seals the reconciliation and agreement" (Boulaga, 154–55).[14] Marie-Soleil Frère has drawn similar analogies to the context of orality:

> There is no doubt that the National Conferences constituted a contemporary manifestation of an organized *palabre*, providing the opportunity for multiple oratorical encounters. . . . Through the staging of dialogue, it has the capacity to promise, engage, and allow an interruption to the endless cycle of violence and counter-violence by aiming for reintegration rather than exclusion.[15]

I discuss this aspect later in this chapter when the analysis shifts to graphic arts and political cartoons.

In *The Burden of Memory, the Muse of Forgiveness*, Wole Soyinka questions the inadequacies and shortcomings of mechanisms or processes that investigate history, yet he nevertheless agrees that such procedures are often essential in order to map "the trajectories of prior monstrosities on a continent's power landscape, their capacity for unthinkable atrocities."[16] In many areas, political developments have pointed to the failure of the reconciliatory impulse, as Mobutu was able to hold on to power in Zaire until 1997, and Sassou Nguesso returned to office in the Congo in 1997. While the transition to a pluralist democracy may have been a fairly peaceful one in the Congo, the initial optimism of some observers—one that was not shared by many insiders—proved premature.

Post–National Conference Transition and Political Restoration

These political processes warrant additional exploration in order to adequately discern those forces that contributed to the rapid disintegration of the democratization impulse. Five stages subsequent to the National Conference in the Congo will inform this analysis: (1) Pascal Lissouba's election; (2) violent civil unrest and clashes between rival groups in 1993–94; (3) the Forum national pour la culture et la paix (National Forum for Culture and Peace), held in Brazzaville between December 19 and December 24, 1994; (4) the civil war that erupted on June 5, 1997; and (5) Sassou Nguesso's restoration.

The most important political constituencies in the Congo after the National Conference were represented by Bernard Kolélas's Mouvement Congolais pour le Développement et la Démocratie Intégrale (MCDDI), Pascal Lissouba's Union Panafricaine pour la Démocratie Sociale (UPADS), and of course the Parti Congolais du Travail (Congolese Workers Party) headed by Sassou Nguesso. In the first round of the August 1992 presidential elections, Lissouba's UPADS received 36 percent of the vote, Kolélas's MCDDI 20 percent, Sassou Nguesso's PCT 17 percent, and Milongo 10 percent. In the second round, principal coalitions were formed by the Union pour le Renouveau Démocratique (URD), made up of Kolélas and his followers, and the Alliance Nationale pour la Démocratie (AND), made up of Lissouba and Sassou Nguesso. Sassou Nguesso endorsed Lissouba, who went on to win with 61.32 percent of the vote to Kolélas's 38.68 percent and took office in August 1992 (Clark, 70–71).[17] Yet, as Clark has underlined, "the ethnoregional character of the vote was notable" (Clark, 71) and "Congo's ethnic cleavages have hindered the process of effective governance in the past, and these cleavages have again proven to be the dominant sociopolitical feature of Congo during its recent experiment in democratization" (Clark, 78).[18] The electoral process had done little to eradicate ethnic alignments and animosity, with the URD's support coming primarily from the southern regions and Brazzaville's concentration of Bakongo and Lari, and the AND's support from the southeastern region of Niari, Bouenza, and Lékoumou, along with Sassou Nguesso's strong northern support (Mbochi, etc.).[19] As Elikia M'Bokolo has observed, "although the different parties carefully chose national names, public opinion identified them quite clearly with the ethnic homelands of their leaders."[20] The next few years can be characterized by constant shifts in alignments, including violent civil unrest in late 1993 and early 1994, and with each new conflict, ethnic divisions were exacerbated and international involvement became more pronounced. Between December 19 and December 24, 1994, the Forum national pour la culture et la paix was held in Brazzaville. The agenda was essentially motivated by the imperatives of peace and reconciliation—a sort of mini–National Conference. Some of the items foregrounded in the forum's agenda are contained in Sassou Nguesso's statement, published in *La Rue Meurt:*

> An ominous threat has been hanging over our society for some time now. Praiseworthy efforts have already been made towards eliminating this threat, but these have only had limited results thus far. Living conditions are becoming increasingly harsh for many of our citizens. Workers are struggling to raise their families. Helped on by tribalistic ideologies, the country's soul has been torn apart. Now, society has the duty to take measures that will safeguard life. . . . These measures confirm without ambiguity the willingness of the political establishment and Congolese civil society to make peace between themselves, and to strive to bring the

country out of the crisis it has been sinking deeper into with each passing day.[21]

By this time, the Congolese were growing increasingly skeptical of such
gatherings, a mood that is captured in the media at the time. Presidential
elections were nevertheless scheduled for July 1997 at the end of Lissouba's
five-year term in office. In the meantime, the leaders of each party remained
active, outlining the coordinates of their respective national projects and circulating them in several books, most notably Lissouba's *Congo: Les fruits de la
passion partagée*, and Sassou Nguesso's *Le manguier, le fleuve et la souris*.[22]
With Sassou Nguesso's return from temporary exile in France and impend-
ing elections, civil war erupted on June 5 and lasted until October 17, 1997.[23]
The death toll is widely accepted as having exceeded 10,000 people. The
country's infrastructure was destroyed and the capital, Brazzaville, razed to
the ground.

Few would argue that it was not without international backing that Sassou
Nguesso was restored to the presidency. The particular appeal of Sassou
Nguesso to the French government resided in the historical ties France had
established with him, and of course his willingness to relinquish control
over offshore oil production. This inaugurated an ongoing pattern of un-
scrupulous behavior that is inseparable from France's relationship with
francophone Africa. In this context, the French authorities have refused to
abandon their influence and to relinquish their economic interest in the
region, preferring instead to capitalize upon and sustain entrenched political corruption, thereby effectively compromising any hope of sociopolitical
stability. Sassou Nguesso sees himself very much as a legitimate leader, and
he remains committed to a rhetoric of National Dialogue in the name of
reconstruction, in which peace and reconciliation are foregrounded. Yet
Lissouba and Kolélas, both living in exile, in the United Kingdom and Côte
d'Ivoire, respectively, have been excluded from this dialogue. Sassou Nguesso
has promised to subject the new constitution to a referendum and to hold
elections, but few observers are optimistic that durable political solutions
will emerge from these measures, and most agree that Sassou Nguesso would
likely be reluctant to leave office anyway should he not emerge victorious.

Media and Decentralization in Francophone Africa

Africa offers a unique model for exploring questions relating to the media,
and the concept of engineering seems particularly useful here, given its as-

sociations with the mechanical aspects of media production and dissemination, and the performative dimension of National Conference proceedings. Furthermore, engineering gains proximity to Noam Chomsky's notion of consent as something that is manufactured through propagandist gestures and connects with practices adopted by the colonial administration and the leaders of newly independent African nations.[24]

In order to consider issues relating to the media in the Congo, a broader contextual framework would seem necessary, one that incorporates more specific notions as they pertain to the distribution, production, and of course political alignment in the non-Western context of both anglophone and francophone Africa. As MacDonald Ndombo Kale has observed, one needs to question "the assumption that the notion of liberty of thought and expression is of universal validity. This paradigm is not only based on a universalistic view of press freedoms as well as other fundamental human rights but is also a largely eurocentric construct."[25] In order to avoid the pitfalls of a Eurocentric paradigm, Kale draws on several media categories as they are elaborated by Dhyana Ziegler and Molefi Asante:

- unrestrained: "operates according to their own values, norms and objectives."
- restrained: "controlled by the government."
- directed: "operates under the influence of the government's stated objectives for national development."[26]

The state's alignment with Marxist ideology and control over political discourse in the Congo in order to promote the unifying model for nation-building have provided the justificatory premise for controlling both literary and journalistic productions. To this extent, the notion of a "restrained" media is more appropriate to the Congolese context, specifically from 1969 to 1991, after which time, and for a brief period, "unrestrained" models were evidenced. My approach incorporates many of the criteria underscored by Kale, but I do make several important distinctions:

- The analysis of African media necessarily needs to be located outside of potentially reductive Eurocentric approaches, which might ignore such factors as literacy, audience, distribution, production, and so on.
- Analysis should attempt to consider the particular circumstances of media production in Africa in general, incorporating similarities and differences in colonial and missionary activity, as well as the intercultural dynamics inside, outside, and between anglophone, francophone,

lusophone, and other European and African language sectors. While countries may share similarities, it would be more appropriate to consider the radical differences that have been evidenced as post-independence nationalistic tendencies have accentuated and exacerbated distinctions (in the same way that variations in colonial experiences could be attributed to respective linguistic and political zones).

- Arguably, investigations during the post-independence era restricted to the national scale will be more productive if, and only if, they consider the specific circumstances of government involvement, ideological choices, and so forth. Naturally, similarities exist with other African countries, but the state's commitment to Marxism-Leninism in the Congo generated very particular circumstances for media development that inevitably inscribed marked distinctions.

- Finally, my position departs from that adopted by Kale, Assante, and Ziegler to the extent that editorial autonomy—the unambiguous ability to function independently of partisan constructs and without fear of persecution—stands for me as an absolute precondition for existence and participation in discourse. Press freedom thus signifies primarily freedom from government control but also, and often more importantly, freedom from economic constraints. Restrictions inherent to a "directed" or "restrained" model have more to do with political circumstances in which dissent and oppositionality are constructed as treasonable offenses. The fact that conditions for press freedom have only briefly been evidenced has everything to do with the political structures in place and the state's insistence on the primacy of its own monolithic discourse.

Naturally, the precedent for these conditions is to be found in the colonial press, which was controlled by the colonial administration and under whose aegis there was no such thing as freedom of speech. Colonial law of July 29, 1881, stated that "all colonial publications should operate under the charge of French nationals."[27] In the Afrique Occidentale Française sector (French West Africa), *Journaux Officiels* were distributed, as Frère has shown, in order to "bring expatriates news from the *metropole*, maintain cohesion among them, and sometimes even to defend their interests with regard to the administration" (Frère, 26). In this framework, however, "the 1881 law on the press (applicable to the colonies through article 69) prevented natives, even those who were *évolués*, from creating their own newspapers because the law stipulated that only those publications edited by 'respectable French citizens' were authorized" (Frère, 27).

After the Second World War, regulations were relaxed, allowing for increased African participation in the media. Nevertheless, this pattern of exclusion was duplicated in the postcolonial era, and with independence, this model provided the framework for nation-building through governmental insistence on a partisan press. As Festus Eribo and William Jong-Ebot have argued, "the media too are a contradiction. Having been organized to serve the needs of the various colonial administrations, they became, at independence, ideological tools of the new African leaders, and were brought under state control and made to sing the praises of dictators in the name of national unity and development."[28] The imperative of nation-building provided the agenda for newspapers and gradually shifted toward adopting party ideology. According to Frère, "After independence, the media played an important role in the authoritarian armory of new African governments. Newspapers were not real vectors of information and did not constitute spaces for exchange since they were at the service of precise ideologies and strategies that imposed significant restrictions on them" (Frère, 30). Perhaps the more interesting approach would be one that identifies those mechanisms employed in order to impose consensus and manipulate power. Educational, religious, and commercial objectives provided the justificatory premise for control over the media during colonial expansionism, a pattern replicated for the purpose of nation-building during the post-independence era, and subsequently for the various restructuring exigencies of the post-Marxist, post–National Conference period.

Earlier in this book, in the discussion of official literature, emphasis was accorded to the state's insistence on a singular discourse, one which Sue Curry Jansen has aptly described as located in "Marxist-Leninist eschatology," given that it "is inherently intolerant of heterodox ideas. For if culture (the superstructure) reflects economic conditions (the substructure), and if proletarian revolution is taken as the inevitable goal of historical progress, then intellectual or artistic currents which impede progress toward that goal can only be seen as 'deviations' which reflect survivals of 'reactionary' economic interests."[29] This paradigm provided Congolese leaders with the ideological framework for prescriptive control over literary productions, but also newspapers in their responsibility to "propagandize," "agitate," and serve as "an 'organ' organizing society along socialist lines and cultivating a socialist consciousness" (Jansen, 107). In a similar fashion, Karl Marx's and Friedrich Engels's emphasis in the *Manisfesto of the Communist Party* on the importance of state centralization of the means of communication generated a "programmatic document" that "authorized and legitimated Lenin's directives" (Jansen, 101) and of course those of the Congolese government authorities, while "official censorship became a necessary constituent principle for the maintenance of that State" (Jansen, 100), and the successful engineering of the nation-building imperative. In fact, from 1969 to 1991, a censorship commission screened editorial matter, all publications had to be submitted to it for approval prior to distribution, and lists of banned texts were kept on record.

Journalists were often trained in the Soviet Union, where they refined their propagandist skills, faithfully adhering upon their return to the official guidelines provided by the various ministers for information and propaganda. Sassou Nguesso was unambiguous in delineating the demands and exigencies of official writing in the Congolese context, and President Kérékou demanded similar media collaboration in Benin, insisting that "The Revolution requires substantial ideological training and the means of communication have an important role to play in achieving this objective. We must draw upon them as a revolutionary weapon, within the context of the class struggle" (Frère, 42).[30] For all aspects of print culture, the model was provided by the Soviet Union, and, accordingly, newspapers were exploited for their revolutionary potential. As Jean-Claude Gakosso has claimed, "Leninist propaganda, that is a component of the 'class struggle,' is considered indispensable to the proletariat's ability to achieve consciousness."[31] By firmly anchoring their narratives in an official reality, these contributions to the nation's revolutionary agenda constitute important documents, since as "historians of the present, journalists are more prosaically technicians of information" (Gakosso, 76). Gakosso's notion of the journalist as a "technician" establishes a striking parallel with the official writer's responsibility of adhering to and promoting party lines in response to the ideological imperative provided by the dictatorship of the proletariat. In turn, each respectively assumes the role of "technician" and "engineer," simultaneously juxtaposing the task of recounting and falsifying history. A further example is provided by Mobutu's legacy of control from 1965 to 1997 in Zaire, where Article 10 of a 1970 governmental decree stated that "Quite apart from legal action, the Minister of Information may suspend for a maximum of six months the publication of any newspaper or periodical liable to endanger public order or the peace. In urgent cases the provincial governor may do the same, provided he informs the Minister of Information immediately."[32] Similarly, Sékou Touré's writings in his legendary multivolume *Révolution Démocra-*

tique Africaine serve to underline the univocal nature of discourse in Guinea under his leadership. The surveillance state he created imposed conditions in which dissent became virtually inarticulable:

> Men and women, young and old, you are assigned the task of observing everyone . . . in each and every activity, whether public or private, in order to identify those subjects likely to bring shame upon Guinea and Africa. . . . Some of you may be surprised that we know everything. As we have said before, nothing can happen in Guinea without us knowing about it. You can be certain of one thing, and that is that those who choose another path but that of honor, will be dealt with accordingly.[33]

Chomsky's notion of "consent" as something that is "manufactured" gains pertinence in the African context, given the degree to which the postcolonial authorities manipulated public opinion for the purpose of serving the specific agenda of those who controlled power. For Chomsky,

> the mass media serve as a system for communicating messages and symbols to the general populace. It is their function to amuse, entertain, and inform, and to inculcate individuals with the values, beliefs, and codes of behavior that will integrate them into the institutional structures of the larger society. In countries where the levers of power are in the hands of a state bureaucracy, the monopolistic control over the media, often supplemented by official censorship, makes it clear that the media serve the ends of a dominant elite. In a world of concentrated wealth and major conflicts of class interest, to fulfil this role requires systematic propaganda.[34]

Of course, the propaganda model Chomsky has in mind refers primarily to the American context in which the conditions under which consent is "manufactured" are quite different, since predominantly de-nationalized private-sector ownership has generated different circumstances for the control of public opinion.

In her study "The Global and the Local in International Communications," Annabelle Sreberny-Mohammadi focuses on the relationship between media and its consumers in a global market.[35] While the historical period covered, 1987–92, is outside the particular time frame considered here, these findings nevertheless serve to underline the massive discrepancy between Africa and other areas of the world in terms of various media constructs—audience, marketing issues, resources, dissemination of information, and so forth. As far as print culture is concerned, copies of daily newspapers reach

25 out of every 100 individuals in the European Community and North America, a figure that drops to 1.2 in Africa, some 8 points lower than the world aggregate; furthermore, 92 books are published for every 100,000 people in the European Community compared to only 2.7 in Africa. Not surprisingly, pronounced differences are to be evidenced in other media categories such as radio and television. These statistics are employed here in a noncritical manner, and while these figure have much to reveal in their use of standardized comparative calculation tools, they fail to consider cultural and social specificities, most significantly the broader implications of literacy and the transmission of information in cultures that have historically relied primarily on orality as opposed to print culture. Yet, even with these shortcomings in mind, the fact remains that whatever comparative indicators one utilizes, Africa clearly enjoys a completely different relationship to print culture and other forms of communication technology than many areas of the world. Of course, one should not underestimate the prevalence and indeed the effectiveness of alternative communication mechanisms located in popular culture and orality. These will be partially addressed later in this chapter in order to establish similarities between these practices and some of the devices employed by caricaturists.

Political reform in francophone Africa generated unique conditions for media, as the editors of newly formed newspapers distanced their publications from the official *langue de bois* rhetoric of the Marxist era. As Frère has shown, "Private newspapers during the transition period broke away from 'authorized' discourse as it was practiced during the years of political monopoly, and defined themselves as truth-bearers" (Frère, 261). The spirit of reform and the accompanying increasingly tolerant sociopolitical environment generated a relaxation of the media for a few years. To this end, new laws were enacted, such as the Loi Congolaise sur la liberté de la presse (Congolese Law on Press Freedom):

> Article 1: Press freedom is guaranteed by the Constitution and provided for within the framework of current legal clauses whose purpose are to establish the rules concerning the right to information access, as well as the rights and duties of journalists in the Republic of the Congo.
>
> Article 2: Access to sources of information is free, and censorship prohibited; this means that individuals should not have to worry about their ideas, opinions, and to research, receive and diffuse . . . information and ideas by whatever means of expression available, within the framework of the limits determined by the present law. (Gakosso, 85)

Newspapers, radio, and television had been controlled by the state in the Congo for several decades, and *La Semaine Africaine*, a Catholic newspaper, was the only so-called independent newspaper circulating (albeit regularly interfered with and harassed by the authorities). News and information were dominated by the PCT's official newspaper, *Etumba*, and by another newspaper, *Mwéti*, that adhered to the party line. Parallels were to be found in many other francophone African countries, with newspapers such as *Ehuzu* in Benin and *Sahel* in Niger. In the immediate aftermath of 1991, decentralization triggered a profusion of post-official publications, including some sixty newspapers in Benin (Frère, 17–18), and according to Gakosso's exhaustive list, the number rose to eighty-six publications in the Congo on either a weekly or biweekly production schedule (Gakosso, 121–23).[36] However, since Sassou Nguesso's restoration in 1997, production has rapidly declined, and most newspapers have interrupted their activities. Nevertheless, those years demarcating the National Conferences and restoration provide a good indication of the remarkable potentiality of African media under conditions in which creative autonomy is fostered. One particularly striking aspect of this phenomenon is contained in some of the work produced by graphic artists and caricaturists.

Radical Graphics and Political Dissidence

Questions of accessibility, distribution, production cost, and of course literacy have generated particular circumstances for print culture and nation-building in the Congo. Somewhat paradoxically, Sassou Nguesso reiterated the importance of print culture to the nation-building imperative at the Forum national pour la culture et la paix, held in Brazzaville between December 19 and December 24, 1994:

> The successful outcome of this national initiative will depend in part on the press, and much is expected of them. Ladies and gentlemen, from tomorrow onwards, you will have your share of responsibility, as much as the politicians, in case of failure. Because information is the blood of democracy; its poor circulation is usually the source of all kinds of disturbances in the social body.[37]

As Manning has observed, "the spread of an active popular press, and the decline of government control of radio and television, characterized this era" across francophone sub-Saharan Africa (Manning, 194). Accordingly, mechanisms for participation were extended to a much broader section of the population, allowing for radically new possibilities for the articulation of political commentary. Article 20 of the National Conference's *Acte Fondamental* of June 4, 1991, had outlined the parameters of such rights: "Every citizen has the right to information. Activities relative to information and communication are exercised in all independence and within the parameters of the law" (Boulaga, 199). One of the most important newspapers to emerge in the Congo during this period was *La Rue Meurt*, an opposition newspaper whose support base was primarily located in the Pool region. The Forum national pour la culture et la paix provides an interesting marker for an analysis of some of these key issues, since it is sufficiently separated in time from both the immediate aftermath of the National Conference and the political disintegration during 1997. Several cartoons published in *La Rue Meurt* at this time also establish points of contact to many of the themes explored in this book—orality, popular culture, official voices, propaganda, and resistance literature—elements that are recuperated by an engaged and confrontational media insistent upon calling attention to the excesses of government and politics.

The specificity of the African context is partly contained in the prevalence of nontraditional forms of communication and information transmission located primarily in the domain of orality and popular culture and exemplified in the phenomenon widely known as *radio-trottoir*.[38] Accounting for these local sociological conditions reveals an effective form of communication in an environment in which official discourse was the privileged domain of a hegemonic, centralized, and monolithic government foregrounding print culture. Indeed, such findings gain proximity to the broader implications of the book's opening epigraph from Ahmadou Hampaté Ba, "when an old person dies in Africa, it is the same thing as a library burning," which has served throughout to underline the multiple discursive realms that inform the African sphere. As Frère has signaled, "In a context in which information was controlled in an official manner and written and telecommunication development are inadequate, the transmission of information was conducted primarily by means of orality" (Frère, 57). The circulation of information in such an undocumented, uncontrolled fashion had all kinds of ramifications for the articulation of dissent:

> *Radio-trottoir* in fact constitutes a direct consequence of censorship and continues to develop, especially given that local media outlets have no credibility. It serves as an indicator of latent conflicts and of the global social dynamic. *Radio-trottoir* is at once a vague form of counter-power,

a means of self-defense, and a social regulator that provides an outlet for certain frustrations. It also contributes to the construction of a country's past by pinning down key elements that can be held on to for posterity. (Frère, 57–58)

Orality, then, may very well constitute the site at which history is to be found—the library of knowledge evoked by Ahmadou Hampaté Ba—where a rectification of the truth and a record for posterity may reside, one that would correct propagandist and official versions. These considerations further underline the imperative of incorporating multiple voices in any consideration of nation-building discourse. But the objective here is not to document that version of history—a task that may in actuality prove to be insurmountable—but rather to explore how these elements have been recuperated into the mainstream in recent newspapers that have exhibited a striking fusion of art, words, and key tenets associated with orality. Indeed, as Théophile Obenga has argued, these serve as "visual archives," given their capacity for documenting and recording history (Obenga, 340).

The semiotic possibilities become enormous through the combination of linguistic and visual components, offering a communicative potential in terms of accessibility across multiple social lines with all sorts of broader implications with regard to the creation of political communities. Premised on public awareness of political events—acquired through oral and print culture, but also from radio and television broadcasts—graphics are able to capitalize upon this in order to guarantee that a given message will be successfully deciphered. For while graphics rely on both the linguistic and the visual, and while part of the message may inevitably be obfuscated for an illiterate individual, the cartoonist's engagement with a given sociopolitical reality allows for a greater communicative potential as the method of communication shifts away from the exclusively privileged domain of the written word toward the image.

Achille Mbembe's work provides a perceptive contextualization of popular culture's anti-hegemonic, resistant, and survivalist qualities, and some of his more recent work on signs produced in Cameroon during the post-1991 era, what he has characterized as a "phase of relaxation,"[39] is relevant to the graphics I want to discuss. For Mbembe, "in spite of its claim to represent presence, immediacy, facticity, what is special about an image is its 'likeness'—that is, its ability to annex and mime what it represents, while, in the very act of representation, masking the power of its own arbitrariness, its own potential for opacity, simulacrum, and distortion" (Mbembe, 142). The image and the word function together for Mbembe, since "the pictographic sign does not belong solely in the field of 'seeing'; it also falls in that of 'speaking.' It is in itself a figure of speech, and this speech expresses itself, not only for itself or as a mode of describing, narrating, and representing reality, but also as a particular strategy of persuasion, even violence" (Mbembe, 142).

The political cartoons I consider were published in 1994–95 in *La Rue Meurt* around the time of the Forum national pour la culture et la paix. They reflect the type of innovative dialogue generated during this period and offer an engaging manner of mixing oral culture and popular discourse. Indeed, as Obenga has commented, "cartoons that represent events in a satirical and sketched format are *archives* of immediate history . . . satirical drawings and cartoons offer a politico-historical language that is accessible to all, in towns as well as the countryside" (Obenga, 339). Anchored in the quotidian experience and the immediacy of the event—prerequisites for understanding each illustration—a symbiotic pact and even complicity is established between the artist/satirist and her/his audience or constituency as they in turn register the words and images in order to arrive at the message formulated. These works are then systematically transformed into revelatory documents with regard to the national sentiment at a particular historical juncture and, in a similar manner to *radio-trottoir* or other forms of counter-hegemonic discourse, undermine power by subjecting it to ridicule. As Gakosso has argued: "Through rumor, the little people can 'bring down' to their level the men in power, sometimes caricaturing them, often parodying them" (Gakosso, 60).[40]

Figure 1, "L'échec de l'idéologie de l'intimidation" (The failure of the ideology of intimidation) by the cartoonist Ray M', published in *La Rue Meurt* (no. 062, December 29, 1994–January 5, 1995), features a congregation of political leaders similar to the one held on the occasion of the Forum national pour la culture et la paix. In the drawing, the setting has been transferred to a M'Bongui, a Kikongo word that designates a gathering place in a Kongo village designed to allow the elders to discuss the village's problems. After the first uprisings in 1993, Lissouba had invoked the need for a "democracy of intimidation"—an oxymoronic construct if ever there was one—and this cartoon represents an indictment of that policy.

In the top left-hand corner, Martin Mberi, Lissouba's former minister of the interior, who was responsible for ordering the government's "ministerial reserve" to attack Kolélas's opposition strongholds in the Brazzaville neighborhoods of Makélékélé and Bacongo, appears in the guise of an owl. The onomatopoeic hoot of an owl characterizes his words, "La paix c'est vous! Moukoukouloukourou la guerre toujouuuuurs! Moukoukoulourououhouuuu!," through which he emphasizes the responsibility of those gathered for achieving peace but also juxtaposes the words "peace" and "war."[41] He is clearly being mocked, given that as a public persona he is inseparable from his war-mongering agenda.

A bespectacled Lissouba appears comfortably positioned, larger than the other caricatured personalities, enjoying his Mbanga-filled (cannabis) professorial pipe, presiding over proceedings and stationed before his cabinet ministers and the leaders of other political parties: clockwise, from the bottom left-hand corner of the cartoon, Kolélas, Sassou Nguesso, Jean-Pierre Thystère-Tchicaya, Justin Lekoundzou (today Sassou Nguesso's minister of defense), unidentified man, and then Victor Tamba-Tamba, Christophe Moukoueke, André Milongo, and Augustin Poignet (president of the Senate). Seated at the back and dressed in traditional clothing is the widely recognized figure of Claudine Munari, Lissouba's head of cabinet, popularly described as his mistress.

Engaged in dialogue with P'tit David (Lil' David), Lissouba signals the end of the Congo's disintegration and his vilification through recourse to the term *M'Bongui*, employed here to designate the new climate of reconciliation brought about by the forum. The exclamation "MP'MP'MP'" after his words onomatopoeically designates the sound associated with pipe-smoking but could also be seen to symbolize the initials of his Mouvance Présidentielle (Presidential Movement). P'tit David speaks directly to Lissouba using one of the many names he has been given, "Lissoubios," and commenting on his growing wisdom, "Tu deviens Mbuta-Muntu" (You are becoming Mbuta-Muntu), that is to say a wise old man in Kikongo, for having agreed to hold a UNESCO-supported forum as a pretext for reconciliation, instead of following Mberi's call to arms.

P'tit David is a fascinating character who appears in all of Ray M's cartoons and who, as Obenga has argued, "in fact incarnates the Congolese people, national consciousness" (Obenga, 343). Sporting a soccer shirt bearing the all-important number 10 that is traditionally worn by the sweeper or playmaker, he is accorded a similar role in these cartoons as he assumes the responsibility of distributing, disseminating, and revealing information, exposing that which is hidden, articulating that which is kept silent, recording and registering injustice and hypocrisy, offering advice, providing direc-

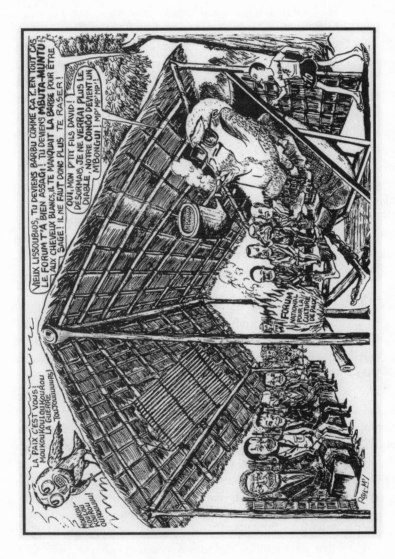

Figure 1. "L'échec de l'idéologie de l'intimidation." *La Rue Meurt*, no. 062, December 29, 1994–January 5, 1995.

tion, and feeding information much like this key player would feed a ball to his team members, transmuted in this case into the national team that is his nation and for whom he has become the spokesperson.

Representing the "rue," the people of the street, P'tit David captures the spirit of the newspaper itself, once distributed as *La Rumeur* and subsequently dismantled because of editorial disagreement, and then later reconfigured as *La Rue Meurt.* With its new name, editors capitalized on the notoriety achieved under the previous name but now underlined the pain and suffering of the masses at the hands of authoritarian rulers in addition to the dimension more closely associated with the transmission of clandestine information contained in the notion of "rumor" and associated with the people's *radio-trottoir.* Whereas people commonly exclaimed during the Marxist era, with reference to the "Big Brother" omnipresence of the *Mwéti* newspaper, which unequivocally supported the ruling PCT, "Mwéti était là" (*Mwéti* was there), this omnipresence is now recuperated by "little brother" as P'tit David—young and wise, the eyes and ears of the new nation, reminding leaders that the people are still watching.

The focus is more specific in figure 2 (*La Rue Meurt,* no. 062, December 29, 1994–January 5, 1995), as the chair of the National Conference, Bishop Ernest Kombo, stands distraught before a crumbling brick citadel shaped like the Congo and whose infrastructure parallels that of the Congo's democratic project ("Congo démocratique" is inscribed on the side of the citadel to emphasize this connection). Atop the citadel rests the tricolor flag (although the cartoon appears in black and white, one must assume that the colors would correspond to the republic's green, yellow, and red flag) adopted at independence in 1960, later abandoned by the Marxist-Leninist authorities during their years of rule, and subsequently reinstated during the National Conference when the Congo relinquished its status as a people's republic in favor of a republic. A number of essential points concerning post–National Conference politics are alluded to here and a familiarity with this context is essential in order to access the cartoon's deeper meaning.

Lissouba's political rhetoric was characterized by its scientific and technological foundations, capitalizing on the professorial authority he commanded and that was premised upon his scientific training as a biologist. This set him apart from his opponents, especially Kolélas, who was better known for his mysticism. The struggle then was between scientific logic and mysticism, and Kombo backed Lissouba. In this cartoon he is seen deploring this choice, invoking the injustice he has suffered: "On a scientifiquement

Figure 2. *La Rue Meurt*, no. 062, December 29, 1994–January 5, 1995.

menti, on a technologiquement volé! On a jordonniquement tué!" (People have lied scientifically, people have lied technologically! People have killed jordonically!). In order to impede civil unrest, Lissouba broadcast a speech over the radio in which he repeated the instruction "j'ordonne" (I command) multiple times, ordering military troops to curb protests in Kolélas opposition strongholds, and thereby obtaining the nickname "Jordonne." Ray M' transforms this appellation into an adverb in order to ridicule Kombo for his misplaced allegiance to Lissouba, while simultaneously indicting Lissouba for his failure to build a post–National Conference democracy. P'tit David's intervention serves to reinforce this message, further emphasizing the precariousness of the foundations upon which the Congo's democracy is erected by affiliating Lissouba's ruling coalition, the Mouvance Présidentielle, with the "sable mouvant" (quicksand) upon which Kombo's symbolic citadel now stands: "Son édifice démocratique qu'il a bâti sur la logique scientifique s'enfonce dans le sable mouvant de la mouvance présidentielle!" (His democratic edifice that he built on scientific logic is now sinking into the quicksand of the *mouvance présidentielle*!).

Figure 3 (*La Rue Meurt*, no. 062, December 29, 1994–January 5, 1995), by the cartoonist Wassemo, juxtaposes two representations of Lissouba standing opposite one another in their respective black and white corners. In the caricature to the left, Lissouba appears with one foot resting on a block inscribed with the word "hier" (yesterday), bearing the traditional iconographic symbols of the devil, including horns on his head and a long tail emerging from under his formal suit. With one hand shaking the outstretched hand his transmuted image holds out to him, the other hand conceals a sign behind his back with the names of the opposition neighborhoods his armed forces bombed. Beneath this sign lies a landscape of skulls and various bones, representing the victims abandoned in the wake of his political machinations. The figure he has been morphed into for the purpose of the forum meeting now holds a peace sign behind his back, with one foot resting on a block that now reads "aujourd'hui" (today), with the traditional symbol of peace in the guise of a dove resting on his head. Yet, a large question mark is superimposed over his lower body, reflecting P'tit David's own skepticism concerning the proceedings and symbolized by the finger he holds to his mouth in an interrogative gesture, and also of course questioning Lissouba's genuineness as his agenda shifts from one of unrestrained violence toward peace. P'tit David's question, "Il suffit d'un centième de forum pour que le professèr fasse sa transmutation! A-t-il vraiment quitté le monde parallèle?"

Figure 3. *La Rue Meurt*, no. 062, December 29, 1994–January 5, 1995.

(All it takes is a hundredth forum for the *professèr* to undertake his transmutation! Has he really left the parallel world?), recuperates language commonly associated with Japanese futurist television series that were very popular in the Congo at the time, and in which transmutations were frequent, in order to characterize the similar qualities of Lissouba's own rapidly mutating policies.[42]

With figure 4 (*La Rue Meurt*, no. 062, December 29, 1994–January 5, 1995), Ray M' explores some of the principal issues associated with coalition formation in the post–National Conference era. On the left, the caricatured men correspond to two key UPADS leaders, the taller Moukoueke and shorter Tamba-Tamba, representatives of the Mouvance Présidentielle and of its majority support in the Niari region that is inscribed on the slightly raised platform they are standing on. The fractured mirror they hold up with "Mouvance Présidentielle" written on the frame conveys the fragility of the alliance they have supported. Imploring Kolélas to come over to their camp with veiled promises of electoral success in the scheduled 1997 elections, they are met with a unified URD-PCT response, "Notre alliance c'est bon" (Our alliance is strong). The strong coalition is exemplified by the embrace Kolélas is enjoying in the arms of Thystère-Tchicaya (on the left) and Sassou Nguesso (to the far right). P'tit David, arms raised, expresses his astonishment with regard to political developments: "Drôles des mouvouziers! On présente à Ya Kolins un miroir qui se brise au moment où son alliance devient plus fort!" (Strange mouvouziers! They go and give Ya Kolins a mirror that cracks just when their alliance is getting stronger!).[43] A neologism, "mouvouziers," is created to enucleate this confusion by combining Lissouba's "mouvance" and the Kikongo word "mouvouze" that describes disturbance, disorder, and chaos, and that is *francisé* here.

Figure 5 (*La Rue Meurt*, no. 062, December 29, 1994–January 5, 1995) presents a grinning Lissouba riding a tractor, with the word "forum" engraved on it as a personalized license plate. "P'tit David, tu vois! Je suis un grand cultivateur de paix! Ah! Ah! Ah!" he exclaims (P'tit David, you see! I'm becoming a great cultivator of peace! Ah! Ah! Ah!). P'tit David may be surprised at the rapidity with which Lissouba's new technology allows for seeds to transform themselves into ripe crops, but the cartoon's political message fastens on the irony of P'tit David's observation revealing that the crops are in fact skulls, while also mocking Lissouba's constant recourse to a pseudoscientific language that exhibits all the attributes of an orthodoxy. Suspicion and distrust are expressed for Lissouba's rhetoric of peace, and

Figure 4. *La Rue Meurt*, no. 062, December 29, 1994–January 5, 1995.

Figure 5. *La Rue Meurt*, no. 062, December 29, 1994–January 5, 1995.

Figure 6. *La Rue Meurt*, no. 062, December 29, 1994–January 5, 1995.

there is little faith that his initiatives will lead to a future any different from the one symbolized by the skulls that his seeds of peace have yielded. For the time being, the Congo's only real fertilizer appears to reside in the corpses of victims of political uncertainty and aggression.[44]

The focus in figure 6 (*La Rue Meurt*, no. 062, December 29, 1994–January 5, 1995) is provided by the image of a suffering, agonizing Congo, symbolized by an ailing man whose physical contours correspond to the topography of the country itself. Lissouba places a bandage inscribed with the word "forum" over the man's wound, but, as P'tit David signals, without appropriate cleansing, antiseptic products, and antibiotics, this course of action will be futile. By analogy, recent attempts at treating the Congo's malady with temporary solutions such as the forum have been equally redundant in their failure to sufficiently address the underlying infectious nature of the sociopolitical malady.

Finally, in figure 7 (*La Rue Meurt*, no. 063, January 6–January 12, 1995), Ray M' takes stock of events of the past year as he declares Lissouba world champion in the super-heavyweight category of an imaginary weight-lifting contest. Lissouba is dressed in a weight-lifter's outfit embossed with three palm trees, the symbol of his ruling UPADS Party, holding in the squat position large weights he has just snatched. His achievements for 1994, ranging from lies, promises, unpaid wages and formulas, to assassinations, genocide, and intimidation, are imprinted on the weights. Once again, Lissouba's legacy of violence is invoked, his politics of intimidation denounced, and his empty scientific formulas and equations exposed for their incapacity to offer solutions.

Conclusion: From *Engineering* to *Reconciliation*

The question then remains as to how one makes the transition from *engineering* toward *reconciliation*. Clearly, Africa offers a striking framework for the exploration of issues relating to postcoloniality, and it continues to do so as observers assiduously monitor events in countries as diverse as Algeria, the Congo, the Democratic Republic of the Congo, Nigeria, Rwanda, Sierra Leone, Somalia, and South Africa. The twentieth century ended with striking new reconfigurations and alignments—as some areas of the world fractured, others came together in newfound alignments and communities. The unpredictability of the sociopolitical context renders prognosis in the African context virtually futile yet serves as confirmation of Africa's vitality and vibrancy. Political transitions and instability seem inevitable in years to come,

Figure 7. *La Rue Meurt*, no. 063, January 6–January 12, 1995.

yet individuals and communities continue to demonstrate remarkable resourcefulness and creativity. While two of the Congo's most important writers died in 1995 (Sony Labou Tansi and Sylvain Bemba), Emmanuel Dongala and Henri Lopes have remained active, and exciting new voices have emerged from within France's postcolonial communities, most notably those of Daniel Biyaoula and Alain Mabanckou.[45] These writers have in turn further emphasized transnational connections between Africa and the Diaspora and have much to contribute to the elaboration of twenty-first-century conceptions of citizenship and nationalism. Furthermore, cultural activity is also to be evidenced in other domains, with actors, musicians, theater directors, and filmmakers active in the Congo and elsewhere.

In the immediate aftermath of independence in the 1960s, responsibility was provided by the imperative of nation-building in the francophone sub-Saharan African context, but emphasis has now shifted toward the dynamic operation of national reconstruction. With this in mind, Mbembe has provided a powerful example of some of globalization's more sinister influences, whereby the Congo "is an example of extraterritorialization. Here, the model is not that of partition proper, but rather of a vortex. Violence is cyclical, and its epicenter is the capital. Located in the hinterland, the capital itself has its center of gravity outside itself, in the relation the state maintains with the oil companies operating offshore."[46] To this end, outsiders as much as insiders must insist on playing an active role in the process of reconstruction, holding governments and multinational organizations accountable for their activities in Africa, demanding that ethical standards be respected and adhered to in a global framework, while preventing external agencies from assisting corrupt authoritarian regimes in the task of developing new technologies of terror and repressing activism.

From slavery to colonialism, from neocolonialism to multinationalism, or other exploitative formations, the fact remains that unless monolithic orthodoxies of national engineering are abandoned, post-democratic transition will be unlikely to generate sociopolitical circumstances conducive to reconciliation. Few would question Africa's ability to negotiate successful transition away from hegemony and to accept history's convoluted trajectories, in order to join one of Emmanuel Dongala's protagonists who finds comfort in renewal: "How could such a world regenerate itself without first destroying itself? . . . Every end contains within itself a hope, that of a beginning."[47] Indeed, the time has come for Africa to be *left alone*—yet, it should not be left *all on its own*—and there is a fundamental difference between the two. Once individuals have accepted their own legacy of complicity and collaboration in the punctuation of history, once the origins have become more transparent, then the journey ahead will be less painful. I think that is what Maya Angelou was trying to tell us at the beginning of this book: "History, despite its wrenching pain, cannot be unlived, and if faced with courage, need not be lived again."

NOTES

1. Introduction

1. Most notably Shu-mei Shih's *The Lure of the Modern: Writing Modernism in Semicolonial China, 1917–1937* (Berkeley: University of California Press, 2001).
2. Benedict Anderson, *Imagined Communities: Reflections on the Origin and Spread of Nationalism* (New York: Verso, 1983).
3. Noam Chomsky and Edward S. Herman, *Manufacturing Consent: The Political Economy of the Mass Media* (New York: Pantheon Books, 1988). Chomsky also discusses the notion of "historical engineering" in *Necessary Illusions: Thought Control in Democratic Societies* (Boston: South End Press, 1989).
4. Edouard Glissant, *Caribbean Discourse: Selected Essays*, trans. J. Michael Dash (Charlottesville: University of Virginia Press, 1989).
5. In recent years, a plethora of stimulating books has been devoted to the region. See Adam Hochschild, *King Leopold's Ghost* (New York: Houghton Mifflin, 1998); Michela Wrong, *In the Footsteps of Mr. Kurz: Living on the Brink of Disaster in Mobutu's Congo* (New York: HarperCollins, 2001); and Ludo de Witte, *The Assassination of Patrice Lumumba*, trans. Ann Wright and Renée Fenby (London: Verso, 2001). See also Raoul Peck's film, *Lumumba* (2000). See also Phyllis M. Martin, *The External Trade of the Loango Coast, 1576–1870* (Oxford: Clarendon Press, 1972); and *Leisure and Society in Colonial Brazzaville* (Cambridge: Cambridge University Press, 1995).
6. All too often, African territorial boundaries are described as "arbitrary," a fact that Achille Mbembe has challenged, arguing that "it is clear that the boundaries inherited from colonization were not defined by Africans themselves. But contrary to common assumption, this does not necessarily mean that they were arbitrary," 264. See Achille Mbembe, "At the Edge of the World: Boundaries, Territoriality, and Sovereignty in Africa," trans. Steven Rendall, *Public Culture* 12, no. 1 (Winter 2000): 259–84. No matter what the origins of territorial borders may have been in their original conception, they nevertheless became political, legal, and administrative realities at independence. The Berlin Conference failed to take into account the traditional boundaries between ethnic groups, and while the colonial period modernized Africa, infrastructures were created that favored a number of regions over and above inland areas. This situation was further complicated since the artificial boundaries demarcated by the colonial powers provided the framework for the emergence of national consciousness as the driving force behind the struggle for independence; once this objective had been instilled, its very continuity depended on the sustained and unified opposition to the colonial powers.
7. Achille Mbembe, *On the Postcolony* (Berkeley: University of California Press, 2001), 103.

8. Mbembe, *On the Postcolony*, 104.

9. Paul N'Da, *Les intellectuels et le pouvoir en Afrique noire* (Paris: L'Harmattan, 1987), 10–11; and *Pouvoir, lutte de classes, idéologie et milieu intellectuel africain* (Paris: Présence Africaine, 1987).

10. On the notion of "promiscuity," see Mbembe, *On the Postcolony*.

11. Tanella Boni, "L'écrivain et le pouvoir," *Notre Librairie*, no. 98 (July–September 1989): 84.

12. This is Richard Bjornson's term from *The African Quest for Freedom and Identity: Cameroonian Writing and the National Experience* (Bloomington: Indiana University Press, 1991), xiii.

13. The situation is somewhat paradoxical, given that non-official authors are compelled to "export" their work because of government control over Congolese publishing, while official writers are rarely read outside of the national context in which their writings are conceived.

14. Jean-Paul Sartre, "Orphée noir," preface to *Anthologie de la nouvelle poésie nègre et malgache de langue française*, ed. Léopold Sédar Senghor (Paris: Presses Universitaires de France, 1948).

15. Camara Laye, *L'enfant noir* (Paris: Plon, 1953); and Mongo Béti, "Afrique noire, littérature rose," *Présence Africaine*, nos. 1–2 (April–July 1955): 133–45.

16. Frantz Fanon, *Les damnés de la terre* (Paris: François Maspéro, 1961).

17. See Ahmadou Kourouma, *Les soleils des indépendances* (Montréal: Presses Universitaires de Montréal, 1968); and Yambo Ouologuem, *Le devoir de violence* (Paris: Seuil, 1968).

18. Guy Ossito Midiohouan, *L'idéologie dans la littérature négro-africaine d'expression française* (Paris: L'Harmattan, 1986). He has in mind Lilyan Kesteloot's classification according to political *engagement*. See Lilyan Kesteloot, *Les écrivains noirs de la langue française: Naissance d'une littérature* (Brussels: Institut Solvay, 1963). Other examples would include Jacques Chevrier, *Anthologie africaine d'expression française*, vol. I: *Le roman et la nouvelle* (Paris: Hatier, 1981); and Séwanou Dabla, *Nouvelles écritures africaines: Romanciers de la seconde génération* (Paris: L'Harmattan, 1986). Dabla's readings are often incisive, but his concern with identifying new trends in African writing does not sufficiently highlight the idiosyncrasies of the various authors. Dabla also has a tendency to overgeneralize; he argues, for example, that "Mongo Béti's and Ousmane Sembène's momentary silence" and the "complete and obstinate silence of Ferdinand Oyono and Cheikh Hamidou Kane" were remedied from 1968 onward only with the publication of a number of works, 16. However, the period which Dabla presents as a creative vacuum (1960 to 1968) witnessed the publication of some thirty-seven novels, fifteen plays, and fifty-two volumes of poetry by authors as diverse as Francis Bebey, Olympe Bhêly-Quenum, Bernard Dadié, Malick Fall, Ahmadou Kourouma, Charles Nokan, Yambo Ouologuem, Guillaume Oyonô-Mbia, and Tchicaya U Tam'si. See Guy Ossito Midiohouan, *Bibliographie chronologique de la littérature négro-africaine d'expression française* (Cotonou: UNB, 1984); and Lilyan Kesteloot, *Anthologie négro-africaine: Panorama critique des prosateurs, poètes et dramaturges noirs du XXème siècle* (Verviers: Marabout, 1981).

19. In his essay "The Postcolonial and the Postmodern," Kwame Anthony Appiah engages in precisely the type of dynamic that has been the subject of a remise-en-question by Midiohouan, when he argues that "Far from being a celebration of the nation, the novels of the second stage—the postcolonial stage—are novels of delegitimation: rejecting the Western imperium, it is true, but also rejecting the nationalist project of the postcolonial national bourgeoisie. . . . Africa's postcolonial novelists . . . are no longer committed to the nation," in *In My Father's House: Africa in the Philosophy of Culture* (New York: Oxford University Press, 1992), 152. There are several problems with the reduction of his investigative framework to a "second stage" that contribute to the oversimplified conclusions he reaches: (1) he ignores the respective historiographies of particular genres; (2) he does not explore writers such as Ousmane Sembène who have published during both stages (colonial and postcolonial); (3) he fails to broaden the analysis in order to include a multiplicity of stages (such as *négritude*, anti-colonialism, etc.); (4) most writers are in fact committed to the reality of the nation—it is the state that provides the subject of their criticism; (5) his pessimism vis-à-vis African fiction fails to incorporate the plethora of recent productions by African women (Mariama Bâ, Calixthe Beyala, Aminata Sow Fall, Werewere Liking, Véronique Tadjo, etc.), as well as exciting new voices (Abdourahman Wabéri).

20. For an overview of this surge in literary production, see Arlette Chemain, "Chroniques, geste épique, récit symbolique: Le roman, 1977–1987," *Notre Librairie*, nos. 92–93 (March–May 1988): 116–22.

21. For more detailed figures, refer to Koffi Anyinefa, "Bibliographie de la littérature congolaise d'expression française," *Research in African Literatures* 20, no. 3 (Fall 1989): 481–88.

22. See, for example, Sylvain Bemba, "La phratrie des écrivains congolais," *Notre Librairie*, nos. 92–93 (March–May 1988): 13–15. The relative absence of women writers in the Congo is not unusual in the francophone sub-Saharan context where access to literacy during the colonial era was for the most part the privileged domain of men, although the Marxist-Leninist elite also restricted the participation of women in public discourse. On the question of women writers in the francophone sub-Saharan African context, see Christopher L. Miller, "Senegalese Women Writers, Silence, and Letters: Before the Canon's Roar," in *Theories of Africans*, 246–93; Nicki Hitchcott, *Women Writers in Francophone Africa* (Oxford: Berg, 2000); Pierrette Herzberger-Fofana, *Littérature féminine francophone d'Afrique noire* (Paris: L'Harmattan, 2001); Jean-Marie Volet, "Romancières francophones d'Afrique noire: Vingt ans d'activité littéraire à découvrir," *French Review* 65, no. 5 (April 1992): 765–73; and *La parole aux africaines ou l'idée de pouvoir chez les romancières d'expression française de l'afrique sub-saharienne* (Amsterdam: Rodopi, 1993). For a broader comparative perspective on women writers, see Françoise Lionnet, *Autobiographical Voices: Race, Gender, Self-Portraiture* (Ithaca: Cornell University Press, 1991); *and Postcolonial Representations: Women, Literature, Identity* (Ithaca: Cornell University Press, 1995). And for a pan-francophone approach, see Mary-Jean Green et al., *Postcolonial Subjects: Francophone Women Writers* (Minneapolis: University of Minnesota Press, 1996).

23. See Jean-Pierre Makouta-M'Boukou, *Introduction à l'étude du roman négro-africain de langue française: Problèmes culturels et littéraires* (Dakar: Nouvelles Editions Africaines, 1980); and Locha Mateso, *La littérature africaine et sa critique* (Paris: ACCT/Karthala, 1986).

24. The most complete guide to the question is provided by Guy Ossito Midiohouan, "Eléments de bibliographie: Pour une approche méthodique de la question des 'littératures nationales' en Afrique," *Notre Librairie*, no. 85 (October–December 1986): 93–97.

25. Timothy Brennan, "The Nation Longing for Form," in *Nation and Narration*, ed. Homi K. Bhabha (London: Routledge, 1990), 58.

26. Edward Said, *Culture and Imperialism* (New York: Alfred A. Knopf, 1993), xxv. See also Sami Zubaida, "Theories of Nationalism," in *Power and the State*, ed. Gary Littlejohn et al. (New York: St. Martin's Press, 1978), who has argued that "For the 'nation' to have a plausible existence and boundaries in the present, its 'essence' has to be demonstrated in its history. The writing of a history in which the national unit is shown to have temporal depth of ancestry, of common experience, consciousness and destiny is an essential part of nationalist enterprise," 53–54.

27. Crawford Young, "Evolving Modes of Consciousness and Ideology: Nationality and Ethnicity," in *Political Development and the New Realism in Sub-Saharan Africa*, ed. David E. Apter and Carl G. Rosberg (Charlottesville: University of Virginia Press, 1994), 72.

28. *République du Congo-Brazzaville: Bulletin d'information de la représentation permanente auprès de l'ONU*, no. 4 (February 1963); no. 5 (March 1963); and no. 8 (June 1963). Also see Michael S. Radu, "Ideology, Parties and Foreign Policy in Sub-Saharan Africa," in *Africa in the Post-Decolonization Era*, ed. Richard Bissell and Michael S. Radu (New Brunswick, N.J.: Transaction Books, 1984), 15–40; and Michael S. Radu and Keith Somerville, *Benin, the Congo, and Burkina Faso* (London: Pinter Publishers, 1988).

29. Appiah, *In My Father's House: Africa in the Philosophy of Culture*, 59.

30. See "Littératures nationales: Mode ou problématique," *Notre Librairie*, no. 83 (April–June 1986); "Littératures nationales: Langues et frontières," *Notre Librairie*, no. 84 (July–September 1986); and "Littératures nationales: Histoire et identité," *Notre Librairie*, no. 85 (October–December 1986).

31. Elikia M'Bokolo, "Ce que dit l'histoire," *Notre Librairie*, no. 83 (April–June 1986): 11–16.

32. Jean-Loup Amselle and Elikia M'Bokolo, eds., *Au cœur de l'ethnie: Ethnies, tribalisme et état en Afrique* (Paris: La Découverte, 1985), 29.

33. Adrien Huannou, *La question des littératures nationales en Afrique noire* (Abidjan: CEDA, 1989). Hereafter cited parenthetically in the text as "Huannou."

34. Alain Rouch and Gérard Clavreuil, *Littératures nationales d'écriture française* (Paris: Bordas, 1986), 3.

35. Huannou fastens on Arlette Chemain and Roger Chemain's *Panorama critique de la littérature congolaise contemporaine* (Paris: L'Harmattan, 1973). The panorama arranges works in chronological order along with a brief synopsis and commentary. Identifying what they consider the most salient distinguishing charac-

teristics of Congolese literature ("lyricism," a supposed "social passion," recourse to a "colonial past" as a source of inspiration, and, above all, a condemnation of *négritude*), their framework becomes increasingly problematic as they make claims such as "the People's Republic of the Congo has some twenty writers for a population of just over a million, which is quite remarkable," 14. The usefulness of such observations needs to be interrogated, given that per capita production proves absolutely nothing, as well as the deeper implications of comparing countries along these lines. Indeed, the inherent dangers of such discourse are contained in Said's warning, whereby "Culture is a sort of theater where various political and ideological causes engage one another. . . . Now the trouble with this idea of culture is that it entails not only venerating one's own culture but also thinking of it as somehow divorced from, because transcending, the everyday world," *Culture and Imperialism*, xiii. See also Adrien Huannou, "Inquiétudes et objections: D'un colloque à l'autre," *Notre Librairie*, no. 83 (April–June 1986): 29–37.

36. Bjornson, *The African Quest for Freedom and Identity*, xi.
37. Guy Ossito Midiohouan, "Le phénomène des littératures nationales," *Peuples noirs, Peuples africains*, no. 27 (1982): 57–70.
38. Midiohouan, *L'Idéologie dans la littérature négro-africaine*, 11.
39. Christopher L. Miller, "Nationalism as Resistance and Resistance to Nationalism in the Literature of Francophone Africa," in *Post/Colonial Conditions: Exiles, Migrations, and Nomadisms, Yale French Studies* 1, no. 82 (1993): 100. There are two convincing studies of national literatures in the francophone sub-Saharan African context: Richard Bjornson's book *The African Quest for Freedom and Identity: Cameroonian Writing and the National Experience*, and Koffi Anyinefa's *Littérature et politique en Afrique noire: Socialisme et dictature comme thèmes du roman congolais d'expression française* (Bayreuth: Eckhard Breitinger, 1990). Focusing on Cameroon, Bjornson has shown how "the circumstances under which its institutions came into being . . . have produced a society with its own distinctive set of cultural references" (xi), in which "writers and intellectuals transform the raw materials suggested by their environments into fictional worlds that reflect the content of a people's collective memory, influence the course of its evolution, and extend its imaginative grasp of its own situatedness in the world," 7. For Bjornson, specificity increases as a national literary culture emerges offering increased common references: "Like national literatures everywhere, then, the nascent literatures of African countries will be recognized by the shared reference points in the spectrum of world views that individual writers project into their works . . . these developments have begun to occur in African countries, suggesting that the term 'national literature' might well provide a legitimate framework for understanding the diversity of literary production in Africa," 17–18. In his comprehensive study of Congolese literature, Anyinefa undertakes insightful critiques of works by what he describes as established writers—Emmanuel Dongala, Henri Lopes, Jean-Pierre Makouta-Mboukou, and Sony Labou Tansi. Recognizing that the "different political experiences . . . have inevitably generated national particularities, thereby breaking with the relative homogeneity of these countries during the colonial era" (Anyinefa, 12), and that "it is not errone-

ous to try and identify a link between a given state's political life and its literature" (12). Yet, having made these observations, he does not then proceed to engage the reader in a discussion of national literatures. The ideology of national
literatures constitutes a major current in literary discourse, and the restricted focus of his study reinforces the viability of such an approach. Yet, his dismissal of
it is too rapid and sweeping a move, particularly given the role which the state
has played in sponsoring an official literature. Many of the issues raised by Anyinefa add to the debate on national literatures: he argues, for example, that Socialism accords specificity to writings from the Congo, while dictatorship represents a point of commonality for francophone postcolonial sub-Saharan African
literature. Socialist ideology is of course a recurring feature in writings from the
Congo, but the same is also true of texts produced in other francophone (Guinea,
Benin, Mali), lusophone (Angola, Mozambique), and anglophone African countries (Kenya, Somalia) in which governments have implemented Socialist or Marxist
models. Thus, Anyinefa includes works in which the subject of Socialism features prominently, but he fails to demonstrate the extent to which the treatment
of Socialist discourse in Congolese writings is any different from that by cultural
practitioners from other countries. See Roger Chemain, Review of *Littérature et
politique en Afrique noire: Socialisme et dictature comme thèmes du roman congolais d'expression française* by Koffi Anyinefa, *Research in African Literatures* 24,
no. 1 (Spring 1993): 124–25.

40. Chemain, "Review," 124.

41. Québec is, of course, the exception. Different demographics are evidenced in
the anglophone context in which established markets are to be found in North
America, Europe, Australia, New Zealand, and South Africa.

42. A recent conference held at the University of California, Los Angeles, explored
some of these issues: "After the End: Hong Kong Culture after 1997," May 25–
26, 2001.

43. The writings of literary and political figures such as Léopold Sédar Senghor and
Aimé Césaire allow us to gauge the complexity of the situation.

44. Léopold Sédar Senghor, *Anthologie de la nouvelle poésie nègre et malgache de
langue française*; Léopold-Pindy Mamonsono, *La nouvelle génération de poètes
congolais* (Brazzaville and Heidelberg: P. Kivouvou Verlag/Editions Bantoues,
1984).

45. Christopher L. Miller, *Nationalists and Nomads: Essays on Francophone African
Literature and Culture* (Chicago: University of Chicago Press, 1998), 20–21.

46. Miller, *Nationalists and Nomads*, 54.

2. Official Writers

The subtitle of this chapter is an adaptation of Stalin's phrase "engineers of the
human soul," coined in the 1930s. See Michael Scriven and Dennis Tate, eds.,
European Socialist Realism (Oxford: Berg Publishers, 1988), 1.

1. Denis Sassou Nguesso, *Sur l'approfondissement du processus révolutionnaire* (Brazzaville: Les Editions du Comité Central du Parti Congolais du Travail, 1984), 44.
Hereafter cited parenthetically in the text as "Sassou Nguesso."

2. Alain Robbe-Grillet, "On Several Obsolete Notions," in *For a New Novel: Essays on Fiction*, trans. Richard Howard (Freeport, N.Y.: Books for Libraries Press, 1970), 37. Hereafter cited parenthetically in the text as "Robbe-Grillet."

3. Variations on this theme are to be found in Partha Chatterjee's work on the "Nationalist Elite." See *The Nation and Its Fragments: Colonial and Postcolonial Histories* (Princeton: Princeton University Press, 1993).

4. Ben Okri, "Listen to My Friend," *The Guardian* (November 1, 1995).

5. Cheikh Hamidou Kane, *L'aventure ambiguë* (Paris: Julliard, 1961).

6. Cheikh Hamidou Kane completed and published *Les Gardiens du Temple* (Paris: Albin Michel) in 1995, a second novel he had started writing several decades earlier.

7. See, for example, Phyllis Peres, *Transculturalism and Resistance in Lusophone African Narratives* (Gainesville: University Press of Florida, 1997).

8. Henri Brunschwig, *Noirs et blancs dans l'Afrique noire française: Ou comment le colonisé devient colonisateur (1870–1914)* (Paris: Flammarion, 1983). Hereafter cited parenthetically in the text as "Brunschwig." See also Joseph-Roger de Benoist, *L'Afrique occidentale française de 1944 à 1960* (Dakar: Les Nouvelles Editions Africaines, 1982); Nazi Boni, *Histoire synthétique de l'Afrique résistante: Les réactions des peuples africains face aux influences extérieures* (Paris: Présence Africaine, 1971); and Catherine Coquery-Vidrovitch, ed., *L'Afrique occidentale au temps des français: Colonisateurs et colonisés, c. 1860–1960* (Paris: Editions de la Découverte, 1992).

9. See Annette Smith, *Gobineau et l'histoire naturelle* (Genève: Droz, 1984).

10. See, for example, Ike Okonta and Oronto Douglas, *Where Vultures Feast: Shell, Human Rights, and Oil in the Niger Delta* (San Francisco: Sierra Club Books, 2001).

11. Paul Gilroy, *Between Camps: Nations, Cultures, and the Allure of Race* (London: Penguin, 2000). Hereafter cited parenthetically in the text as "Gilroy."

12. Joseph Stalin, *Marxism and the National and Colonial Question* (New York: International Publishers, 1913); and Vladimir Ilich Lenin, *Imperialism, the Highest Stage of Capitalism* (New York: International Publishers, 1969).

13. Omafume F. Onoge, "The Crisis of Consciousness in Modern African Literature," in *Marxism and African Literature*, ed. Georg M. Gugerberger (London: James Currey, 1985), 38. Hereafter cited parenthetically in the text as "Onoge."

14. Ahmadou Mapaté Diagne, *Les trois volontés de Malic* (Nendeln: Kraus Reprints, 1973 [first published in 1920]). Mongo Béti's criticism of Camara Laye's novel *L'enfant noir* for what he perceived as its lack of an explicit political agenda is somewhat indicative of the situation. See Alexandre Biyidi (pseudonym of Mongo Béti), Review of *L'enfant noir* by Camara Laye, *Présence Africaine* 16 (1954): 419–22; and "Afrique noire, littérature rose," *Présence Africaine* 1–2 (1955): 133–45.

15. Frantz Fanon, *Les damnés de la terre* (Paris: François Maspéro, 1961); *The Wretched of the Earth*, trans. Constance Farrington (New York: Grove Press, 1963), 206. See also David Macey's biography of Fanon, *Frantz Fanon* (New York: Picador, 2001).

16. See, for example, Aimé Césaire, *Une saison au Congo* (Paris: Seuil, 1965); *Discours*

sur le colonialisme (Paris: Présence Africaine, 1955); and *La tragédie du roi Christophe* (Paris: Présence Africaine, 1963).

17. See Régine Robin, *Le réalisme socialiste: Une esthétique impossible* (Paris: Payot, 1986). Hereafter cited parenthetically in the text as "Robin." One should note that Robin is herself a well-known francophone author from Québec.

18. Scriven and Tate, eds., *European Socialist Realism*, 2. In various ways, these criteria were recuperated by official writers in formulating a specifically African model.

19. Onoge is quoting Ernst Fischer, *The Necessity of Art* (London: Penguin, 1963), 108.

20. Georg M. Gugelberger, ed., *Marxism and African Literature* (London: James Currey, 1985), 5. See also Chidi Amuta, *The Theory of African Literature: Implications for Practical Criticism* (London: Zed Books, 1989).

21. Emmanuel Ngara, *Art and Ideology in the African Novel: A Study of the Influences of Marxism on African Writing* (London: Heinemann, 1985), 3. Hereafter cited parenthetically in the text as "Ngara." See also Lucien Goldmann, *Pour une sociologie du roman* (Paris: Presses Universitaires de France, 1964).

22. Raymond Williams, *Marxism and Literature* (Oxford: Oxford University Press, 1977). Hereafter cited parenthetically in the text as "Williams." See also Ayi Kwei Armah, "Masks and Marx: The Marxist Ethos vis-à-vis African Revolutionary Theory and Praxis," *Présence Africaine* 131, no. 3 (1984): 35–65.

23. See Vladimir Ilich Lenin, *On Literature and Art* (Moscow: Progress Publishers, 1975).

24. Gugelberger, ed., *Marxism and African Literature*, xiv.

25. Léopold-Pindy Mamonsono, *La nouvelle génération de poètes congolais* (Brazzaville and Heidelberg: P. Kivouvou Verlag/Editions Bantoues, 1984). Hereafter cited parenthetically in the text as "Mamonsono."

26. Sikhé Camara, *Somme de la poésie guinéenne de combat ou la sirène de la révolution africaine* (Casablanca, Morocco: Imprimerie Eddar El Be ida, 1982). Hereafter cited parenthetically in the text as "Sikhé Camara." See also *Poèmes de combat et de vérité* (Paris: P. J. Oswald, 1967); and *Clairière dans le ciel* (Paris: Présence Africaine, 1973). Djigui Camara, *Chronique de la révolution* (Conakry, Guinea: Bureau de Presse de la Présidence Conakry R.P.R. de Guinée, 1982). Hereafter cited parenthetically in the text as "Djigui Camara."

27. See Roger Goto Zomou, "Les auteurs guinéens de l'intérieur: Notes bio-bibliographiques," *Notre Librairie*, nos. 88–89 (July–September 1987): 153–55; and John Victor Singler, "The Role of the State in the Development of Literature: The Liberian Government and Creative Fiction," *Research in African Literatures* 11, no. 4 (Winter 1980): 511–28. Singler describes the government's need to "preclude writing that is antigovernment in tone and content. Also unacceptable would be literature at variance with the government's Unification and Integration Policy," 511.

28. Paul N'Da, *Pouvoir, lutte de classes, idéologie et milieu intellectuel africain* (Paris: Présence Africaine, 1987), 22.

29. See, for example, the work of the French writer Paul Nizan. See also Michael

Scriven, "Paul Nizan and Socialist Realism: The Example of *Le Cheval de Troie*" in *European Socialist Realism,* ed. Michael Scriven and Dennis Tate, 128–45.

30. Roland Barthes, "Ecrivains et écrivants," in *Essais critiques* (Paris: Seuil, 1964), 147–54. In Richard Howard's translation of this text, "écrivains" becomes "authors," while "écrivants" is translated as "writers." See Roland Barthes, *Critical Essays,* trans. Richard Howard (Evanston, Ill.: Northwestern University Press, 1972), 143–50. Hereafter cited parenthetically in the text as "Barthes."

31. See Robbe-Grillet's discussion of "engagement," *Pour un nouveau roman* (Paris: Les Editions de Minuit, 1963), specifically 33–39. In translation, see *For a New Novel: Essays on Fiction,* 37–41.

32. For an analysis of the debate between "committed and autonomous literature," see, for example, T. W. Adorno, "Commitment," trans. Francis McDonagh, from Ernst Bloch and others, *Aesthetics and Politics* (London: NLB, 1977), 177–95, and also in Terry Eagleton and Drew Milne, eds., *Marxist Literary Theory: A Reader* (Oxford: Blackwell, 1996), 187–203.

33. Steven Ungar, introduction to Jean-Paul Sartre, *"What Is Literature" and Other Essays* (Cambridge, Mass.: Harvard University Press, 1988), 12. Jean-Paul Sartre, "Qu'est-ce que la littérature," *Situations* II (Paris: Editions Gallimard, 1948); "Orphée noir," preface to Léopold Sédar Senghor's *Anthologie de la nouvelle poésie nègre et malgache de langue française* (Paris: Editions PUF, 1948); and "Orphée noir," *Situations* III (Paris: Editions Gallimard, 1949).

34. Ungar, *"What Is Literature" and Other Essays,* 330.

35. Bernard Geniès, "Africain d'accord, écrivain d'abord," *Le Nouvel Observateur* (August 15–25, 1988): 58–61.

36. Tanella Boni, "L'écrivain et le pouvoir," *Notre Librairie,* no. 98 (July–September 1989): 86–87.

37. In an interview I conducted with the Congolese novelist and playwright Sylvain Bemba in December 1994, he objected to his novel *Le dernier des cargonautes* (Paris: L'Harmattan, 1984) being labeled by L'Harmattan publishers as a "roman congolais."

38. Salman Rushdie, "In Good Faith," in *Imaginary Homelands* (London: Granta, 1991), 412.

39. Elisabeth Mudimbe-Boyi, "Langue violée, langue volée: Pouvoir, écriture et violence dans le roman africain," in *La deriva della francophonie: Figures et fantasmes de la violence dans les littératures de l'Afrique subsaharienne et des Antilles* (Bologna, Italy: Editrice CLUEB, 1991), 103.

40. Ngũgĩ wa Thiong'o, *Barrel of a Pen: Resistance to Repression in Neo-Colonial Kenya* (Trenton, N.J.: Africa World Press, 1983), 69.

41. Alexandre Mboukou, "The Rise of Anti-Intellectualism among the Modern African Elite," *Journal of African Studies* 9, no. 4 (Winter 1982–83): 185.

42. Sue Curry Jansen, *Censorship: The Knot That Binds Power and Knowledge* (New York: Oxford University Press, 1991), 194. Hereafter cited parenthetically in the text as "Jansen."

43. In Ousmane Sembène's novels, whether it be Diaw Falla, the dock-worker in the novel by that name, the idealist Oumar Faye in *O pays mon beau peuple!,* or the

enlightened, visionary strike leader Bakayoko during the 1947 strike by the Dakar-Niger railway workers in *Les bouts de bois de dieu,* the oppression of the proletarian worker by the colonizer or postcolonial political elite is denounced, and resolution to this alienation is presented through revolutionary class struggle. See Ousmane Sembène, *Le docker noir* (Paris: Ed. Debresse, 1956); *O pays mon beau peuple!* (Paris: Ed. Buchet-Chastel, 1957); and *Les bouts de bois de dieu* (Paris: Le Livre Contemporain, 1960).

44. Walter Benjamin, "The Work of Art in the Age of Mechanical Reproduction," in *Illuminations,* trans. Harry Zohn (New York: Schocken Books, 1977), 234.

45. For detailed commentary on the specificity of literature and politics in Guinea, see *Notre Librairie* 88–89 (July–September 1987); Claude Rivière, *Guinea: The Mobilization of a People,* trans. Virginia Thompson and Richard Adloff (Ithaca: Cornell University Press, 1977); W. A. E. Skurnik, ed., *African Political Thought: Lumumba, Nkrumah, and Touré* (Denver: University of Denver, 1968); Sidiki Kob el e Keita, *Ahmed Sékou Touré, l'homme du 28 septembre 1958* (Conakry, Guinea: I.N.R.D.G., Bibliothèque nationale, 1977); Mahmoud Bah, *Construire la Guinée après Sékou Touré* (Paris: L'Harmattan, 1990); Ladipo Adamolekun, *Sékou Touré's Guinea: An Experiment in Nation Building* (London: Methuen, 1976).

46. Selected titles of *Révolution Démocratique Africaine* include vol. 6: La révolution guinéenne et le progrès social; vol. 14: Le plan septennial guinéen; vol. 20: Pour une économie populaire et révolutionnaire; vol. 23: Informer et former pour transformer; and vol. 27: Le plan quinquennal (1982–85). See also Ahmed Sékou Touré, *Action politique du parti démocratique de Guinée* (Paris: Présence Africaine, 1959); *La Guinée et l'émancipation africaine* (Paris: Présence Africaine, 1959); *L'Afrique et la révolution* (Paris: Présence Africaine, 1966); *La révolution culturelle* (Conakry, Guinea: Imprimerie Nationale Patrice Lumumba, 1969); *Technique de la révolution* (Conakry, Guinea: Imprimerie Nationale Patrice Lumumba, 1960); *Expérience guinéenne et unité africaine* (Paris: Présence Africaine, 1982).

47. Ahmed Sékou Touré, *Révolution Démocratique Africaine,* no. 21, *Poèmes militants* (Conakry, Guinea: Imprimerie Nationale Patrice Lumumba, 1977), 10. Hereafter cited parenthetically in the text as "*Poèmes militants.*" See also *La révolution culturelle.*

48. Ahmed Sékou Touré, *La Guinée et l'émancipation africaine: L'action politique du Parti Démocratique de Guinée* (Paris: Présence Africaine, 1959), 169. Hereafter cited parenthetically in the text as "*La Guinée et l'émancipation.*" See Bernard Mouralis, "Sékou Touré et l'écriture; Réflexions sur un cas de scribomanie," *Notre Librairie,* nos. 88–89 (July–September 1987): 76–85; and Lansiné Kaba, "The Cultural Revolution, Artistic Creativity, and Freedom of Expression in Guinea," *Journal of Modern African Studies* 14, no. 2 (June 1976): 201–18.

49. Sékou Touré, preface, in Camara, *Somme de la poésie guinéenne de combat ou la sirène de la révolution africaine,* n.p.

50. Sékou Touré, preface, in Camara, *Somme de la poésie guinéenne de combat ou la sirène de la révolution africaine,* n.p.

51. Djigui Camara, preface, *Chronique de la révolution,* 12–13.

52. Camara Laye, *Dramouss* (Paris: Plon 1966); Alioum Fantouré, *Le cercle des tropiques* (Paris: Présence Africaine, 1972) and *Le récit du cirque . . . de la vallée des morts* (Paris: Editions Buchet-Castel, 1975); Tierno Monénembo's *Les crapauds-brousse* (Paris: Seuil, 1979); and Williams Sassine, *Saint-Monsieur Baly* (Paris: Présence Africaine, 1973).

53. Sikhé Camara, *Somme de la poésie guinéenne de combat*, 11–29. Ilya Ehrenbourg, *Un écrivain dans la révolution* (Paris: Gallimard, 1963). See also Michael Heim, "La littérature soviétique et la guerre d'Espagne," in *Les écrivains et la guerre d'Espagne* (Paris, 1975), 89–99.

54. Sikhé Camara, *Somme de la poésie guinéenne de combat*, 15.

55. Nenekhaly Condetto Camara, "Conscience nationale et poésie négro-africaine d'expression française," in *La Pensée: Revue du Rationalisme Moderne*, no. 3 (June 1962), cited in Sikhé Camara, *Somme de la poésie guinéenne de combat*, 18. See also selected poems, "Souvenir du Che," in *Horoya-Hebdo*, no. 3 (Conakry, February 15–21, 1969); and "Salut Viet-nam," in *Horoya-Hebdo*, no. 8 (Conakry, March 20–26, 1969).

56. See also "Le message de la révolution culturelle" (Sikhé Camara, 77); and "Les héritiers de la révolution" (Sikhé Camara, 36–37).

57. Ibrahima Khalil Diaré, *Chants et larmes, de foi et de joie* (Conakry, Guinea: INPL, 1972); and *Les dits de nul et de tous* (Conakry, Guinea: INPL, 1981).

58. Ibrahima Khalil Diaré, preface, in Djigui Camara, *Chronique de la révolution*, 13.

59. See also "Révolution" and "Etre révolutionnaire," *Chronique de la révolution*, 34 and 31–32 respectively.

60. Christopher L. Miller, *Theories of Africans: Francophone Literature and Anthropology* (Chicago: University of Chicago Press, 1990), 60.

61. Marien Ngouabi, *Vers la construction d'une société socialiste en Afrique* (Paris: Présence Africaine, 1975), 3. Hereafter cited parenthetically in the text as "Ngouabi." See also Théophile Obenga, *La vie de Marien Ngouabi: 1938–1977* (Paris: Présence Africaine, 1977).

62. Other examples would include "Tout pour le Peuple / Rien que pour le Peuple / Classe Ouvrière / Unité–Lutte–Socialisme / Pour le Drapeau Rouge / Nous vaincrons! Nous vaincrons!" or "Un seul Peuple / Un seul Parti / Un seul Idéal / Un seul Combat." See Samuel Decalo, "Ideological Rhetoric and Scientific Socialism in Benin and Congo/Brazzaville," in *Socialism in Sub-Saharan Africa: A New Assessment*, ed. Carl G. Rosberg and Thomas Callaghy (Berkeley: Institute of International Studies, 1979), 231–64.

63. Cited in Xavier Okotaka-Ebale, *Tous solidaire pour un Congo radieux* (Brazzaville: Imprimerie Nationale, 1987), 6.

64. *Etumba*, no. 462 (October 1977), cited in Emmanuel Boundzéki Dongala, "Littérature et société: Ce que je crois," *Peuples noirs, Peuples africains*, no. 9 (May–June 1979): 59.

65. Denis Sassou Nguesso, *Message du président du comité central du Parti Congolais du Travail à l'occasion du 20ème anniversaire des trois glorieuses (1963–1983)* (Brazzaville: Imprimerie Nationale du Congo, 1983), 18. See also his *Pour l'Afrique* (ABC Groupe Média International, 1987).

66. In order to legitimate the validity of this struggle, attentive listeners are informed of other countries within the international political community that can be considered ideological allies. One of these was Romania: "if there is a country the People's Republic of the Congo can feel close to . . . it must surely be the Socialist Republic of Romania" (Ngouabi, 676). Audience members are also handed pictures of Ngouabi enjoying a few moments with his many children after a long day at the office confronting his "weighty historical responsibilities" (Ngouabi, 528). The objective is to portray a leader fully engaged in legitimate political rule, at the head of a country that is recognized by the international community.

67. There are obvious parallels to be drawn here both historically and of course ideologically with Eastern European countries. Sanda Golopentia has written on this question with regard to post–World War II Romania and described events which led writers to "desert their talent" and "void their voices" when the "new regime dissected Romania's instituting Pre-War literature into those tendencies that could help in the development of a new, 'politically correct' literature," and those that "were not perceived as 'politically' and ideologically sound or 'constructive.'" Sanda Golopentia, "Battles of Silence: The Institution of Literature in Post–World War II Romania," in *Tradition and Change in Central and Eastern Europe*, ed. Henrietta Mondry and Paul Schveiger (Johannesburg, South Africa: University of the Witwatersrand, 1993), 78.

68. Sassou Nguesso, *Sur l'approfondissement du processus révolutionnaire*, 17. This division has become increasingly clear-cut since the Republic of the Congo became a pluralist democracy in 1991, allowing for the creation of independent writers' unions. The old Union Nationale des Ecrivains, Artistes, et Artisans Congolais (UNEAC), established by Sassou Nguesso under the one-party Marxist-Leninist system, still exists, but the majority of "unofficial" writers are now members of the Association Nationale des Ecrivains Congolais (ANEC). See also Bayo Ogunjimi, "The Military and Literature in Africa," *Journal of Political and Military Sociology* 18 (Winter 1990): 327–41.

69. Denis Sassou Nguesso, cited in Xavier Okotaka-Ebale, *Tous solidaires pour un Congo radieux* (Brazzaville: Imprimerie Nationale, 1987), 7. Musicians were also active in promoting party ideology. See, for example, the recordings of the Group-Rouge de Brazzaville, and one of their songs, "Alliance des opprimés": "L'Afrique s'éveille poignard au dos / L'Asie sous le napalm / l'Amérique latine sous l'oppression / Tricontinentale / Fusil en bandoulière / Le soleil des opprimés s'est levé." Recorded by Sonafric.

70. Sylvain Bemba, Emmanuel Dongala, Henri Lopes, and Sony Labou Tansi were published by Albin Michel, L'Harmattan, Seuil, and Présence Africaine in Paris, and NEA and CLE in Senegal and Cameroon, while Claude-Emmanuel Eta-Onka, Léopold-Pindy Mamonsono, J.-F. Obembe, and Xavier Okotaka-Ebale were published in Brazzaville by P. Kivouvou, Editions Bantoues, Editions Littéraires Congolaises, Editions et Publication Premières, Editions Héros dans l'Ombre, Editions INRAP, the Imprimerie des Armées, and the Imprimerie Nationale.

71. As I have already mentioned, numerous writers exceed the categories I have established. There are variations in degrees of commitment, whether this be to government paradigms or individual approaches to literature or nationalism. Some

narratives exhibit certain patriotic patterns to the extent that they engage in the glorification of leaders (past and present) or emphasize a common Congolese ancestry or heritage, but lack the type of revolutionary ideological structure that interests me here.

72. Adrien Huannou, *La littérature béninoise de langue française des origines à nos jours* (Paris: Karthala/ACCT, 1984), 264.

73. Maxime N'Debeka, *Soleils neufs* (Yaoundé: CLE, 1969); and *Les signes du silence* (Paris: Editions Saint-Germain-des-Prés, 1978).

74. Maxime N'Debeka, *L'oseille des citrons* (Paris: P. J. Oswald, 1975).

75. Maxime N'Debeka, cited in Femi Osofian et al., *Proceedings of the International Symposium on African Literatures. Theme: African Literature Before and After the 1986 Nobel Prize* (Lagos: Centre for Black and African Arts and Civilization, 1991), 252.

76. Jean-François Obembe, *Problèmes liés à l'édification du Parti Congolais du Travail: Premier parti marxiste-léniniste au pouvoir en Afrique* (Paris: Présence Africaine, 1987). See also his *Nouveau regard sur les certitudes d'hier* (Brazzaville: Editions Héros dans l'Ombre, 1991); *Vivre et mourir selon son style* (Paris: La Pensée Universelle, 1984); and *Philosophie marxiste-léniniste en bref* (Brazzaville: Editions de l'INRAP, 1985).

77. I have translated the French word "cautionné," meaning "supported" and "backed," as "sponsored."

78. Léopold-Pindy Mamonsono, *Héros dans l'ombre* (Kinshasa: Editions Pelamo, 1979), 21. He has also published *Light-Houses* (Brazzaville: Editions Héros dans l'Ombre, 1978); and *Equinoxes* (Brazzaville: Editions Littéraires Congolaises, 1983).

79. Huannou, *La littérature béninoise de langue française des origines à nos jours*, 272. As I have repeatedly stated, a certain caution must be exercised in any discussion as to what is "aesthetically worthwhile." For, while Huannou foregrounds stylistic criteria in his appraisal of literature, it is important to underline the fact that official writers *also* adhere to a carefully formulated aesthetic theory.

80. Xavier Okotaka-Ebale, *La femme africaine* (Brazzaville: Imprimerie des Armées, 1993), 6.

81. Xavier Okataka-Ebale, *La pensée conscientisante d'un progressiste* (Brazzaville: Imprimerie Nationale, 1982). Hereafter cited parenthetically in the text as "Okotaka-Ebale." The credential "Membre du Parti Congolais du Travail" appears under his name on the cover of the book.

82. The interview was conducted in Brazzaville, Republic of the Congo, in January 1995.

83. During the interview I conducted with him in Brazzaville, he claimed to be the Congo's equivalent to the American General Colin Powell!

84. Claude-Emmanuel Eta-Onka, *Insomnies* (Brazzaville: Edition et Publication Premières, 1991); and *Les tandaliennes* (Brazzaville: Edition Le Bélier, 1993). In Lari and Kutuba, "Tanda" designates Brazzaville, and rather than calling the collection "Les Brazzavilloises," which would have suggested that the subject concerned "the women of Brazzaville," Eta-Onka chose "*Les Tandaliennes*" instead. Hereafter cited parenthetically in the text as "*Insomnies*" and "*Tandaliennes*," respectively.

85. Terry Eagleton, *Criticism and Ideology: A Study in Marxist Literary Theory*, first published in 1976 (London: Verso, 1995), 178.
86. Huannou, *La littérature béninoise de langue française des origines à nos jours*, 272.
87. Sony Labou Tansi, *L'état honteux* (Paris: Seuil, 1981), 5.
88. Robert Porter, "Soviet Perspectives on Socialist Realism," in *European Socialist Realism*, ed. Michael Scriven and Dennis Tate (Oxford: Berg Publishers, 1988), 53.
89. Guy Menga, *Congo: La tradition escamotée* (Paris: L'Harmattan, 1993). See also Jean-Pierre Makouta-Mboukou, *La destruction de Brazzaville ou la démocratie guillotinée* (Paris: L'Harmattan, 1999); and Patrick Quantin, "Congo: Les origines politiques de la décomposition d'un processus de libéralisation (août 1992–décembre 1993)," in *L'Afrique politique 1994: Vue sur la démocratisation à marée basse* (Paris: Karthala/CEAN, 1994), 167–90. Jean-Claude Willame has remained skeptical with regard to these National Conferences and the feasibility of pluralist democracies in the African context. See his *Pouvoir et gouvernance au Zaïre* (Paris: Karthala, 1993).
90. Recent novels by young Congolese authors residing in France have appeared. Among the most notable of these writers are Daniel Biyaoula, who was awarded the 1997 Grand Prix Littéraire de l'Afrique Noire for his first novel, *L'impasse* (Paris: Présence Africaine, 1996), and his fellow countryman, Alain Mabanckou, who received the Grand Prix Littéraire de l'Afrique Noire in 1998 for his novel *Bleu-Blanc-Rouge* (Paris: Présence Africaine, 1998). See also the posthumous publication of Sony Labou Tansi's novel *Le commencement des douleurs* (Paris: Editions du Seuil, 1995); Tchichelle Tchivela, *Les fleurs des lantanas* (Paris: Présence Africaine, 1998); Henri Lopes, *Dossier classé* (Paris: Editions du Seuil, 2002); and Emmanuel Dongala, *Johnny, chien méchant* (Paris: Editions Le Serpent à Plumes, 2002).
91. Théophile Obenga has provided a survey of recent writings by writers he describes as "la classe politique congolaise." For him, "Les réflexions politiques d'un homme d'Etat congolais sont, en soi, une précieuse contribution à la vie publique congolaise. Le débat politique national est mieux nourri, approfondi, s'il dispose de documents écrits, d'idées publiquement exprimées, de dossiers accessibles, pour faire fructifier les discussions," *L'histoire sanglante du Congo-Brazzaville (1959–1997): Diagnostic d'une mentalité politique africaine* (Paris: Présence Africaine, 1998), 299. Sample works by key political figures include Jean-Pierre Thystère-Tchicaya, *Itinéraire d'un Africain vers la démocratie* (Genève: Editions du Tricone, 1992); Itihi Ossetoumba Justin Lekoundzou, *Pour bâtir la richesse nationale du Congo* (self-financed, 1995); and Victor Tamba-Tamba, *Le parti de mon choix: Contribution à l'édification d'un parti* (Brazzaville: Editions Mationgo, 1995).
92. Nurrudin Farah, *Sweet and Sour Milk* (St. Paul, Minn.: Graywolf Press, 1992), 190.
93. Edward Said, "Challenging Orthodoxy and Authority," *Culture and Imperialism* (New York: Alfred A. Knopf, 1993), 304.

3. Sony Labou Tansi

1. Sony Labou Tansi, quoted in *Equateur*, no. 1 (October–November 1986), 32.
2. Sony Labou Tansi, *Les sept solitudes de Lorsa Lopez* (Paris: Seuil, 1985): 11; *The Seven Solitudes of Lorsa Lopez*, trans. Clive Wake (Portsmouth, N.H.: Heinemann, 1995), foreword. Hereafter cited parenthetically in the text as *"The Seven Solitudes."*
3. Tchicaya U Tam'si, in Maximin, "Tchicaya/Sony: Le dialogue interrompu," 91.
4. The Congolese author Sylvain Bemba has provided an explanation of this pseudonym: *"Labou* is the name of the father. . . . *Tansi* is a tribute to a distinguished elder, the tremendous poet Tchicaya U Tam'si, as a discreet wink at him. Sony is actually a harmless cannibal who has often pulled off the conjurer's trick," "Sony Labou Tansi et moi," *Equateur*, no. 1 (October–November 1986): 52. This has generated much confusion. In his book *Sony Labou Tansi: Ecrivain de la honte et des rives magiques du Kongo* (Paris: L'Harmattan, 1996), Jean-Michel Dévésa contradicts Bemba's explanation, arguing that "Sony Labou Tansi did not give himself a pseudonym evoking by euphony Tchicaya U Tam'si," 78; instead, he locates the change as a marker of his Kongo lineage: *"Sony* is simply the Westernized form of the Kikongo *Ntsoni* . . . the 'y' is ultimately decorative; it gives the writer's name a diminutive appearance by analogy with Anglo-Saxon turns of phrase . . . as for the *Labou* component, this derives from the Kikongo term *Laboula* that designates the costume worn by men to emphasize, as they dance, the liberal movements of the thighs that are characteristic of Kongo choreographies. . . . And finally, *Tansi* refers to the novelist's grandmother . . . thereby perpetuating the memory of his grandmother but also specifying the lineage to which she belonged," 79–80. Hereafter cited parenthetically in the text as "Dévésa." This confusion is perhaps best exemplified in the various ways in which critics and scholars have referred to him. Jacques Chevrier indexes him under T, in *Littérature nègre* (Paris: Armand Colin, 1984), as does Séwanou Dabla in *Nouvelles écritures africaines: Romanciers de la seconde génération* (Paris: L'Harmattan, 1986). Koffi Anyinefa, however, indexes him under L, in *Littérature et politique en Afrique noire: Socialisme et dictature comme thèmes du roman congolais d'expression française* (Bayreuth: Eckhard Breitinger, 1990). In 1979 the Nouvelles Editions Africaines-CLE edition of *Conscience de tracteur* listed the author as SONY Lab'OU Tansi; by 1981, the Hatier edition of *La parenthèse de sang* and *Je soussigné cardiaque* had transformed his name to Sony Lab'ou Tansi; hereafter cited parenthetically in the text following the title of the work. Since the "nom de plume" Sony Labou Tansi modifies the original parameters of the name, ambiguity can be eliminated by listing him under S. The Editions du Seuil have been the most consistent in this matter, since his name has appeared under this format on the six novels they published between 1979 and 1995. Kenneth W. Harrow refers to him consistently as "Sony Labou Tansi" and indexes him under "S" in his book *Thresholds of Change in African Literature: The Emergence of a Tradition* (Portsmouth, N.H.: Heinemann, 1994). Hereafter, references to Dabla's, Anyinefa's,

and Harrow's books are cited parenthetically in the text following their respective names.

5. Critics have often referred to Sony Labou Tansi as Zairian. Kenneth Hammond, for example, categorized Sony Labou Tansi as a Zairian author in his review of *L'anté-peuple* for *World Literature Today* 58 (1984). The blurb on Heinemann's recent translation of *The Seven Solitudes of Lorsa Lopez* (1995) incorrectly claims that Sony Labou Tansi resided in the Republic of Zaire.

6. For additional biographical information, refer to Dévésa, *Sony Labou Tansi: Ecrivain de la honte et des rives magiques du Kongo*; Alain Rouch and Gérard Clavreuil, *Littératures nationales d'écriture française* (Paris: Bordas, 1986); "Sony Labou Tansi," *Equateur*; and Drocella Mwisha Rwanika and Nyunda ya Rubango, eds., *Francophonie littéraires en procès: Le destin unique de Sony Labou Tansi* (Paris: Silex/Editions Nouvelles du Sud, 1999).

7. *La vie et demie* (Paris: Seuil, 1979); *L'état honteux* (Paris: Seuil, 1981); *L'anté-peuple* (Paris: Seuil, 1983); *Les yeux du volcan* (Paris: Seuil, 1988); *Le commence-ment des douleurs* (Paris: Seuil, 1995); *Le coup de vieux*, with Caya Makhele (Paris: Présence Africaine, 1988). Hereafter cited parenthetically in the text following the title of the work.

8. Sony Labou Tansi, *Antoine m'a vendu son destin*, in *Equateur*, no. 1 (1986): 66–104. For a detailed history of the Rocado Zulu Theater, see Dévésa, *Sony Labou Tansi: Ecrivain de la honte et des rives magiques du Kongo*, 163–213; Marie-Léontine Tsibinda, "Petite histoire du Rocado Zulu Théâtre," *Notre Librairie*, no. 102 (July–August 1990): 184–85; and Sony Labou Tansi: "'Rocado,' comes from the word by-pass, the detour we have to take to get things done," quoted in "Du 'symbole à la scène.'" Interview with Jean-Gabriel Carasso, *Théâtre/Public*, no. 76–77 (1987), from the Dossier de Presse, 4th Festival International des Francophonies, October 3–16, 1987: 70.

9. Dévésa has also shown how Sony Labou Tansi managed to secure funding for his cultural projects from the Elf-Congo petroleum consortium and Italian-based AGIP research group by insisting on the importance of such organizations committing themselves to broader cooperative projects. See Dévésa, *Sony Labou Tansi: Ecrivain de la honte et des rives magiques du Kongo*, 21.

10. "Speaking with Sony Labou Tansi." Interview with David Applefield, *Frank: An International Journal of Contemporary Writing and Art*, no. 14 (1993): 94–95. Hereafter cited parenthetically in the text as "Applefield."

11. Abel Kouvouama, "Sony Labou Tansi ou l'utopie pratiquée," in *Sony Labou Tansi ou la quête permanente du sens*, ed. Mukala Kadima-Nzuji, Abel Kouvouama, and Paul Kibangou (Paris: L'Harmattan, 1997), 97. Hereafter cited parenthetically in the text as "Kouvouama."

12. Interview with Carasso, "Du 'symbole à la scène,'" 70.

13. Bernard Magnier, Interview: "Un citoyen de ce siècle," *Equateur*, no. 1 (October–November 1986): 18–19.

14. Magnier, Interview: "Un citoyen de ce siècle," 19.

15. Jean-Pierre Guingané, "De Ponty à Sony: Représentations théâtrales en Afrique," *Notre Librairie*, no. 102 (July–August 1990): 8–9. Jean-Pierre Guingané, *Le fou* (Abidjan: CEDA, 1986). See also "Jean-Pierre Guingané, un 'fou' de théâtre au

Burkina Faso." Interview with Wolfgang Zimmer, *Notre Librairie*, no. 102 (July–August 1990): 48–53.

16. Sony Labou Tansi, "Qui sera libre demain?" *Libération*, November 5, 1994. See my Letter to the Editor, "Sony Labou Tansi," *Times Literary Supplement* (December 16, 1994). There remains some question as to whether Sony Labou Tansi's passport was in fact ever withdrawn by the authorities. Given his health at the time and reluctance to travel, some have suggested that this was part of an elaborate scheme to discredit Pascal Lissouba's government; such an argument is implied by Dévésa's comment: "I *now* know that in September 1994, André Milongo certified to Henri Lopes that the Congolese authorities had not withheld his passport," *Sony Labou Tansi: Ecrivain de la honte et des rives magiques du Kongo*, 30.

17. See Howard W. French, "A Dying Writer Finds Solace in the Heart of Africa," *New York Times* (June 7, 1995).

18. Sony Labou Tansi, *Equateur*, 30.

19. Bernard Dadié, *Un Nègre à Paris* (Paris: Présence Africaine, 1959); Ferdinand Oyono, *Une vie de boy* (Paris: Julliard, 1956); Cheikh Hamidou Kane, *L'aventure ambigüe* (Paris: Julliard, 1962); and Ahmadou Kourouma, *Les soleils des indépendances* (Montréal: Presses Universitaires de Montréal, 1968). On the question of titles, see also Chevrier, *Littérature nègre*, 148, and Dabla, *Nouvelles écritures africaines*, 66.

20. Lydie Moudileno, "Labou Tansi's *La vie et demie*, or The Tortuous Path of the Fable," *Research in African Literatures* 29, no. 3 (Fall 1998): 23. Hereafter cited parenthetically in the text as "Moudileno."

21. As is often the case with Sony Labou Tansi's writing, given the remarkable degree to which he experimented with language, the playfulness and innovative dimension is lost in translation. The word "maux" in this case replaces the French word "mots" (words) that one would have expected to find here. By substituting "maux" (troubles, ills), Sony Labou Tansi underlines his concern with exposing sociopolitical injustice.

22. According to *Le grand Robert de la langue française* dictionary (1985), the word "Flamant" derives from the Latin "flamma" (flame) and is the name given to "un oisier échassier palmipède, au plumage généralement rose." It functions as a homonym for the word "Flamand" (the Flemish), which in this particular instance designates the Belgian colonizers and thus serves to further ridicule President Lopez.

23. For a convincing analysis of these issues, see Kenneth W. Harrow, Jonathan Ngate, Clarisse Zimra, eds., *Crisscrossing Borders in African Literatures* (Washington, D.C.: Three Continents Press, 1991).

24. Jonathan Ngate, *Francophone African Fiction: Reading a Literary Tradition* (Trenton, N.J.: Africa World Press, 1988): 154.

25. Michel Foucault, *Surveiller et punir: Naissance de la prison* (Paris: Gallimard, 1975).

26. Achille Mbembe, *De la postcolonie: Essai sur l'imagination politique dans l'Afrique contemporaine* (Paris: Karthala, 2000); *On the Postcolony* (Berkeley: University of California Press, 2001). Hereafter cited parenthetically in the text as "Mbembe."

Mbembe concentrates "on those elements of the obscene and the grotesque that Mikhail Bakhtin claims to have located in 'non-official' cultures but that, in fact, are intrinsic to all systems of domination and to the means by which those systems are confirmed or deconstructed" (Mbembe, 102), thereby attributing the notion of "non-officialdom" to a counter-hegemonic domain.

27. Most notably, Mikhail Bakhtin's *L'œuvre de François Rabelais et la culture populaire au moyen âge et sous la renaissance* (Paris: Gallimard, 1970).

28. Mbembe, 105. Although Mbembe's work was not available to Anyinefa when he wrote his book, Bakhtin's work on the grotesque and carnivalesque provides a crucial critical framework with which to contextualize the interplay of culture and politics in francophone sub-Saharan Africa.

29. János Riesz, "From *L'état sauvage* to *L'état honteux*," *Research in African Literatures* 31, no. 3 (Fall 2000): 124.

30. See Alexis Gabou, "Des libertés publiques et de la personne humaine," *Les constitutions congolaises* (Paris: Librairie générale de droit et de jurisprudence, 1984), 486. This is based on the constitution of July 8, 1979.

31. See also Bernard Mouralis, "La figuration de la violence et ses enjeux dans la fiction africaine," in *La deriva della francophonie: Figures et fantasmes de la violence dans les littératures de l'Afrique subsaharienne et des Antilles* (Bologna, Italy: Editrice CLUEB, 1991), 69–84; and Jacques Chevrier, "Visages de la tyrannie dans le roman africain contemporain," in *La deriva della francophonie*, 33–53.

32. Page duBois, *Torture and Truth* (London: Routledge, 1991), 148.

33. Sony Labou Tansi, *Parentheses of Blood*, trans. Lorraine Alexander Veach (New York: Ubu Repertory Theater Publications, 1985, 43). Hereafter cited parenthetically in the text as *"Parentheses of Blood."*

34. Arlette Chemain-Degrange, "Violence destructrice, violence régénératrice: Originalité de la littérature africaine subsaharienne," in *La deriva della francophonie*, 28.

35. See also Alpha-Noël Malonga, "Martillimi Lopez, les corps des femmes et *L'état honteux*," in *Sony Labou Tansi ou la quête permanente du sens*, ed. Mukala Kadima-Nzuji, Abel Kouvouama, and Paul Kibangou, 167–76.

36. This dimension receives additional treatment in chapter 4 with particular reference to the character "Tonton" in Henri Lopes's novel *Le Pleurer-Rire* (Paris: Présence Africaine, 1982).

37. Sony Labou Tansi and Caya Makhele, *Le coup de vieux*, 40–41.

38. Impotence provides the subject matter of Ousmane Sembène's novel and film *Xala*, in which a newly appointed member of the elitist Chamber of Commerce is cursed by impotence in the company of his new wife. This emasculation impacts his ability to function in the professional and social environment to which he has grown accustomed, culminating in his downfall. Ousmane Sembène, *Xala* (Paris: Présence Africaine, 1973).

39. For what is arguably the most complete and insightful study of francophone African theater, see John Conteh-Morgan, *Theatre and Drama in Francophone Africa: A Critical Introduction* (Cambridge: Cambridge University Press, 1994).

40. Patrick Chabal, "Pouvoir et violence en Afrique postcoloniale," *Politique Africaine*

42 (June 1991): 58–59; see also his *Power in Africa: An Essay in Political Interpretation* (Basingstoke, Hampshire: Macmillan, 1992).

41. Sony Labou Tansi, in *Equateur*, 60.

42. Other plays by Sony Labou Tansi include "Antoine m'a vendu son destin," *Equateur*, no. 1 (October–November 1986); "Moi, veuve de l'empire," *L'Avant-Scène Théâtre*, no. 815 (October 1, 1987); *Qui a tué Madame d'Avoine Bergotha* (Brussels: Editions Promotion Théâtre, "Collection Théâtre en Tête," 1989). The first of these plays focuses on a dictator who plots to overthrow himself in order to ferret out his enemies. Through the reenactment of Julius Caesar's murder, the second play denounces the violence that has come to define contemporary governments, while the final one takes sexual empowerment to its extreme, when President Wallante exiles all men from his territory so that he can become the "Country's exclusive Father-Inseminator," 95. See also *Qu'ils le disent, qu'elles le beuglent* (Carnières-Morlanwelz, Belgium: Editions Lansman, 1995); *Monologues d'or et noces d'argent* (Carnières-Morlanwelz, Belgium: Editions Lansman, 1998); *Le trou* (Carnières-Morlanwelz, Belgium: Editions Lansman, 1998); *Une chouette vie bien osée* (Carnières-Morlanwelz, Belgium: Editions Lansman, 1992); *Une vie en arbre et chars . . . bonds* (Carnières-Morlanwelz, Belgium: Editions Lansman, 1995). Unpublished plays include *Franco; Confession nationale; La peau cassée; Béatrice au Congo; La coutume d'être fou;* and *Les enfants du champignon.*

43. Sony Labou Tansi, *La parenthèse de sang*, 3. This is my translation.

44. Pius Ngandu Nkashama, "La mémoire du temps . . . Le temps de la mémoire dans le théâtre de Sony Labou Tansi," *Notre Librairie*, no. 102 (July–August 1990): 33–36. He also refers us to J. Van Wing, *Etude Bakongo: Sociologie, religion, magie* (Louvain, Desclée et Brouwer, 1959). See also Ange-Séverin Malanda and James Tshiatshimo, "La question Kongo," *Nouvelles Congolaises* no. 023/024 (January–April 1999), 61–80.

45. Nkashama, "La mémoire du temps," 34–35.

46. Sony Labou Tansi, "Les Kongo: Cinq formes de théâtre essentiel (22 octobre 1992)," in Dévésa, *Sony Labou Tansi: Ecrivain de la honte et des rives magiques du Kongo*, 353. See also Sony Labou Tansi, "Les sources Kongo de mon imagination (23 avril 1993)," in Dévésa, *Sony Labou Tansi: Ecrivain de la honte et des rives magiques du Kongo*, 359–62; and Dévésa, *Sony Labou Tansi: Ecrivain de la honte et des rives magiques du Kongo*, 315–33.

47. Sony Labou Tansi, "Les Kongo: Cinq formes de théâtre essentiel," in Dévésa, *Sony Labou Tansi: Ecrivain de la honte et des rives magiques du Kongo*, 353–54. These performances incorporate, respectively, "The public insult is a kind of *happening* that was played at the *lumbu* (royal court). . . . It is based on the antagonism between those who liked the new elected King and those who decried him"; "*Kingizila*, or the theater of madmen (of healing) consisted in giving a role to a sick person—usually a mentally ill person—in a story the whole village had to act out for entire moon cycles, until the afflicted person finds a suitable place in society"; "*Lemba* was the theater of the rich. Wealth was considered a marginalization risk. A person recently named by that calamity had to

organize a grandiose spectacle for his initiation to humility and death. The great feast that came at the end of the spectacle led the initiated person to die from drinking and eating in order for the *nganga* (wise men) to speak to his subconscious mind prior to his resurrection (his second birth)"; "The *Yala-Yala* theater (Nsimba: hold me) was played in honor of new-born twins. . . . If they were not given this honor, the twins ran the risk of returning from where they had come"; "*Nkoloba* (theater of the little wooden men) has its origin in the rice, millet, groundnut, or yam fields. To frighten off the wild creatures that destroyed crops, marionettes and scarecrows were built," 354–55. See also the categories provided by Kouvouama, "Sony Labou Tansi ou l'utopie pratiquée," in *Sony Labou Tansi ou la quête permanente du sens*, 95–106. Hereafter cited parenthetically in the text as "Kouvouama."

48. Salman Rushdie has talked about magic realism and surrealism with reference to events in Eastern European countries. For Rushdie, the "real" is constantly changing, so that reality, the "world," take on a somewhat surrealistic dimension, which only an extremely imaginative writer (such as Sony Labou Tansi) would be able to project. Salman Rushdie talking to Michael Ignatieff on "The Late Show," BBC2, September 30, 1989.

49. Bernard Magnier, Interview: "Je ne suis pas à développer mais à prendre ou à laisser," *Notre Librairie*, no. 79 (April–June 1985): 6.

50. Tchicaya U Tam'si, in "Tchicaya/Sony: Le dialogue interrompu. Rencontre animée par Daniel Maximin," *Notre Librairie*, nos. 92–93 (March–May 1988): 89.

51. Indeed, a tragi-comic dimension permeates Sony Labou Tansi's treatment of the postcolony. See Pierre Monsard's analysis, "Sony Labou Tansi: Esquisse d'une poétique du comique," in *Sony Labou Tansi ou la quête permanente du sens*, ed. Mukala Kadima-Nzuji, Abel Kouvouama, and Paul Kibangou, 47–60.

52. Jean-Paul Sartre, *Huis-Clos* (Paris: Gallimard, 1944).

53. I was faced with this dilemma when I directed the play in 1987 and finally decided that the paratextual devices were too significant to be ignored. The prologues to the Premier Soir, Troisième Soir, and Premier Matin were recorded and played at the appropriate moment. This served, I believe, to reinforce the tenuous relationship between the two worlds alluded to in the play.

54. See in particular chapter 13, "Wordplay at the Water's Edge," 315–41, in which Harrow examines the phenomenon he has described as "postoxymoron writing" (to designate works "in which the paradoxes of contemporary life do not lead inevitably to the blockage of an unsynthesized, endless dialectical struggle," x) in three of Sony Labou Tansi's novels: *La vie et demie*, *Les sept solitudes de Lorsa Lopez*, and *Les yeux du volcan*.

55. Nicolas Martin-Granel finds this refusal to die indicative of Sony Labou Tansi's own literary trajectory, given the attention that continues to be accorded to his work posthumously. See his "Sony *in Progress*," in *Sony Labou Tansi ou la quête permanente du sens*, ed. Mukala Kadima-Nzuji, Abel Kouvouama, and Paul Kibangou, 211–28, and "*Le quatrième côté du triangle*, or Squaring the Sex: A Genetic Approach to the 'Black Continent' in Sony Labou Tansi's Fiction," *Research in African Literatures* 31, no. 3 (Fall 2000): 69–99.

56. Sylvain Bemba, *Léopolis* (Paris: Hatier, 1986).

57. Aimé Césaire, *Une saison au Congo* (Paris: Seuil, 1965).
58. Jean-Paul Sartre, "The Political Thought of Patrice Lumumba," *Colonialism and Neocolonialism*, trans. Azedine Haddour, Steve Brewer, Terry McWilliams (London: Routledge, 2001), 156.
59. Pius Ngandu Nkashama, "La mémoire du temps," 34–35.
60. For other representations of oppressive bureaucratic infrastructures in francophone sub-Saharan African literature, see Emmanuel Dongala, "Une journée dans la vie d'Augustine Amaya," in *Jazz et vin de palme* (Paris: Hatier/Monde Noir, 1982): 35–43; Jean-Marie Adiaffi, *La carte d'identité* (Paris: Hatier/Monde Noir, 1980); and Ousmane Sembène, *Le mandat* (Paris: Présence Africaine, 1965).
61. David Mavouangui, "Sony Labou Tansi ou le refus 'd'exister sur commande,'" in *Sony Labou Tansi ou la quête permanente du sens*, ed. Mukala Kadima-Nzuji, Abel Kouvouama, and Paul Kibangou, 294–97.
62. Makhtar Diouf, "La marginalisation de l'Afrique dans le système-monde," in *L'intégration régionale dans le monde: Innovations et ruptures* (Paris: Karthala, 1994), 65.
63. Jean-Claude Willame, *Pouvoir et Gouvernance au Zaïre* (Paris: Karthala, 1993), 87. See also Jean-François Bayart, *L'état en Afrique: La politique du ventre* (Paris: Fayard, 1989); and Michela Wrong, *In the Footsteps of Mr. Kurz: Living on the Brink of Disaster in Mobutu's Congo* (New York: HarperCollins, 2001).
64. Jean-Claude Willame, *L'automne d'un despotisme: Pouvoir, argent et obéissance dans le Zaïre des années quatre-vingt* (Paris: Karthala, 1992), 212.
65. Achille Mbembe, *Les jeunes et l'ordre politique en Afrique noire* (Paris: L'Harmattan, 1985), 234–35.
66. The acronym is lost in translation: "villas, cars, wine, women."
67. Mbembe, *Les jeunes et l'ordre politique*, 237.
68. Jean-Loup Amselle and Elikia M'Bokolo, *Au cœur de l'ethnie: Ethnies, tribalisme et état en Afrique* (Paris: La Découverte, 1985).
69. Willame, *L'automne d'un despotisme*, 59.
70. There are times when translating Sony Labou Tansi's work becomes an almost insurmountable task, a fact that serves as confirmation of his creative aptitude and that is underlined in this statement in which Sony Labou Tansi conveys the inability of language itself to fulfill the needs of communication: "A une époque où l'homme est plus que jamais résolu à tuer la vie, comment voulez-vous que je vous parle sinon en *chair-mots-de-passe?*" (*La vie et demie*, 9, emphasis mine).
71. Ahmadou Kourouma, *Allah n'est pas obligé* (Paris: Seuil, 2000), 11. The word "toubab" essentially designates French colonials residing in francophone Africa.
72. Lopes, for example, has stated that "je n'écris pas français, mais en français" (I do not write French but rather in French), cited in Michel Tétu, *La Francophonie: Histoire, problématique et perspectives* (Montréal: Guérin Littérature, 1987), 297.
73. Bemba, "Sony Labou Tansi et moi," 50.
74. Bemba, "Sony Labou Tansi et moi," 50. Séwanou Dabla explores these linguistic devices exhaustively in *Nouvelles écritures africaines*. See also Paul Nzete, "Les jeux de mots dans les romans de Sony Labou Tansi," in *Sony Labou Tansi ou la quête permanente du sens*, ed. Mukala Kadima-Nzuji, Abel Kouvouama, and Paul Kibangou, 61–74.

75. The question as to "why" has been addressed comprehensively in a number of studies that have focused specifically on the polemics of language, and I do not believe that it is necessary to add to this debate at this juncture. See, for example, Richard Bjornson, ed., "The Language Question," *Research in African Literatures* 23, no. 1 (Spring 1992); Emmanuel N. Obiechina, *Language and Theme: Essays on African Literature* (Washington, D.C.: Howard University Press, 1990); and Christopher L. Miller, "*Les soleils des indépendances* and francophone dialogue," in *Theories of Africans: Francophone Literature and Anthropology in Africa* (Chicago: University of Chicago Press, 1990), 181–245.

76. See, for example, Emily Apter, "On Translation in a Global Market," *Public Culture* 13, no. 1 (Winter 2001): 1–12.

77. See, for example, "Rencontre avec Sony Labou Tansi," *Bingo* (September 1987): 58–59; and Calixthe Beyala's epigraph to *Les honneurs perdus*, "Le français est francophone, mais la francophonie n'est pas française" (The French language is francophone but *la francophonie* is not French) (Paris: Albin Michel, 1996).

78. Alain Ricard, *Littératures d'Afrique noire, des langues aux livres* (Paris: Karthala, 1995), 248.

79. Bernard Magnier, Interview: "Un citoyen de ce siècle," 16.

80. *Bingo*, "Rencontre avec Sony Labou Tansi," 59.

81. Kwame Anthony Appiah, *In My Father's House: Africa in the Philosophy of Culture* (New York: Oxford University Press, 1992), 53.

82. Quoted in *Equateur*, no. 1 (October–November 1986): 30.

83. Quoted in Tétu, *La francophonie: Histoire, problématique, perspectives*, 207.

84. Elisabeth Mudimbe-Boyi, "Langue volée, langue violée: Pouvoir, écriture et violence dans la roman africain," in *La deriva della francophonie*, 104. See also the parallels Daniel-Henri Pageaux establishes between the literary projects of Sony Labou Tansi and Gabriel García Márquez, "Entre le renouveau et la modernité: Vers de nouveaux modèles?" *Notre Librairie*, no. 78 (January–March 1985): 31–35.

85. Bernard Geniès, "Africain d'accord, écrivain d'abord," *Le Nouvel Observateur* (August 19–25, 1988): 60.

86. Dabla, *Nouvelles écritures africaines*, 144. See also Ngate, *Francophone African Fiction: Reading a Literary Tradition*; and Gilbert Lombalé-Baré, "Une lecture de *L'état honteux*: Essai d'analyse syntaxique," in *Sony Labou Tansi ou la quête permanente du sens*, ed. Mukala Kadima-Nzuji, Abel Kouvouama, and Paul Kibangou, 107–23.

87. Mudimbe-Boyi, "Langue volée, langue violée," 103.

88. Harrow, *Thresholds of Change*, 336.

89. Georges N'Gal, "Sony Labou Tansi et l'engendrement du sens," in *Sony Labou Tansi ou la quête permanente du sens*, ed. Mukala Kadima-Nzuji, Abel Kouvouama, and Paul Kibangou, 39–46; and also his pioneering book, *Création et rupture en littérature africaine* (Paris: L'Harmattan, 1994). André-Patient Bokiba extends this experimentation with language to an analysis of various naming processes in Sony Labou Tansi's work. See his "L'identité dans les romans de Sony Labou Tansi," in *Sony Labou Tansi ou la quête permanente du sens*, ed. Mukala Kadima-Nzuji, Abel Kouvouama, and Paul Kibangou, 255–75.

90. For one of the earliest studies of Sony Labou Tansi's language, see Eileen Julien, "Dominance and Discourse in *La vie et demie* or How to Do Things with Words," *Research in African Literatures* 20, no. 3 (1989): 371–84.

91. Justin Kalulu Bisanswa, "Life Is Not a Book. Creuse: Literature and Representation in Sony Labou Tansi's Work," *Research in African Literatures* 31, no. 3 (Fall 2000): 136–37.

4. Henri Lopes

1. Marie-Clotilde Jacquey, Interview, "Henri Lopes africain, métis et congolais," *Notre Librairie*, no. 83 (April–June 1986): 50. See also J.-L. Aka-Evy, "Interview," *Etudes Littéraires Africaines* 4 (1997): 3–8.

2. J. M. Coetzee, "Confession and Double Thoughts: Tolstoy, Rousseau, Dostoevsky," *Doubling the Point: Essays and Interviews*, ed. David Attwell (Cambridge, Mass.: Harvard University Press, 1992), 280. Hereafter cited parenthetically in the text as "Confession and Double Thoughts."

3. Henri Lopes, *The Laughing Cry: An African Cock and Bull Story*, trans. Gerald Moore (London: Readers International, 1987). Hereafter cited parenthetically in the text as "*The Laughing Cry.*"

4. Jacquey, Interview, 47. I have retained the self-referential French term *métisse* that Lopes uses rather than *mestizo* or *hybrid*. For a detailed account of Lopes's childhood, see his "Maluku au temps des bateaux à roues," in *Une enfance d'ailleurs: 17 écrivains racontent*, ed. Nancy Huston and Leïla Sebbar (Paris: Belfond, 1993), 125–41.

5. Henri Lopes, *Le chercheur d'Afriques* (Paris: Seuil, 1990). On the question of *métissage*, see Kenneth W. Harrow, "The Dance of the Creole," *Thresholds of Change in African Literature: The Emergence of a Tradition* (Portsmouth, N.H.: Heinemann, 1994), 291–313; and Françoise Lionnet, *Postcolonial Representations: Women, Literature, Identity* (Ithaca: Cornell University Press, 1995).

6. Bessie Head, *A Gesture of Belonging: Letters from Bessie Head, 1965–1979*, ed. Randolph Vigne (London: 1991), 55, quoted in Jacqueline Rose, "On the 'Universality' of Madness: Bessie Head's *A Question of Power*," *Critical Inquiry* 20 (Spring 1994): 412.

7. Jacqueline Rose, "On the 'Universality' of Madness: Bessie Head's *A Question of Power*," 412–13.

8. More recently, Henri Lopes has actively sought the nomination as Boutros Boutros-Ghali's successor for the post of secretary-general of the Organisation Internationale de la Francophonie (OIF). To this end, he has established his own web site (http://www.henri-lopes.org), while also drawing irascible letters of opposition from prominent Congolese personalities, such as novelist and critic Jean-Pierre Makouta-Mboukou's "Francophonie: Lettre ouverte à propos de la candidature d'Henri Lopes," August 24, 2001: <http://www.rezoweb.com/forum/politique/brazzamfoayikoba/359.html>.

9. Arlette Chemain has underlined the importance of considering these dual careers. See "Henri Lopes: Engagement civique et recherche d'une écriture," *Notre Librairie* 92–93 (March–May 1988): 123–28.

10. Henri Lopes, *Tribaliques* (Yaoundé: CLE, 1971); *Tribaliks: Contemporary Congolese Stories*, trans. Andrea Leskes (London: Heinemann, 1987); *La nouvelle romance* (Yaoundé: CLE, 1976); *Sans tam-tam* (Yaoundé: CLE, 1977); *Le chercheur d'Afriques* (Paris: Seuil, 1990); *Sur l'autre rive* (Paris: Seuil, 1992); *Le lys et le flamboyant* (Paris: Seuil, 1997); *Le Pleurer-Rire* (Paris: Présence Africaine, 1982), and *Dossier classé* (Paris, Editions du Seuil, 2002).

11. Edouard Maunick, "Le territoire d'Henri Lopes: Propos recueillis par Edouard Maunick," *Notre Librairie*, nos. 92–93 (March–May 1988): 130.

12. Henri Lopes, "My Novels, My Characters, and Myself," *Research in African Literatures* 24, no. 1 (Spring 1993): 84. Hereafter cited parenthetically in the text as "My Novels."

13. Achille Mbembe, *On the Postcolony* (Berkeley: University of California Press, 2001), 108. Hereafter cited parenthetically in the text as "Mbembe." Koffi Anyinefa has argued that "By multiplying the narrative voices, Lopes forces different points of view to enter the novel: one can read a democratic principle in this polyphony," in "Postcolonial Postmodernity in Henri Lopes's *Le Pleurer-Rire*," *Research in African Literatures* 29, no. 3 (Fall 1998): 14. Hereafter cited parenthetically in the text as "Postcolonial Modernity." While this essay does indeed achieve its objective of contributing to the debate surrounding the pertinence of the term *postmodernism* to a critique of African literature, the omission of Kwame Anthony Appiah's important essay on the subject, "The Postcolonial and the Postmodern," is somewhat unfortunate. See *In My Father's House: Africa in the Philosophy of Culture* (New York: Oxford University Press, 1992), 137–57.

14. Quoted in Sue Curry Jansen, *Censorship: The Knot That Binds Power and Knowledge* (New York: Oxford University Press, 1991), 197.

15. Anyinefa has described this as "a kind of chronological anarchy," "*Postcolonial Postmodernity*," 12. See also his earlier work on Lopes's novel in his book *Littérature et politique en Afrique noire: Socialisme et dictature comme thèmes du roman congolais d'expression française* (Bayreuth: Eckhard Breitinger, 1990), 179–223. Hereafter cited parenthetically in the text as "Anyinefa." The very structure of Lopes's novel serves to underline the multiplicity of perspectives available, and for Anyinefa, "The aesthetic functions of the novel's form are evident. By multiplying narrative instances, Lopes introduces different points of view on a given subject, thereby suggesting its complexity" and "conferring a density and complexity on *Le Pleurer-Rire*" (Anyinefa, 184–85).

16. This became a common device for Lopes's *avant-gardist* peers, notably in Sony Labou Tansi's *La vie et demie*, *La parenthèse de sang*, and *Je soussigné cardiaque*. For an analysis of novelistic techniques, see Ange-Séverin Malanda, *Henri Lopes ou l'impératif romanesque* (Paris: Silex, 1987).

17. Nicolas Martin-Granel, "Le crier-écrire," *Notre Librairie* 78 (January–March 1985): 47–55. See also his *Rires noirs: Anthologie romancée de l'humour dans le roman africain* (Paris: Editions SEPIA, 1991).

18. M. H. Abrams, *A Glossary of Literary Terms* (Harcourt Brace College Publishers, 1993), 64.

19. Denis Diderot, *Jacques le fataliste et son maître*, in *Œuvres romanesques* (Paris: Editions Garnier Frères, 1981), 521–808.

20. See, for example, Sony Labou Tansi's "Avertissement" to his first novel, *La vie et demie* (Paris: Seuil, 1979), where he writes: "this is not a fable."

21. Lydie Moudileno, "Labou Tansi's *La vie et demie*, or The Tortuous Path of the Fable," *Research in African Literatures* 29, no. 3 (Fall 1998): 24. Hereafter cited parenthetically in the text as "Moudileno."

22. Tvetan Todorov, *The Morals of History*, trans. Alyson Waters (Minneapolis: University of Minnesota Press, 1995), 90.

23. Alice Green Fredman, *Diderot and Sterne* (New York: Columbia University Press, 1954), 93.

24. Lopes's novel contains elements that one could easily attribute to a multitude of genres. See, for example, the pertinence of Abrams's definition of "autobiography," "biography," and "memoir": "Autobiography is a biography written by the subject about himself or herself. It is to be distinguished from the *memoir*, in which the emphasis is not on the author's developing self but on the people and events that the author has known or witnessed," *A Glossary of Literary Terms*, 15.

25. Shoshana Felman, "After the Apocalypse: Paul de Man and the Fall to Silence," in *Testimony: Crises of Witnessing in Literature, Psychoanalysis, and History* (New York: Routledge, 1992), 93. Hereafter cited parenthetically in the text as "Felman."

26. Charles S. Maier, "Doing History, Doing Justice: The Narrative of the Historian and of the Truth Commission," in *Truth v. Justice: The Morality of Truth Commissions*, ed. Robert I. Rotberg and Dennis Thompson (Princeton: Princeton University Press, 2000), 271.

27. On this matter, see J. Robert Loy, *Diderot's Determined Fatality* (New York: King's Crown Press, 1950), 10.

28. Lopes, *Sans tam-tam*, 62.

29. I am reminded of Ferdinand Oyono's novel, *Une vie de boy* (Paris: Julliard, 1956), as I explore Lopes's choice of the Maître d'Hôtel as the central narrative voice. Whereas Oyono's "houseboy," Toundi, held a position that afforded him a unique perspective on colonial mechanisms, Lopes's Maître d'Hôtel enjoys a similar position from which to judge the manner in which power mechanisms are manipulated in a postcolonial government.

30. Another such instance is provided by the inclusion of a reference to a book (*Dark Days on Uganda*, Wallgren Publishing House, London, 1974) in a footnote to one of the exiled friend's letters to the narrator, in which one of Idi Amin Dada's government ministers gave an account of a meeting between Bwakamabé and the Ugandan dictator.

31. Jacquey, "Interview," 49.

32. See, for example, Frédéric Grah-Mel, "Henri Lopes: L'écrivain doit prendre position ou se taire," *Fraternité-Matin* (October 6, 1976): 17; and Christine Falgayrettes, "Lopes: Poser la révolte avec *Le Pleurer-Rire*," *Afrique-Asie*, no. 282 (1982): 50–51.

33. Aimé Césaire, *Cahier d'un retour au pays natal* (Paris: Présence Africaine, 1939); Jean-Paul Sartre, "Orphée noir," preface to *Anthologie de la nouvelle poésie nègre et malgache de langue française*, ed. Léopold Sédar Senghor (Paris: Presses Universitaires de France, 1948). For other Congolese examples, see Sony Labou Tansi, *La vie et demie*; *L'état honteux* (Paris: Seuil, 1981); and *Les sept solitudes*

de Lorsa Lopez (Paris: Seuil, 1985); Tchichelle Tchivela's "starting block" in his collection of short stories *L'exil ou la tombe* (Paris: Présence Africaine, 1986); and Caya Makhele's novel *Le cercle des vertiges* (Paris: L'Harmattan, 1992). For a compelling study of prefaces in francophone literature, see Richard Watts, "'The Politics of Prefaces: Patronage, Self-Promotion, and the Colonial/Metropolitan Relationship in Prefaces to Francophone Literary Texts" (dissertation, Yale University, 1998).

34. Josaphat B. Kubayanda, "Dictatorship, Oppression, and New Realism," *Research in African Literatures* 21, no. 2 (Summer 1990): 7.

35. Cheikh Hamidou Kane published his second novel in 1995, *Les gardiens du temple* (Paris: Albin Michel).

36. J. M. Coetzee, "The Work of the Censor: Censorship in South Africa," in *Giving Offense: Essays on Censorship* (Chicago: University of Chicago Press, 1996), 200.

37. Lopes, *Tribaliques*, 63.

38. Tchichelle Tchivela, "Ilotes et martyrs," in *Longue est la nuit* (Paris: Hatier, 1980), 89–90.

39. Personal communication, Brazzaville, Republic of the Congo, January 2, 1995.

40. Jacquey, "Interview," 50.

41. Sony Labou Tansi, interview with David Applefield, *Frank: An International Journal of Contemporary Writing and Art*, no. 14 (1992): 101–102.

42. Applefield, "Interview," 101.

43. Dori Laub, in Felman, *Testimony: Crises of Witnessing in Literature, Psychoanalysis, and History*, 70. Hereafter cited parenthetically in the text as "Laub."

44. Wole Soyinka, *The Burden of Memory, the Muse of Forgiveness* (New York: Oxford University Press, 1999), 31.

45. Jean-Michel Dévésa, *Sony Labou Tansi: Ecrivain de la honte et des rives magiques du Kongo* (Paris: L'Harmattan, 1996), 18.

46. David N'Zitoukoukou, "*Le Pleurer-Rire* de Henri Lopes," *Peuples noirs, Peuples africains*, no. 35 (September–October 1983): 115–16.

47. Mark Behr, "Fault Lines Speech," South Africa, 1996. Personal communication. *The Smell of Apples* (London: Little, Brown, 1995), and *Embrace* (London: Little, Brown, 2000).

48. Robert I. Rotberg, "Truth Commissions and the Provision of Truth, Justice, and Reconciliation," in *Truth v. Justice: The Morality of Truth Commissions*, ed. Robert I. Rotberg and Dennis Thompson (Princeton: Princeton University Press, 2000), 6.

49. Njabulo S. Ndebele, *South African Literature and Culture: Rediscovery of the Ordinary* (Manchester: Manchester University Press, 1994), 155. Arguably, the most powerful and complete exploration of this question was undertaken by the South African journalist and poet Antjie Krog and published as *Country of My Skull: Guilt, Sorrow, and the Limits of Forgiveness in the New South Africa* (New York: Random House, 1999).

50. J. M. Coetzee, "Confession and Double Thoughts: Tolstoy, Rousseau, Dostoevsky," 251–93.

51. Coetzee introduces Paul de Man's reading of Rousseau's *Confessions* to the dis-

cussion here. See Paul de Man, *Allegories of Reading: Figural Language in Rousseau, Nietzsche, Rilke, and Proust* (New Haven: Yale University Press, 1979).

52. For Coetzee, *confessor* is used "to denote the one to whom the confession is addressed," while *confessant* designates "the one who confesses" ("Confession and Double Thoughts," 419n).

53. See Jacques Chevrier, "Henri Lopes et son 'tonton,'" *Jeune Afrique*, no. 1141 (1982): 105–107. See also Anyinefa, who has drawn on T. Zezeze Kalonji's work to comment on the etymological significance of Bwakamabé's name, in *Littérature et Politique en Afrique Noire*, 186. See T. Zezeze Kalonji, "Eléments pour une analyse plurielle du *Pleurer-Rire* d'Henri Lopes," *Peuples noirs, Peuples africains*, no. 37 (1984): 34.

54. Hergé, *Les aventures de Tintin au Congo* (Belgium: Casterman, 1930; 1946 for the color edition).

55. Philippe Met, "Of Men and Animals: Hergé's *Tintin au Congo*, a Study in Primitivism," *Romanic Review* 87, no. 1 (1995): 131.

56. This is another instance when the conflation between the real and fictive dimension is underlined. Bwakamabé's "Country," described as an ex-French colonial territory, serves to further restrict the narrative to francophone sub-Saharan Africa and, in theory at least, excludes the possibility of the setting being Zaire (Democratic Republic of the Congo), which was of course an ex-Belgian colony. However, this technique highlights the tenuousness of these political constructs since Bwakamabé's rhetoric is at times closer to that of former Zairian leader President Mobutu than to the scientific-Socialist discourse associated with Marien Ngouabi or Denis Sassou Nguesso, among others, in the People's Republic of the Congo (Republic of the Congo).

57. George Orwell, *1984* (London: Penguin, 1948).

58. Monsieur Gourdain was included in Bwakamabé's administration because of his ability to establish a rule of fear. He is widely recognized as "the chief of all our torturers" (*The Laughing Cry*, 55) and nicknamed "Bazooka Commando" (*The Laughing Cry*, 246). The name Gourdain is close enough to the French "gourdin," which is a "club" or "bludgeon," to function homonymously.

59. After the 1991 National Conference was held in the Congo, the newly drafted constitution underlined the need to respect civil and human rights as outlined by international charters. Yet, while claiming to embrace the principles of democratic pluralism, the actualization of these statements remains to be seen. Until this happens, Susan E. Waltz's words of caution in her book *Human Rights and Reform: Changing the Face of North African Politics* apply to the Congo: "so long as authority has effective control in a non-democratic regime, it is difficult to imagine that such groups (i.e., human rights organizations, etc.) will be appreciated" (Berkeley: University of California Press, 1995), 14.

60. J. M. Coetzee, *Disgrace* (New York: Viking Penguin, 1999), 172.

5. Emmanuel Dongala

1. See Julie Michaels, "Writer in Exile," *Boston Globe Magazine* (February 6, 2000): 12–31.

2. Emmanuel Dongala, *Un fusil dans la main, un poème dans la poche* (Paris: Albin Michel, 1973); *Jazz et vin de palme* (Paris: Hatier, 1982); *Le feu des origines* (Paris: Albin Michel, 1987), 215; *The Fire of Origins*, trans. Lillian Corti and Yuval Taylor (Chicago: Lawrence Books, 2000); *Les petits garçons naissent aussi des étoiles* (Paris: Editions Le Serpent à Plumes, 1997): 251–52; *Little Boys Come from the Stars*, trans. Joël Réjouis and Val Vinokurov (New York: Farrar, Straus and Giroux, 2001); and *Johnny, chien méchant* (Paris: Editions Le Serpent à Plumes, 2002). Hereafter cited parenthetically in the text following the title of the work. Koffi Anyinefa has written incisively on Dongala's first novel in *Littérature et politique en Afrique noire: Socialisme et dictature comme thèmes du roman congolais d'expression française* (Bayreuth: Eckhard Breitinger, 1990). See also his article "Intertextuality in Dongala's 'Un fusil dans la main, un poème dans la poche,'" *Research in African Literatures* 24, no. 1 (1993): 5–17; hereafter cited parenthetically in the text as "Intertextuality."

3. See Wyatt MacGaffey, *Kongo Political Culture: The Conceptual Challenge of the Particular* (Bloomington: Indiana University Press, 2000); and Johannes Fabian, *Out of Our Minds: Reason and Madness in the Exploration of Central Africa* (Berkeley: University of California Press, 2000).

4. All interviews with Emmanuel Dongala were conducted in Brazzaville in December 1994 and January 1995.

5. Simon Bockie, *Death and the Invisible Powers: The World of Kongo Belief* (Bloomington: Indiana University Press, 1993), 139. Hereafter cited parenthetically in the text as "Bockie."

6. Wyatt MacGaffey, *Modern Kongo Prophets: Religion in a Plural Society* (Bloomington: Indiana University Press, 1983), 12. Hereafter cited parenthetically in the text as "*Modern Kongo Prophets.*"

7. Emmanuel Dongala, "Emmanuel Dongala: Rire pour ne pas pleurer," interview with Alain Brezault and Gérard Clavreuil, *Notre Librairie*, nos. 92/93 (March–May 1988): 135.

8. Ahmadou Kourouma, *Les soleils des indépendances* (Montréal: Presses de l'Université de Montréal, 1968); Aminata Sow Fall, *La grève des bàttu ou les déchets humains* (Dakar: Nouvelles Editions Africaines, 1979); Alioum Fantouré, *Le cercle des tropiques* (Paris: Présence Africaine, 1972); Ibrahima Ly, *Toiles d'araignées* (Paris: L'Harmattan, 1982); and Calixthe Beyala, *Tu t'appelleras Tanga* (Paris: Stock, 1988).

9. Henri Lopes, *Le Pleurer-Rire* (Paris: Présence Africaine, 1982); Sony Labou Tansi, *La vie et demie* (Paris: Seuil, 1979); Tchichelle Tchivela, *Longue est la nuit* (Paris: Hatier, 1980), and *L'exil ou la tombe* (Paris: Présence Africaine, 1986).

10. Tierno Monénembo, *Les crapauds-brousse* (Paris: Seuil, 1979), 8.

11. There are a number of autobiographical elements in these stories which one can deduce from biographical information about the author (who was a professor of chemistry at the Marien Ngouabi University in Brazzaville), or because Dongala is directly describing his experiences, as is the case with the jazz musician John Coltrane in the final story. In the case of the penultimate story, "Mon métro fantôme," the narrator is clearly Dongala himself, who through an extra-textual

act that is justified by its productivity allows the reader to deduce that it is in fact the author that is in question.

12. Sue Curry Jansen, *Censorship: The Knot That Binds Power and Knowledge* (New York: Oxford University Press, 1991), 196.

13. Brezault and Clavreuil, "Interview," 136.

14. Brezault and Clavreuil, "Interview," 137.

15. Jean-Claude Willame, *Pouvoir et gouvernance au Zaïre* (Paris: Karthala, 1993), 209.

16. A similar situation played an important role in Ahmadou Kourouma's novel *Les soleils des indépendances*. In this novel, Fama and Salimata were unable to have children. Kourouma's text leaves the responsibility for the sterility somewhat ambiguous. Clearly, sterility functions as a metaphor for the social and political sterility of the post-independence era.

17. See also J. Van Wing, *Etudes bakongo* (Brussels: Desclée de Brouwer, 1959); and Georges Balandier, *La sociologie de l'Afrique noire* (Paris: Presses Universitaires de France, 1955).

18. Wyatt MacGaffey, *Art and Healing of the Bakongo Commented by Themselves* (Bloomington: Indiana University Press, 1991), 4. This is a complete study of *nkisi*, accompanied by detailed explanations of their respective functions and attributes. See also Buakasa Tulu Ria Mpansu, "Les discours de la kindoki ou sorcellerie," *Cahiers des Religions Africaines* 4, no. 11 (1972): 5–67.

19. The *Webster's Dictionary* definition of "leviathan" reveals its pertinence to this context: "a totalitarian state having a vast bureaucracy."

20. For other examples of bureaucratic oppression, see Ousmane Sembène, *Vehi-Ciosane ou blanche-genèse suivi du mandat* (Paris: Présence Africaine, 1965). In the short story entitled "Le mandat," the central protagonist, Ibrahima Dieng, receives a money order from France. He is unable to cash it without first obtaining official identification papers. See also Sony Labou Tansi, *Je soussigné cardiaque* (Paris: Hatier, 1981). In this play, Mallot is a victim of a number of bureaucratic maneuvers and processes from which he is excluded.

21. Sony Labou Tansi, *L'anté-peuple* (Paris: Seuil, 1983).

22. The *mbouloumboulou* were African colonial militiamen.

23. For further examples in African literature of the status that ownership of a vehicle confers on individuals, see Nkem Nwankwo, *My Mercedes Is Bigger Than Yours* (London: André Deutsch, 1975).

24. Ousmane Sembène, *Les bouts de bois de dieu* (Paris: Le Livre Contemporain, 1960).

25. Wyatt MacGaffey, *Custom and Government in Lower Congo* (Berkeley: University of California Press, 1970), 299.

26. MacGaffey, *Art and Healing*, 9.

27. André Matsoua (1899–1942) is a symbol of anti-colonial resistance, particularly among the Kongo. He was imprisoned by the colonial authorities.

28. A translation of this story appeared as "The Man," trans. Clive Wake, in *Contemporary Short Stories*, ed. Chinua Achebe and C. L. Innes (Portsmouth, N.H.: Heinemann, 1992), 81–86.

29. For one of the most remarkable and incisive studies of the theme of "cruelty," and of what Kanan Makiya has described as a "new literary genre: cruelty's litera-ture of witness" (cover blurb), see Kate Millett, *The Politics of Cruelty: An Essay on the Literature of Political Imprisonment* (New York: W. W. Norton, 1994).

30. The French expression "avoir le trouillomètre à zéro" can be translated in a number of ways: "to be scared stiff" or "to be in a blue funk" would be the clos-est. The word "trouille" also describes a state of fear that is usually attributed to people who are not only afraid but who also lack courage. It thus serves to under-mine the earlier descriptions and image which propaganda has created of the leader as a constituent part to the rule of fear.

31. "Jazz and Palm Wine," in *Jazz and Palm Wine and Other Stories*, edited and with an introduction by Willfried F. Feuser (Harlow, Essex: Longman, 1981), 194–202. Hereafter cited parenthetically in the text as "Jazz and Palm Wine"). It should be noted that Emmanuel Dongala was not asked for permission to use the title of his collection of short stories for the actual volume published by Longman.

32. When Dongala was a student in America in the 1960s, he published a short story called "The D Train" which "Mon métro fantôme" is based on. One of the most memorable works in terms of its treatment of similar issues is Louis-Ferdinand Céline's *Voyage au bout de la nuit* (Paris: Denoël, 1932). See also Bernard Dadié, *Patron de New York* (Paris: Présence Africaine, 1964).

33. Brezault and Clavreuil, "Interview," 136.

34. Séwanou Dabla, *Jazz et vin de palme de Emmanuel Boundzéki Dongala* (Paris: Fernand Nathan, 1986), 11.

35. Anna Ridelagh, "Emmanuel Boundzéki Dongala," in *The New Oxford Compan-ion to Literature in French*, ed. Peter France (Oxford: Oxford University Press, 1995), 252.

36. Emmanuel Boundzéki Dongala, "Littérature et société: Ce que je crois, *Peuples noirs, Peuples africains*, no. 9 (May–June 1979): 63.

37. Dabla, *Jazz et vin de palme de Emmanuel Boundzéki Dongala*, 56. See also "L'univers nord-américain," 40–43.

38. Homi K. Bhabha, *The Location of Culture* (London: Routledge, 1994), 9.

39. Edouard Glissant, *Caribbean Discourse: Selected Essays*, trans. J. Michael Dash (Charlottesville: University of Virginia Press, 1989), 258–59.

40. Glissant, *Caribbean Discourse*, 258–59.

41. Wole Soyinka, *The Burden of Memory, the Muse of Forgiveness* (New York: Ox-ford University Press, 1999), 58, paraphrasing Elie Wiesel and Danielle Mitter-rand. Hereafter cited parenthetically in the text as "Soyinka."

42. Achille Mbembe, *Notes on the Postcolony* (Berkeley: University of California Press, 2001).

43. Interestingly enough, Dongala draws on the Chinese writer Lu Xun's (1881–1936) collection of poems *Yecao* for his epigraph to the seventh chapter. See *Complete Works of Lu Xun* (Beijing: Renmin wenxue chubanshe, 1981). Ac-cording to Shu-mei Shih's discussion of Lu Xun's poems, "although the prevail-ing mood seems pessimistic, hope is ultimately sustained through relentless

struggle against the pessimism engendered by both social corruption and individual existential anguish," 90. See Shu-mei Shih, *The Lure of the Modern: Writing Modernism in Semicolonial China, 1917–1937* (Berkeley: University of California Press, 2001).

44. In highlighting the complicity of Africans in colonial expansionism, Dongala is also careful to point out the fact that Western representations and responses to Africa were not themselves monolithic. Two contradictory examples cited by Dongala follow:

- "There are territories for the taking, servants at our pleasure. The rights of man do not apply to Negroes. Besides, the natives have no right to anything, whatever one gives them is a genuine gratuity" (*The Fire of Origins*, 78).
- "We've seen nothing which justifies the hypothesis of the native inferiority of the Negro, nothing which proves that he is of a different species than the most civilized. The African is a man endowed with all the attributes characteristic of the human race" (*The Fire of Origins*, 79).

45. Mbembe, *Notes on the Postcolony*, 104.

46. The italicization of the original French term *évolué* serves to underline its untranslatability. The term is used to designate those Africans who had achieved a degree of success in the assimilationist *evolutionary* ladder (primarily determined through one's proximity to French language literacy) that separates Africanness from Frenchness. This type of movement from "indigènes" to *évolués* constitutes the ideological agenda of the Tintin narratives I discussed in the previous chapter.

47. Paul Gilroy, *The Black Atlantic: Modernity and Double Consciousness* (Cambridge, Mass.: Harvard University Press, 1993), 3.

48. Charles S. Maier, "Doing History, Doing Justice: The Narrative of the Historian and of the Truth Commission," in *Truth v. Justice: The Morality of Truth Commissions*, ed. Robert I. Rotberg and Dennis Thompson (Princeton: Princeton University Press, 2000), 264.

49. Cited in Elizabeth Kiss's brilliant reading of the subject, "Moral Ambition within and beyond Political Constraints: Reflections on Restorative Justice," in *Truth v. Justice: The Morality of Truth Commissions*, ed. Robert I. Rotberg and Dennis Thompson (Princeton: Princeton University Press, 2000), 79.

50. Kiss, "Moral Ambition within and beyond Political Constraints," 79.

51. Nadine Gordimer, "Living in the Interregnum," *The Essential Gesture* (London: Penguin, 1988), 269–70. See also André Brink, *Reinventing a Continent: Writing and Politics in South Africa* (Cambridge, Mass.: Zoland Books, 1998).

52. Njabulo Ndebele, *South African Literature and Culture: Rediscovery of the Ordinary* (Manchester: Manchester University Press, 1994), 157. See also the recent book by the vice chairperson of the Truth and Reconciliation Commission, Alex Boraine, *A Country Unmasked: Inside South Africa's Truth and Reconciliation Commission* (Oxford: Oxford University Press, 2001).

53. Carolyn Toll Oppenheim, "Witnesses to History," *The Berkshire Eagle*, Sunday, February 25, 2001. The Dowmel Lecture was delivered on February 8, 2001.

54. Mark Behr, *Embrace* (London: Little, Brown, 2000), "Dedication."

55. Ousmane Sembène, *Xala* (Paris: Présence Africaine, 1973); Sony Labou Tansi, *L'état honteux* (Paris: Seuil, 1981); and Alioum Fantouré, *Le cercle des tropiques*.

6. National Conferences and Media Decentralization in Francophone Africa

1. Henri Lopes, *The Laughing Cry: An African Cock and Bull Story*, trans. Gerald Moore (London: Readers International, 1987), 42.
2. Antjie Krog, *Country of My Skull: Guilt, Sorrow, and the Limits of Forgiveness in the New South Africa* (New York: Random House, 1999), 364.
3. The most comprehensive studies available that address political transition in francophone Africa are John A. Wiseman, ed., *Democracy and Political Change in Sub-Saharan Africa* (London: Routledge, 1995); and John F. Clark and David E. Gardinier, eds., *Political Reform in Francophone Africa* (Boulder, Colo.: Westview Press, 1997). Clark suggests that "reform" is perhaps a more appropriate and cautious term as well as a more encompassing one in order to reflect the various transitions he and Gardinier have characterized as "peaceful regime change," "moderate reform," "opposition without reform," and "civil war and political change," rather than "democratization" and "liberalization," given the inherent difficulty of predicting the lasting outcome of these transitions; see introduction to *Political Reform in Francophone Africa*, 1–5. This period in history also coincided with the deaths of many of francophone Africa's longtime leaders, notably Ahmed Sékou Touré of Guinea in 1984, Félix Houphouët-Boigny of Côte d'Ivoire in 1993, and Joseph Désiré Mobutu (Mobutu Sese Seko) of Zaire in 1997.
4. Patrick Manning, *Francophone Sub-Saharan Africa 1880–1995* (New York: Cambridge University Press, 1998), 194. Hereafter cited parenthetically in the text as "Manning."
5. Clark, introduction to *Political Reform in Francophone Africa*, 2. See also Jean-François Bayart, Stephen Ellis, and Béatrice Hibou, *The Criminalization of the State in Africa* (Bloomington: Indiana University Press, 1999).
6. John F. Clark, "Congo: Transition and the Struggle to Consolidate," *Political Reform in Francophone Africa*, ed. John F. Clark and David E. Gardinier (Boulder, Colo.: Westview Press, 1997), 65. Hereafter cited parenthetically in the text as "Clark."
7. Denis Sassou Nguesso speaking in an interview with Christian Castéran and Blaise-Pascal Talla, "Denis Sassou Nguesso: 'Rendez-vous avec la paix et la démocratie,'" *Jeune Afrique Economie*, no. 330 (June 4–17, 2001): 58–67.
8. Fabien Eboussi Boulaga, *Les conférences nationales en Afrique noire: Une affaire à suivre* (Paris: Karthala, 1993), 195–96. Hereafter cited parenthetically in the text as "Boulaga."
9. Emmanuel Dongala, *Les petits garçons naissent aussi des étoiles* (Paris: Albin Michel, 1998).
10. Antjie Krog, *Country of My Skull*, x.
11. Desmond Tutu, *Truth and Reconciliation Commission of South Africa Report*, vol. 1 (London: Macmillan, 1998), 5.
12. Tutu, *Truth and Reconciliation Commission*, 17.

13. Njabulo S. Ndebele, *South African Literature and Culture: Rediscovery of the Ordinary* (Manchester: Manchester University Press, 1994), 158.

14. The word "palabre" is employed in a number of referential contexts and signifies dialogue and debate here.

15. Marie-Soleil Frère, *Presse et démocratie en Afrique francophone: Les mots et les maux de la transition au Bénin et au Niger* (Paris: Karthala, 2000), 258–59. Hereafter cited parenthetically in the text as "Frère."

16. Wole Soyinka, *The Burden of Memory, the Muse of Forgiveness* (New York: Oxford University Press, 1999), 9. Hereafter cited parenthetically in the text as "Soyinka."

17. See also Grégoire Biyoko, "La République du Congo," in *Afrique centrale: Des médias pour la démocratie* (Paris: Editions Karthala/Institut Panos de Paris, 2000), 101–15.

18. Indeed, as early as 1971, the focus of Henri Lopes's collection of short stories *Tribaliques* had been provided by tribalism. See Henri Lopes, *Tribaliques* (Yaoundé: CLE, 1971).

19. The Congo is divided into thirteen regions (Bouenza, Brazzaville, Cuvette, Kouilou, Lékoumou, Likouala, Loubomo, Niari, Nkayi, Plateaux, Pointe-Noire, Pool, and Sangha), represented by six main ethnic groups (Kongo, Lari, Mbochi, Sanga, Teke, and Vili).

20. Elikia M'Bokolo, "Comparisons and Contrasts in Equatorial Africa: Gabon, Congo and the Central African Republic," *History of Central Africa: The Contemporary Years since 1960*, ed. David Birmingham and Phyllis M. Martin (New York: Longman, 1998), 92. In fact, these distinctions manifested themselves in pernicious ways through the creation of armed militias divided according to territorial and ethnic configurations. These included Kolélas's *Ninjas*, Sassou Nguesso's *Cobras*, and Lissouba's *Zoulous*. Other militias included the "Aubevillois," "Cocoyes," and "Mambas." See Rémy Bazenguissa-Ganga, "Les milices politiques dans les affrontements," *Afrique Contemporaine*, no. 186 (April–June 1998): 46–57; and also Théophile Obenga, *L'histoire sanglante du Congo-Brazzaville (1959–1997): Diagnostic d'une mentalité politique africaine* (Paris: Présence Africaine, 1998), 179–81. Hereafter cited parenthetically in the text as "Obenga."

21. Denis Sassou Nguesso, *La Rue Meurt*, no. 062, December 29, 1994–January 5, 1995.

22. Pascal Lissouba, *Congo: Les fruits de la passion partagée* (Editions Odilon Média, 1997); and Denis Sassou Nguesso, *Le manguier, le fleuve et la souris* (Paris: Editions Jean-Claude Lattès, 1997).

23. See, for example, Géraldine Faes, "Brazza perd la raison," *L'Autre Afrique*, no. 4 (June 11–17, 1997): 15–18.

24. Noam Chomsky and Edward S. Herman, *Manufacturing Consent: The Political Economy of the Mass Media* (New York: Pantheon Books, 1988). See also *Necessary Illusions: Thought Control in Democratic Societies* (Boston: South End Press, 1989); and *Deterring Democracy* (New York: Hill and Wang, 1992).

25. MacDonald Ndombo Kale, "Deconstructing the Dialectics of Press Freedom in Cameroon," in *Press Freedom and Communication in Africa*, ed. Festus Eribo

and William Jong-Ebot (Trenton, N.J.: Africa World Press, 1997), 264. See also Jean Tudesq, "Problems of Press Freedom in Côte d'Ivoire," in *Press Freedom and Communication in Africa*, ed. Festus Eribo and William Jong-Ebot, 291–302.

26. Dhyana Ziegler and Molefi Asante, *Thunder and Silence: The Mass Media in Africa* (Trenton, N.J.: Africa World Press, 1992), cited in Kale, "Deconstructing the Dialectics of Press Freedom in Cameroon," in *Press Freedom and Communication in Africa*, ed. Festus Eribo and William Jong-Ebot, 275–76.

27. Allen W. Palmer, "Reinventing the Democratic Press of Benin," in *Press Freedom and Communication in Africa*, ed. Festus Eribo and William Jong-Ebot, 247. The most significant publications included the *Bulletin Official Administratif du Gabon-Congo* (1849–97), *Journal Officiel du Congo Français* (1888–1904), *Journal Officiel des Possessions du Congo Français et Dépendances du Moyen-Congo* (1904–1909).

28. Festus Eribo and William Jong-Ebot, *Press Freedom and Communication in Africa*, x.

29. Sue Curry Jansen, "The Marxist-Leninist Paradigm of Power-Knowledge as Auspices for Prescriptive Control of Literature," *Censorship: The Knot That Binds Power and Knowledge* (New York: Oxford University Press, 1991), 105. Hereafter cited parenthetically in the text as "Jansen."

30. Frère is citing Rogatien Biaou, "Les moyens de communication de masse et la politique de l'information en république populaire du Bénin" (thesis, Cotonou, Université nationale du Bénin, 1979).

31. Jean-Claude Gakosso, *La nouvelle presse congolaise: Du goulag à l'agora* (Paris: L'Harmattan, 1997), 69. Hereafter cited parenthetically in the text as "Gakosso."

32. Cited in Minabere Ibelema and Ebere Onwudiwe, "Congo (Zaire): Colonial Legacy, Autocracy and the Press," in *Press Freedom and Communication in Africa*, ed. Festus Eribo and William Jong-Ebot, 316.

33. Ahmed Sékou Touré, *La Révolution Démocratique Afrique: Revue Mensuel du Parti Démocratique de Guinée* (1966–1984, vols. 1–224).

34. Chomsky, *Manufacturing Consent*, 2.

35. Annabelle Sreberny-Mohammadi, "The Global and the Local in International Communications," in *Mass Media and Society*, ed. James Curran and Michael Gurevitch (London: Arnold, 1996), 177–203.

36. Other titles included *L'Arc-en-Ciel*, *La Boussole*, *Brazza-Hebdo*, *La Colombe*, *Le Gardien*, *Maintenant*, *La Nation*, *L'Observateur Congolais*, *Le Patriote*, *Le Pays*, *Le Soleil*, *Le Temps*, *Le Vagabond*. See also Biyoko, *Afrique centrale: Des médias pour la démocratie*, 106.

37. Denis Sassou Nguesso, *La Rue Meurt*, no. 062, December 29, 1994–January 5, 1995.

38. As Frère has pointed out, this phenomenon is also evidenced in anglophone Africa, where it is known as "bush telegraph" or "pavement radio," *Presse et démocratie en Afrique francophone*, 57.

39. Achille Mbembe, *On the Postcolony* (Berkeley: University of California Press, 2001), 143.

40. Similar devices are exemplified in the Caribbean context through various devices employed by storytellers in order to critique power. See, for example, the Martinican writer Patrick Chamoiseau, notably *Creole Folktales*, trans. Linda Coverdale (New York: The New Press, 1994).

41. The owl is informing the leaders gathered that they represent the hope for peace ("La paix c'est vous"), while his own war-mongering tendencies are veiled in the sounds of an owl, whereby "la guerre toujours" (always war) becomes "la guerre toujouuuuurs."

42. Lissouba was sometimes referred to as *Professèr*.

43. "Ya Kolins," essentially meaning "big brother Kolélas," is one of the many terms of endearment used as a substitute for his legal name.

44. There is a striking parallel to be drawn here to the work of a young writer from Djibouti, Abdourahman Wabéri, whose absorbing and sensitive book on the genocide in Rwanda is titled *Moisson de crânes* (Paris: Le Serpent à Plumes, 2000).

45. See, for example, Daniel Biyaoula's novels, *Impasse* (Paris: Présence Africaine, 1996) and *Agonies* (Paris: Présence Africaine, 1998); and Alain Mabanckou's collections of poetry, *Au jour le jour* (Paris: Maison Rhodanienne, 1993), *L'usure des lendemains* (Paris: Nouvelles du Sud, 1995), *La légende de l'errance* (Paris: L'Harmattan, 1995), *Les arbres aussi versent des larmes* (Paris: L'Harmattan, 1997), *Quand le coq annoncera l'aube d'un autre jour* (Paris: L'Harmattan, 1999), and two novels, *Bleu-Blanc-Rouge* (Paris: Présence Africaine, 1998), and *Et dieu seul sait comment je dors* (Paris: Présence Africaine, 2001). Henri Lopes published his seventh novel in 2002, *Dossier classé* (Paris: Editions du Seuil, 2002), and Emmanuel Dongala's fourth novel is forthcoming from Le Serpent à Plumes publishers in Paris.

46. Achille Mbembe, "At the Edge of the World: Boundaries, Territoriality, and Sovereignty in Africa," trans. Steven Rendall, *Public Culture* 12, no. 1 (Winter 2000): 282.

47. Emmanuel Dongala, *The Fire of Origins*, trans. Lillian Corti and Yuval Taylor (Chicago: Lawrence Hill Books, 2001), 247.

BIBLIOGRAPHY

Abrams, M. H. *A Glossary of Literary Terms*. Fort Worth, Tex.: Harcourt Brace College Publishers, 1993.

Adamolekun, Lapido. *Sékou Touré's Guinea: An Experiment in Nation Building*. London: Methuen, 1976.

Adiaffi, Jean-Marie. *La carte d'identité*. Paris: Hatier/Monde Noir, 1980.

Adorno, T. W. "Commitment." Translated by Francis McDonagh. In *Aesthetics and Politics*, edited by Ernst Bloch and others, 177–95. London: NLB, 1977.

Africa Insight 17, no. 4 (1987).

Aka-Evy, J.-L. "Interview." *Etudes Littéraires Africaines* 4 (1997): 3–8.

Amselle, Jean-Loup, and Elikia M'Bokolo. *Au cœur de l'ethnie: Ethnies, tribalisme et état en Afrique*. Paris: La Découverte, 1985.

Amuta, Chidi. *The Theory of African Literature: Implications for Practical Criticism*. London: Zed Books, 1989.

Anderson, Benedict. *Imagined Communities: Reflections on the Origin and Spread of Nationalism*. New York: Verso, 1983.

Anyinefa, Koffi. "Bibliographie de la littérature congolaise d'expression française." *Research in African Literatures* 20, no. 3 (Fall 1989): 481–88.

———. "Intertextuality in Dongala's 'Un fusil dans la main, un poème dans la poche.'" *Research in African Literatures* 24, no. 1 (Spring 1993): 5–17.

———. *Littérature et politique en Afrique noire: Socialisme et dictature comme thèmes du roman congolais d'expression française*. Bayreuth: Eckhard Breitinger, 1990.

———. "Postcolonial Postmodernity in Henri Lopes's *Le Pleurer-Rire*." *Research in African Literatures* 29, no. 3 (Fall 1998): 8–20.

Appiah, Kwame Anthony. *In My Father's House: Africa in the Philosophy of Culture*. New York: Oxford University Press, 1992.

Applefield, David. Interview. "Jean-Baptiste Tati-Loutard." Translated by John Archibald and Emily Eakin. *Frank: An International Journal of Contemporary Writing and Art*, no. 14 (1992): 157–62.

———. Interview. "Speaking with Sony Labou Tansi." Translated by Tanya Leslie. *Frank: An International Journal of Contemporary Writing and Art*, no. 14 (1992): 91–109.

Apter, Emily. "On Translation in a Global Market." *Public Culture* 13, no. 1 (Winter 2001): 1–12.

Area Handbook for the People's Republic of the Congo (Congo-Brazzaville). Washington D.C.: Foreign Area Studies of the American University, 1971.

Arlinghaus, Bruce. *Military Development in Africa: The Political and Economic Risks of Arms Transfers*. Boulder, Colo.: Westview Press, 1984.

———, ed. *African Security Issues: Sovereignty, Stability, and Solidarity.* Boulder, Colo.: Westview Press, 1984.

Armah, Ayi Kwei. "Masks and Marx: The Marxist Ethos vis-à-vis African Revolutionary Theory and Praxis." *Présence Africaine* 131, no. 3 (1984): 35–65.

Attwell, David, ed. *Doubling the Point: Essays and Interviews.* Cambridge, Mass.: Harvard University Press, 1992.

Austin, Denis. "Pax Africa." In *Military Power and Politics in Black Africa,* edited by Simon Baynham, 166–76. London: Croom Helm, 1986.

Badian, Seydou. *Les dirigeants africains face à leur peuple.* Paris: François Maspéro, 1964.

Bah, Mahmoud. *Construire la Guinée après Sékou Touré.* Paris: L'Harmattan, 1990.

Bakhtin, Mikhail. *L'œuvre de François Rabelais et la culture populaire au moyen âge et sous la renaissance.* Paris: Gallimard, 1970.

Balandier, Georges. *La sociologie de l'Afrique noire.* Paris: Presses Universitaires de France, 1955.

Bambi, Jean-Guy. *Chronologie des principaux faits et évènements au Congo: 1482–1979.* Imprimerie du Centre National du Zaïre, 1980.

Bamboté, Makombo. *Princesse Mandapu.* Paris: Présence Africaine, 1972.

Barthes, Roland. *Critical Essays.* Translated by Richard Howard. Evanston: Northwestern University Press, 1972.

———. *Essais critiques.* Paris: Seuil, 1964.

Baxandall, S., and S. Morawski, eds. *Marx and Engels on Literature and Art.* St. Louis, Mo.: Telos Press, 1973.

Bayart, Jean-François. *L'état en Afrique: La politique du ventre.* Paris: Fayard, 1989.

Bayart, Jean-François, Stephen Ellis, and Béatrice Hibou, eds. *The Criminalization of the State in Africa.* Bloomington: Indiana University Press, 1999.

Baynham, Simon, ed. *Military Power and Politics in Black Africa.* London: Croom Helm, 1986.

Bazenguissa-Ganga, Rémy. "Les milices politiques dans les affrontements." *Afrique Contemporaine,* no. 186 (April–June 1998): 46–57.

Behr, Mark. *Embrace.* London: Little, Brown, 2000.

———. "Fault Lines Speech." South Africa, 1996.

———. *The Smell of Apples.* London: Little, Brown, 1995.

Béji, Hélé. *Désenchantement national: Essai sur la décolonisation.* Paris: François Maspéro, 1982.

Belyaev, A. *The Ideological Struggle and Literature.* Moscow: Progress Publishers, 1978.

Bemba, Sylvain. *Le dernier des cargonautes.* Paris: L'Harmattan, 1984.

———. *Léopolis.* Paris: Hatier, 1986.

———. "La phratrie des écrivains congolais." *Notre Librairie,* nos. 92–93 (March–May 1988): 13–15.

———. *Rêves portatifs.* Dakar: Nouvelles Editions Africaines, 1979.

———. *Le soleil est parti à M'Pemba.* Paris: Présence Africaine, 1982.

———. "Sony Labou Tansi et Moi." *Equateur*, no. 1 (October–November 1986): 48–54.

Benjamin, Walter. "The Work of Art in the Age of Mechanical Reproduction." In *Illuminations*. Translated by Harry Zohn, 219–53. New York: Schocken Books, 1977.

Benoist, Joseph-Roger de. *L'Afrique occidentale française de 1944 à 1960*. Dakar: Les Nouvelles Editions Africaines, 1982.

Béti, Mongo. "Afrique noire, littérature rose." *Présence Africaine*, nos. 1–2 (April–July 1955): 133–45.

———. *La France contre l'Afrique: Retour au Cameroun*. Paris: La Découverte, 1993.

———. *Main basse sur le Cameroun: Autopsie d'une décolonisation*. Paris: François Maspéro, 1972.

———. *Le pauvre Christ de Bomba*. Paris: Robert Laffont, 1956.

———. Review of *L'enfant noir* by Camara Laye. *Présence Africaine* 16 (1954): 419–22.

Beyala, Calixthe. *Les honneurs perdus*. Paris: Albin Michel, 1996.

———. *Tu t'appelleras Tanga*. Paris: Stock, 1988.

Bhabha, Homi K. *The Location of Culture*. London: Routledge, 1994.

———, ed. *Nation and Narration*. London: Routledge, 1990.

Biaou, Rogatien. *Les moyens de communication de masse et la politique de l'information en république populaire du Bénin*. Thesis, Cotonou, Université nationale du Bénin, 1979.

Bisanswa, Justin Kalulu. "Life Is Not a Book. Creuse: Literature and Representation in Sony Labou Tansi's Work." *Research in African Literatures* 31, no. 3 (Fall 2000): 129–46.

Biyaoula, Daniel. *Agonies*. Paris: Présence Africaine, 1998.

———. *L'impasse*. Paris: Présence Africaine, 1996.

Biyidi, Alexandre. *See* Béti, Mongo.

Biyoko, Grégoire. *Afrique centrale: Des médias pour la démocratie*. Paris: Editions Karthala/Institut Panos de Paris, 2000.

Bjornson, Richard. *The African Quest for Freedom and Identity: Cameroonian Writing and the National Experience*. Bloomington: Indiana University Press, 1991.

———, ed. "The Language Question." *Research in African Literatures* 23, no. 1 (Spring 1992).

Blancq, Bernard. "Corruption et résistance au changement." In *L'Afrique politique 1994: Vue sur la démocratisation à marée basse*. Paris: Karthala/CEAN, 1994, 191–98.

Bockie, Simon. *Death and the Invisible Powers: The World of Kongo Belief*. Bloomington: Indiana University Press, 1993.

Bokiba, André-Patient. "L'identité dans les romans de Sony Labou Tansi." In *Sony Labou Tansi ou la quête permanente du sens*, edited by Mukala Kadima-Nzuji, Abel Kouvouama, and Paul Kibangou, 255–75. Paris: L'Harmattan, 1997.

Boni, Tanella. "L'écrivain et le pouvoir." *Notre Librairie*, no. 98 (July–September 1989): 82–87.

Boni, Nazi. *Histoire synthétique de l'Afrique résistante: Les réactions des peuples africains face aux influences extérieures.* Paris: Présence Africaine, 1971.

Bonnafé, Pierre. "Une classe d'âge politique: La JMNR de la République du Congo-Brazzaville." *Cahiers d'Etudes Africaines* 31, no. 8 (1968): 327–68.

Boraine, Alex. *A Country Unmasked: Inside the South African Truth and Reconciliation Commission.* Oxford: Oxford University Press, 2001.

Borgeaud, Pierre-Yves. "Les médias dans *Le Pleurer-Rire* d'Henri Lopes." *Les Cahiers du Cedaf,* nos. 1–3 (1987): 139–58.

Boulaga, Fabien Eboussi. *Les conférences nationales en Afrique noire: Une affaire à suivre.* Paris: Karthala, 1993.

Boutet, Rémy. *Les trois glorieuses ou la chute de Fulbert Youlou.* Dakar: Editions Chaka, 1990.

Brayton, Abbot. "Arms Control in Africa." In *Military Power and Politics in Black Africa,* edited by Simon Baynham. London: Croom Helm, 1986.

Brennan, Timothy. "The Nation Longing for Form." In *Nation and Narration,* edited by Homi K. Bhabha, 44–70. London: Routledge, 1990.

Bretton, Henry. *Power and Politics in Africa.* Chicago: Aldine Publishing Company, 1973.

Brezault, Alain, and Gérard Clavreuil. "L'écriture au bistouri de Tchichelle Tchivela." *Notre Librairie,* nos. 92–93 (March–May 1988): 139–43.

———. Interview. "Emmanuel Dongala 'Rire pour ne pas pleurer.'" *Notre Librairie,* nos. 92–93 (March–May 1988): 135–38.

Brink, André. *Reinventing a Continent: Writing and Politics in South Africa.* Cambridge, Mass.: Zoland Books, 1998.

Brunschwig, Henri. *Brazza Explorateur: L'Ogooué 1875–1879.* Paris: Mouton, 1966.

———. *Brazza Explorateur: Les traités de Makoko 1880–1882.* Paris: Mouton, 1972.

———. *Noirs et blancs dans l'Afrique noire française: Ou comment le colonisé devient colonisateur (1870–1914).* Paris: Flammarion, 1983.

Buakasa Tulu kia Mpansu. "Les discours de la kindoki ou sorcellerie." *Cahiers des Religions Africaines* 4, no. 11 (1972): 5–67.

Buijtenhuijs, Robert. *La conférence nationale souveraine du Tchad.* Paris: Karthala, 1993.

Bulletin official administratif du Gabon-Congo (1849–1897).

Cahen, M. "Le socialisme, c'est les Soviets plus l'ethnicité." *Politique Africaine* 42 (June 1991): 87–107.

Camara Laye. *Dramouss.* Paris: Plon, 1966.

———. *L'enfant noir.* Paris: Plon, 1953.

Camara, Djigui. *Chronique de la révolution.* Conakry, Guinea: Bureau de Presse de la Présidence Conakry R.P.R. de Guinée, 1982.

Camara, Nenekhaly Condetto. "Salut Viet-nam." *Horoya-Hebdo,* no. 8, Conakry (March 20–26, 1969).

———. "Souvenir du Che." *Horoya-Hebdo,* no. 3. Conakry (February 15–21, 1969).

Camara, Sikhé. *Clairière dans le ciel.* Paris: Présence Africaine, 1973.

———. *Poèmes de combat et de vérité.* Paris: P. J. Oswald, 1967.

———. *Somme de la poésie guinéenne de combat ou la sirène de la révolution africaine*. Casablanca, Morocco: Imprimerie Eddar El Be ida, 1982.

Carasso, Jean-Gabriel. "Du 'symbole à la scène.'" *Théâtre/Public*, no. 76–77 (1987). Dossier de Presse. 4th Festival International des Francophonies, October 3–16, 1987, 70.

Castéran, Christian, and Blaise-Pascal Talla. Interview. "Denis Sassou Nguesso: 'Rendez-vous avec la paix et la démocratie.'" *Jeune Afrique Economie*, no. 330 (June 4–17, 2001): 58–67.

Céline, Louis-Ferdinand. *Voyage au bout de la nuit*. Paris: Denoël, 1932.

Césaire, Aimé. *Cahier d'un retour au pays natal*. Paris: Présence Africaine, 1939.

———. *Discours sur le colonialisme*. Paris: Présence Africaine, 1955.

———. *Une saison au Congo*. Paris: Seuil, 1965.

———. *La tragédie du roi Christophe*. Paris: Présence Africaine, 1963.

Chabal, Patrick. "Pouvoir et violence en Afrique postcoloniale." *Politique Africaine* 42 (June 1991): 51–64.

———. *Power in Africa: An Essay in Political Interpretation*. Basingstoke, Hampshire: Macmillan, 1992.

Chamoiseau, Patrick. *Creole Folktales*. Translated by Linda Coverdale. New York: The New Press, 1994.

Chatterjee, Partha. *The Nation and Its Fragments: Colonial and Postcolonial Histories*. Princeton: Princeton University Press, 1993.

Chemain, Arlette. "Chroniques, geste épique, récit symbolique: Le roman, 1977–1987." *Notre Librairie*, nos. 92–93 (March–May 1988): 116–22.

———. "Henri Lopes: Engagement civique et recherche d'une écriture." *Notre Librairie* 92–93 (March–May 1988): 123–28.

———. "Sur l'image des pygmées dans 'La vie et demie' de Sony Labou Tansi: De l'oralité à l'écriture." *Cahiers Congolais d'Anthropologie et d'Histoire*, no. 9 (1984): 31–36.

———. "Violence destructrice, violence régénératrice: Originalité de la littérature africaine subsaharienne." In *La deriva della francophonie: Figures et fantasmes de la violence dans les littératures de l'Afrique subsaharienne et des Antilles*, 13–32. Bologna, Italy: Editrice CLUEB, 1991.

Chemain, Arlette, and Roger Chemain. *Panorama critique de la littérature congolaise contemporaine*. Paris: L'Harmattan, 1973.

Chemain, Roger. "Autour de la revue *Liaison*." *Notre Librairie*, nos. 92–93 (March–May 1988): 74–75.

———. Review of *Littérature et politique en Afrique noire: Socialisme et dictature comme thèmes du roman congolais d'expression française* (Bayreuth: Eckhard Breitinger, 1990) by Koffi Anyinefa. *Research in African Literatures* 24, no. 1 (Spring 1993): 124–27.

Chevrier, Jacques. *Anthologie africaine d'expression française*. Volume 1: *Le roman et la nouvelle*. Paris: Hatier, 1981.

———. "Henri Lopes et son 'tonton.'" *Jeune Afrique*, no. 1141 (1982): 105–107.

———. *Littérature nègre*. Paris: Armand Colin, 1984.

———. "Visages de la tyrannie dans le roman africain contemporain." In *La deriva della francophonie: Figures et fantasmes de la violence dans les littératures de l'Afrique subsaharienne et des Antilles*, 33–53. Bologna, Italy: Editrice CLUEB, 1991.

Chomsky, Noam. *Chronicles of Dissent*. Monroe, Maine: Common Courage Press, 1992.

———. *Deterring Democracy*. New York: Hill and Wang, 1992.

———. *Necessary Illusions: Thought Control in Democratic Societies*. Boston: South End Press, 1989.

Chomsky, Noam, and Edward S. Herman. *Manufacturing Consent: The Political Economy of the Mass Media*. New York: Pantheon Books, 1988.

Chrétien, J.-P. "Les racines de la violence contemporaine." *Politique Africaine* 42 (June 1991): 15–27.

Clark, John F., and David E. Gardinier, eds. *Political Reform in Francophone Africa*. Boulder, Colo.: Westview Press, 1997.

Coetzee, J. M. "Confession and Double Thoughts: Tolstoy, Rousseau, Dostoevsky." In *Doubling the Point: Essays and Interviews*, edited by David Attwell, 251–93. Cambridge, Mass.: Harvard University Press, 1992.

———. *Disgrace*. New York: Viking Penguin, 1999.

———. *Giving Offense: Essays on Censorship*. Chicago: University of Chicago Press, 1996.

Cohen, William B. *The French Encounter with Africans: White Response to Blacks, 1530–1880*. Bloomington: Indiana University Press, 1980.

Conteh-Morgan, John. *Theatre and Drama in Francophone Africa: A Critical Introduction*. Cambridge: Cambridge University Press, 1994.

Coquery-Vidrovitch, Catherine, ed. *L'Afrique occidentale au temps des français: Colonisateurs et colonisés, c. 1860–1960*. Paris: Editions de la Découverte, 1992.

Crowder, Michael. *Senegal: A Study of French Assimilation Policy*. London: Methuen, 1967.

Curran, James, and Michael Gurevitch, eds. *Mass Media and Society*. London: Arnold, 1996.

Dabla, Séwanou. *Jazz et vin de palme de Emmanuel Boundzéki Dongala*. Paris: Fernand Nathan, 1986.

———. *Nouvelles écritures africaines: Romanciers de la seconde génération*. Paris: L'Harmattan, 1986.

Dadié, Bernard. *Un Nègre à Paris*. Paris: Présence Africaine, 1959.

———. *Patron de New York*. Paris: Présence Africaine, 1964.

Davies, Ioan. *Writers in Prison*. Oxford: Basil Blackwell, 1990.

Davis, David Brion. *The Problem of Slavery in the Age of Revolution, 1770–1823*. Ithaca: Cornell University Press, 1975.

———. *The Problem of Slavery in Western Culture*. Ithaca: Cornell University Press, 1966.

Decalo, Samuel. *Coups and Army Rule in Africa*. New Haven: Yale University Press, 1976.

——. "Ideological Rhetoric and Scientific Socialism in Benin and Congo/ Brazzaville." In *Socialism in Sub-Saharan Africa: A New Assessment*, edited by Carl G. Rosberg and Thomas Callaghy. Berkeley: Institute of International Studies, 1979.

——. "Military Rule in Africa: Etiology and Morphology." In *Military Power and Politics in Black Africa*, edited by Simon Baynham. London: Croom Helm, 1986.

DeLillo, Don. *Mao II*. New York: Viking Penguin, 1991.

De Man, Paul. *Allegories of Reading: Figural Language in Rousseau, Nietzsche, Rilke, and Proust*. New Haven: Yale University Press, 1979.

Dévésa, Jean-Michel. *Sony Labou Tansi: Ecrivain de la honte et des rives magiques du Kongo*. Paris: L'Harmattan, 1996.

Diagne, Ahmadou Mapaté. *Les trois volontés de Malic*. Nendeln: Kraus Reprints, 1973 [first published in 1920].

Diallo, Siradiou. *Les armées africaines*. Paris: Economica, 1986.

Diaré, Ibrahima Khalil. *Chants et larmes, de foi et de joie*. Conakry, Guinea: INPL, 1972.

——. *Les dits de nul et de tous*. Conakry, Guinea: INPL, 1981.

Diderot, Denis. *Jacques le fataliste et son maître*. In *Œuvres romanesques*. Paris: Editions Garnier Frères, 1981, 521–808.

Diouf, Mahktar. "La marginalisation de l'Afrique dans le système monde." In *L'intégration régionale dans le monde: Innovations et ruptures*, 63–75. Paris: Karthala, 1994.

Diouf, Mamadou. "Les paroles politiques africaines: Des luttes anticoloniales aux conférences nationales." In *L'intégration régionale dans le monde: Innovations et ruptures*, 263–72. Paris: Karthala, 1994.

Dongala, Emmanuel Boundzéki. *Le feu des origines*. Paris: Albin Michel, 1987.

——. *The Fire of Origins*. Translated by Lillian Corti and Yuval Taylor. Chicago: Lawrence Books, 2000.

——. *Un fusil dans la main, un poème dans la poche*. Paris: Albin Michel, 1973.

——. "Jazz and Palm Wine." *Jazz and Palm Wine and Other Stories*. Edited and with an introduction by Willfried F. Feuser, 194–202. Harlow, Essex: Longman, 1981.

——. *Jazz et vin de palme*. Paris: Hatier, 1982.

——. "Littérature et société: Ce que je crois." *Peuples noirs, Peuples africains*, no. 9 (May–June 1979): 58–64.

——. *Little Boys Come from the Stars*. Translated by Joël Réjouis and Val Vinokurov. New York: Farrar, Straus and Giroux, 2001.

——. "The Man." Translated by Clive Wake. *Contemporary Short Stories*, edited by Chinua Achebe and C. L. Innes, 81–86. Portsmouth, N.H.: Heinemann, 1992.

——. *Les petits garçons naissent aussi des étoiles*. Paris: Editions Le Serpent à Plumes, 1998.

——. *Johnny, chien méchant*. Paris: Editions Le Serpent à Plumes, 2002.

DuBois, Page. *Torture and Truth*. London: Routledge, 1991.

Eagleton, Terry. *Criticism and Ideology*. London: Verso, 1978.

——. *Marxism and Literary Criticism*. London: Methuen, 1976.

Eagleton, Terry, and Drew Milne, eds. *Marxist Literary Theory: A Reader.* Oxford: Blackwell, 1996.

Ehrenbourg, Ilya. *Un écrivain dans la révolution.* Paris: Gallimard, 1963.

Elébé, Philippe. *Uhuru.* Paris: Debresse, 1970.

Equateur. "Sony Labou Tansi," no. 1 (October–November 1986).

Eribo, Festus, and William Jong-Ebot, eds. *Press Freedom and Communication in Africa.* Trenton, N.J.: Africa World Press, 1997.

Ermalaev, H. *Soviet Literary Theories 1917–1934: The Genesis of Socialist Realism.* Berkeley: University of California Press, 1973.

Eta-Onka, Claude-Emmanuel. *Insomnies.* Brazzaville: Edition et Publication Premières, 1991.

———. *Les tandaliennes.* Brazzaville: Edition Le Bélier, 1993.

Fabian, Johannes. *Out of Our Minds: Reason and Madness in the Exploration of Central Africa.* Berkeley: University of California Press, 2000.

Faes, Géraldine. "Brazza perd la raison." *L'Autre Afrique,* no. 4 (June 11–17, 1997): 15–18.

Falgayrettes, Christine. "Lopes: Poser la révolte avec 'Le Pleurer-Rire.'" *Afrique-Asie,* no. 282 (1982): 50–51.

Fall, Aminata Sow. *La grève des bàttu ou les déchets humains.* Dakar: Nouvelles Editions Africaines, 1979.

Fanon, Frantz. *Les damnés de la terre.* Paris: François Maspéro, 1961.

———. *The Wretched of the Earth.* Translated by Constance Farrington. New York: Grove Press, 1963.

Fantouré, Alioum. *Le cercle des tropiques.* Paris: Présence Africaine, 1972.

———. *Le Récit du cirque . . . de la vallée des morts.* Paris: Editions Buchet-Castel, 1975.

Farah, Nurrudin. *Sweet and Sour Milk.* Saint Paul, Minn.: Graywolf Press, 1992 [first published 1979].

Felman, Shoshana. *Testimony: Crises of Witnessing in Literature, Psychoanalysis, and History.* New York: Routledge, 1992.

First, Ruth. *The Barrel of a Gun: Political Power in Africa and the Coup d'Etat.* London: Penguin, 1970.

Fischer, Ernst. *The Necessity of Art.* London: Penguin, 1963.

Flower J. E. "Socialist Realism without a Socialist Revolution: The French Experience." In *European Socialist Realism,* edited by Michael Scriven and Dennis Tate, 99–110. Oxford: Berg Publishers, 1988.

Foltz, William J., and Henry S. Bienen. *Arms and the African: Military Influences on Africa's International Relations.* New Haven: Yale University Press, 1985.

Fortes, M., and E. E. Evans-Pritchard, eds. *African Political Systems.* London: Oxford University Press, 1940.

Foucault, Michel. *Discipline and Punish: The Birth of the Prison.* Translated by Alan Sheridan. New York: Vintage Books, 1979.

———. *Surveiller et punir: Naissance de la prison.* Paris: Gallimard, 1975.

Foutou, Celestin Goma. *Histoires des civilisations du Congo*. Paris: Editions Anthropos, 1981.

Fredman, Alice Green. *Diderot and Sterne*. New York: Columbia University Press, 1954.

Frère, Marie-Soleil. *Presse et démocratie en Afrique francophone: Les mots et les maux de la transition au Bénin et au Niger*. Paris: Karthala, 2000.

French, Howard W. "A Dying Writer Finds Solace in the Heart of Africa." *New York Times* (June 7, 1995).

———. "An Ignorance of Africa as Vast as the Continent." *New York Times* (November 20, 1994).

Gabou, Alexis. *Les constitutions congolaises*. Paris: Librairie générale de droit et de jurisprudence, 1984.

Gakosso, Jean-Claude. *La nouvelle presse congolaise: Du goulag à l'agora*. Paris: L'Harmattan, 1997.

Gandoulou, Justin-Daniel. *Au cœur de la Sape: Mœurs et aventures de congolais à Paris*. Paris: L'Harmattan, 1989.

Gauze, René. *The Politics of Congo-Brazzaville*. Translated by Virginia Thompson and Richard Adloff. Stanford: Hoover Institution Press, 1973.

Geniès, Bernard. "Africain d'accord, écrivain d'abord." *Le Nouvel Observateur* (August 19–25, 1988): 58–61.

Géographie de la République Populaire du Congo. Brazzaville: Office Nationale des Librairies, 1976.

Giddens, Anthony. *The Nation-State and Violence: Volume Two of A Contemporary Critique of Historical Materialism*. Berkeley: University of California Press, 1985.

Gikandi, Simon. *Reading the African Novel*. London: James Currey, 1987.

Gilroy, Paul. *Between Camps: Nations, Cultures, and the Allure of Race*. London: Penguin, 2000.

———. *The Black Atlantic: Modernity and Double Consciousness*. Cambridge, Mass.: Harvard University Press, 1993.

Glissant, Edouard. *Caribbean Discourse: Selected Essays*. Translated by J. Michael Dash. Charlottesville: University of Virginia Press, 1989.

Goldmann, Lucien. *Pour une sociologie du roman*. Paris: Presses Universitaires de France, 1964.

Golopentia, Sanda. "Battles of Silence: The Institution of Literature in Post–World War II Romania." In *Tradition and Change in Central and Eastern Europe*, edited by Henrietta Mondry and Paul Schveiger, 59–97. Johannesburg, South Africa: University of Witwatersrand, 1993.

Gonidec, P.-F. *Les systèmes politiques africains*. Paris: Librairie générale de droit et de jurisprudence, 1978.

Goody, Jack. *Technology, Tradition, and the State in Africa*. London: Oxford University Press, 1971.

Gordimer, Nadine. *The Essential Gesture*. London: Penguin, 1988.

Gorky, Maxim. *On Literature*. Seattle: University of Washington Press, 1973.

Grah-Mel, Frédéric. "Henri Lopes: L'écrivain doit prendre position ou se taire." *Fraternité-Matin* (October 6, 1976): 17.

Grand Robert de la langue française. 1985.

Green, Mary-Jean, et al. *Postcolonial Subjects: Francophone Women Writers.* Minneapolis: University of Minnesota Press, 1996.

Gugelberger, Georg M., ed. *Marxism and African Literature.* London: James Currey, 1985.

Guingané, Jean-Pierre. *Le fou.* Abidjan: CEDA, 1986.

———. "De Ponty à Sony: Représentations théâtrales en Afrique." *Notre Librairie,* no. 102 (July–August 1990): 6–11.

Hamilton, Russell G. "Class, Race, and Authorship in Angola." In *Marxism and African Literature,* edited by Georg M. Gugelberger, 136–49. London: James Currey, 1985.

Hammond, Kenneth. "L'anté-peuple." *World Literature Today* 58, no. 2 (Spring 1984): 316.

Hamza, Kaidi, and Djamila Bitat. "L'armée, une école pour chefs d'états." *Jeune Afrique,* nos. 389–90 (August 1987): 36–40.

Harrow, Kenneth W. *Thresholds of Change in African Literature: The Emergence of a Tradition.* Portsmouth, N.H.: Heinemann, 1994.

Harrow, Kenneth W., Jonathan Ngate, and Clarisse Zimra. *Crisscrossing Borders in African Literatures.* Washington, D.C.: Three Continents Press, 1991.

Hazoumé, Guy. *Idéologies tribalistes et nation en Afrique.* Paris: Présence Africaine, 1972.

Heim, Michael. "La littérature soviétique et la guerre d'Espagne." In *Les écrivains et la guerre d'Espagne,* 89–99. Paris, 1975.

Hergé. *Les aventures de Tintin au Congo.* Belgium: Casterman, 1930 [1946 for the color edition].

Herzberger-Fofana, Pierrette. *Littérature féminine francophone d'Afrique noire.* Paris: L'Harmattan, 2001.

Hettne, Björn. "Afrique: Régionalisme et échec du projet d'état-nation." In *L'intégration régionale dans le monde,* 167–74. Paris: Karthala, 1994.

Historical Dictionary of the People's Republic of the Congo (Congo-Brazzaville). Metuchen, N.J.: Scarecrow Press, 1974.

Hitchcott, Nicki. *Women Writers in Francophone Africa.* Oxford: Berg, 2000.

Hochschild, Adam. *King Leopold's Ghost.* New York: Houghton Mifflin, 1998.

Hodder-Williams, Richard. *An Introduction to the Politics of Tropical Africa.* London: George Allen and Unwin, 1984.

Howe, Marvin. "French Influence Pervades Marxist Congo." *New York Times* (July 17, 1972).

Huannou, Adrien. "Inquiétudes et objections: D'un colloque à l'autre." *Notre Librairie* 83 (April–June 1986): 29–37.

———. *La littérature béninoise de langue française des origines à nos jours.* Paris: Karthala/ACCT, 1984.

———. *La question des littératures nationales en Afrique noire.* Abidjan: CEDA, 1989.

Ibelema, Minabere, and Ebere Onwudiwe. "Congo (Zaire): Colonial Legacy, Autocracy and the Press." In *Press Freedom and Communication in Africa*, edited by Festus Eribo and William Jong-Ebot, 303–21. Trenton, N.J.: Africa World Press, 1997.

Jacquey, Marie-Clotilde. Interview. "Henri Lopes africain, métis et congolais." *Notre Librairie*, no. 83 (April–June 1986): 47–51.

James, C. Vaughan. *Soviet Socialist Realism: Origins and Theory.* New York: St. Martin's Press, 1973.

Jansen, Sue Curry. *Censorship: The Knot That Binds Power and Knowledge.* New York: Oxford University Press, 1991.

Journal Officiel des Possessions du Congo Français et Dépendances du Moyen-Congo (1904–1909).

Journal Officiel du Congo Français (1888–1904).

Julien, Eileen. "Dominance and Discourse in *La vie et demie* or How to Do Things with Words." *Research in African Literatures* 20, no. 3 (1989): 371–84.

Kaba, Lansiné. "The Cultural Revolution, Artistic Creativity, and Freedom of Expression in Guinea." *Journal of Modern African Studies* 14, no. 2 (June 1976): 201–18.

Kadima-Nzuji, Mukala, Abel Kouvouama, and Paul Kibangou, eds. *Sony Labou Tansi ou la quête permanente du sens.* Paris: L'Harmattan, 1997.

Kale, MacDonald Ndombo. "Deconstructing the Dialectics of Press Freedom in Cameroon." In *Press Freedom and Communication in Africa*, edited by Festus Eribo and William Jong-Ebot, 263–89. Trenton, N.J.: Africa World Press, 1997.

Kalonji, T. Zezeze. "Eléments pour une analyse plurielle du *Pleurer-Rire* d'Henri Lopes." *Peuples noirs, Peuples africains*, no. 37 (1984): 30–54.

Kane, Cheikh Hamidou. *L'aventure ambiguë.* Paris: Julliard, 1961.

———. *Les gardiens du temple.* Paris: Albin Michel, 1995.

Kasenda, Mpinga. "Le mobutisme." *Remarques Africaines*, no. 451 (January 1, 1975): 8–12.

Keita, Sidiki Kobélé. *Ahmed Sékou Touré, l'homme du 28 septembre 1958.* Conakry, Guinea: I.N.R.D.G., Bibliothèque nationale, 1977.

Kennedy, Paul. *Preparing for the Twenty-First Century.* New York: Random House, 1993.

Kesteloot, Lilyan. *Anthologie négro-africaine: Panorama critique des prosateurs, poètes et dramaturges noirs du XXème siècle.* Verviers: Marabout, 1981.

———. *Les écrivains noirs de la langue française: Naissance d'une littérature.* Brussels: Institut Solvay, 1963.

Kiss, Elizabeth. "Moral Ambition within and beyond Political Constraints: Reflections on Restorative Justice." In *Truth v. Justice: The Morality of Truth Commissions*, edited by Robert I. Rotberg and Dennis Thompson, 68–98. Princeton: Princeton University Press, 2000.

Kourouma, Ahmadou. *Allah n'est pas obligé.* Paris: Seuil, 2000.

———. *Les soleils des indépendances.* Montréal: Presses Universitaires de Montréal, 1968.

Kouvouama, Abel. "Sony Labou Tansi ou l'utopie pratiquée." In *Sony Labou Tansi ou la quête permanente du sens*, edited by Mukala Kadima-Nzuji, Abel Kouvouama, and Paul Kibangou, 95–106. Paris: L'Harmattan, 1997.

Krog, Antjie. *Country of My Skull: Guilt, Sorrow, and the Limits of Forgiveness in the New South Africa*. New York: Random House, 1999.

Kubayanda, Josaphat. "Dictatorship, Oppression, and New Realism." *Research in African Literatures* 21, no. 2 (Summer 1990): 5–11.

Kuper, Leo, and M. G. Smith, eds. *Pluralism in Africa*. Berkeley: University of California Press, 1969.

Leclercq, Claude. *L'ONU et l'Affaire du Congo*. Paris: Payot, 1964.

Lekoundzou, Itihi Ossetoumba Justin. *Pour bâtir la richesse nationale du Congo*. Self-financed, 1995.

Lenin, Vladimir Ilich. *Imperialism, the Highest Stage of Capitalism*. New York: International Publishers, 1969.

——. *On Literature and Art*. Moscow: Progress Publishers, 1975.

Liebenow, J. Gus. "The One-Party State in West-Africa: Its Strengths and Weaknesses in the Nation-Building Process." In *French-Speaking Africa: The Search for Identity*, edited by William H. Lewis, 45–57. New York: Walker, 1965.

Lionnet, Françoise. *Autobiographical Voices: Race, Gender, Self-Portraiture*. Ithaca: Cornell University Press, 1991.

——. *Postcolonial Representations: Women, Literature, Identity*. Ithaca: Cornell University Press, 1995.

Lissouba, Pascal. *Congo: Les fruits de la passion partagée*. Editions Odilon Média, 1997.

"Littératures nationales: Histoire et identité." *Notre Librairie*, no. 85 (October–December 1986).

"Littératures nationales: Langues et frontières." *Notre Librairie*, no. 84 (July–September 1986).

"Littératures nationales: Mode ou problématique?" *Notre Librairie*, no. 83 (April–June 1986).

Loango, Dominique. *La cité flamboyante*. Paris: Editions du Scorpion, 1959.

Lombalé-Baré, Gilbert. "Une lecture de *L'état honteux*: Essai d'analyse syntaxique." In *Sony Labou Tansi ou la quête permanente du sens*, edited by Mukala Kadima-Nzuji, Abel Kouvouama, and Paul Kibangou, 107–23. Paris: L'Harmattan, 1997.

Lopes, Henri. *Le chercheur d'Afriques*. Paris: Seuil, 1990.

——. *The Laughing Cry: An African Cock and Bull Story*. Translated by Gerald Moore. London: Readers International, 1987.

——. *Le Lys et le Flamboyant*. Paris: Seuil, 1997.

——. "Maluku au temps des bateaux à roues." In *Une enfance d'ailleurs: 17 écrivains racontent*, edited by Nancy Huston and Leïla Sebbar, 125–41. Paris: Belfond, 1993.

——. "My Novels, My Characters, and Myself." *Research in African Literatures* 24, no. 1 (Spring 1993): 81–86.

——. *La nouvelle romance*. Yaoundé: CLE, 1976.

———. *Le Pleurer-Rire.* Paris: Présence Africaine, 1982.

———. *Sans tam-tam.* Yaoundé: CLE, 1977.

———. *Sur l'autre rive.* Paris: Seuil, 1992.

———. *Tribaliks: Contemporary Congolese Stories.* Translated by Andrea Leskes. London: Heinemann, 1987.

———. *Tribaliques.* Yaoundé: CLE, 1971.

———. *Dossier classé.* Paris: Editions du Seuil, 2002.

Low, Alfred D. *Lenin on the Question of Nationality.* New York: Bookman Associates, 1958.

Loy, J. Robert. *Diderot's Determined Fatality.* New York: King's Crown Press, 1950.

Lu Xun. *Complete works of Lu Xun.* Beijing: Renmin wenxue chubanshe, 1981.

Ly, Ibrahima. *Toiles d'araignées.* Paris: L'Harmattan, 1982.

Lynch, Hollis, ed. *Black Africa.* New York: New York Times Company, 1973.

Mabanckou, Alain. *Les arbres aussi versent des larmes.* Paris: L'Harmattan, 1997.

———. *Au jour le jour.* Paris: Maison Rhodanienne, 1993.

———. *Bleu-Blanc-Rouge.* Paris: Présence Africaine, 1998.

———. *Et dieu seul sait comment je dors.* Paris: Présence Africaine, 2001.

———. *La légende de l'errance.* Paris: L'Harmattan, 1995.

———. *Quand le coq annoncera l'aube d'un autre jour.* Paris: L'Harmattan, 1999.

———. *L'usure des lendemains.* Paris: Nouvelles du Sud, 1995.

Macey, David. *Frantz Fanon.* New York: Picador, 2001.

MacGaffey, Wyatt. *Art and Healing of the Bakongo Commented by Themselves.* Bloomington: Indiana University Press, 1991.

———. *Custom and Government in Lower Congo.* Berkeley: University of California Press, 1970.

———. *Kongo Political Culture: The Conceptual Challenge of the Particular.* Bloomington: Indiana University Press, 2000.

———. *Modern Kongo Prophets: Religion in a Plural Society.* Bloomington: Indiana University Press, 1983.

Magnier, Bernard. "Un citoyen de ce siècle." *Equateur,* no. 1 (October–November 1986): 12–20.

———. Interview. "Sony Labou Tansi: Je ne suis pas à développer mais à prendre ou à laisser." *Notre Librairie,* no. 79 (April–June 1985): 5–7.

Maier, Charles S. "Doing History, Doing Justice: The Narrative of the Historian and of the Truth Commission." In *Truth v. Justice: The Morality of Truth Commissions,* edited by Robert I. Rotberg and Dennis Thompson, 261–78. Princeton: Princeton University Press, 2000.

Makhele, Caya. *Le cercle des vertiges.* Paris: L'Harmattan, 1992.

———. *Le coup de vieux.* Paris: Présence Africaine, 1988.

———. *L'homme au fardeau.* Paris: L'Harmattan, 1988.

Makouta-M'Boukou, Jean-Pierre. *La destruction de Brazzaville ou la démocratie guillotinée.* Paris: L'Harmattan, 1999.

———. *En quête de la liberté.* Yaoundé: CLE, 1970.

———. *Les exilés de la forêt vierge.* Paris: P. J. Oswald, 1974.

———. *Les initiés*. Yaoundé: CLE, 1970.

———. *Introduction à l'étude du roman négro-africain de langue française: Problèmes culturels et littéraires*. Dakar-Abidjan: Nouvelles Editions Africaines, 1980.

Malanda, Ange-Séverin. *Henri Lopes et l'impératif romanesque*. Paris: Silex, 1987.

Malanda, Ange-Séverin, and James Tshiatshimo. "La question Kongo." *Nouvelles Congolaises*, no. 023/024 (January–April 1999): 61–80.

Malonga, Alpha-Noël. "Martillimi Lopez, les corps des femmes et *L'état honteux*." In *Sony Labou Tansi ou la quête permanente du sens*, edited by Mukala Kadima-Nzuji, Abel Kouvouama, and Paul Kibangou, 167–76. Paris: L'Harmattan, 1997.

Malonga, Jean. *Cœur d'aryenne*. *Présence Africaine*, no. 16 (1954).

———. *La légende de M'Pfoumou Ma Mazono*. Paris: Présence Africaine, 1954.

Mamonsono, Léopold-Pindy. *Equinoxes*. Brazzaville: Editions Littéraires Congolaises, 1983.

———. *Héros dans l'ombre*. Kinshasa: Editions Pelamo, 1979.

———. *Light-Houses*. Brazzaville: Editions du Héros dans l'Ombre, 1978.

———. *La nouvelle génération de poètes congolais*. Brazzaville and Heidelberg: P. Kivouvou Verlag/Editions Bantoues, 1984.

Manning, Patrick. *Francophone Sub-Saharan Africa: 1880–1985*. Cambridge: Cambridge University Press, 1998.

Mao Tse-Tung. "Talks at the Yenan Forum on Art and Literature." In *Mao-Tse Tung: An Anthology of His Writings*, edited by Anne Freemantle. A Mentor Book, The New American Library, 1962.

Markov, Dmitry. *Socialist Literatures: Problems of Development*. Translated by Catherine Judelson. Moscow: Raduga Publishers, 1984.

Markovitz, Irving. *Léopold Sédar Senghor and the Politics of Negritude*. New York: Atheneum, 1969.

Martin, Phyllis M. *The External Trade of the Loango Coast, 1576–1870*. Oxford: Clarendon Press, 1972.

———. *Leisure and Society in Colonial Brazzaville*. Cambridge: Cambridge University Press, 1995.

Martin-Granel, Nicolas. "Le crier-écrire." *Notre Librairie* 78 (January–March 1985): 47–55.

———. "*Le quatrième côté du triangle*, or Squaring the Sex: A Genetic Approach to the 'Black Continent' in Sony Labou Tansi's Fiction." *Research in African Literatures* 31, no. 3 (Fall 2000): 69–99.

———. *Rires noirs: Anthologie romancée de l'humour dans le roman africain*. Paris: Editions SEPIA, 1991.

———. "Sony in Progress." In *Sony Labou Tansi ou la quête permanente du sens*, edited by Mukala Kadima-Nzuji, Abel Kouvouama, and Paul Kibangou, 211–28. Paris: L'Harmattan, 1997.

Mateso, Locha. *La littérature africaine et sa critique*. Paris: ACCT/Karthala, 1986.

Maunick, Edouard. Interview. "Le territoire d'Henri Lopes." *Notre Librairie*, nos. 92–93 (March–May 1988): 128–31.

Mavouangui, David. "Sony Labou Tansi ou le refus 'd'exister sur commande.'" In *Sony Labou Tansi ou la quête permanente du sens*, edited by Mukala Kadima-Nzuji, Abel Kouvouama, and Paul Kibangou, 291–97. Paris: L'Harmattan, 1997.

Maximin, Daniel. "Tchicaya/Sony: Le dialogue interrompu." Rencontre animé par Daniel Maximin. *Notre Librairie*, nos. 92–93 (March–May 1988): 88–91.

Mazrui, Ali. "On Poet-Presidents and Philosopher-Kings." *Research in African Literatures* 21, no. 2 (Summer 1990): 13–19.

———. "Pluralism and National Integration." In *Pluralism in Africa*, edited by Leo Kuper and M. G. Smith, 333–49. Berkeley: University of California Press, 1969.

Mbembe, Achille. *Afriques indociles: Christianisme, pouvoir et état en société post-coloniale*. Paris: Karthala, 1988.

———. "At the Edge of the World: Boundaries, Territoriality, and Sovereignty in Africa." Translated by Steven Rendall. *Public Culture* 12, no. 1 (Winter 2000): 259–84.

———. "Déflation de l'état, civilité et citoyenneté en Afrique noire." In *L'intégration régionale dans le monde*, 273–86. Paris: Karthala, 1994.

———. *De la postcolonie: Essai sur l'imagination politique dans l'Afrique contemporaine*. Paris: Karthala, 2000.

———. "Désordres, résistances et productivité." *Politique Africaine* 42 (June 1991).

———. *Les jeunes et l'ordre politique en Afrique noire*. Paris: L'Harmattan, 1985.

———. *On the Postcolony*. Berkeley: University of California Press, 2001.

———. "Pouvoir, violence et accumulation." In *La politique par le bas en Afrique noire: Contributions à une problématique de la démocratie*, edited by Jean-François Bayart, Comi Toulabor, and Achille Mbembe. Paris: Karthala, 1992.

M'Bokolo, Elikia. *Affonso 1er: Le roi chrétien de l'ancien Congo*. Paris: ABC; Dakar/Abidjan: Nouvelles Editions Africaines; Yaoundé, CLE: 1975.

———. *L'Afrique au XXème siècle: Le continent convoité*. Paris/Montréal: Etudes Vivantes, 1980.

———. "Ce que dit l'histoire." *Notre Librairie*, no. 83 (April–June 1986): 11–16.

———. "Comparisons and Contrasts in Equatorial Africa: Gabon, Congo and the Central African Republic." In *History of Central Africa: The Contemporary Years since 1960*, edited by David Birmingham and Phyllis M. Martin, 67–95. New York: Longman, 1998.

Mboukou, Alexandre. "The Rise of Anti-Intellectualism among the Modern African Elite." *Journal of African Studies* 9, no. 4 (Winter 1982–83): 180–86.

Menga, Guy. *La case de Gaulle*. Paris: Karthala, 1984.

———. *Congo: La transition escamotée*. Paris: L'Harmattan, 1993.

———. *L'oracle*. Yaoundé, CLE, 1967.

———. *La palabre stérile*. Yaoundé, CLE, 1969.

Mercier, P. "Elites et forces politiques." In *New Elites in Tropical Africa*, edited by P. C. Lloyd. London: Oxford University Press, 1966.

Met, Philippe. "Of Men and Animals: Hergé's *Tintin au Congo*, a Study in Primitivism." *Romanic Review* 87, no. 1 (1995): 131–44.

Meya, Fabrice. *Poèmes inutiles*. Paris: La Pensée Universelle, 1987.

Michaels, Julie. "Writer in Exile." *Boston Globe Magazine* (February 6, 2000): 12–31.

Midiohouan, Guy Ossito. *Bibliographie chronologique de la littérature négro-africaine d'expression française*. Cotonou: UNB, 1984.

———. "Eléments de bibliographie: Pour une approche méthodique de la question des 'littératures nationales' en Afrique." *Notre Librairie*, no. 85 (October–December 1986): 93–97.

———. *L'idéologie dans la littérature négro-africaine d'expression française*. Paris: L'Harmattan, 1986.

———. "Le phénomène des littératures nationales." *Peuples noirs, Peuples africains*, no. 27 (1982): 57–70.

Miller, Christopher L. "Literary Studies and African Literature: The Challenge of Intercultural Literacy." In *Africa and the Disciplines*, edited by Robert H. Bates, V. Y. Mudimbe, and Jean O'Barr, 213–31. Chicago: University of Chicago Press, 1993.

———. *Nationalists and Nomads: Essays on Francophone African Literature and Culture*. Chicago: University of Chicago Press, 1998.

———. "Nationalism as Resistance and Resistance to Nationalism in the Literature of Francophone Africa." *Post/Colonial Conditions: Exiles, Migrations, and Nomadisms. Yale French Studies* 1, no. 82 (1993): 62–100.

———. *Theories of Africans: Francophone Literature and Anthropology in Africa*. Chicago: University of Chicago Press, 1990.

Millett, Kate. *The Politics of Cruelty: An Essay on the Literature of Political Imprisonment*. New York: W. W. Norton, 1994.

Missiata, Ngolaono. "La vérité sur le 'socialisme scientifique' du Congo-Brazzaville." *Peuples noirs, Peuples africains*, no. 23 (1981): 11–18.

Monénembo, Tierno. *Les crapauds-brousse*. Paris: Seuil, 1979.

Monsard, Pierre. "Sony Labou Tansi: Esquisse d'une poétique du comique." In *Sony Labou Tansi ou la quête permanente du sens*, edited by Mukala Kadima-Nzuji, Abel Kouvouama, and Paul Kibangou, 47–60. Paris: L'Harmattan, 1997.

Morgenthau, Ruth. *Political Parties in French-Speaking Africa*. Oxford: Clarendon Press, 1964.

Moudileno, Lydie. "Labou Tansi's *La vie et demie*, or The Tortuous Path of the Fable." *Research in African Literatures* 29, no. 3 (Fall 1998): 21–33.

Moudileno-Massengo, Aloïse. *République populaire du Congo: Une escroquerie idéologique ou Au cœur du long drame*. Paris: Editions G.-P. Maisonneuve et Larose, 1975.

Mouralis, Bernard. "La figuration de la violence et ses enjeux dans la fiction africaine." In *La deriva della francophonie: Figures et fantasmes de la violence dans les littératures de l'Afrique subsaharienne et des Antilles*, 69–84. Bologna, Italy: Editrice CLUEB, 1991.

———. "Sékou Touré et l'écriture: Réflexions sur un cas de scribomanie." *Notre Librairie*, nos. 88–89 (July–September 1987): 76–85.

Mpansu, Buakasa Tulu Ria. "Les discours de la kindoki ou sorcellerie." *Cahiers des Religions Africaines* 4, no. 11 (1972): 5–67.

Mudimbe, V. Y. *The Invention of Africa: Gnosis, Philosophy, and the Order of Knowledge*. Bloomington: Indiana University Press, 1988.

——, ed. *The Surreptitious Speech: Présence Africaine and the Politics of Otherness, 1947–1987*. Chicago: University of Chicago Press, 1992.

Mudimbe-Boyi, Elisabeth. "Langue violée, langue volée: Pouvoir, écriture et violence dans le roman africain." In *La deriva della francophonie: Figures et fantasmes de la violence dans les littératures de l'Afrique subsaharienne et des Antilles*. Bologna, Italy: Editrice CLUEB, 1991, 101–18.

Nazareth, Peter. "Survive the Peace: Cyprian Ekwensi as a Political Novelist." In *Marxism and African Literature*, edited by Georg M. Gugelberger, 118–29. London: James Currey, 1985.

N'Da, Paul. *Les intellectuels et le pouvoir en Afrique noire*. Paris: L'Harmattan, 1987.

——. *Pouvoir, lutte de classes, idéologie et milieu intellectuel africain*. Paris: Présence Africaine, 1987.

N'Debeka, Maxime. *L'oseille des citrons*. Paris: P. J. Oswald, 1975.

——. *Les signes du silence*. Paris: Editions Saint-Germain-des-Prés, 1978.

——. *Soleils neufs*. Yaoundé: CLE, 1969.

Ndebele, Njabulo S. *South African Literature and Culture: Rediscovery of the Ordinary*. Manchester: Manchester University Press, 1994.

Neto, Agostinho. "On Literature and National Culture." *Lavra & Oficina*, Luanda, no. 20 (1979).

——. *Sacred Hope*. Dar es Salaam: Tanzania Publishing House, 1974.

N'Gal, Georges. *Création et rupture en littérature africaine*. Paris: L'Harmattan, 1994.

——. "Sony Labou Tansi et l'engendrement du sens." In *Sony Labou Tansi ou la quête permanente du sens*, edited by Mukala Kadima-Nzuji, Abel Kouvouama, and Paul Kibangou, 39–46. Paris: L'Harmattan, 1997.

——. "Les 'tropicalités' de Sony Labou Tansi." *Silex*, no. 23 (1982): 134–43.

Ngal, M. a M. "Nationalité, résidence, exil." *Notre Librairie*, no. 83 (April–June 1986): 42–46.

Ngampika-Mperet, Jean-Pierre. *Flamme de Sang*. Brazzaville: Editions Littéraires Congolaises, 1981.

Ngara, Emmanuel. *Art and Ideology in the African Novel: A Study of the Influence of Marxism on African Writing*. London: Heinemann, 1985.

Ngate, Jonathan. *Francophone African Fiction: Reading a Literary Tradition*. Trenton, N.J.: Africa World Press, 1988.

Ngouabi, Marien. *Vers la construction d'une société socialiste en Afrique*. Paris: Présence Africaine, 1975.

Ngũgĩ wa Thiong'o. *Barrel of a Pen: Resistance to Repression in Neo-Colonial Kenya*. Trenton, N.J.: Africa World Press, 1983.

——. *Decolonizing the Mind: The Politics of Language and in African Literature*. London: James Currey, 1986.

——. *Detained: A Writer's Prison Diary*. London: Heinemann, 1981.

———. *Devil on the Cross*. London: Heinemann, 1982.

———. *Ngaahika Ndeenda* [I Will Marry When I Want]. London: Heinemann, 1982.

———. *Petals of Blood*. London: Heinemann, 1977.

Nkashama, Pius Ngandu. "La mémoire du temps . . . Le temps de la mémoire dans le théâtre de Sony Labou Tansi." *Notre Librairie*, no. 102 (July–August 1990): 33–36.

Nkounkou-Mbecko-Senga, Dieudonné. *Tam-Tam Noir*. Paris: Le Méridien Editeur, 1988.

Nwankwo, Nkem. *My Mercedes Is Bigger Than Yours*. London: André Deutsch, 1975.

Nwoye, Rosaline Eredepa. *The Public Image of Pierre Savorgnan de Brazza and the Establishment of French Imperialism in the Congo*. Aberdeen: Aberdeen University African Studies Group, 1981.

Nzete, Paul. "Les jeux de mots dans les romans de Sony Labou Tansi." In *Sony Labou Tansi ou la quête permanente du sens*, edited by Mukala Kadima-Nzuji, Abel Kouvouama, and Paul Kibangou, 61–74. Paris: L'Harmattan, 1997.

N'Zitoukoukou, David. "*Le Pleurer-Rire* de Henri Lopes." *Peuples noirs, Peuples africains*, no. 35 (September–October 1983): 113–16.

Obembe, Jean-François. *Nouveau regard sur les certitudes d'hier*. Brazzaville: Editions Héros dans l'Ombre, 1991.

———. *Philosophie marxiste-léniniste en bref*. Brazzaville: Editions de l'INRAP, 1985.

———. *Problèmes liés à l'édification du Parti Congolais du Travail: Premier parti marxiste-léniniste au pouvoir en Afrique*. Paris: Présence Africaine, 1987.

———. *Vivre et mourir selon son style*. Paris: La Pensée Universelle, 1984.

Obenga, Théophile. *L'histoire sanglante du Congo-Brazzaville (1959–1997): Diagnostic d'une mentalité politique africaine*. Paris: Présence Africaine, 1998.

———. *La vie de Marien Ngouabi: 1938–1977*. Paris: Présence Africaine, 1977.

Obiechina, Emmanuel N. *Language and Theme: Essays on African Literature*. Washington, D.C.: Howard University Press, 1990.

Ogunjimi, Bayo. "The Military and Literature in Africa." *Journal of Political and Military Sociology* 18 (Winter 1990): 327–41.

Okonta, Ike, and Oronto Douglas. *Where Vultures Feast: Shell, Human Rights, and Oil in the Niger Delta*. San Francisco: Sierra Club Books, 2001.

Okotaka-Ebale, Xavier. *La femme africaine*. Brazzaville: Imprimerie des Armées, 1993.

———. *La pensée conscientisante d'un progressiste*. Brazzaville: Imprimerie nationale, 1982.

———. *Tous solidaires pour un Congo radieux*. Brazzaville: Imprimerie nationale, 1987.

Okri, Ben. "Listen to My Friend." *The Guardian* (November 1, 1995).

Onoge, Omafume F. "The Crisis of Consciousness in Modern African Literature." In *Marxism and African Literature*, edited by Georg M. Gugelberger, 21–49. London: James Currey, 1985.

Oppenheim, Carolyn Toll. "Witnesses to History." *The Berkshire Eagle*, February 25, 2001.

Orwell, George. *1984*. London: Penguin, 1948.

Osofian, Femi, et al. *Proceedings of the International Symposium on African Literatures. Theme: African Literature Before and After the 1986 Nobel Prize*. Lagos: Centre for Black and African Arts and Civilization, 1991.

Ouali, Kamadini Sylvestre. "L'intégration régionale en Afrique." In *L'intégration régionale dans le monde*, 153–66. Paris: Karthala, 1994.

Ouologuem, Yambo. *Le devoir de violence*. Paris: Seuil, 1968.

Ovcharenko, A. *Socialist Realism and the Modern Literary Process*. Moscow: Progress Publishers, 1978.

Oxford Latin Dictionary (1977).

Oyono, Ferdinand. *Une vie de boy*. Paris: Julliard, 1956.

Pabanel, Jean-Pierre. *Les coups d'état militaires en Afrique noire*. Paris: L'Harmattan, 1984.

Pageaux, Daniel-Henri. "Entre le renouveau et la modernité: Vers de nouveaux modèles?" *Notre Librairie*, no. 78 (January–March 1985): 31–35.

Paillet, Michel. "L'idéologie d'un régime 'militaire': Le cas de la République Populaire du Congo." *Armée en Afrique* (1974): 121–37.

Pakenham, Thomas. *The Scramble for Africa 1876–1912*. London: Abacus, 1992.

Palmer, Allen W. "Reinventing the Democratic Press of Benin." In *Press Freedom and Communication in Africa*, edited by Festus Eribo and William Jong-Ebot, 243–61. Trenton, N.J.: Africa World Press, 1997.

Peres, Phyllis. *Transculturalism and Resistance in Lusophone African Narratives*. Gainesville: University Press of Florida, 1997.

Pfaff, William. *The Wrath of Nations: Civilization and the Furies of Nationalism*. New York: Simon and Schuster, 1993.

Pierré-Caps, Stéphane. *Nation et peuples dans les constitutions modernes*. Paris: Presses Universitaires de Nancy, 1987.

Porter, Robert. "Soviet Perspectives on Socialist Realism." In *European Socialist Realism*, edited by Michael Scriven and Dennis Tate, 49–59. Oxford: Berg Publishers, 1988.

Quantin, Patrick. "Congo: Les origines politiques de la décomposition d'un processus de libéralisation (août 1992–décembre 1993)." In *L'Afrique politique 1994: Vue sur la démocratisation à marée basse*, 167–90. Paris: Karthala/CEAN, 1994.

Rabut, Elisabeth. *Brazza commissaire général: Le Congo Français de 1886 à 1897*. Paris: Editions de l'Ecole des Hautes Etudes en Sciences Sociales, 1989.

Radu, Michael S. "Ideology, Parties, and Foreign Policy in Sub-Saharan Africa." In *Africa in the Post-Decolonization Era*, edited by Richard Bissell and Michael S. Radu, 15–40. New Brunswick, N.J.: Transaction Books, 1984.

Radu, Michael S., and Keith Somerville. *Benin, the Congo, and Burkina Faso*. London: Pinter Publishers, 1988.

Ravenhill, John. "Redrawing the Map of Africa." In *The Precarious Balance: State and Society in Africa*, edited by D. Rothchild and Naomi Chazan, 282–306. Boulder, Colo.: Westview Press, 1988.

"Rencontre avec Sony Labou Tansi." *Bingo* (September 1987): 58–59.

La République du Congo a trois ans. Brazzaville: Imprimerie Officielle, c. 1963.

République du Congo-Brazzaville: Bulletin d'information de la représentation permanente auprès de l'ONU. No. 4 (February 1963); no. 5 (March 1963); and no. 8 (June 1963).

Ricard, Alain. *Littératures d'Afrique noire, des langues aux livres.* Paris: Karthala, 1995.

Ridelagh, Anna. "Emmanuel Boundzéki Dongala." In *The New Oxford Companion to Literature in French,* edited by Peter France, 252. Oxford: Oxford University Press, 1995.

Riesz, János. "From *L'état sauvage* to *L'état honteux." Research in African Literatures* 31, no. 3 (Fall 2000): 100–28.

Rivière, Claude. *Guinea: The Mobilization of a People.* Translated by Virginia Thompson and Richard Adloff. Ithaca: Cornell University Press, 1977.

Robbe-Grillet, Alain. *For a New Novel: Essays on Fiction.* Translated by Richard Howard. Freeport, N.Y.: Books for Libraries Press, 1970.

———. *Pour un nouveau roman.* Paris: Les Editions de Minuit, 1963.

Robin, Régine. *Le réalisme socialiste: Une esthétique impossible.* Paris: Payot, 1986.

Rosberg, Carl G., and Thomas Callaghy, eds. *Socialism in Sub-Saharan Africa: A New Assessment.* Berkeley: Institute of International Studies, 1979.

Rose, Jacqueline. "On the 'Universality' of Madness: Bessie Head's A *Question of Power." Critical Inquiry* 20 (Spring 1994): 401–18.

Rotberg, Robert I. "Truth Commissions and the Provision of Truth, Justice, and Reconciliation." In *Truth v. Justice: The Morality of Truth Commissions,* edited by Robert I. Rotberg and Dennis Thompson, 3–21. Princeton: Princeton University Press, 2000.

Rouch, Alain, and Gérard Clavreuil. *Littératures nationales d'écriture française.* Paris: Bordas, 1986.

Rousseau, Jean-Jacques. *Discours sur l'inégalité parmi les hommes.* Paris: Flammarion, 1971.

Roy, Maurice-Pierre. *Les régimes politiques du tiers-monde.* Paris: Librairie générale de droit et de jurisprudence, 1977.

Rushdie, Salman. *Imaginary Homelands.* London: Granta, 1991.

———. *The Satanic Verses.* London: Viking, 1988.

Rwanika, Drocella Mwisha, and Nyunda ya Rubango, eds. *Francophonie littéraires en procès: Le destin unique de Sony Labou Tansi.* Paris: Silex/Editions Nouvelles du Sud, 1999.

Said, Edward. *Culture and Imperialism.* New York: Alfred A. Knopf, 1993.

Samatar, Ahmed. *Socialist Somalia: Rhetoric and Reality.* London: Zed Books, 1988.

Sartre, Jean-Paul. *Huis-Clos.* Paris: Gallimard, 1944.

———. "Orphée noir." Introduction to *Anthologie de la nouvelle poésie nègre et malgache,* edited by Léopold Sédar Senghor. Paris: Presses Universitaires de France, 1948.

———. "Orphée noir." *Situations* III. Paris: Editions Gallimard, 1949.

———. "La pensée politique de Patrice Lumumba." In *Colonialisme et Néo-Colonialisme. Situations* V (1964).

———. "The Political Thought of Patrice Lumumba." In *Colonialism and Neocolonialism*. Translated by Azedine Haddour, Steve Brewer, Terry McWilliams, 156–200. London: Routledge, 2001.

———. "Qu'est-ce que la littérature." *Situations* II. Paris: Editions Gallimard, 1948.

Sassine, Williams. *Saint-Monsieur Baly*. Paris: Présence Africaine, 1973.

Sassou Nguesso, Denis. *Le manguier, le fleuve et la souris*. Paris: Editions Jean-Claude Lattès, 1997.

———. *Message du président du comité central du Parti Congolais du Travail à l'occasion du 20ème anniversaire des trois glorieuses (1963–1983)*. Brazzaville: Imprimerie Nationale du Congo, 1983.

———. *Pour l'Afrique*. ABC Groupe Média International, 1987.

———. *Sur l'approfondissement du processus révolutionnaire*. Brazzaville: Les Editions du Comité Central du Parti Congolais du Travail, 1984.

Scriven, Michael. "Paul Nizan and Socialist Realism: The Example of *Le cheval de troie*." In *European Socialist Realism*, edited by Michael Scriven and Dennis Tate, 128–45. Oxford: Berg Publishers, 1988.

Scriven, Michael, and Dennis Tate, eds. *European Socialist Realism*. Oxford: Berg Publishers, 1988.

Seeber, Edward. *Anti-Slavery Opinion in France during the Second Half of the Eighteenth Century*. Baltimore: The Johns Hopkins Press, 1937.

Sembène, Ousmane. *Les bouts de bois de dieu*. Paris: Le Livre Contemporain, 1960.

———. *Le docker noir*. Paris: Ed. Debresse, 1956.

———. *O pays mon beau peuple!* Paris: Ed. Buchet-Chastel, 1957.

———. *Vehi-Ciosane ou blanche-genèse suivi du mandat*. Paris: Présence Africaine, 1965.

———. *Xala*. Paris: Présence Africaine, 1973.

Senghor, Léopold Sédar. *African Socialism: A Report to the Constitutive Congress of the Party of the African Federation*. Translated and edited by Mercer Cook. New York: American Society of African Culture, 1959.

———. *Anthologie de la nouvelle poésie nègre et malgache de langue française*. Paris: Presses Universitaires de France, 1948.

———. *Ce que je crois*. Paris: Bernard Grasset, 1988.

———. *Liberté I: Négritude et humanisme*. Paris: Seuil, 1964.

———. *Liberté II: Nation et voie africaine du socialisme*. Paris: Seuil, 1971.

———. *Liberté III: Négritude et civilisation de l'universel*. Paris: Seuil, 1977.

———. *Nation et voie africaine du socialisme*. Paris: Présence Africaine, 1961.

Shapiro, Michael J. "Moral Geographies and the Ethics of Post-Sovereignty." *Public Culture: Society for Transnational Cultural Studies* 6, no. 3 (Spring 1994): 479–502.

Shih, Shu-mei. *The Lure of the Modern: Writing Modernism in Semicolonial China, 1917–1937*. Berkeley: University of California Press, 2001.

Signaté, I. *Une aube si fragile.* Dakar/Abidjan: Les Nouvelles Editions Africaines, 1977.

Sinda, Martial. *André Matsoua: Fondateur du mouvement de libération du Congo.* Dakar/Abidjan: Nouvelles Editions Africaines, 1977.

———. *Premier chant du départ.* Paris: Seghers, 1955.

Singler, John Victor. "The Role of the State in the Development of Literature: The Liberian Government and Creative Fiction." *Research in African Literatures* 11, no. 4 (Winter 1980): 511–28.

Skurnik, W. A. E., ed. *African Political Thought: Lumumba, Nkrumah, and Touré.* Denver: University of Denver, 1968.

Smith, Annette. *Gobineau et l'histoire naturelle.* Genève: Droz, 1984.

Sony Labou Tansi. *L'anté-peuple.* Paris: Seuil, 1983.

———. "Antoine m'a vendu son destin." *Equateur,* no. 1 (October–November 1986): 66–104.

———. *Béatrice au Congo.* Unpublished.

———. *Une chouette petite vie bien osée.* Editions Lansman, 1992.

———. *Une chouette vie bien osée.* Carnières-Morlanwelz, Belgium: Editions Lansman, 1992.

———. *Le commencement des douleurs.* Paris: Seuil, 1995.

———. *Confession nationale.* Unpublished.

———. *Conscience de tracteur.* Dakar-Yaoundé: Nouvelles Editions Africaines/CLE, 1979.

———. *Le coup de vieux.* Paris: Présence Africaine, 1988.

———. *La coutume d'être fou.* Unpublished.

———. *Les enfants du champignon.* Unpublished.

———. *L'état honteux.* Paris: Seuil, 1981.

———. *Franco.* Unpublished.

———. *Je soussigné cardiaque.* Paris: Hatier, 1981.

———. "Les Kongo: Cinq formes de théâtre essentiel (22 octobre 1992)." In Jean-Michel Dévésa, *Sony Labou Tansi: Ecrivain de la honte et des rives magiques du Kongo.* Paris: L'Harmattan, 1996, 353–55.

———. "Moi, veuve de l'empire." *L'Avant-Scène Théâtre,* no. 815 (October 1, 1987).

———. *Monologues d'or et noces d'argent.* Carnières-Morlanwelz, Belgium: Editions Lansman, 1998.

———. *La parenthèse de sang.* Paris: Hatier, 1981.

———. *Parentheses of Blood.* Translated by Lorraine Alexander Veach. New York: Ubu Repertory Theater Publications, 1985.

———. *La peau cassée.* Unpublished.

———. *Qui a tué Madame d'Avoine Bergotha.* Bruxelles: Editions Promotion Théâtre, 1989.

———. *Qu'ils le disent, qu'elles le beuglent.* Carnières-Morlanwelz, Belgium: Editions Lansman, 1995.

———. "Qui sera libre demain?" *Libération,* November 5, 1994.

———. "La résurrection rouge et blanche de Roméo et Juliette." Supplément à *La Revue Acteurs*, no. 83 (1990).

———. *Les sept solitudes de Lorsa Lopez*. Paris: Seuil, 1985.

———. *The Seven Solitudes of Lorsa Lopez*. Translated by Clive Wake. Portsmouth, N.H.: Heinemann, 1995.

———. "Les sources Kongo de mon imagination (23 avril 1993)." In Jean-Michel Dévésa, *Sony Labou Tansi: Ecrivain de la honte et des rives magiques du Kongo*. Paris: L'Harmattan, 1996, 359–62.

———. *Le trou*. Carnières-Morlanwelz, Belgium: Editions Lansman, 1998.

———. *Une vie en arbre et chars . . . bonds*. Carnières-Morlanwelz, Belgium: Editions Lansman, 1995.

———. *La vie et demie*. Paris: Seuil, 1979.

———. *Les yeux du volcan*. Paris: Seuil, 1988.

Soret, Marcel. *Histoire du Congo, capitale Brazzaville*. Paris: Editions Berger-Levrault, 1978.

Soyinka, Wole. *The Burden of Memory, the Muse of Forgiveness*. New York: Oxford University Press, 1999.

———. *A Man Died: Prison Notes*. New York: Noonday Press, 1972.

———. *A Shuttle in the Crypt*. New York: Hill and Wang, 1972.

Sreberny-Mohammadi, Annabelle. "The Global and the Local in International Communications." In *Mass Media and Society*, edited by James Curran and Michael Gurevitch, 177–203. London: Arnold, 1996.

Stalin, Joseph. *Marxism and the National and Colonial Question*. New York: International Publishers, 1913.

Stengers, Jean. *Congo, Mythes et Réalités: 100 ans d'histoire*. Paris: Editions Duculot, 1989.

Suchkov, Boris. *A History of Realism*. Moscow: Progress Publishers, 1973.

Tamba-Tamba, Victor. *Le parti de mon choix: Contribution à l'édification d'un parti*. Brazzaville: Editions Mationgo, 1995.

Tam'si, Tchicaya U. *Les cancrelats*. Paris: Albin Michel, 1980.

———. *Le destin glorieux du maréchal Nnikon Nniku prince qu'on dort*. Paris: Présence Africaine, 1979.

———. *Feu de brousse*. Paris: Ed. Caractères, 1957.

———. *Légendes africaines*. Paris: Editions Seghers, 1969.

———. *La main sèche*. Paris: Albin Michel, 1980.

———. *Le mauvais sang*. Paris: Ed. Caractères, 1955.

———. *Les méduses ou les orties de mer*. Paris: Albin Michel, 1982.

———. *Les phalènes*. Paris: Albin Michel, 1984.

Tati-Loutard, Jean-Baptiste. *Anthologie de la littérature congolaise d'expression française*. Paris: Présence Africaine, 1979.

———. *Chroniques congolaises*. Paris: P. J. Oswald, 1974.

———. *Le dialogue des plateaux*. Paris: Présence Africaine, 1982.

———. *Les racines congolaises*. Paris: P. J. Oswald, 1968.

————. *La tradition du songe*. Paris: Présence Africaine, 1985.

Tchichelle Tchivela. *L'exil ou la tombe*. Paris: Présence Africaine, 1986.

————. *Les fleurs des lantanas*. Paris: Présence Africaine, 1998.

————. *Longue est la nuit*. Paris: Hatier: 1980.

Tchivounda, Guillaume. *Essai sur l'état postcolonial*. Paris: Librairie générale de droit et de jurisprudence, 1982.

Tétu, Michel. *La francophonie: Histoire, problématique et perspectives*. Montréal: Guérin Littérature, 1987.

Thomas, Dominic. Interview. "Claude-Emmanuel Eta-Onka." Brazzaville, Republic of the Congo, January 1995.

————. Interview. "Emmanuel Dongala." Brazzaville, Republic of the Congo, December 1994–January 1995.

————. Interview. "Sylvain Bemba." Brazzaville, Republic of the Congo, December 1994–January 1995.

————. Letter to the Editor. "Sony Labou Tansi." *Times Literary Supplement* (December 16, 1994).

————. "Sony Labou Tansi." In *Postcolonial African Writers: A Bio-Bibliographical Sourcebook*, edited by Pushpa N. Parekh and Siga F. Jagne, 460–65. Westport, Conn.: Greenwood Press, 1998.

Thystère-Tchicaya, Jean-Pierre. *Itinéraire d'un Africain vers la démocratie*. Genève: Editions du Tricorne, 1992.

Todorov, Tvetan. *The Morals of History*. Translated by Alyson Waters. Minneapolis: University of Minnesota Press, 1995.

Tounda, Joseph. "Marx et l'ombre des fétiches: Pouvoir local contre *ndjobi* dans le Nord-Congo." *Politique Africaine* 31 (1988): 73–78.

Touré, Ahmed Sékou. *Action politique du parti démocratique de Guinée*. Paris: Présence Africaine, 1959.

————. *L'Afrique et la révolution*. Paris: Présence Africaine, 1966.

————. *Des Etats-Unis d'Afrique*, Tome 15. Conakry, Guinea: Imprimerie Nationale Patrice Lumumba, 1980.

————. *Expérience guinéenne et unité africaine*. Paris: Présence Africaine, 1982.

————. *La Guinée et l'émancipation africaine: L'action politique du Parti Démocratique de Guinée*. Paris: Présence Africaine, 1959.

————. *Poèmes militants*. Conakry, Guinea: Imprimerie Nationale Patrice Lumumba, 1977.

————. *La révolution culturelle*. Conakry, Guinea: Imprimerie Nationale Patrice Lumumba, 1969.

————. *Technique de la révolution*. Conakry, Guinea: Imprimerie Nationale Patrice Lumumba, 1960.

Trotsky, Leon. "Art and Politics." In *Writers and Politics: A Partisan Review Reader*, edited by Edith Kurzweil and William Phillips, 56–63. London: Routledge and Kegan Paul, 1983.

Tshiyembe, Mwayila. *L'état postcolonial, facteur d'insécurité en Afrique*. Paris: Présence Africaine, 1990.

Tshiyembe, Mwayila, and Mayele Bukasa. *L'Afrique face à ses problèmes de sécurité et de défense.* Paris: Karthala, 1989.

Tsibinda, Marie-Léontine. *Demain un autre jour.* Paris: Editions Silex, 1987.

——. *Une lèvre naissant d'une autre.* Brazzaville and Heidelberg: P. Kivouvou Verlag and Editions Bantoues, 1984.

——. *Mayombe.* Paris: Editions Saint-Germain-des-Près, 1980.

——. "Petite histoire du Rocado Zulu Théâtre." *Notre Librairie,* no. 102 (July–August 1990): 184–85.

Tudesq, Jean. "Problems of Press Freedom in Côte d'Ivoire." In *Press Freedom and Communication in Africa,* edited by Festus Eribo and William Jong-Ebot, 291–302. Trenton, N.J.: Africa World Press, 1997.

Tutu, Desmond. *Truth and Reconciliation Commission of South Africa Report.* London: Macmillan, 1998.

Ungar, Steven. Introduction. *"What Is Literature" and Other Essays.* Cambridge, Mass.: Harvard University Press, 1988.

Van Wing, J. *Etudes Bakongo: Sociologie, religion, magie.* Brussels: Desclée de Brouwer, 1959.

Vignondé, Jean-Norbert. "Littératures nationales ou cri pluriels." *Notre Librairie,* no. 85 (October–December 1986): 85–91.

Ville de Brazzaville, Un lustre d'action municipale: 1956 à 1961. Brazzaville: Imprimerie Officielle, 1961.

Volet, Jean-Marie. *La parole aux africaines ou l'idée de pouvoir chez les romancières d'expression française de l'afrique sub-saharienne.* Amsterdam: Rodopi, 1993.

——. "Romancières francophones d'Afrique noire: Vingt ans d'activité littéraire à découvrir." *French Review* 65, no. 5 (April 1992): 765–73.

Wabéri, Abdourahman. *Moisson de crânes.* Paris: Le Serpent à Plumes, 2000.

Wallerstein, I. *The Politics of Unity.* London: Pall Mall Press, 1968.

Waltz, Susan E. *Human Rights and Reform: Changing the Face of North African Politics.* Berkeley: University of California Press, 1995.

Watts, Richard. "The Politics of Prefaces: Patronage, Self-Promotion, and the Colonial/Metropolitan Relationship in Prefaces to Francophone Literary Texts." Dissertation, Yale University, 1998.

Wauthier, Claude. "Négritude, 'tigritude' et indépendance: Conscience nationale et littérature." *Notre Librairie,* no. 85 (October–December 1986): 16–22.

Webster's Ninth New Collegiate Dictionary. 1984.

Willame, Jean-Claude. *L'automne d'un despotisme: Pouvoir, argent et obéissance dans le Zaïre des années quatre-vingt.* Paris: Karthala, 1992.

——. *Patrice Lumumba: La crise congolaise revisitée.* Paris: Karthala, 1990.

——. *Pouvoir et gouvernance au Zaïre.* Paris: Karthala, 1993.

Williams, Raymond. *Marxism and Literature.* Oxford: Oxford University Press, 1977.

Wiseman, John A., ed. *Democracy and Political Change in Sub-Saharan Africa.* London: Routledge, 1995.

Witte, Ludo de. *The Assassination of Patrice Lumumba.* Translated by Ann Wright and Renée Fenby. London: Verso, 2001.

Wrong, Michela. *In the Footsteps of Mr. Kurz: Living on the Brink of Disaster in Mobutu's Congo.* New York: HarperCollins, 2001.

Yoka, Lye M. "Radio-Trottoir: Le discours en camouflage." *Le Mois en Afrique*, nos. 225/226 (1984): 154–60.

Young, Crawford. "Evolving Modes of Consciousness and Ideology: Nationality and Ethnicity." In *Political Development and the New Realism in Sub-Saharan Africa*, edited by David E. Apter and Carl G. Rosberg, 61–86. Charlottesville: University of Virginia Press, 1994.

Zhdanov, A. *Sur la littérature, la philosophie et la musique.* Paris: Editions de la Nouvelle Critique, 1948.

Ziegler, Dhyana, and Molefi Asante. *Thunder and Silence: The Mass Media in Africa.* Trenton, N.J.: Africa World Press, 1992.

Zimmer, Wolfgang. Interview. "Jean-Pierre Guingané, un 'fou' de théâtre au Burkina Faso." *Notre Librairie*, no. 102 (July–August 1990): 48–53.

Zomou, Roger Goto. "Les auteurs guinéens de l'intérieur: Notes bio-bibliographiques." *Notre Librairie*, nos. 88–89 (July–September 1987): 153–55.

Zubaida, Sami. "Theories of Nationalism." In *Power and the State*, edited by Gary Littlejohn et al., 52–71. New York: St. Martin's Press, 1978.

INDEX

Page numbers in italics refer to illustrations.

DOMINIC THOMAS

is Assistant Professor in the Department of French and
Francophone Studies at the University of California, Los Angeles.

AEF-3531